The Undead
in World Mythology
and Folklore

The Undead in World Mythology and Folklore

An Encyclopedia

THERESA BANE

McFarland & Company, Inc., Publishers

Jefferson, North Carolina

LIBRARY OF CONGRESS CATALOGING-IN-PUBLICATION DATA

Names: Bane, Theresa, 1969– author
Title: The undead in world mythology and folklore : an encyclopedia / Theresa Bane.
Description: Jefferson, North Carolina : McFarland & Company, Inc., Publishers, 2025. |
Includes bibliographical references and index.
Identifiers: LCCN 2025021784 | ISBN 9781476695617 paperback ∞
ISBN 9781476656069 ebook
Subjects: LCSH: Zombies—Encyclopedias | BISAC: SOCIAL SCIENCE / Folklore & Mythology |
LITERARY CRITICISM / Horror & Supernatural | LCGFT: Encyclopedias
Classification: LCC GR581 .B36 2025 | DDC 398.21—dc23/eng/20250602
LC record available at https://lccn.loc.gov/2025021784

ISBN (print) 978-1-4766-9561-7
ISBN (ebook) 978-1-4766-5606-9

Front cover image: *The Teacher* by Timothy Glenn Bane.

Printed in the United States of America

*McFarland & Company, Inc., Publishers
Box 611, Jefferson, North Carolina 28640
www.mcfarlandpub.com*

To my brother,
Vincenzo L. Falcone

Table of Contents

Preface

There was a time, back when I was known as the "vampire lady," when I would have opened the preface to my work with an introduction of myself, detailing my title and role as a professional vampirologist. I felt such introductions were necessary because at the heart of the job was a profound understanding of the mythological and cross-cultural study of vampires. I felt compelled to clarify the academic relevance because of the assumptions that came with the territory. It was assumed I wore dramatic black attire, red contact lenses, and prosthetic fangs. I never appeared at any speaking engagement so attired; I have always been Goth in spirit only.

Over the years, however, perceptions have shifted. The community no longer points me out as the "vampire lady" when I shop, and the media's seasonal Halloween articles have ceased to cast me as a novelty feature. These changes, while subtle, mark a departure from earlier days when such labels often defined me in the public eye. Yet, despite the evolution in how others see me, I continue to hold on to that part of my identity. Even as I've grown and deepened my understanding of the undead in broader contexts, I still think of myself as the "vampire lady." Thus, when the topic of the undead presented itself, I could not resist revisiting what once felt like my own shadowed corner of mythology. To return to those familiar subjects was, in a way, like retracing steps to an old haunt.

The idea of creating an "encyclopedia of the undead" had been simmering in my mind ever since I penned *Encyclopedia of Vampire Mythology* in 2010. Back then, I was cautiously optimistic that if I were fortunate, I might extend my scholarly pursuits to encompass other enigmatic subjects within the realm of the folkloric supernatural. It is with great satisfaction that I can look back and see how that aspiration has been realized. Since that time, I have authored numerous encyclopedic tomes on various subjects, all deeply rooted in folklore and mythology. Each work has been devoted to a specific subject matter of narrow focus, be it artifacts, beings, creatures, or locations, reflecting the myriad beliefs and stories across different cultures and religions worldwide.

In tackling this particular subject matter, I endeavored to create a comprehensive resource that captures the essence and spirit of undead creatures and entities. My approach was meticulous and thorough. I immersed myself fully in each entry, venturing "down the rabbit hole," as they say. My goal was to uncover and include every possible risen monstrosity, ranging from the most popular and well-known entities to those obscure and elusive figures that might otherwise be forgotten.

To achieve this, I relied heavily on a broad spectrum of references. My fondness for the printed form, particularly older texts, has served me well. Delving into books dating back to the 1800s, I found a treasure trove of insights. These works, being closer to the source material, offer a glimpse into the past, where authors were unfiltered in their documentation of factual history. They presented knowledge fearlessly, even when it challenged prevailing norms. This candidness is invaluable, especially considering how folklore and mythology evolve with the times. It's fascinating to observe how beings adapt to the eras they inhabit.

I did not include those undead horrors from popular culture that exist in movies, novels, television shows, and the like. Those abominations were the creation of writers, directors, and producers and are worthy of a book all their own. So, this is why AMC's *Walking Dead* walkers are not included. Yes, they are zombies, but also the creation of Robert Kirkman. I remember seeing his comic years ago at New York Comic Con, and I remember stealing away time from my table to read the first issue. I remember how much I enjoyed the story and wished the artwork were different, but yet somehow it worked with that postapocalyptic work. Likewise, you will not find Imhotep, the mummy from Universal Pictures. The Mummy franchise was created by Nina Wilcox Putnam (November 28, 1888–March 8, 1962) and her coauthor, Richard Schayer (December 13, 1880–March 13, 1956) back in the 1930s. Truly the brainchild of Putman–Schayer has withstood the test of time. And the portrayal of the character has changed little over the years, I feel, due to Boris Karloff's initial portrayal. The idea of the mummy has manifested in untold remakes that have expanded upon the initial story but never strayed too far from the original. But again, that creative team invented the mythology for the sake of developing a story to entertain. It was sort of based on some actual historical facts, true, but was never a part of the beliefs of the ancient Egyptians or their religious beliefs as portrayed in the film.

In developing this encyclopedia, my goals were clear. I sought to provide an authoritative, objective, and expansive examination of the undead, presenting each entry with the neutrality and precision it deserves. As with all my encyclopedic works, an even hand was applied. The book's structure is designed to be accessible yet detailed, offering readers a reliable reference that caters to both casual enthusiasts and dedicated researchers. The bibliography is complete, and the index is exhaustive.

Throughout this project, I have been incredibly fortunate to receive assistance from a myriad of individuals. Their support has been instrumental, whether in providing feedback, offering fresh perspectives, or simply being there through the inevitable challenges of such an ambitious endeavor. I am deeply grateful to my friends and colleagues, whose insights and encouragement have been invaluable. Additionally, I extend my heartfelt thanks to the librarians and archivists who facilitated access to rare and essential resources. But above all, the truest and deepest thanks go to my devoted and long-suffering husband, T. Glenn Bane. Without him, not only would none of this be possible, but also it would all be pointless.

In closing, I invite you, dear reader, to turn these pages with an open mind and a spirit of inquiry. Whether you are an academic, horror fan, researcher, or writer, I hope this encyclopedia enriches your understanding of the undead and inspires further exploration into the wondrous world of myth and folklore.

Introduction

Death. The end of life. It is clinically defined as what happens after crucial functions cease, namely when all brain activity has stopped, respiration has come to a complete halt, and no vital signs, such as a pulse, are detected.

Not so long after the last breath is expelled, the eyes begin to gray over. Within 10 minutes, a paleness (*pallor mortis*) creeps over the body; the corpse's temperature has been steadily decreasing (*algor mortis*) and will continue to do so until it reaches ambient temperature. The blood begins to pool in the lower portions of the body, causing a purplish-red discoloration of the skin (*livor mortis*) within 20 minutes of the heart stopping; these patches will grow for the next six hours. In about an hour, the limbs start to become stiff and more difficult to move as *rigor mortis* sets in; this can last for up to 36 hours. Putrefaction, the decomposition process, is apparent as soon as 12 hours after death. Depending on the circumstance, the body will be reduced to a SKELETON in about a year.

And yet, very little, if any, of this process applies to the undead. In addition to the cessation of life as we know it, there are some corpses that, according to cultural beliefs, folklore, legend, and mythology, somehow animate and return—be it as a physical REVENANT or as a ghostly presence—to the living world.

The idea of the undead, those individuals who were once alive or had the potential for life, returning to some semblance of life to act out, usually with malicious intent, on the living, is an idea as old as civilization. How they return (be it due to a curse, demonic possession, or sheer force of will) or why they return (to kill a clearly defined specific type of human prey) is never nearly as important in the end as the fact that they *did* return.

For much of civilization, death has been seen as a rite of passage, and it was the responsibility of the family or at the very least the community to prepare the person, body and soul, for its next stage of being. This was a serious undertaking, as failure to fulfill this obligation always resulted in dire consequences. To have the undead return was a violent reminder to adhere to tradition as well as a punishment for breaking with the old ways.

Archaeological evidence has shown that even the earliest humans, *Homo naledi*, who walked the Earth between 335 and 236 thousand years ago, had some sort of funeral rites, as they purposefully interred their dead.

These ancient graves are rare finds, and research is still ongoing into the subject. What we can do, however, is a deep dive into the funerary rites and beliefs about life and death and the realm of the supernatural of the ancient Greeks.

As in many other cultures, it was believed among the ancient Greeks that souls not yet admitted to the underworld had both the ability and the desire to compel the gods to bring harm upon the living who had wronged them. The dead, especially those who were unhappy about their situation, were assumed to harbor envy towards the living, as they were still able to enjoy life. Success and joy were often shadowed by a heightened awareness of the potential misfortune a jealous spirit might bring.

Such beliefs in the vengeful dead were deeply woven into the cultural fabric. Greek literature is rife with incidents where the living interact with the dead. Ghosts were thought to retain the emotions they had in life, feeling the same about good and bad treatment. In death, however, their responses to these feelings changed. Some ghosts were predisposed to unhappiness and vindictiveness, usually due to unresolved issues from when they were alive. Even the kindest soul, if left unhonored, could turn angry and make its displeasure known.

The ancient Greeks believed that the dead were particularly active on the night of the new moon, making this the most opportune, and necessary, time to appease them. Ghosts were imagined working more through mental or psychological means rather than physical ones. Their subtle attacks were seen as an excellent explanation for aberrant behavior among the living, often raising suspicions that the afflicted party was either guilty of some wrongdoing or the victim of a ghostly attack.

Contradictory views were held about the disembodied soul. The Greeks imagined it sometimes in Hades and at other times lingering at its tomb. Ghosts were often described in this period as sooty black or transparently pale—reflecting either the grim, menacing nature of many apparitions or the washed-out appearance of a corpse.

The Greeks believed in an enduring link between the body and soul, even after death. They held that affliction to one would automatically affect the other. This belief is underscored by the fact that funerary cults honored the dead even in the absence of their bodies.

The restless dead, particularly the violently departed, were seen as a constant source of danger, especially when another soul was transitioning. The Greek belief system assumed a connection between the state of the corpse and the strength of the ghost. For instance, a body with severed hands and feet was thought to result in a weaker ghost. After Achilles killed Hector before the gates of Troy, he tied the body to his chariot and dragged it across the battlefield and around the walls of Troy. In this act of disrespect and revenge, Achilles was doing far more than desecrating the body and raising the ire of the god, Zeus; he was also torturing the soul of the man he speared through the neck, weakening Hector's spirit so that if it returned seeking revenge, it would be unable.

Interestingly, the Greek dead often served dual roles—as scapegoats bearing the blame for disasters, and as mirrors reflecting the fears and desires of the living. This led to a belief that souls, regardless of their nature, could become dangerously active within the world of the living and could even be manipulated. It was also widely accepted, however, that contacting and directing the power of these less familiar, departed souls required the expertise of a specially trained individual.

The ancient Greeks' views on death did little to alter the essential features of human personality. The key difference lay in what the dead could do about their unspent feelings.

In the Homeric perception of the afterlife, the dead inhabit a twilight state, not entirely devoid of sensation but incapable of substantial interaction with the living. They exist in a realm separated from the world of the living by formidable rivers, forming an uncrossable barrier between the two worlds.

These spectral inhabitants require special nourishment before they can engage even with those who manage to reach their doorstep from the land of the living. It is only through the consumption of blood that they temporarily gain the capability for human-like communication. Despite this temporary ability, however, these souls remain physically intangible, unable to physically connect or influence those still among the living.

Interestingly, Homer acknowledges exceptions to this general rule. Certain departed souls, specifically those who have not yet crossed the five rivers into the underworld (Acheron, Cocytus, Lethe, Phlegethon, and Styx), can interact with the living. This implies that the recently deceased retain some capacity to watch the living and receive their offerings.

Yet, this connection is fleeting. Over time, the dead become increasingly isolated from the living, and their ability, or perhaps desire, to interact significantly diminishes. They maintain their earthly appearances but are unable to engage in meaningful conversation without the aid of blood.

It was not just the Greeks who had to appease ghosts; most cultures feared their angry dead. They're a mirror reflecting the values and fears of the culture they originate from. Every tiny detail a culture has about its beliefs about the dead can tell us something about the living. What kind of misfortune is attributed to the anger of the dead? Most often, the things that the culture deeply fears losing and therefore values the most.

Additionally, blaming the dead can be a clever way to avoid explanations that may shake up the social structure or question divine justice. For instance, if without explanation or any signs of trauma, a child tragically dies, and you blame your neighbor for casting the magical spell that made it happen, relationships between families could be irreparably damaged. If you put the death down to divine wrath, you're admitting either that you deserved such a loss, or that the deity is capricious. But, if you blame the angry dead for the loss of the child, you neatly sidestep all these issues. The dead make perfect scapegoats, carrying the weight of blame too heavy for others to bear, making sense of the senseless.

Many cultures also believe that dying under certain circumstances, or before reaching particular life milestones, could damn the soul to become a restless ghost. Although death was considered to be a rite of passage, as mentioned earlier, it was meant to be the *final* rite, after other essential milestones were achieved. A fulfilled life meant a happy and peaceful death.

In ancient Rome, people held a rather grim view of the deceased. They were seen as impure and dangerous and were blamed for epidemics, female sterility, madness, and possession. The word *larvaetus*, meaning to be possessed by a dead person, was used to describe such cases. It was believed that the dead continued to live within their tombs and therefore could gain power over the living. They could return and act if the manner of their death or the behavior of the living displeased them. Violently deceased individuals were deemed dangerous because they existed in a liminal state, neither fully in the world of the living nor completely incorporated into the underworld. Those who died before completing their life were said to linger, unable to pass on because their lives were unfinished.

In ancient Scandinavia, there is a rich tapestry of tales about revenants and ghosts. The Norse language is brimming with words that describe these beings, reflecting a prevalent belief in their existence and activities.

In medieval Europe, a world steeped in Christian beliefs and homespun folklore, societies recognized death as a transitional phase, a departure, and believed it was the duty of the living to assist the deceased in reaching the afterlife. Their monsters were categorized into three broad groups based on their physical nature and the ability to shape-shift: disembodied creatures from the afterlife, embodied creatures from the afterlife capable of assuming human form, and humans who had morphed into monsters.

In the tenth and eleventh centuries, there was a shift in perception. The "good dead" were no longer feared but revered as tutelary spirits, offering guidance and protection.

As time marched on, people's views on death and the supernatural changed as well; the tradition of the vigil also evolved.

This tradition of maintaining watch over the deceased has deep historical roots, though its purpose and symbolism have evolved across different cultures and epochs. In ancient Rome, the practice was primarily aimed at safeguarding the physical integrity of the deceased's body, a protective measure to deter witches from desecrating the corpse.

Among the ancient Germans, the vigil took on a more celebratory form, manifesting as a feast to honor the departed. This ritual implies a different perspective on death, viewing it not merely as an end but also as an occasion for commemoration and homage.

By the twelfth century, the rationale for a vigil over the dead had evolved further. It was now believed that it could prevent spirits from possessing the deceased, underscoring the preoccupation with the potential intrusion of supernatural entities into the mortal realm.

The response to revenants during the fifteenth century varied across regions, reflecting different cultural practices and beliefs. In the city of Riga, in Latvia, communal laws dictated that the bodies of the deceased be bound in their graves. Meanwhile, on Rügen Island in the Baltic Sea, it was recommended to place three stones on the cadaver during burial—one on the head, one on the torso, and one on the feet. This practice was likely intended to physically restrain the spirit within the grave.

In northern Germany during this time, cremation was employed to deal with corpses, potentially signifying a ritualistic purification process through fire. In contrast, in southern Germany, the bodies were discarded into rivers, perhaps symbolizing a journey or transition into the afterlife.

By the nineteenth century, the attitude toward the dead had changed severely. Ghosts and revenants became more of an annoyance than a source of fear or reverence. People distanced themselves from their ancestors, dismissing apparitions as diabolical illusions. The dead had become undesirable, and the sense of dread associated with them lessened. Ghosts were seen as mere ectoplasms, manifesting at the moment of death to bid farewell to loved ones. The final metamorphosis saw revenants reduced to cursory signs, no longer worthy of their names. These spectral figures were most common among those living close to nature, like farmers, mountain dwellers, and sailors.

But how are the undead created, exactly? What conditions or circumstances cause the dead to rise?

It depends on the society and their culture, but one of the more common causes is to have been an individual with a difficult and disagreeable nature. People who were malicious or quarrelsome in life posed a challenge to the integration of the family and clan. Their disruptive behaviors relegated them to the social margins, and their presence, both in life and death, incited fear. Their character flaws or malevolent tendencies are what prevent them from finding eternal peace, suggesting that tranquility in the afterlife is denied to those who fail or refuse to assimilate into the community.

So now, these deceased individuals, discontented and envious, seek vengeance or someone to avenge them. They inspired ritual burials intended to make one last push at integrating them and making them if not happy, at least content enough to stay buried.

There is also the prevalent belief that a person who buried their money would return undead until their hidden wealth was discovered.

Many revenants and angry spirits are created when they die abnormally or prematurely, thereby missing key rites of passage; such triggers are being stillborn, being unbaptized, committing suicide, drowning, dying a virgin, dying in childbirth, dying on one's wedding day, dying unmarried, dying without heirs, being executed, or having been a murder victim, to name the most popular.

Premature death was considered a curse, and the belief in revenants and ghosts stemmed primarily from the fear of the departed and the upheaval caused by any abnormal death. They were believed to linger between the worlds of the living and the dead, posing potential threats to the living.

To note, suicide, in certain historical contexts, was perceived not merely as an act of self-destruction but also as a means of revenge. The ghost of the individual who committed suicide would return to torment the person responsible for their despair.

Additionally, suicides presented a unique set of challenges. They were often buried where they were found, necessitating specific precautionary measures to ensure they did not return to torment the living. Because they took their own life, they were denied holy rites and burial in consecrated grounds, under Christian dogma, and so, sometimes they were buried at the crossroads, a magical and mystical place, where the barrier between realms was thin.

These varying practices reflect the societal efforts to contain the potential threat posed by these restless spirits, demonstrating the profound influence of supernatural beliefs on societal norms and rituals surrounding death.

If the rites of the deceased were disrespected or not performed at all, the angry dead could find a way to return. This included those without a grave, such as drowning victims whose bodies were never recovered.

Hauntings, a classification of manifesting undeath, were also triggered by an abnormal death. A ghost pursuing an individual could by extension attack those around the individual they seek to have their vengeance on, especially if they failed to punish the offender.

The cause of a haunting was not solely the *violence* of a death, but also the *reason* or *manner* of death. Dishonorable deaths were problematic and a potential cause for the dead to return. Death in battle, though regrettable, was considered honorable and glorious, but a cowardly end could trigger UNDEATH.

Vengeance is a recurring theme in tales of hauntings. The departed exacted revenge, either personally or through an intermediary, or served as messengers announcing imminent death or conveying news of a death that had occurred.

And with vengeance comes fear—fear of justice, of being held accountable. And fear leads to horror. The pursuit of vengeance is a dark path and can quickly spiral out of control. Vengeance is not a singular, standalone action. It is a part of an emotional cycle that evokes dread and terror in not just the avenger but also those who are affected by this pursuit.

It's all intertwined in the complex tapestry of human emotions. To understand their relationship to the undead, it's necessary to dip into psychological and sociological perspectives.

Fear is a primal human emotion, an evolutionary response designed to protect us from danger. It triggers our "fight, flight, or fawn" mechanism. When we experience fear, we perceive a threat to our safety.

Ann Radcliffe (1764–1823), a prominent Gothic author of the late eighteenth and early nineteenth centuries, provides a compelling distinction between terror and horror. According to her, "terror expands the soul and awakens the faculties to a high degree of life; the other [horror] contracts, freezes, and nearly annihilates them." In essence, horror diminishes human nature, while terror expands it.

Terror is the tension-filled anticipation leading up to a horrifying event or realization. It's that unsettling, creepy feeling that keeps you on edge. Horror, on the other hand, is our reaction to the event once it has occurred; it's the aftermath of a terrible event.

Our real-world fears often fuel fictional undead terrors. Yet, if these fears are shaped into compelling images and narratives, they can persist in our cultural memory for extended periods. There are four broad domains of the monstrous and fearsome, each corresponding to a significant area of cultural anxiety in the Western world from the eighteenth century to now: monsters from nature, like the shark from the popular movie *Jaws*; created monsters, like Dr. Frankenstein's creation; the monster within, like Hannibal Lecter; and the monster from our past, like Dracula. From these flow virtually all varieties of monsters.

To explain, natural monsters embody fears of a physical world spiraling out of control, while created monsters represent fears of human ambition and scientific progress. The monster from within symbolizes the fear of the resurgence of a suppressed, dark inner self, while the monster from the past reflects fears that the present has lost the vibrancy of more ancient times.

These four basic types are not entirely distinct but often intersect or overlap, much like Venn diagrams, giving rise to new manifestations of the monstrous. Thus, the figure of the monster is a dynamic symbol, continually evolving in response to shifting societal fears and anxieties.

When confronted with the unknown, our first instinct is to try to understand it using familiar words and images. This process gives rise to what is known as "uncanniness," which elicits that cocktail of disgust, fear, hate, nervousness, and shock associated with novelty or unfamiliarity. It's essentially a facsimile of life.

Eastern Orthodox theologian John Damascene (circa 676–749) categorized fear into six types: anxiety, consternation, disgrace, panic, shame, and shrinking.

Of these, only anxiety, disgrace, shame, and shrinking are fears rooted in reality, while consternation and panic are products of the imagination. This analysis mirrors the distinction John Trusler (1735–1820) draws between fear, which acts upon the mind; consternation, which affects the heart and disorders the senses; and terror, which disrupts the senses.

The paradoxical pleasure principle, a form of benign masochism, explains our love for being scared. It's why we flock to horror movies, scream in haunted attractions, and immerse ourselves in terrifying tales. This craving for fear, as psychologist Bruno Bettelheim (1903–1990) argued, can be seen as either an escape from the real world or a form of training for its conflicts.

Despite advancements in reason-based politics and science since the eighteenth century's political and industrial revolutions, the undead have persisted in our consciousness. Far from vanquishing them, these developments seem to have amplified our fears, providing a continuous counterpoint to the ambitious assertions of the modern world. But the question remains—why?

I suspect it's all in the storytelling.

The genre of horror, like all artistic and literary genres, is underpinned by two essential elements. The first is its traditional narrative structure, characterized by recurring characters, plot twists, and motifs. The second is the interaction of these patterns and ritualized stories with the dynamics of history, including specific historical events and individuals.

At its core, horror elicits a primarily physical response in the body, while the intricate blend of awe and dread associated with terror infiltrates the soul, making terror essentially a spiritual reaction. This distinction traces back to the Latin roots of the word *horror*, which refer to the physical fear manifested, such as hair standing on end. This raw, immediate fear triggers the instinctual fight, flight, or fawn response. In contrast, *terror* denotes a more abstract, ambiguous fear, characterized by trembling or shuddering, but it also encompasses a sense of awe at whatever is causing that fear.

In the realm of horror, optimism about the future is often rejected, along with the notion of progress defined solely in terms of scientific, social, or technological advancements. Instead, horror forces us to confront repressed realities, primarily death, but also the world of spirits, which cannot be enhanced or improved upon like an automobile or computer microchip.

Horror, therefore, places the human body under attack, with the bedroom—a place of intercourse and sleep—becoming a location of heightened vulnerability. The experience of horror triggers a visceral fear for one's safety.

On the other hand, terror, shaded with awe, is felt when beholding the grandeur of nature, the immense mountains of the Alps. In this way, terror can be uplifting. It can make you feel insignificant yet connected to the universe.

The horror genre often grapples with the ineffable and unspeakable. The transformation of the unnatural or peculiar into the horrifying necessitates an interpreter who perceives it as a harbinger of doom, rather than a mere anomaly. Thus, the horror story serves as a conduit for confronting our deepest fears and anxieties, casting light on the darker corners of the human psyche.

Genres, by their very nature, create a community of viewers or readers with shared experiences. They're powerful mediums that tell similar or overlapping stories, ones that fans desire to relive again and again. However, a genre cannot simply rely on endless repetition and expect its audience to respond similarly each time. For a genre to have longevity and outlast others of its kind, it must contain a certain level of originality. This repetition satisfies audiences until societal changes and shifts in human consciousness render the stories no longer engaging or amusing.

To survive and retain its power for future generations, the genre must evolve and interpret new traditions as they emerge. Its meaning must adapt and transform to respond to new contexts. While the basic story and characters may remain the same, different elements are emphasized depending on the period in which the story appears. The circumstances of the story may be altered, or it may explore different aspects or viewpoints that were previously overlooked or ignored.

The most enduring genres embody cultural myths, the stories we tell to make sense of our world but that are not so factual as to be emotionally charged. It's important to note that all genres depend on the repetition and formulation of basic elements such as characters, plots, symbols, and phrases. The horror genre is unique, however. Unlike other genres that raise and then resolve expectations, fears, and apprehension, horror often leaves you hanging, unable to fully resolve the fear it instills. Even when the story ends, the fears it raises can never be entirely banished.

This leads us to the intriguing question of whether we can ever truly triumph over the monsters, fictional or real. This unresolved issue makes the horror genre particularly conducive to never-ending stories.

And this brings us to the heart of the matter. The monster itself.

The word *monster* originates from the Latin words *monstrum*, meaning "an omen," and *monere*, which translates as "to warn." It is used in English and, to some extent, all the Romance languages, to describe anything that deviates from the norm or incites repulsion. The original connotation of the word is considerably more specific, however, often referring to entities that are large, potentially dangerous, and peculiar but notably visible.

Monsters represent a breach of the natural order, embodying chaos. They emerge as aberrations, originating from alien realms—hell, outer space, or any place considered beyond the norm. Such creatures often surface from boundary zones shrouded in night, fog, and mist, such as marshes, swamps, and fens, places where the boundaries between man and nature blur.

Natural monsters, owing to their diversity, defy easy categorization, unlike the undead. They are the earliest instances of the feared and malformed, often representing outsize versions of natural or unnatural beings.

The figure of the monster is a complex, multifaceted symbol that distinguishes the horror genre from its counterparts. It invariably embodies a threat, either as a direct danger or as a metaphorical menace to societal norms. The monster's defining characteristic is its deviation from the conventional social order, a difference that induces fear and trepidation.

The monster is often depicted as a peculiar, disoriented entity that straddles the divide between the past and an uncertain future. This creature, a conglomeration of the animal, the diabolical, the divine, and the human, is always an amalgamation of contradictory traits. Its existence disrupts the rational categories of order, creating its unique logic and dominating the space it occupies. Whether portrayed as a medieval aristocrat wielding power ruthlessly, a physically deformed being, or a supernatural demon, the monster is a symbol of uniqueness. As the world grows increasingly complex, the monster continues to captivate us with its absolute difference.

Although it may be relatively straightforward to trace contemporary monsters back to their ancient origins, a more intriguing question is why monsters lie dormant in certain eras and proliferate in others. Each age has its unique fears, and monsters often serve to characterize the emergent threats on the horizon. For example, the 1980s churned out an untold number of slasher films, and novelist Stephen King told tales that required only the slightest bit of interference from the supernatural. What did this say about our society, then? Later, in the late 1990s and throughout the 2000s, vampires became all the rage. From *Buffy the Vampire Slayer* to the Twilight Saga, the undead were not just popular but wildly so. This led to the emergence of a newly defined genre, urban fantasy. Why were we so attracted to the vampire, then? What was it about a vampire that spoke to the soul of that era?

It matters not. The habit of categorizing monsters as either products of eternal human fears or specific historical periods is unnecessary. Monsters derive their forms from the interplay between inherent fears of an unseen world and the distinct fears of a particular era.

An enduring trope in the annals of early cinematic horror is that of the monster abducting a woman, pursued by a group of armed men brandishing pitchforks and torches, the very symbols of agriculture and civilization. Do they ever ask what motivates the monster? Does it intend to violate or venerate its captive? This image may be interpreted as a manifestation of the fear of *the other*, who threatens our society by targeting our women. This scene often evokes the imagery of a lynching, underscoring the societal fear of otherness.

And this image of mobs of pitchfork-carrying and torch-toting peasants calls to mind Doctor Frankenstein's cadaverous creation.

Mary Wollstonecraft Shelley's *Frankenstein*, first published in 1818, introduces us to a creature of an extraordinary yet grotesque nature. It was constructed from human remains and stood eight feet tall, with black hair and lips, glowing eyes, and transparent yellow skin. And despite its obviously horrific physical appearance, this flesh GOLEM had not just a complex personality but also the capacity for love.

The novel is renowned for its exploration of the dangers of scientific experimentation and man's overreach into the realm of God. Science can benefit man, but it can also create a danger as wild and uncontrollable as any force of nature. This theme is so resonant that utterance of the words "I've created Frankenstein's monster" is instantly received as an admission of profound regret due to unwanted and unanticipated byproducts of a scientific undertaking.

There are many books and essays written on the subject, so I will not linger here, except to draw attention to the fact that this fictional narrative about the undead monster draws on a long-standing tradition in folklore of artificial servants created through mystical knowledge. Whether it's the GOLEM, the MOMMET, or the ghoul, the idea of a figure constructed from clay, rags, sticks, or cadaverous flesh continues to hold power over our collective imagination. In Shelley's novel, the act of constructing a living being from the parts of the dead becomes a kind of Holy Grail of science, foreshadowing contemporary pursuits in robotics, cloning, artificial intelligence, and mind-body dichotomies (ghost in the machine).

And, having explored the topics of ghosts and monsters as much as one can in an introduction to the undead, it is fitting to move on to the subject of vampires and zombies.

I find the lore of the vampire to be riveting, as it is steeped in folklore, mythology, and religion across various cultures down the timeline of civilization. Of all the types of undead, vampires, I suspect, will always be with mankind; they have been depicted in many ways, ranging from the bloodthirsty monsters of ancient civilizations to the charismatic, complex, emotionally damaged beings worthy of salvation of contemporary media.

The vampire can be traced back to the earliest stories of the Assyrians, Hebrews, Romans, and ancient Greeks. Their legends permeate myths and religions, indicating their deep-rooted presence in human consciousness.

They were regarded as transdimensional beings in medieval times, bridging the gap between this world and the next.

Vampires are traditionally associated with disease and death. The word *nosferatu* is derived from the Slavonic expression "*nosufur atu,*" which itself originates from the Greek word *nosophoros*, meaning "plague carrier." Many vampire legends are attributed to improper burial practices, which led to the spread of dangerous bacteria escaping from decomposing corpses.

Traditionally, vampires were portrayed as monstrous beings, devoid of any sympathetic qualities and universally feared. They were unattractive, unwanted, and reviled for their bloodsucking activities, a trait echoed in various other cultures. They were seen as the embodiment of evil, targeting children—an attempt by mankind to rationalize the tragic phenomenon of childhood mortality.

Zombies, in contrast, represent a collective entity with a shared consciousness, making them particularly prone to embody contemporary anxieties regarding the encroachment of inexorable masses. They are devoid of an apparent leader and lack the individual charisma that characterizes the vampire. This absence of leadership and personal allure differentiates them significantly from their vampiric counterparts.

Identification of a zombie is straightforward due to their distinct attributes: decaying skin and an insatiable craving for human flesh. This contrast to the vampire, who can seamlessly blend into society until their true nature is revealed, underscores the different fears these creatures symbolize. While vampires are often linked to fears of a concealed, sexually arousable self, zombies embody societal apprehensions about being overwhelmed by impersonal, faceless multitudes.

In essence, the dichotomy between vampires and zombies mirrors distinct facets of human fear; the former represents the dread of the covert and personal, while the latter encapsulates the terror of overt, impersonal threats.

As the Texan American necromancer Lisa Lee Harp Waugh (b. 1967) defines it, "a zombie is a soulless human corpse still dead but taken from the grave and endowed by sorcery with a mechanical semblance of life. It is a dead body which is made to walk and act and move as if it were alive." This definition underscores the uncanny nature of zombies, beings that blur the line between life and death.

Zombies have their origin in the ancient lore of Egyptian, Sumerian, and Babylonian cultures. These early depictions of zombies involved the use of magic to control these reanimated corpses.

Vodou lore of Haiti had much to do with the slave trade and was prevalent from 1625 to the 1800s. The history here is complex and sensitive but has to do with the revivification of the dead to be enslaved to work on plantations. Scholars believe these people were trapped under the influence of a concoction of burundanga and puffer fish poison, among other drugs, which caused stupefaction and likely permanent brain damage.

Regardless of their origin, zombies as they have come to be known and accepted pose a singular threat to humanity—extinction. They currently symbolize the potential to overthrow societal structures, a lumbering swarm consuming and contributing only to the apocalypse. Thus, the evolution of the zombie narrative from controlled servants to harbingers of global annihilation reflects shifting societal fears and anxieties.

There is some good news in all talk of the undead—decapitation. This tried-and-true ancient practice is a cure-all for virtually all types of unwanted undead.

It is believed in many cultures throughout time that a decapitated being, be it alive or undead, can no longer act. Furthermore, if the head was then placed in the grave at the feet of the corpse or thereabouts, the deceased would not be able to get ahold of it to reattach to their neck, thereby keeping the undead in the grave where they belong. Some cultures took it a step further and wrapped the body in a shroud to limit movement, or they placed a cairn of stones atop the grave to weigh the body down. And just to err on the side of caution, staking the corpse to the earth with a branch of sacred wood, such as ash or rowan, cannot be overstressed. Best practices recommended all of the aforementioned measures.

But, it never worked, not really. The dead always found a way to haunt us. It was all just an illusion, a temporary comfort. Decapitation was a common, but not a foolproof preventative for someone who had the potential to arise as the undead. It may prevent the body from arising, a REVENANT, but it did nothing to stop the creation of a ghost of a restless soul.

So, what then?

Cremation. That is, reducing the body and bones to ash and then either spreading them into the wind or scattering them into moving water. Perhaps this method is the only real way to prevent the undead of any sort from returning and acting against the living.

And yet, still, we have ghosts, monsters, vampires, and the assorted undead. Man has at best a temporary, imagined say in who or what comes back from the dead.

Fortunately, there are "good undead," those folks who were lucky enough to die of natural, acceptable circumstances and who, with proper funeral and burial rites, can rest in peace. Should they return, they do so as ancestral spirits and guard over their clan and family, adhering to the concept of *do ut des* ("I give so that you may give").

This only serves as further proof that death can never separate the living from the dead. The living need their ancestors to protect them, and the dead need the living to perform their sacred duties of final rites of passage so their souls can pass into the next realm where they can best assist those they left behind. It was practiced by pagan traditions and was later adopted and modified by the Christians. A circular, symbiotic relationship was created, when it worked.

Friendly ghosts, spirits, and hauntings remain the exception, not the rule. It drives home the importance of honoring the dead, celebrating their memories, and inviting them to feasts and festivals. Failure to do so openly invites their wrath and potential revenge, and it has been established how difficult they are to vanquish.

So, it is not *death* that is to be feared, but rather the dead themselves. All we, the living, can do is provide the deceased with everything they need to remain in their graves and go to their eternal reward. If they should visit, we should welcome their company and make sure to give them a proper send-off when the time has come for them to leave again. To deliberately choose to do otherwise or act improperly out of ignorance, well, it's the stuff of cautionary tales and horror stories.

Admittedly, it can be a challenge to distinguish between reverence and fear of the dead. Are we performing these rites of passage for their benefit or our own? Does it matter? I will end with this often-cited truth: Death—it is only the beginning.

The Encyclopedia

Abhartach (Ah-BART-tig)

Variation: Murbhheo

Perhaps the oldest known vampire narrative in Western European history originates from ancient Celtic mythology and is situated in the rural parish of Glenullin, within the town of Slaghtaverty, Ireland. The town's name translates to "Abhartach's grave." Abhartach, a ruthless ruler and potent magician, is traditionally described as a short individual or dwarf, with an assortment of additional physical abnormalities.

The narrative tells that, one evening, Abhartach, driven by jealousy and suspicion, convinced himself of his wife's infidelity. Rather than confronting her directly, he sought to catch her in the act. He climbed through his bedroom window, balanced carefully on the ledge, and inched along towards his wife's bedroom. However, he slipped and fell to his death before reaching his destination. His cold and lifeless body was found the next morning. Although Abhartach was feared and disliked in life, the townsfolk buried him upright in his grave, as befitting a king.

The next day, Abhartach returned to Slaghtaverty as NEAMH-MHAIRBH ("the undead" or "walking dead"), demanding daily blood offerings from each resident for him to drink so as to maintain his undead existence. He was referred to as a *dearg-diulai* ("blood-drinker"). The townspeople obeyed, as they were now more frightened of Abhartach in death than they ever were in his life.

The people soon decided they could not endure the reign of a REVENANT, so they hired an assassin to eliminate him. Despite the initial success, Abhartach returned from his grave yet again, demanding his usual daily blood quota. Even after multiple failed assassination attempts, the townsfolk remained undeterred; they employed another assassin, only to achieve the same, disappointing results.

Eventually, a druid stepped forward, promising to rid the people of Abhartach permanently. He explained that due to the magic initially utilized to resurrect the tyrant along with the particular species he had become, a *murbhheo* (ancient Gaelic for vampire), their malevolent ruler could not be permanently destroyed but only trapped in his grave. Using a yew wood sword, the druid stabbed Abhartach and, while he was in a weakened state, buried the tyrant ruler upside down in a grave covered with ash branches, thorn bramble, and a large boulder.

According to local legend, Abhartach still has enough power to attack anyone who ventures too close to his grave site in Slaghtaverty, although he cannot fully escape it. A large thorn tree, growing from his burial site next to the imprisoning boulder, pins him to the earth.

In some variations of the tale, the mythical Irish hero Finn MacCool (Fionn Mac

Cumhail, Fionn mac Cumhaill) is the savior of the townsfolk. At the request of the citizens living under Abhartach's reign of terror, he intervened. After his first two unsuccessful attempts to destroy the vampire, he then consulted a druid, who advised him to slay the creature with a wooden sword and bury the monstrosity upside down to negate its magical powers. With this advice, Finn MacCool triumphed, and the vampire ceased to feed upon and trouble the people.

In another version, a local chieftain named Cathan was the hero who put Abhartach to his true and final rest. As in other versions, his initial attempts were unsuccessful, but before his third try, he consulted an early Catholic saint named Eoghan (pronounced "Owen"). He too recommended slaying the vampire with a wooden sword and burying him "head downwards" to neutralize his powers and keep him beneath his thorn-covered cairn.

Sources: Borlase, *The Dolmens of Ireland*, 825; Cork Historical Society, *Journal of the Cork Historical*, 350; Harris, *Folklore and the Fantastic*, 135; Hayward, *In Praise of Ulster*, 263; MacKillop, *Dictionary of Celtic Mythology*, 1; Russo, *Vampire Nation*, 38

acheri

In both Chippewa Indigenous American narratives and Hindu folklore, there is a recurring character of a malevolent, mountain-residing, nocturnal entity known as an "acheri." This entity is believed to be the manifestation of the spirit of a young girl who has met an unfortunate and premature death. Her spirit is said to return to the physical realm with the intent to torment others, inflicting upon them the same suffering she endured until she successfully causes their demise. The acheri primarily targets children.

The acheri is said to possess theriomorphic (shape-shifting) capabilities, often appearing as a frail, thin girl with pale skin. By masquerading as a child, it gains the trust of other children, interacting with them as one of their own. The creature then casts its shadow over a child, which results in the victim contracting a highly infectious respiratory disease. As the illness spreads and human suffering escalates, the acheri becomes increasingly powerful, drawing strength from the despair, misery, and sorrow it generates.

An acheri is regarded as a psychopomp (harbinger of death); hearing an acheri's song is considered a warning of imminent death or sickness in a family or district. These entities typically inhabit the hills and mountains, descending to lower regions only to wreak havoc on communities. However, it is believed that the acheri can be warded off using sacred amulets. Protective measures such as red ribbons or threads tied around the neck are also thought to provide protection against this child-hating entity.

According to Hindu tradition, acheri are always female spirits who prefer to stay in secluded mountaintops during the day. They descend to chosen clearings at twilight to gather. Crossing paths with a group of acheri or traversing their meeting spot, even in their absence during daylight, is perceived as a sure sign of impending death. They exhibit particular hostility towards young girls and individuals who wear red clothing, a color they detest. Any unusual optical phenomena are attributed to the activities of the acheri.

Sources: Crooke, *Introduction to the Popular Religion and Folklore of Northern India*, 87, 164; Johnston, *Acheri Demon Haunting*, 8–9; Latham, *Descriptive Ethnology*,

Volume 2, 400; Maberry, *They Bite!*, 51; MacDougall, *Vampire Slayers' Field Guide to the Undead*, 552

Adam Kadmon

Variations: Adamas, Adam Kadem, First Man, God's Firstborn, Heavenly Man, Light Man

In Semitic and Jewish mythology, the entity known as Adam Kadem represents an early endeavor by the Creator in the formation of humankind. This figure, referenced within the Nag Hammadi texts, including the "Gospel of the Egyptians," is also referred to as Adamas. Meanwhile, in kabbalistic literature, the same entity is identified as Adam Kadmon. Both sources propose that Adam Kadmon was fundamentally flawed, resulting in his rejection. Descriptions of this figure vary significantly, with some likening him to an inelegant mass of semi-shaped mud, while others describe him as a crude prototype of *Homo sapiens*.

An alternative interpretation suggests that Adam Kadmon may not be a physical entity but rather a constellation shaped like a man. This interpretation parallels the pareidolia—the phenomenon of seeing familiar patterns in random or unrelated stimuli—of constellations, such as Taurus, perceived as a bull, and the Pleiades, visualized as seven sisters. This perspective contends that Adam Kadmon should not be interpreted literally and asserts that there was never a physical form. Instead, it proposes that Adam Kadmon serves as a cosmic metaphor for the universe. Additional interpretations propose that he is a giant, a semidivine being, a GOLEM, or a fusion of these characterizations.

Sources: Curran, *Man-Made Monsters*, 50; Schwartz, *Tree of Souls*, 16, 124, 128

adas

Among the Buryat people of the Buryat Republic, Siberia, the adas are the returned souls of children. They have the propensity for being both evil and good.

These undead appear as miniature humans, but their mouths open from left to right; when meeting people, they try to hide this by covering the lower part of their face with their sleeves. Sightings of the adas are common, especially among shamans. All adas fear horned owls, and in households where children are present, the pelts of this bird are oftentimes hung.

Adas are known to assault and harm children; they will drink their milk, eat their food, and otherwise deprive the child of nutrients. When an ada becomes too dangerous to the child, a shaman will be called in to rid the family of it. There is one tale of a shaman finding and capturing 14 adas in one home, placing them all in a pot with a heavy lid, and roasting them in a fire. Once they are dead, their bodies look like small animals.

Some adas will take on the role of family protector and keep the home safe from thieves. Should anyone attempt to steal from the family home, the adas will raise an alarm, shouting, *"Mania! Mania!"* ("Ours! Ours!").

The adas and all the other souls of the dead have an unnamed one-eyed chief who rules over them. This overseer of wandering souls can be killed only if shot in the eye. Once dead, he will transform into a pelvis bone, which must then be burned.

Sources: Hastings, *Encyclopædia of Religion and Ethics*, Volumes 3–4, 9

afrit (AFF-reet), plural afriti

Variations: afreet, afreeti, afrite, efreet, efreeti, efrit, ifreet, ifrit

African and Muslim folklore alike speak of a vampiric spirit called the afrit ("blood-drinking nomad"); it is a species of jinn. It is said that when a person is murdered, their spirit returns to the place of their death. At the very spot where the last drop of their lifeblood fell, a newly created afrit rises. Descriptions vary, saying it looks like a larger version of the jinni, a desert dervish, a ghostlike form, a tall column of smoke, or a being resembling the Christian devil complete with cloven hooves, horns, and tail. Seeing one will cause a person to be overcome with fear. To prevent this vampiric spirit from entering into existence, a nail must be driven into the exact spot where the last drop of lifeblood fell. This will force the spirit to remain in the earth.

In all, there are five types of jinn, and although the afrit is the second most powerful of its kind, it is the most ruthless and cruel toward its victims.

Sources: Hoiberg, *Students' Britannica India*, 5–6; Jacobs, *Folklore*, vol. 11, 389–94; Philp, *Jung and the Problem of Evil*, 56–57; Rose, *Giants, Monsters, and Dragons*, 6

Ahkiyyini

In the traditional narratives of the Inuit community in Alaska, USA, a spectral figure known as Ahkiyyini is spoken of. The tale suggests that this entity was once a living being who had a predilection for dance and music. Following his demise, he is said to have reemerged in the form of a skeletal apparition. They utilize a bone from their own arm as a drumstick, creating rhythmic beats against their shoulder blade, or scapula. The narrative attributes the occurrence of seismic activity and substantial waves, potent enough to overturn boats, to the energetic dancing of this specter.

Sources: Cotter, *A World Full of Ghosts*, n.p.

airi

In the folklore from northern India, the airi is said to be the ghost of someone who was killed while hunting; it will haunt the general area in which its death occurred. Similar to the Wild Huntsman of European lore, the airi is accompanied by two litter bearers and a pack of hunting dogs wearing bells upon their collars; to hear the baying of these hounds is an ill omen signifying an imminent catastrophe. The saliva of an airi is venomous; anyone who touches it will become sick, and incantations must be chanted while brushing the infected area with the branch of a tree. Assuming this remedy was applied quickly enough to save the person's life, the victim must then abstain from rich food for several days to ensure good health returns.

Anyone who has a face-to-face encounter with an airi will suffer a horrible demise, dying either by being immolated by its fiery eye, by being torn asunder by its hunting dogs, or by having their liver ripped from their body and fed to the nature spirits accompanying it.

Sources: Bonnerjea, *L'Ethnologie du Bengale*, 100; Crooke, *Introduction to the Popular Religion and Folklore of Northern India*, 163

akakharu (Oak-a-CAH-roo)

Variations: akakarm, akakhura, akhkharu (Assyrian), rapganmekhab (Akkadian)

An ancient Chaldean epic written in the third millennium BC tells the tale of the akakharu, a species of vampiric REVENANT. When the goddess Ishtar journeyed into the underworld to rescue her son and lover Tammuz, she said aloud, "I will cause the dead to arise and devour the living." And so, it came to pass; these vampiric, lesser demons or semisolid ghosts came into being, seeking human flesh. Interestingly, the word *devour* translated initially to mean "waste away," as in from an illness.

Sources: Cramer, *Devil Within*, 104; Jones, *On the Nightmare*, 121; Masters, *Eros and Evil*, 187

alp (ALP)

Variations: alb, alf, alfemoe, alpdaemon, alpen, alpes, alpmann, apsaras, BOCK-SHEXE, bocksmarte, cauquemare, chauche vieille, dochje, dockele, dockeli, doggi, druckerl, drude, drut, drutt, elbe, fraueli, inuus, leeton, lork, maar, mahr, mahrt, mahrte, mar, MARA (female), mare, mart (female), moor, mora, morous, mura, murawa, nachtmaennli, nachtmahr, nachtmanndli, nachtmannlein, nachtmerrie, nachtschwalbe, nachttoter, nielop, nightmare, night terror, old hag, quauquemaire, racking one, ratzel, schratlein, schrattel, schrattele, schratteli, schrattl, schrettele, schrotle, schrotlein, schrsttel, stampare, stampen, stampfen, stempe, sukkubus, toggeli, trampling, trempe, trud, trude, trutte, tryd, tudd, vampyr, walrider, walriderske, wichtel, and numerous others through history and geographic region

The lecherous and ravenous alp of Germany is difficult to classify, falling somewhere in the realm of a demonic, ghostly, fairylike, vampiric being. Typically, demons are infernal, immortal beings that were never human, but this is not the case here. An alp is created through the uncommon but mundane act of having been born male and with a caul (an embryotic sack) over its face, or when a child whose mother went through a particularly long and painful childbirth dies, or when a family member dies and their spirit simply returns with no further explanation added. In each of these instances, when the child dies, they will return as an alp.

Throughout the ages, the only consistency in its description is that it is said to wear a white hat called a *tarnkapp*; this article is especially important in retaining its supernatural abilities. Generally, the alp is described as being male, and although there are a few reports of it being female, it should be noted that this creature is an exceptional theriomorph (shape-shifter). It can assume the form of any animal it pleases, but lore claims that it prefers birds, cats, demon dogs, dogs, mist, pigs, and snakes. Additionally, it is very strong, can become invisible, can fly, and has the unique ability to spit butterflies and moths from its mouth. Because it is a theriomorph, it has been linked to the werewolf folklore in Cologne, Germany.

At night, an alp seeks out its typical prey, a sleeping woman, although it has been known to attack cattle, geese, horses, men, rabbits, and young boys. Once its prey is selected, the alp shape-shifts into mist and slips into the person's home completely undetected. Next, it sits upon the victim's chest and compresses the air out of their lungs so they cannot scream. Then the alp will drink blood (and milk if the victim is a lactating woman), which will cause them to have both horrible nightmares and erotic dreams. The alp feeds off the terror and ecstasy of these dreams. The next day the victim will have vivid memories of the attack and be left feeling drained of energy and miserable. The attack event in its entirety is called an *alpdrucke* ("elf pressure"). It is interesting to note that if a woman intentionally calls an alp to her, it will be a gentle lover.

When an alp victimizes a horse, the event is referred to as a *mare*. It will mount up and ride the animal to death but may choose to crush the animal instead, as it is known to do to geese and rabbits in their pens. When an alp crushes cattle to death, the event is called a *schrattl*.

Fortunately, as powerful as the alp is, its attacks can be easily thwarted. To protect horses and cattle from being ridden or crushed to death, the appropriate apotrope is a hanging pair of crossed measuring sticks in the barn. Placing a broom in the animal's stall is also believed to ward the being off.

There are numerous preventative measures to employ to protect yourself or others from an *alpdrucke*. Folklore tells us the alp's power is linked to its *tarnkapp*. If you can steal the hat off its head, the alp will lose its superhuman strength and the ability to become invisible. Desperate to have its hat once again, the alp will greatly reward anyone who returns it, although with what or how is not mentioned in the lore.

When not feeding off its victims, an alp will also play cruel tricks on them, such as knotting the hair of horses, pulling out nose hairs, souring breast milk, tangling the hair of women, and the like.

Another way to keep an alp at bay is to draw a magical hexagram on your bedroom door with chalk and imbue it with the names of the three magi—Balthasar, Caspar, and Melchior—who visited the Christ child after his birth during the Festival of the Three Kings (January 6). Variations of this preventative method say the head of the household must make a pentagram on the bedroom door and empower it with names of the patriarchic prophets, Elias and Enoch.

Burying a stillborn child under the front door of your home will protect all the occupants who sleep within not only from *alpdrucke*, but also from other species of vampires.

A less invasive defensive method is to keep your shoes at the side of your bed at night when you sleep. If the toes are pointed toward the bedroom door, it will keep the alp from entering. Also, sleeping with a mirror on your chest will scare it off.

At one time there was the practice of singing a specific song at the hearth before the last person in the house retired for the night. Sadly, this method is no longer employed, as the words, melody, and even the name of the song have been lost to history; only the memory of the tradition remains.

If, despite your best attempts, all preventative measures have been taken and *alpdrucke* persist, there is hope. If you should awaken while being pressed down upon, put your thumb in your hand and it will flee.

Occasionally, a witch binds an alp to her in order to inflict harm upon others. Witches who have an alp in their possession have the telltale sign of letting their eyebrows grow together. They allow this to happen because the alp, in this instance, lives inside the witch's body when not in use. When it leaves her through an opening in her eyebrow, it takes on the guise of a moth or white butterfly. If it ever happens that you awaken in the night and see such an insect upon your chest, say to it, "Trud, come back tomorrow and I will lend you something." The insect should immediately fly away, and the next day the alp, in the guise of a human, will come to your home looking to borrow something. When this happens, give it nothing, but say to it, "Come back tomorrow and drink with me." The alp will leave, and the following day the witch who sent the alp will come to your home, seeking a drink. Give it to her, and the attacks should stop.

Sometimes an alp will return night after night to assault the same person. Fortunately, there is a powerful, if not bizarre, way to prevent this. The victim needs to urinate into a clean, new bottle, which is then hung in a place where the sun can shine upon it for three days. Then, without saying a single word, carry the bottle to a running stream and throw it over your head, into the water.

For all the trouble an alp can prove to be, it is as easy to kill. Once captured, place a lemon in its mouth and then set the creature ablaze.

Sources: Grimm, *Teutonic Mythology*, 423, 442, 463; Jones, *On the Nightmare*, 126; Maberry, *They Bite!*, 52–3; MacDougall, *Vampire Slayers' Field Guide to the Undead*, 655; Nuzum, *Dead Travel Fast*, 234, Riccardo, *Liquid Dreams*, 139

alvantin (AL-von-tin)

Variations: CHUREL, jakhai, jakhin, MUKAI, nagulai

This vampire from India is created when a woman dies unnaturally, such as in childbirth.

Sources: Hastings, *Encyclopædia of Religion*, 481; Melton, *Vampire Book*, 323; Verma, *Social, Economic, and Cultural*, 199–200

alwantin

In India an alwantin is a GHOST or returned spirit of a pregnant woman who died while attempting to give birth. Manifesting as a beautiful woman with backward-turned feet, this spirit is considered to be especially dangerous to its family members. When forced to appear at the summoning of an exorcist, the alwantin manifests in the flame of his lamp looking like a dakini (a species of female ogre).

Sources: Bonnerjea, *Allborough New Age Guide*, 18; Khanam, *Demonology*, 24–5

anaikatoumenos

Variation: anakathoumenos

Specifically from the Tenos region of Greece; it is like many other GREEK VAMPIRES in that blood drinking is not required to sustain its unlife, nor is it susceptible to sunlight.

Its name, *anaikatoumenos*, translates to mean "one who has sat back up" and may have originally meant that the position of the corpse had changed from how it was laid in its grave. Movement from a corpse is not only possible but probable after rigor mortis has occurred.

Another possible explanation as to how the anaikatoumenos received its name may have to do with an ancient hatred the Greeks had at one time for the Turks. Many GREEK VAMPIRE stories begin with a person being cursed to UNDEATH because they had a heretical religious belief or had converted to Islam. According to Islamic beliefs, after death, two angels, Munkar and Nakeer, come to question the departed, who must sit upright in their presence. There is a Romanian story of how a man happened upon an undead being while it was still in its grave "sitting upright like a Turk."

Source: Summers, *Vampire: His Kith and Kin*, XXX

ancestral spirit

Ancestral spirits hold a significant place in the folklore, myths, religions, and spiritual traditions of many cultures worldwide. Their influence is particularly prominent in Buddhism, Hinduism, and the spiritual practices of China, Japan, and Korea. They are also deeply rooted in the indigenous faiths of Africa, Oceania, Native America, and Native Australia. This belief is most common in societies where kinship is important, such as with tribal groups. Those who believe in interaction with ancestral spirits do not necessarily worship them, although this interaction is present in most religions in some fashion even if it manifests only as a remembrance, offering of prayer, or simply lighting a candle. Veneration is given to those who in life held a position of importance or rank, for example, clan leaders, heads of families, heroes, kings, lineage founders, political leaders, royalty, tribal elders, and other such groups. Common venerations are attendance of the grave site and monuments, commemorative services, festivals of honor, maintenance of moral standards, offerings, prayers, and sacrifices.

Ancestral spirits are best described as being the deceased members of one's family or tribe and are similar to angels, bodhisattvas, lesser gods, nature spirits, and saints; they may even share similar abilities, features, and responsibilities. These spirits concern themselves with looking after the well-being of their descendants; this manifests as blessing those who keep with traditions and reverence and punishing those unworthies who break social and spiritual laws, practices, or taboos.

Often, shamans or the comparable like are utilized to speak with these spirits in order to seek guidance or discover what had occurred to offend them. Ancestral spirits, like lesser gods with high powers, have the ability to cause illness and misfortune, manifesting in a number of ways; they expect to receive proper treatment and to be shown respect. When this occurs, the people are blessed with health and material happiness.

Sources: Doniger, *Merriam-Webster's Encyclopedia of World Religions*, 54; Ellwood, *Encyclopedia of World Religions*, 14–5

anchimayen

Variations: anchimalguen, anchimallen

The undead creation known as the anchimayen from the mythology of the native people of Argentina and Chile is the reanimated corpse of a child who died suddenly. They have the theriomorph ability to transform into a glowing ball of light or fireball. This undead being has no autonomy and must obey the will of its creator. If is created by an evil sorcerer, a *kalku* (or *calcu*), it will be used to harm or kill others by spreading disease. In the rare instances when the sorcerer who created it is not malevolent, the anchimayen is utilized as a protector or guardian.

Sources: Markowitz, *Robots That Kill*, 4, 5, 66; Woog, *Zombies*, 43

Ancient Babylonian and Assyrian vampires

Variations: LAMIA, lilatou, lilats, lilit, Lilith

As far back as the twenty-fourth century BCE, the people of Babylon, and later Assyria, supposed that vampires were demonic beings who were not of this plane of existence. Therefore, in order for them to interact with and assault humans, the demons had to possess corpses. As an even greater insult to humanity proving how evil these beings were, the demons specifically chose to inhabit the corpses of women. To these ancient people, women were considered to be the living symbol of life, this concept was a near-sacred thing—their menstrual cycles, which were in rhythm with the cycles of the moon, were linked to the planting and harvesting of crops. Nothing in the world of these ancient peoples could have been more perverse than the very symbols of life and life-giving beings turning into violent monstrosities that sought to consume the flesh and blood of children. These vampires were further described as being very fast and shameless in their pursuit of destruction. They needed to feed in order to maintain the capability of the corpse they utilized.

Sources: Budge, *Babylonian Life and History*, 142–3; Campbell, *Masks of Gods*; Hayes, *Five Quarts*, 187; Summers, *Vampire: His Kith and Kin*; Summers, *Vampire in Lore and Legend*, 267; Thompson, *Devils and Evil Spirits of Babylonia*; Varner, *Creatures in the Mist*, 93

Andaokut

The Tsimshian people live along the Pacific Northwest Coast of Alaska and British Columbia; in their folklore comes the story of Andaokut ("Mucus Boy"). He is a HOMUNCULUS-like being created from the accumulation of four days' worth of mucus a woman generated while mourning the loss of her child who was stolen by the Great Woman of the Wood, the cannibal witch, Malahas. This witch was well known for abducting children and smoking them alive over a fire pit so she could eat them at her leisure. Andaokut grew quickly and soon asked its new parents for a bow and an arrow. After discovering why his foster mother cried so often, Andaokut set out to find Malahas. Through a series of carefully played tricks, he managed to kill the old witch the only way she could be—by finding her small black heart (*ti-tema*) where she hid it—hanging by a string in the corner of her house—and piercing it with an arrow. Once Malahas was destroyed, Andaokut gathered up the bodies of the children, laid them out carefully on the ground, and urinated all over them; this process brought them all back to life.

Source: Boas, *Tsimshian Mythology*, 903–7

angiak

In the folklore of the Inuit of Greenland, the angiak was said to be the returned angry spirits of unwanted children or children who were born in secrecy and not given a name (*utburden*) who were left out on the open snowfields to die of exposure. They were known to seek out the skulls of dogs to use as kayaks in order to relentlessly pursue their would-have-been-uncles who shamed their mother for her pregnancy and pressured her to commit infanticide. When these spirits would return to their family's camp, the GHOST would seek out its mother and suckle from her breast while she slept in order to increase its strength. When the angiak grew strong enough, it gained the power to transform into various forms. While it often took the shape of an animal, some stories recount it changing into a feather or even a mitten. The angiak would use this new form to attack the elders of its family.

Sources: Avant, *Mythological Reference*, 466; Buckland, *Weiser Field Guide to Ghosts*, 32; Maberry, *Vampire Universe*, 17; Nansen, *Eskimo Life*, 293–4

anito

Variations: anitu, cancaniaos, mamangkiks

From Filipino folklore comes an aggressive ancestral spirit known as an anito. It rises from its burial mound as a gaseous vapor, and although it seldom ventures too far from its grave, it will assault anyone who enters its domain. Its gaseous form clings to the victim and allows itself to be inhaled. Although not consumed, the anito will infect the person with an illness presenting as an outbreak of boils. Eventually, the disease spreads through the blood and enters the lungs. Many people who fall victim to the attack die, especially children. Highly territorial, the anito can be appeased with offerings of fruit left on top of its burial mound. There is a chant that offers protection for those who need to walk through an area an anito is known to defend: "Honored spirit, please step aside, I am just passing through."

The anito does not seem to gain any apparent means of nourishment or sustenance from these aggressive assaults, however, this does not disqualify it as a vampiric being as many species of vampires are plague carriers and gain no benefits from the death they cause from the illnesses they spread. Likewise, there seems to be neither a method nor a desire to vanquish anitos, for as aggressive as they are, they are also ancestral spirits and revered.

Sources: Benedict, *Study of Bagobo*, 115–6, 123–9; Blair, *Philippine Islands*, 170–3; Kroeber, *People of the Philippines*, 175–82; Maberry, *Vampire Universe*, 18–19

aoroi, fay (OW-roy)

In the British Isles, the aoroi is a species of ghostlike fay. They are created whenever a man dies in battle before his proper time or when a woman dies in childbirth. The babies who are born to deceased mothers as well as those who die before they can be named are immediately transformed into this type of fay. Historically, these children were seen as bad omens, and their bodies were usually taken outside of the town's limits and left to the elements as soon as the events of the birth were duly noted and recorded. Lore has it that these children cannot be intentionally slain or buried once deceased or else they will return to haunt the living, vengeful and angry. They can be captured, however, and their magical properties tapped into and used in the casting of spells. The magic that an aoroi possesses will last until the day that its natural death would have occurred, had it lived out its full human life.

Sources: Collins, *Magic in the Ancient Greek World*, 70–2; Johnston, *Restless Dead*, 71; Meyer, *Mythologie der Germanen*, 94

aoroi, ghost (OW-roy)

In ancient Greece, the aoroi ("untimely dead") is a species of ghost created when a person dies prematurely. Like the aoroi of the British Isles, it can be captured, and its magical abilities tapped into and used in the casting of spells. Also, the magic that the ghost possesses will last only until the day that its natural death would have occurred, had it lived.

Sources: Johnston, *Restless Dead*, 10, 61, 71, 73; Meyer, *Mythologie der Germanen*, 94; Ogden, *Companion to Greek Religion*, 95–6

aptrgangr

Variations: HAUGBUI ("howe," or "barrow")

A fierce monstrosity from Norse legend, an aptrgangr ("again walker" or "one who walks after death") is a demonic spirit that inhabits a recently deceased human corpse. Similar to the draugr, the aptrgangr seldom leaves the vicinity of its cairn. When it becomes angry, it has the ability to grow to a gigantic size with proportional strength. It will drink the blood and consume the flesh of anyone it catches. The only way to temporally be rid of it is to defeat it in a wrestling match, forcing it back into its cairn.

Sources: Cohen, *Prismatic Ecology*, n.p.; Hamilton, *The World of Horror*, 19; Maberry, *They Bite!*, 54

aptrgongumenn (apt-tra-go-GIM-in)

There is little known about the aptrgongumenn ("walking dead"), a REVENANT vampire from Norse mythology, except for the very specific way it must be slain. First, its grave must be found and the corpse exhumed. Then, it must be beheaded. Next, one of its feet must be severed. The two parts are then put in each other's place and the body reburied. If this method of binding it to its grave should fail, again exhume the corpse and set it ablaze, destroying it down to ash alone. Like many vampires from this region, the aptrgongumenn rises up from the grave when summoned by the powerful magic of a sorcerer to do his bidding.

Sources: Belanger, *Sacred Hunger*, 110; Flowers, *Runes and Magic*, 131

aswang tiyanak (AZ-wang TEA-ya-nak)

Variations: anak ni janice, tyanak

Aswang, the Tagalog word for "dog," is applied to anything and everything that is considered a vampire. There are seven different types of aswang vampires, the aswang mandurugo, aswang mannananggal, aswang shape-shifter, aswang tik-tik, aswang tiyanak, aswang witch, and the tanggal. Of these, only the tiyanak is undead.

Generally, the aswang can be found on Mindanao, the second-largest island in the Philippines. Most often they are described as being female and zombielike in appearance, incredibly thin and dressed in rags. Their favorite prey are newborn babies and children, as it is easy to catch them, drain their blood, and consume their tender flesh. They are particularly fond of organ meat.

Of the tiyanak, it is a vampiric demon, born from the union between a demon and a human woman; however, it can also come into being when a child dies without having been baptized or when a mother aborts her unborn child. In this latter instance, it will single out its mother, bringing her nothing but hardship and misery for the rest of her life.

The tiyanak is hairless and red-skinned and has glowing red eyes. It hunts by shape-shifting itself in the guise of an adorable baby and placing itself in a location where it is certain to be discovered. When it is in the home of its rescuer, it waits until the Samaritan is asleep and then, reverting back to its true form, will attack, draining the victim of blood.

Sources: Cannell, *Power and Intimacy*, 144–5, 277; Demetrio, *Encyclopedia of Philippine Folk Beliefs*, 398; Hufford, *Terror That Comes*, 236–7; Jocano, *Folk Medicine*, 109,

169; Lopez, *Handbook of Philippine Folklore*, 146, 221, 227; Ramos, *The Aswang Syncrasy*, 39; Redfern, *The Zombie Book*, 18; *Asian Studies*, 297

Aswid and Asmund (Ah-swayed and Az-mon)

Variations: Assueit and Asmund

In book two of the Icelandic Eyrbyggja Saga ("Saga of the People of Eyri") there is the legend of two blood brothers, Aswid and Asmund, each a great warrior, general, and constant companion to the other. They swore an oath between them that whoever died first, the other would follow him to the grave. As it happened, Aswid grew ill and died. True to his word, Asmund had himself entombed with his friend's body within his crypt along with all the honors they deserved and the treasures they had accumulated over the years, including their dogs, horses, and favorite weapons.

Before Asmund could decide how best to commit suicide, Aswid awoke as an undead vampire, ravenous from his rebirth. He immediately attacked, killed, and consumed the dogs before moving on to the horses. Only then did Aswid seek out the only other living being in the crypt—his brother-in-arms, Asmund.

Three hundred years later, a group of friends had set out to find the now legendary tomb and resting place of the warriors, even though there had been stories that their barrow was haunted. Undaunted, the friends found the site and, despite the religious implications of doing so, opened the tomb.

From within, they heard the sounds of battle. One of the friends volunteered to be lowered into the tomb to scout ahead and see what was causing the noise. A few moments later the friends felt a mighty tug on the rope and together they quickly began to pull it back up. Hanging onto the other end they found a man wearing old-style armor.

The man they had rescued was none other than Asmund. He struggled to catch his breath and explained as best he could the story of how he had been fighting for his life these last three hundred years. It was only when the young thrill seeker was lowered into the tomb and caused a distraction that he, Asmund, was finally able to defeat his undead friend. Having told his tale, Asmund then died. The group of friends found the body of Aswid, beheaded it, and then burned the remains, scattering the ashes to the wind. Then, they reburied Asmund in the tomb with full honors.

Sources: Cox, *An Introduction to Folk-lore*, 52, 58, 151; Elton, *The First Nine Books of the Danish History*, 331–4; Grammaticus, *The Danish History*, 210–1, 237–8; Masters, *Natural History of the Vampire*, 23–4

ataphoi

In the literature and folklore of the ancient Greeks and Romans, if a person died and was not properly buried, they would return as a ghost known as an ataphoi. These restless spirits were particularly aggressive and bitter because they were no longer among the living but, due to lack of funeral rites, were also not among the dead in Hades. Because these souls linger, they can be called upon and used in magical ceremonies. The proper burial and funeral rites performed for the deceased would almost always stop their haunting.

Possibly related or connected to the ataphoi are the *apoaphoi*; it is uncertain but speculated they are a classification of ataphoi, the deceased who were buried but in a state of disfavor or under undesirable circumstances.

Sources: Garland, *The Greek Way of Death*, 101, 103; Johnston, *Restless Dead*, 127, 151; Ogden, *Companion to Greek Religion*, 96–7

ayakashi

Variation: ayakashi no kaika ("atmospheric ghost lights of ayakashi")

Yōkai is the collective name for the assorted myriad creatures of Japanese folklore; they have no set form or purpose and are morally ambiguous. They usually have the ability to shape-shift and an assortment of other supernatural powers. Ayakashi is the collective name for yōkai that appear above the surface of a body of water. They are believed to be the vengeful spirits of those who died at sea, and they are attempting to lure others to their death to join their ranks.

Specifically, on Tsushima Island, the ayakashi appear on the beach and are described as looking like children walking amidst flames. In other places along the Japanese coast, they take on the form of a mountain blocking the trade route; it is believed steering your ship directly towards one will cause it to disappear.

In the *Kaidanoi no Tsue*, a collection of ghost stories from the Edo period, there is a story that takes place in Taidōzaki, Chōsei District, Chiba Prefecture involving an ayakashi. Once, it says, a ship in need of water landed on an island and sent a man ashore to fetch some. When he returned, he told his shipmates how a beautiful woman scooped water from a well for him. One of the crew immediately informed everyone there wasn't a well on this island and the woman was an ayakashi. The crew set sail immediately, and as they went out to sea, the woman appeared and chased them. She came alongside the boat and began to bite into it. The men were able to beat her with their oars and drive her off.

Sources: Murakami, *Yoki Jiten*, 28; Wikipedia, "Ayakashi (yōkai)"

baital

Variations: baitala, baitel, baitol, bay valley, betail, katakhanoso, vetal, VETALA

The baital is a divine, vampiric race of being first mentioned in *Bar-do thos-grol* (*Liberation Through Hearing During the Intermediate State*), better known in the Western world as *The Tibetan Book of the Dead* (circa eighth century). These therianthropes of humans and bats have stubby tails, stand anywhere between four and seven feet tall, and are so horrific in appearance to look upon, that even brave men may become dizzy, grow weak, lock up in fear, or faint.

In artwork, the baital are pictured holding drinking cups made of human skulls filled with blood. When they are not supping upon the sacrificial flesh of humans, they rest by hanging upside down from trees in the jungle near cemeteries. Despite their appearance and appetite for human flesh, they are not mindless monsters.

With their innate ability to possess a corpse, the baital involve themselves in human affairs. For example, the baital from the story *Vetala Panchavimshati* (*Twenty-five tale of Betal*) but internationally known as *Vikram and the Vampire*, decides he will assist the hero, Rajah Vikram. It possesses the body of a murder victim and, through it, reminds the hero of the good advice given to him by the giant—to slay the sorcerer—and encourages him to follow it. Vikram, however, was frightened by the entire event and believed the animated corpse was possessed by a devil.

Sources: Burton, *Vikram and the Vampire*, 11; Icon Group, *Hanging: Webster's Quotations*, 400; Making of America Project, *The Atlantic Monthly*, vol. 49, 69–72; Melton, *Vampire Book*, 322; Stefoff, *Vampires, Zombies, and Shape-Shifters*, 16

bajang

Variation: badjang

In Malaysian folklore, the bajang is a malignant being whose presence foretells disaster. Opinion is divided as to its appearance and origins. Some claim it is a spirit of nonhuman origin that possesses the corpse of a stillborn child and has the ability to take on the appearance of a polecat. Others describe it as having long, pendulous breasts and a penchant for attacking pregnant women; it is believed the stretch marks on a mother's belly are claw marks left behind from an attack. Yet, other sources claim it can be brought into being through incantations. Some tales suggest that the bajang is the male version of the female LANGSUIR.

What is agreed upon is that a bajang can be captured and become a witch's familiar; it can then be passed down to other witches for generations. The familiar is always kept in a bamboo cage specially constructed and ensorcelled with charms and spells called a *tabong* when not in active use. The cage is locked with a stopper made of a particular blend of lead. It is fed a diet of eggs and will turn on its witch if not given enough to eat.

When weaponized, the bajang does not attack its master's enemies with a physical assault but rather inflicts them with a horrible wasting disease; if it is not properly and quickly diagnosed, it is fatal.

Sources: Chopra, *Academic Dictionary of Mythology*, 47; Coulter, *Encyclopedia of Ancient Deities*, 90; Laderman, *Wives and Midwives*, 128; Maberry, *They Bite!*, 57

baka

Variation: benin

When a *bocor* (a Vodou priest) who has led a life of evil dies, they may return as a vampiric spirit known as a baka; it has the natural ability to shape-shift into any animal it desires, and when it does so, it will then have a physical body. No matter what animal it chooses, the baka is especially dangerous because it retains its supernatural strength and will be able to assault and kill a healthy adult man. Bakas are known to prey upon humans to consume their flesh and drink their blood. If the bocor was murdered, as a baka it would be especially vengeful and meticulously hunt down those responsible for its death. It may even decide to spread a fatal disease throughout a community to ensure that its revenge is complete.

Sources: Davis, *Passage of Darkness*, 51, 293; Malbrough, *Hoodoo Mysteries*, 3–4, 131, 180; Owusu, *Voodoo Rituals*, 54, 79

banshee

Variations: bean chaointe ("keening woman"), bean si, BEAN-NIGHE, bean-sidhe ("woman of the fairy" or "woman of the mounds"), bean shith, beansidhe, benshi, caoineag, cointeach, cyhiraeth, cyoerraeth, eur-cunnere noe, gwrach y rhibyn, kannerez-noz, lady of death, little washer by the ford, spirit of the air, washer at the banks, washer at the ford, washer of the shrouds, white lady of Ireland, white lady of sorrow, woman of peace

In Irish folklore, the banshee was originally a singular entity, an ANCESTRAL SPIRIT wailing to announce an upcoming death for one of the five major families: the Kavanaghs, the O'Briens, the O'Connors, the O'Gradys, and the O'Neills.

In modern times, it is still believed the mournful cry of the banshee can be heard; it is considered to be a psychopomp (death omen), and those who hear it know someone who will die the following night. When a chorus of banshees gathers and wails together it is said that someone great or holy is going to die.

Seldom seen, the banshee appeared naked when washing shrouds at the riverbank, its long, pendulous breasts getting in her way. When not at the river it would don a gray cloak over its green gown and let its long white hair hang loose so it could blow in the wind as it hunted for young men near lakes and running water. If it could, a banshee lured its victim to a secluded place and drained him of his blood.

If you caught a glimpse of a banshee as it was washing shrouds, it was advised not to run from it. Rather, wait quietly until it slings its breasts over its shoulder and carefully sneak up behind it. Then, place one of its nipples in your mouth and pretend you are nursing from it. As soon as you are caught, declare to the banshee that it is your foster mother; should it accept you as its foster child, it will answer any question you have. A far less intimate way of gaining information from a banshee is to capture it and threaten it at the point of a sword.

Should you happen upon a banshee while it is washing a shirt at the river and it sees you before you can act, it may speak, saying it is washing the shirt of an enemy. Name an enemy of yours aloud and then do not try to stop it from finishing its task or else the person you named will most certainly die. If you do not name an enemy for it, the banshee will attack and drain you of your blood.

Sources: Maberry, *Cryptopedia*, 101–2; Rose, *Spirits, Fairies, Leprechauns, and Goblins*, 33, 351; Yeats, *Fairy and Folk Tales of the Irish Peasantry*, 108–12

bantu (Ban-TOO), Africa

The people of the Republic of Zambia in South Africa fear a vampiric REVENANT known as a bantu; it is created when an evil person dies or when someone feels they were denied proper respect during their funeral. Spirits are believed to linger near their corpses, sometimes witnessing how survivors honor them—or don't. An offended spirit can return, reanimating its corpse to seek vengeance.

The bantu is mystically drawn to blood, even a single drop, and drinks it out of both a compulsion and necessity, for without the blood, its corpse will begin the natural process of decomposition. Many victims of the bantu survive the experience, waking up with a fresh wound on their body and no memory of the attack.

The Zambian people are largely hemophobic, as even a single drop of blood on the ground will alert the vampire, who will then come when night falls. The only way to stave off the arrival of the vampire is to dig up the area where the blood fell and bury it in a secret location. The person from whom the blood came must go through an elaborate ritual purification process.

Sources: Melland, *In Witch-Bound Africa*, 188; Peek, *African Folklore*, 105, 153; Summers, *Vampire: His Kith and Kin*, 10, 15–6; White, *Speaking with Vampires*, 9–12, 18–22, 51–4

bantu dodong (Ban-TOO Doe-DONG)

The bantu dodong is a vampiric REVENANT from India. It lives in caves and survives off animal blood.

Sources: Konstantinos, *Vampires*, 25; Summers, *Vampire: His Kith and Kin*, 15–6

bantu parl (Ban-TOO PARL)

Variations: han parl, hantu parl

The bantu parl is a vampiric REVENANT from India that preys on people who are too weak to defend themselves, consuming their blood. Typically, its victims are infants, the elderly, and those who are very ill.

Sources: Konstantinos, *Vampires*, 25; Summers, *Vampire: His Kith and Kin*, 15–6; Wright, *The Book of Vampires*, 64

bantu saburo (Ban-TOO Sa-BAH-roo)

Variations: hanh saburi, hanh saburo, hantu saburo

The bantu saburo is a vampiric REVENANT from India that has command over dogs. It lures humans into the jungle and then has its pack of dogs attack and kill its prey. The bantu saburo then drinks up the blood from the corpses.

Sources: Bunson, *Vampire Encyclopedia*, 133; Konstantinos, *Vampires*, 25; Wright, *The Book of Vampires*, 64

baobham sith (BAA-van SITH or BO-vun SITH)

Variations: baobhan sith, bean-fionn, bean si, oinopole ("she with an ass's leg"), onosceles, Sybils, WHITE LADIES

When a woman dies in childbirth, according to Scottish folklore, the woman may return as a type of REVENANT vampiric fay called a baobham sith. According to the original and ancient myth, the baobham sith mingled with humans regularly, even becoming attached to a particular family. It was considered a sign of high status to have one in the family. It was not until after the introduction of Christendom that the baobham sith became an evil being.

Similar to the BANSHEE, the baobham sith is more often heard than seen and will *keen* ("wail") in sorrow, predicting the death of someone who heard its call. If many baobham siths gather together and keen as one, they are foretelling the death of a great person.

It is normally a solitary creature, described as being a tall, pale, beautiful young woman wearing a green dress. In its human guise, it has deer hooves rather than feet that it keeps hidden under its dress. This is especially important as it will often lure young men, particularly shepherds who are up in the highlands, to a secluded place and offer to dance with them. Often it will do this in the guise of someone the man knows, trusts, or lusts after. It will dance wildly until the man is exhausted, then it will attack, draining him of his blood.

In addition to being able to shape-shift into women that their victims know, baobham siths can also change into crows and have the ability to create a thick fog.

Like all fay, the baobham sith can be warded off by iron, but this particular type of fay is also afraid of horses. Carrying a pair of iron scissors in one's pocket while traveling through the highlands will also prevent it from attacking.

Sources: Heldreth, *The Blood Is the Life*, 200; MacKillop, *Dictionary of Celtic Mythology*, 30; Masters, *Natural History of the Vampire*, 139; Senf, *Vampire in Nineteenth-Century English Literature*, 18; Turner, *Dictionary of Ancient Deities*, 92

barabarlakos (BEAR-bur-lock-kose)

According to GREEK VAMPIRE lore, there are a number of ways that a person can have the misfortune of becoming the vampiric REVENANT known as a barabarlakos. One can become a barabarlakos by being someone who was particularly evil in life, by having a cat jump over their corpse, by having been a murder victim, or by having committed suicide. Further, there is the additional rare creation method of having had the misfortune of having eaten, knowingly or not, meat from a sheep that had been slain by a wolf.

No matter how the barabarlakos came into being, it will return with its skin drawn tight as a drum over the body but otherwise looking as it did in life with no other signs of decomposition.

Each night the vampire leaves its grave and goes from house to house knocking on doors or ringing the bell and calling the names of the people who live within. If no one quickly answers the door, it will not linger and move on to the next house, never to return to the home that did not answer its summons. Because this vampire does not have the patience to wait and knock a second time, it is customary in Greece not to open the door until there is a second round of knocking. It is said by some scholars that in this custom may be the origin of the belief that a vampire cannot enter into one's home unless invited. Nevertheless, if someone should answer the door before the second attempt, the vampire will immediately attack, knocking them to the ground as quickly as possible. Then, it will mantle over its prey and pin them to the ground, crushing them to death. Once the person is deceased, the vampire will drain the blood from the corpse.

This vampire is not susceptible to sunlight, and blood drinking is not a requirement for it to sustain its unlife. And the very presence of a barabarlakos can be deadly: should a person see one, he may die on the spot.

The only way to destroy this vampire is to find its grave, exhume the REVENANT, and burn it to ash.

Source: Borrmann, *Vampirismus oder die Sehnsucht nach Unsterblichkeit*, n.p.

Baykok

Variations: Baguck, Bakaak, Paguk, Pakak, Pau'guk

In the Great Lakes region of the United States of America, the Ojibwa folklore includes a being known as the Baykok ("skin draped bones" or "skeletal decomposed remains"); he is undead and wanders the woods at night compelled by hunger, attacking only lone travelers and eating their livers. Wielding a bludgeoning club and invisible spirit arrows, Baykok will incapacitate his victims before consuming them.

According to folkloric *aadizookaan* (traditional stories), a highly skilled and proud hunter became hopelessly lost in the woods while tracking a large buck. Unable to find his way home or catch any food to eat, the hunter began to die of starvation. The hunter swore with his last breath his spirit would never leave his body. Sometime after his death a hunting party passed by his emaciated skeletal remains and roused his spirit. He was described as having glowing red eyes, tight translucent skin, and a shrill cry. Baykok attacked the group, eating them; thereafter he wandered the woods, continuing his hunt for more to eat. He is partial to livers and has the supernatural ability to sneak up upon a sleeping hunter and remove his liver or a slice of his stomach—sources vary—without ever waking the victim.

Sources: Brown, *Complete Idiot's Guide to Zombies*, n.p.; Ingpen, *Ghouls and Monsters*, 43; McGowen, *Encyclopedia of Legendary Creatures*, 12

bean nighe

Variations: an nighechain ("little washerwoman"), nigheag na h-ath ("little washer at the ford"), washer at the ford

The bean nighe ("washer wife") of Irish and Scottish fairy folklore was similar to the BANSHEE, as it too could be found at isolated streams washing the bloodstained garments of those who were about to die. According to folklore, a bean nighe was created when a woman died in childbirth; she became this sort of fairy ghost and remained in such a state until the day she normally would have died. These creatures were described as being small in stature, dressing all in green, and having webbed red feet.

If a person could find a bean nighe and get between it and the river before it sees them, the bean nighe would grant them three wishes. It would also answer any three questions put to it on the provision that it could ask, and expect to receive honest answers to, three questions back.

Sources: Campbell, *Superstitions of the Highlands and Islands of Scotland*, 42–3; Eason, *Complete Guide to Faeries and Magical Beings*, 196; Froud, *Faeries*, 105; Spence, *Minor Traditions of British Mythology*, 22

begierig (bur-GEAR-eg)

Variations: nachttoter, nachtzer, NACHZEHRER, NEUNTOTER

A German vampire, the begierig ("avid chewer"), appeared in one of the series of reports from the minister George Rohrer to the theologian Martin Luther.

One can become a begierig in any of three eclectic ways: by being born with a caul, by drowning, or by being buried in clothes that have one's name sewn into them.

Although this vampire is blamed for tying cows' tails together, it actually never physically leaves its grave. The begierig lies in its grave with its left eye open, chewing on its burial shroud. When its shroud is consumed, it begins to gnaw on its own body, all the while making piglike grunting noises. Every night the begierig uses its psychic powers to drain away the energy, both physical and emotional, from its family members. Garlic, if heavily consumed by the family, is a known repellent—but not a permanent fix to their problem.

The begierig is a known plague carrier, and its body is covered with open sores, so one has to be especially careful when exhuming the body. Some object—such as a brick, a stone, or a coin—must be placed in its mouth to keep it from its incessant chewing. Another method is to tie the mouth closed with clean white linen. As is the case with so many species of vampires, beheading and burning the body to ash will destroy it.

Sources: Dundes, *Vampire Casebook*, 4; Hock, *Die Vampyrsagen*, 33–4; Perkowski, *Vampires of the Slavs*, 162

begu mentas (bee–GOO man-TIS)

In Bataks, Indonesia, begu mentas ("wild spirit") is a specific species of vampiric spirit; it is created when a person commits suicide or dies suddenly and unwillingly, without time to prepare for their death.

Source: Rae, *Breath Becomes the Wind*, 22, 46

Berwick Vampire (Bur-LICK Vam-pire or BER-ik Vam-pire)

Variation: Vampire of Berwick-Upon-Tweed

In 1196, in the village of Berwick, England (or Scotland; sources conflict), a corrupt, excommunicated, and rich merchant died of the plague and was not buried in hallowed ground. There are many variations of the tale, but the earliest source was recorded by a man named William, a canon of Newburgh Priory, Coxwold.

The basic story is a tale of a merchant whose real name has been lost to time but who was referred to as The Wolf for his greedy and merciless nature. Late into his years, he contracted a plague, grew sick, and died in great pain. No one was there to comfort him in death save for his four large dogs. The faithful animals bayed unceasingly for three days after their master died, but it was yet another week before anyone in town went to see why. The townspeople found the dogs emaciated and dying yet guarding the remains of their master. The dogs were killed and their carcasses, as well as the remains of The Wolf, were dragged into the woods and left, forgotten and without funeral rites.

Just after midnight on the next full moon, the townspeople heard the four large dogs baying. What surprised them even more than this, however, was the sight of the dogs' master, The Wolf, running through the town hollering, "Until my body is burnt, you folk of Berwick shall have no peace!" Nearly half of the village died of the plague before the people of the town found the merchant's body, severed the limbs and head, and burned the body down to ash.

Sources: Aylesworth, *Story of Vampires*, 49–50; McNally, *A Clutch of Vampires*, 40–1; Summers, *Vampire in Europe*, 82; Twitchell, *The Living Dead*, 32; White, *Ghost Stories from the North of England*, n.p.

bhut, plural bhutas

Variations: bhoot, Bhuta

In the mythology of India, the bhutas are a type of spirit created when a person dies by accident, execution, or suicide; inadequate or incomplete funeral rites as well as worshiping the bhutas in life will also cause a person to transform into this sort of being after death. Typically, the bhutas live in the mountains and are described as being invisible but large and strong. There are three main classifications of bhutas: hostile, indifferent, and kind. They all accept offerings of black and red flowers, sesame, sugar, and the burning of deodar pine and vatica robusta scented incense. Gandharvas, PISA-CAS, pishacha, PRETA, and yatus are all species of bhutas.

Hostile bhutas will work with rakshasa, attacking and harassing travelers. All bhutas who are active during the night are malicious and associated with demons; some nocturnal bhutas are flesh-eaters.

The kind bhutas will honor and look after the well-being of heroes, lamenting their death or fall from grace.

Indifferent bhutas will dwell alongside man and do no harm so long as they are properly respected; because their presence is sometimes made apparent, they are occasionally confused with GHOSTs.

Sources: Hopkins, *Epic Mythology*, 37, 72, 79; Zelliot, *Experience of Hinduism*, 28–30

bhuta (BOO-ta)

Variation: Brahmaparusha

A vampiric spirit from India, a bhuta ("bad nature spirit") is created when a person who has a physical deformity dies or when a person dies before their proper time, such as in suicide. It is described as looking like a shadow or a flickering light and has the supernatural ability to possess a corpse. Once it has a body, the bhuta spreads sickness and disease. It is also able to shape-shift into a bat or an owl.

Although the bhuta feeds primarily on human corpses, it gets the occasional craving for milk. When this happens, the vampire is known to attack infants who have been recently fed.

Typically, this species of vampire is found in cemeteries, but there are occasions of a bhuta being sighted in places that would have interested it when it was a living person. For instance, if the person whose body the bhuta possesses was an active alcoholic at the time of his death, the vampire may be spotted frequenting bars. No matter what area the bhuta haunts, its presence will permeate the area and people will experience an uncomfortable feeling there; it may even be strong enough to keep animals away. If a Mecaru ceremony is celebrated every 15 days to honor and show respect to the bhuta, then it will not attack anyone and will find a way to be at peace with its environment.

Considered to be a companion of the Shiva, the bhuta casts no shadow, cannot stand on the ground, and is so susceptible to the smell of burning turmeric that if it is in its presence for too long, the vampire will dissipate.

Small shrines called *bhandara* can be found throughout India, especially in regions where the bhuta are revered. These shrines are places of worship, and sacrifices are left to placate the vampires. There is no specific design the shrine must have, but there is always a cradle or some similar device allowing the bhuta to rest so that it does not touch the ground, as the earth is sacred.

Sources: Crooke, *Popular Religion and Folk-lore*, 243; Encyclopedia Americana Corp, *Encyclopedia Americana*, 609; Folklore, *Folklore Society of Great Britain*, vol. 4, 217–8; MacDougall, *Vampire Slayers' Field Guide to the Undead*, 655; Saletore, *Indian Witchcraft*, 99–105

biaiothanatoi

Variation: biaiothanatoz

In the literature and folklore of the ancient Greeks and Romans, if a person died violently and returned as a ghost, they were known as a biaiothanatoi; types of deaths that can trigger their return are death by execution, murder, plague, suicide, or by being a child or virgin at the time of demise. If a person was murdered *and* left unburied (see ATAPHOI), they were particularly violent and vengeful.

Magical papyri have been discovered pressing into service the AOROI and the biaiothanatoi to perform malicious acts, usually insomnia, physical maladies, and loss of appetite. One such text bade the ghost Myrtilus, a murdered charioteer, to jump up from the track and startle the horses during an Olympic race.

Sources: Johnston, *Restless Dead*, xvii; Ogden, *Companion to Greek Religion*, 96, 106

black dog

Variations: bakgest, barghest, barguest, capelthwaite, choin dubh ("muckle black tyke"), devil dog, black angus, Black Shuck, Black Shug, gurt dog, gwyllgi, Gytrash, hell hound, hounds of Annwn, mauthe dhoog, morphing shuck, Padfoot, pooka, rizos, rongeur d'os, skriker, Shuck, suicide shuck, tchian du boulay, Trash

There are many different species of black dogs in mythology, especially on the British Isles; generally, these injurious fairy animals are described as being large, fierce dogs with black coats. Their eyes are said to glow red or yellow, and their mouths are filled with vicious teeth. Regional traditions of their origin vary, but in some places, they are believed to be the returned spirits of the recently deceased. To see one or hear its howl is a psychopomp (death omen); only a few rare stories exist of the black dog playing the role of guardian and protector. Black dogs patrol deserted roads usually invisible right up until the moment they attack; prior to that, only the clicking of their claws can be heard. Crossroads and midnight are also common additions to black dog folklore.

In the British Isles, the black dog is described as being shaggy and the size of a calf, while in German folklore it is equally as large, but its topcoat is dense and wiry with a woolly undercoat, much like a poodle. Appearance and size differ only slightly from region to region; black dogs are reported in some fashion or another throughout the world.

Although traveling alone at night is never a good idea in fairy-country, having a companion offers no protection from the black dog either, as one person may see and hear it while the companion does not. Folklore tells us that the only true protection from one of these creatures is to travel with a descendant of Ean MacEndroe of Loch Ewe; lore has it that he once saved the life of a grateful fairy, who, in return, granted him and his family line perpetual and eternal immunity from black dogs.

Sources: Bois, *Jersey Folklore and Superstitions*, 103; Budd, *The Weiser Field Guide to Cryptozoology*, 98–9; Choron, *Planet Dog*, 28; Godfrey, *Mythical Creatures*, 92–3; Redfern, *The Zombie Book*, 29

black dog, David Suter

In Scottish folklore, there is the tale of a black dog said to the spirit of a man named David Suter. The story has it that in December of 1728 a man by the name of William

Suter heard what he described as unearthly shrieks and cries; he also claims he spotted a dog far larger than any he had ever seen, dark colored and with bright, glowing red eyes. This spectral visitation continued to haunt the Suter family until one night in November of 1730. On that evening the black dog appeared to William and claimed to be the returned spirit of his late brother, David. The specter confessed that, 35 years prior, in a fit of cruelty, he had ordered his hunting dogs to kill a man and that, after they did so, he left the remains unburied. He begged his brother to find the bones and give them the proper burial he once denied the man. William did as his brother asked. After the burial of the remains in consecrated ground, the spectral black dog was seen no more.

Sources: Redfern, *The Zombie Book*, 248

black dog of London's Newgate Jail, the

In the folklore of the city of London, England, it was said that at one time, the lack of food was so pronounced in Newgate Prison that the prisoners would gang up, turn on weaker inmates, and resort to cannibalism.

Luke Hutton, a criminal there, wrote a poem sometime in the 1590s titled "The Discovery of a London Monster Called the Black Dog of Newgate." Hutton died in 1598, hanged on the gallows in York for robbery, but his poem of the event was published in 1638. A pamphlet telling the tale was published in 1812. The verse tells the details of an event that was said to have taken place during the reign of King Henry III (1216–1272) during a severe famine.

The sad and horrific prose relates how a scholar was imprisoned under charges of conjuration and witchcraft; soon thereafter, he was assaulted by his fellow inmates, viciously beaten, and cannibalized. The poem even remarked that the scholar was "passing good meat." Then, from the mutilated remains, a black dog with angry, glowing red eyes arose. No longer weak and incapable of defending himself, the beast violently slaughtered those who had slain and supped upon him, ripping out their bowels and throats. A riot ensued and some prisoners escaped the jail, but not their fate at the maw of the black dog. After its revenge was complete, the black dog vanished and was never seen again.

Sources: Clark, *Haunted London*, n.p.; Pye, *Exposed, Uncovered and Declassified*, n.p.; Redfern, *The Zombie Book*, 247–248

blautsauger

Found throughout Austria, Bosnia Herzegovina, and Germany, the word *blautsauger* ("bloodsucker") encapsulates a species of vampires. The Austrian blautsauger is a REVENANT described as having gaunt features; pale, rotting skin; and a zombielike appearance. It comes into being after the death of a person who had consumed meat that had been slain by a wolf. It is both a blood drinker and a consumer of human flesh.

The blautsauger of Bosnia is said not to have a SKELETON; it is able to hold onto its hair-covered, humanlike form through sheer force of its supernatural will. A theriomorph, it can transform into a gray wolf or rat. This species of vampire comes into being by trickery. The blautsauger takes some dirt from its grave and tricks someone into believing it is a bit of candy or other sort of treat. Once the dirt has been consumed, the transformation begins almost immediately—the victim's bones melt, and hair grows across the surface of the body. Although it sleeps the day away in its grave it does so not out of fear or some sort of vulnerability to sunlight, but because it is a nocturnal predator using the cover of night to hide its movements and better enabling it to approach its prey by stealth. Rarely is it merciful. It can, however, be prevented from entering a home by smearing a mixture of garlic and hawthorn on all the windows and doors. The most effective method of killing this version of the blautsauger is by ritual exorcism performed over its grave during daylight hours as it sleeps.

Sources: Maberry, *They Bite!*, 58–9; MacDougall, *Vampire Slayers' Field Guide to the Undead*, 655

blud

Variations: dickenpoten, irrlicht, Will the Smith

Wendish folklore tells us that the blud ("wanderer"), a type of will o' the wisp, is believed to be the returned soul of an unbaptized child.

Sources: Bonnerjea, *Allborough New Age Guide*, 43; Hastings, *Encyclopædia of Religion and Ethics*, Volumes 3–4, 629

blut aussauger (BLOOT AUS-ah-gr)

Variations: BLAUTSAUGER, nachtzutzler, totbeisser

A vampiric REVENANT, the blut aussauger ("drinker of blood") comes from the folklore in the countries of Bavaria, Bosnia, and Germany. Although similar to the BLAUTSAUGER in some respects, this vampire differs enough to argue it is a separate species.

Like the BLAUTSAUGER, the blut aussauger becomes a vampire by having been force-fed or tricked into eating dirt from the grave of a blut aussauger; however, a person could also become this type of vampire if they had ever consumed meat from an animal that a wolf killed, had committed suicide, died unbaptized, died an unrepentant witch, led an immoral life, or if a nun walked over their grave.

With pale, waxy skin and large eyes, and being only slightly hairier than the average person, the blut aussauger leaves its grave every night in search of human blood. With its supernatural strength and complete lack of a skeletal system to hinder the movements of its body, a blut aussauger can attack from any location or angle. Being a theriomorph, it can shape-shift into a bat, dog, rat, snake, or wolf.

Repelled by garlic and sunlight alike, the blut aussauger also has a curious fear of black dogs that have had eyes drawn in white paint on the top of their heads. Smearing garlic paste or hanging hawthorn on the windows will prevent this species of vampire from entering, and planting hawthorn around the house will keep it off the property.

Garlic plays a vital role in the destruction of the blut aussauger. If someone can force-feed or trick it into eating a garlic bulb, the blut aussauger will be in a weakened state, and a competent combatant should be able to stake it through its heart. Then, garlic and holy water must be put in its grave while incense is burning. Long-term exposure to direct sunlight will also destroy this REVENANT, as long as garlic is placed in the mouth of the remains.

Sources: Dundes, *Vampire Casebook*, 10–1; McNally, *In Search of Dracula*, 117; Petzoldt, *Demons*, 161; Summers, *Vampire: His Kith and Kin*, 315

bockshexe

Variations: bochshexe, bocksmarte

This demonic, vampiric alp comes from the folklore of Germany; therianthropic in appearance, it is described as a large, dark-haired goat. A subspecies of the alp, it is created when a male child is born with a caul (an embryotic sack) over its face or when the mother of a male child goes through a particularly long and painful childbirth and dies. In both of these instances, when the child dies, they will return as an alp.

Sources: Maberry, *They Bite!*, 59; Meyer, *Mythologie der Germanen*, 505

bokholdoys

The bokholdoys are returned souls that are feared by the Buryat people of the Buryat Republic, Siberia, as they steal souls.

In one folktale, the hero, Upitel Khubun ("Orphan"), discovers the means by which to cure the son of the king. He is summoned to court and heals the boy but tells the king he must restore the child's soul for the cure to be complete. He searches the countryside, and because he has the ability to speak the language of the birds, is able to see a gathering of bokholdoys dragging away the soul of the king's son. Pretending not to be interested in what they are doing, he approaches them and strikes up a conversation. In it, he asks what it is they are most afraid of. They reply that thorny and prickly shrubs is the only thing they fear. In turn, they ask Upitel Khubun why it is that when he walks, he does not trample the grass beneath his feet and that branches break as he moves past them. The hero replies that he is still learning to move as they do, as he is newly dead. Believing the lie, the bokholdoys then ask what it is that he fears. The hero replies that he is terrified of fatty meat. Upitel believes he has gained their trust and asks the bokholdoys to teach him how to steal souls. They agree and tell him he can start by carrying this one for them. Upitel takes the soul of the child and runs with it into some thornbushes. The angry bokholdoys give chase and, unable to follow him into the bush, throw fatty meat into it believing it will compel him to leave the safety of the bush. Eventually, the ghosts realize they have been deceived and, unable to do anything about their situation, and leave. Upitel then carries the soul of the child back to the king and completes the cure, restoring the child to full life.

The bokholdoys and all the other souls of the dead have an unnamed one-eyed chief who rules over them. This overseer of wandering souls can be killed only if shot in the eye. Once dead, he will transform into a pelvis bone, which must then be burned.

Source: Hastings, *Encyclopædia of Religion and Ethics*, Volumes 3–4, 8–9

Bourbon Street Devil Baby, the

Variations: Devil Baby of Bourbon Street, Devil Baby of New Orleans

From the folklore of the French Quarter of New Orleans, Louisiana, comes the story of the Bourbon Street Devil Baby. There are many variations of the story, but, in essence, they all claim it began in the early 1800s. Its story has many similarities to the DEVIL BABY OF HULL HOUSE.

According to local legend, a wealthy plantation owner was desperate for a male heir; between his first and second wife (different stories explain away their demise) he had six daughters. For his third wife, he married a beautiful Creole woman, and when she became pregnant with who was to be his seventh child, she immediately sought the assistance of a midwife who also happened to be the area's Vodou queen. Unfortunately, and unbeknownst to the wife, the Vodou queen had a profound hatred for the plantation owner and cursed the child as it grew in its mother's womb.

The child was born on Mardi Gras day, and it was a male, the heir the husband had long desired, but it had claws, cloven hooves, horns, red eyes, and a ratlike tail. A wild thing from birth, it developed quickly, baring its teeth at its terrified siblings; it was locked in the home's attic. It was not long before the devil baby escaped its prison in the family home. It made its way to the neighbor's property, where it stalked, killed, and consumed their children. Evading capture, it is said to now reside somewhere in Saint Anthony Garden located behind the Saint Louis Cathedral. This beautiful fenced-in area has since become known as the Devil's Playpen and the Devil's Garden. Local legend also says this garden is situated directly over a portal to hell. The Devil Baby has been blamed for assaulting people in the gardens.

Lore tells us that the now-adult Devil Baby stands only about three feet tall and is bald. In addition to the above description, he is also said to have pointed ears and "hands like a raccoon."

Ever the menace to the French Quarter, the Devil Baby uses its supernatural charms to make those who see it believe they are looking into the face of the most beautiful child they have ever seen, right up to the point where it bares its teeth and attacks. It survives by drinking blood from its victims and consuming the flesh of the dead. Rumor has it a lock of its hair—presumably not from the top of its head—can cure blindness.

In addition to mesmerizing people into believing it is an adorable child and having the gift of seeing into the future, it can also climb and swim exceedingly well and run incredibly fast. Because it abhors the light of day, it will only prowl the streets from dusk to dawn. Some stories claim that when it is near, crosses and crucifixes will fall off the wall, rosary beads will break in your hands, and water will boil.

On Mardi Gras, he can change his physical being into that of a man and walk among the crowd. If you can find him and confront him with his true identity, he will truthfully answer any one question put to him. At midnight he will revert to his true form.

It is also believed that should the Devil Baby ever kiss you, you are doomed not only to become a ghost when you die but also to do its bidding.

Variations of the Devil Baby's origin claim its mother was a slave who was raped by the plantation owner; another version says the mother was the absinthe-addicted daughter of a wealthy French aristocrat. In this version, she was inebriated the entirety of her pregnancy and, immediately after the child was delivered a horrid, twisted abomination, she abandoned it in Pirate's Alley, located directly across the street from the Saint Louis Cathedral. The story adds that the infant's demonic cries disrupted the Ash Wednesday mass.

Sources: Redfern, *The Zombie Book*, 33; Steiger, *Real Zombies*, 33, 133–134, 256

brahmadaityas

Variation: brahma-daityas

A class of benign ghost, the brahmadaityas of Hindu mythology are the returned spirits of Brahmin priests; they never appear with the intent to frighten or to do harm, nor do they ever enter into the body of a living person in order to possess them. Also, unlike other classes of ghost, they only eat food that would be considered religiously clean. Generally innocuous, the brahmadaityas take up residence in the branches of the *gaya-asvatha* (*Ficus cordifolia*), the most sacred species of the *Ficus religiosa* trees. However, if ever the dignity of one of the brahmadaityas becomes contemned or their tree is desecrated or harmed, their rage will know no bounds; the ghost will find the offender and ruthlessly wring their neck until it is broken.

Sources: Bonnerjea, *Allborough New Age Guide*, 44; Dey, *Govinda Sámanta*, Volume 1, 154–5

broucolaque, ancient (BROW-co-look)

Variations: broncolakas, broucolaca, broucolacchi, broucolacco, broucolokas, broucoloques, broukolakes, brukulaco, brukolak, burcolakas, drakaena, drakos, mulo, timpanita, tumpaniaïoi, vrykolaka

In the mythology of ancient Greece, if a hero or brigand is going to die but fights against the inevitable hard enough, through sheer force of will, they will return as an undead vampiric REVENANT called a broucolaque. Condemned to wander the world as an undead being, this bloodthirsty creature is a gluttonous blood-drinker and revels in its atrocities. For hundreds of years, the belief in the existence of this vampire was held as a steadfast truth. It was so ingrained in Greek society that even the Catholic Church did not try to dissuade it; in fact, they embraced it and added onto the mythology. The Church promised protection to its followers if they made offerings to the Church and paid to have masses said for the broucolaque on the anniversary of its death. Over the centuries the stories of the broucolaque have changed and evolved in order to remain culturally relevant to the people who feared it (see GREEK VAMPIRES).

Sources: Guiley, *Complete Vampire Companion*, 55; Masters, *Natural History of the Vampire*, 169; Stewart, *Romantic Movement*, 137; Voltaire, *Philosophical Dictionary*, 560–1

broucolaque, modern (BROW-co-look)

Variations: broncolakas, broucolaca, broucolacchi, broucolacco, broucolokas, broucoloques, broukolakes, brukulaco, brukolak, burcolakas, drakaena, drakos, mulo, timpanita, tumpaniaïoi, vrykolaka

The broucolaque of today is the result of the social evolution from the broucolaque of ancient times. This modern-day vampiric REVENANT rises from the grave of particularly evil individuals, such as those who have been excommunicated from the Church.

Like most other GREEK VAMPIRES, the broucolaque is described as looking like the person did in life but with its skin drawn so tightly over its body that when it is slapped, it sounds like a drum. Also, like other Greek vampires, it will knock on the doors of those it knew in life, trying to lure them out so that it can attack them, draining them of their blood. The modern broucolaque is something of a stalker, for if it cannot get an answer at a person's home, it will then go to the fields in an attempt to intercept farmers on their way to work. If it should meet a person during its travels, it will ask them a question. Should that person answer, they will die the next day.

Perhaps in an attempt to appeal to the minds of more modern people, the broucolaque is able to rise from its grave without disturbing the ground.

Sources: *Encyclopedia Americana*, vol. 6, 504–5; Whitelaw, *Popular Encyclopedia*, 778

Brown, Mercy

First reported in 1892 by the *Providence Journal* newspaper, this was the highly editorialized story of the alleged vampiric REVENANT known as Ms. Mercy Lena Brown (1872–1892) of Exeter, Rhode Island; family and friends knew her as Lena. This story broke a full four years before Bram Stoker's novel *Dracula* was published. Exeter was a developing town of 2,500 residents in 1820, but tuberculosis set in and the community's population had dropped to 960 by 1890.

Mercy Brown had pulmonary tuberculosis; her mother, Mary Elizabeth (née Arnold) Brown, passed on December 8, 1883, with the disease, and her sister, Mary Olive, followed on June 6, 1884.

In 1890 Mercy's brother, Edwin, began to grow sick; he and his wife moved to Colorado Springs, where the climate seemed to help.

All her life, Mercy had been asymptomatic, but when the disease began to show signs in 1891, it overtook her rapidly; her strength failed, her skin grew pale, and, eventually, she stopped eating. At night her condition always worsened. From time to time, she would awaken in the morning panting heavily with traces of blood on her mouth and bed sheets. She died on January 17, 1892.

Mercy's father, George Thomas Brown, after having lost a wife and two daughters in such a short period of time, was seriously concerned about the health and well-being of his only son, Edwin, whose health had been stabilized since the move; however, when he returned home for Mercy's funeral, the disease returned in full force. It is said he cried out, in fevered dreams, "She haunts me! She wants me to come with her!"

On March 17, 1892, George led a mob of fellow farmers and townsfolk to the Brown family's graves, convinced that one of the deceased had to be a vampire. Both Mary and Mary Olive's bodies had decomposed to the mob's approval. Mercy's body was, however, in their opinion too well preserved for the length of time she had been deceased. Mercy's corpse was cut open and examined. The mob decided that her liver and heart were full of blood. This was evidence enough to them that Mercy must be a vampire. Her heart was removed and rendered to ash and then given to Edwin to consume. It was hoped this would cure him of the curse that his sister had laid upon him. Sadly, Edwin died on May 2, 1892.

Perhaps the "vampire" Mercy Brown had been slain, but the Brown family deaths continued. Annie Laura (née Brown) Taylor died August 9, 1895, at the age of 25; Jennie Adeline (née Brown) Edwards died October 2, 1895, at the age of 18; Myra Frances (née Brown) Caswell died June 25, 1899, at the age of 18.

The last remaining Brown daughter, Hattie May, survived. She married twice; with her first husband, Alvin Luke Clark, she had four children: Hattie, Myra Susan, Janette "Nettie," and Alvin Junior. She was granted a divorce in 1910 and remarried in 1920 to Frank Everette Pierce. She passed in 1954 at the age of 79.

Sources: Belanger, *World's Most Haunted Places*, 121–25; Bell, *Food for the Dead*; Brennan, *Ghosts of Newport*, 113–16; Stefoff, *Vampires, Zombies, and Shape-Shifters*, 17

brucolaco (BRUKE-oh-lock-oh)

Variations: broucalaque, brucolak, bruculaco, BRUCULACAS, timpanita

Strictly from the lore of the Epirus, Thessaloniki, and Thessaly regions of Greece, this vampire answers the age-old question "Can a werewolf become a vampire?"

In life, the person accused of being a brucolaco can fall into a state of being where all the muscles in his body will become rigid and remain in a fixed position. This person will show no reaction to painful stimuli, and the limbs are said to feel "waxy."

Today, we know this to be a nervous condition called catalepsy caused by disorders such as epilepsy or Parkinson's disease, but it was once believed that this was a curse sent by God. It was believed that while a person lay in this state, a wolf spirit left his body and went on the hunt, seeking human flesh and blood. When the person with catalepsy eventually died, or, when a person who was excommunicated by the Church died, they would then rise up, undead, as a vampiric REVENANT. It was described as looking the way many GREEK VAMPIRES do, with its skin pulled so tightly over its body that it sounded like a drum when slapped. However, it rises from its grave as a therianthrope with many wolflike characteristics, such as, barrel chest, canine claws, muscular arms, powerful jaws, and vicious claws the length of steak knives. At night, it lets loose with a piercing cry, akin to the wail of the BANSHEE. Whoever answers the call of the brucolaco will then die of plague.

Fortunately, the vampire can be destroyed if the Church can be convinced to recant the excommunication. If this is not possible, then the brucolaco must be captured and beheaded. Then, the head must be boiled in wine. Finally, it and the body must be rendered to ash. Because it was so firmly believed that a werewolf would become a vampire upon death, the Church made it common practice to burn at the stake anyone who was convicted of being a brucolaco in an attempt to prevent vampiric resurrection. Because of this, more than 30 thousand people were burned as werewolves during the Inquisition.

Sources: Calmet, *Dissertation sur les apparitions*, 237; Maberry, *They Bite!*, 60; Riccardo, *Vampires Unearthed*, 5; Volta, *Vampire*, 148

bruculacas

Variation: brukulaco

A vampiric REVENANT from Thessaly and Epirus, Greece, the bruculacas, like many GREEK VAMPIRES, looks like a corpse with tightly drawn, red skin. It is created when a person who has been excommunicated from the Church passes; in some cases, this vampiric curse can be passed from father to son. A foul-smelling and filthy creature, its body cavity is filled with slime and excrement, spreading the plague wherever it goes. It preys on humans for their blood.

Sources: Maberry, *They Bite!*, 60; Maberry, *Vampire Universe*, 57

buau (BWOW)

Variation: buo

The Dayak people of the island of Borneo have a vampiric spirit that they fear called a buau. Created when an enemy of theirs is slain in battle, the spirit returns as a warrior ghost to haunt those who caused its death, attack them, and drink their blood. It is described as having large eyes and fangs and a thirst for blood. To be rid of this enemy once and for all, the body of the warrior must be dismembered and each part separately cremated.

Sources: Maberry, *They Bite!*, 62; Roth, *The Natives of Sarawak*, 167; Saunders, *Borneo Folktales and Legends*, 67–68; Wood, *Uncivilized Races of Men*, 1157

caballi (cab-ALI)

Variation: cabales

This astral vampire exists solely in the astral plane; from there, it preys on other astral beings, the occasional human passing through the astral plane, and sexually driven mediums. Similar to the incubus and succubus, the caballi seeks out humans who share a passion for satisfying voracious needs, latches on to them, and utilizes their bodies during sexual activity.

A caballi is created when a man dies before it is his natural time to do so. His soul travels to the astral plane, retaining its intellect and a desire to do nothing more than interact with the world again. For this purpose, a caballi will possess a psychic medium, so that for a little while at least, it will have some sense of sensation. Fortunately, the caballi will only exist until the day arrives that it would have died naturally.

Sources: Drury, *Dictionary of the Esoteric*, 40; Gaynor, *Dictionary of Mysticism*, 31; Masters, *Eros and Evil*, 181; Rulandus, *Lexicon of Alchemy*, 77

callicantzaro (Cal-ah-KIN-zaro)

Variations: callicantzari, kalikandsaros, kallicantzaros, kallikantzaros, kapaconcolos, karaconcolos

The callicantzaro is different from the other Greek vampires that hunt the islands, most obviously in its method of creation. It does not matter how good a life someone lived or even if they were a devout Christian—all that matters is when they were born. Any child who had the misfortune of being born between Christmas Day (December 25) and the Feast of the Twelfth Night (January 5) will rise from its grave as a callicantzaro when it eventually dies. These children are called "Feast Blasted" and are pitied by all who know the circumstances of their birth. The only method of saving the child from its fate of UNDEATH is to hold the newborn's feet over a fire until its toenails burn and blacken. If this is not done, there is no chance of later salvation.

If the child is not saved and returns from death as a callicantzaro, fortunately, it can only survive in our world on the days between Christmas and either New Year's Day (January 1) or the Feast of the Epiphany (January 6). The rest of the year, it dwells in a nearby dimension or underworld realm. This belief is as old as Christianity. It is possible that in the pre–Christian era, the vampires could only walk in our world from the winter solstice to the next full moon.

Nevertheless, when the callicantzaro does return, it is now a horrific creature, looking nothing like the other numerous vampires that roam the Greek countryside. This therianthrope has a black face, red eyes, very long ears, clawed hands, and sharp teeth. The first time it returns to our world, it will seek out its surviving family members, ripping them apart with its clawed hands. Although blood drinking is not a requirement for its survival, it is something the callicantzaro revels in. As soon as its family members are slain, it will move on to targets of opportunity.

As the time for it to return to its own dimension draws near, the male callicantzaro will try to capture a woman to take back with it in order to sire children with her, forcibly if necessary. The offspring of this union will be born callicantzaro. When not seeing to its parental duties, it sleeps in caves by day and terrorizes villages by night.

Sources: Barber, *Dictionary of Fabulous Beasts*, 34; Bryant, *Handbook of Death*, 99; Georgieva, *Bulgarian Mythology*, 90; Jackson-Laufer, *Encyclopedia of Traditional Epics*, 321; Maberry, *They Bite!*, 62; Senn, *Were-wolf and Vampire in Romania*, 30

cauga

Variation: lau

In the Hindu mythology from the Andaman Islands, cauga ("ancestors" or "spirits") is the general name for spirits living in the sea; they are believed to be the ghosts or returned spirits of deceased islanders who have returned to live among people. The cauga is known to spread disease; however, they are not to be confused with the *cauga tabnja*, the returned spirits of important tribal members who take on a heroic, mythical status in death. These ancestral spirits of legendary status would not harm their descendants.

Sources: Angell, *Principles of Sociology*, 234; Radcliffe-Brown, *Andaman Islanders*, 136, 190, 285

cel-rau (cell-ROO)

Variations: concealmentrau, ieli, orgoi, strigoii

In Romania, people are careful not to say the true name of this vampiric REVENANT aloud as the cel-rau ("the bad" or "wrong-doer") has incredible hearing and can hear its name uttered from any distance. It will appear near the person who has said it within moments.

As the ieli, it is strictly nocturnal and said to look like a hag and an ugly cat that lingers near crossroads waiting for someone to attack. Interestingly, it cannot enter into the center of the crossroads.

Sources: Cremene, *Mythologie du Vampire en Roumanie*; Nash, *Once Upon a Fairies Wing*, 79

chedipe (CHA-dippy)

Variations: ALVANTIN, CHUREL, jakhai, jakhin, mukhai, nagulai

In India, there is the folkloric believe that when a woman dies in an unnatural way, such as in childbirth or by suicide, she may return as a vampiric REVENANT witch known as a chedipe ("prostitute"). Nude, and riding upon a tiger at night, the chedipe selects a home and places all who are within into a deep sleep. Then, it brazenly enters and bites a hole in the big toe of all the male occupants so as to drink their blood. In addition, the vampire feeds off misery and sorrow and takes great delight in destroying the family's bonds of love and trust. Those men who survive the night awaken the following morning feeling as if they had been intoxicated the night before. The chedipe is associated with a discriminated-against caste of people known as the *devadasi*, those who work in the sex industry.

Sources: Crooke, *Religion and Folklore*, 194; Duprae, *The Vampires*, 61; Maberry, *They Bite!*, 63; Riccardo, *Liquid Dreams of Vampires*, 51; Thurston, *Omens and Superstitions*, 261–2

cheonyeo gwisin

Variations: cheonyeogwisin, Korean virgin ghost, maiden specters, malmyeong, sonmalmyeong, songaksi

The cheonyeo gwisin ("virgin ghost") is a figure seen in Korean folklore. It is characterized by its long, flowing black hair; pale complexion; and traces of blood at the corners of its mouth. The ghost is often depicted in a traditional Korean funeral dress called a *hanbok*. There are indications that this spectral entity retains some semblance of life, as evidenced by its continuously growing hair and fresh blood on its lips.

This ghostly REVENANT bears similarities to the BANSHEE from Irish mythology, as it is believed to curse a family lineage until it has been eradicated through exorcism or posthumously married off to a deceased bachelor from the family.

A cheonyeo gwisin comes into existence when a young, unmarried, school-aged girl, subjected to misery within her highly regimented societal structure, passes away. In life, she would have experienced ostracization, school bullying, oppressive class structures, cruelty from a stepparent, and victimization within the hierarchical high school system. Unfulfilled love is occasionally cited as a contributing factor.

Reports often place cheonyeo gwisin sightings in graveyards; on desolate roads; near water bodies; and, intriguingly, in school bathrooms. Their activity peaks between midnight and dawn. Despite their neat and well-maintained appearance that makes them almost indistinguishable from living humans, their presence can be identified by a sudden temperature drop or a gust of wind. These revenants harbor vengeful intentions, seeking retribution against those who wronged them in life by causing accidents and illnesses.

A less commonly encountered male counterpart of this ghost is referred to as the chonggak gwishin.

Sources: Fee, *American Myths, Legends, and Tall Tales*, 212; Lee, *Encyclopedia of Asian American Folklore and Folklife*, 660

ch'iang shih

In Chinese folklore, it is believed that leaving a corpse unburied is not only unlucky but also dangerous as it invites evil spirits to possess the body. There are many tales of stories involving unburied and unguarded bodies, but a popular one tells the tale of four travelers who stop for the night at an inn in Shandong, a northern coastal province.

In the story, they arrive at the inn late in the evening, but the innkeeper tells them he has no room. They are tired and beg for any space he can provide. With great reluctance, the innkeeper offers them a place to spend the night in a shed in his courtyard. Graciously they accept, but the innkeeper does not tell them that behind a curtain, laid out on a plank, is the body of his daughter-in-law, who died earlier in the day.

Three of the men fell asleep quickly, but the fourth, sensing something was not quite right, lay awake, unable to dismiss a feeling of danger. Then, to his horror, he saw a skeletal pale green hand slowly begin to part the curtain. It stealthily moved to where the travelers lay and mantled over them, its horrid, death-spreading breath filling the air. The fourth traveler recognized what was happening and, closing his eyes, held his breath so as not to breathe in the toxic air. The ch'iang shih, believing its evil work was done, crept back to its plank. His life saved, the man panicked. He shot up and fled the shed as quickly as he could, but the vampire was attracted to the movement and gave chase. He tried to hide behind a willow tree but the ch'iang shih found him. It gave a loud shriek and lunged at him; terrified, the man fainted. This saved his life, as the claws of the vampire sunk so deeply into the tree it could not be removed.

When the morning came, the innkeeper cautiously went to check in on his late-night travelers. He discovered three of the men dead in the shed and the fourth still passed out beneath the willow tree. The remains of his daughter-in-law were on the ground next to him, the evil spirits that possessed her body dissipated with the rising of the sun.

Sources: Guiley, *Encyclopedia of Ghosts and Spirits*, 92–93; MacDougall, *Vampire Slayers' Field Guide to the Undead*, 655

chindi

Variation: ch'indi

In the Navajo tribal mythology of North America, the chindi ("evil spirit") is believed to be the ghost of a person who was not properly buried. This spirit is comprised of all evil remnants of the person and preys upon its surviving relatives, causing illness and making mischief. The chindis are also known to prey upon those who profit by taking advantage of others and those people who chose to do harm when they could have chosen to do something good. A complex ritual known as a sing can cleanse the chindi, causing it to dissipate into the night wind.

Sources: Chopra, *Academic Dictionary of Mythology*, 69; *Ethnologic Dictionary of the Navaho Language*, 445; Maberry, *Vampire Universe*, 77, 80–81; Steiger, *Real Zombies*, 121

ch'ing shih (cha-ing SHE)

Variations: chiang-shi, chiang shih, CH'IANG-SHIH, ch'ing-shih, ch'ling shih, gaing shi, "the hopping vampire of Asia," kiang-kouei, kiang shi, kiang-shi, kiangshi, kouei, kuang-shi, kuang-shii, kyonshi, xianhshi

Known the world over as the "hopping vampire," the mythology specifically regarding the ch'ing shih originates in the lands between Siberia and China. This vampiric revenant is created in the typical fashion of most Chinese vampires—when a cat jumps over a corpse, if a person has been cursed to rise as the undead, or if a person has the misfortune of dying far from home and not being returned for burial. More like a zombie, this vampire has only animal-level intelligence and is only motivated to hunt for blood and life-force energy.

The vampire gets its "hopping" name from having the misfortune to have died while far from home. The bodies of travelers were wrapped in a burial shroud and bound tightly for transportation to the person's hometown if it were known. Should the corpse animate before it could be returned for burial, it was so tightly wrapped it was unable to move and only had the ability to hop after prey.

No matter how it is created, the ch'ing shih will arise with curved fingernails, pale green skin giving off a phosphorescent glow, red eyes, and serrated teeth. As it ages, its hair continues to grow, changing from its original color to pure white. When it has a long and full mane, it is considered physically mature. At this point, its breath will be so foul that it can kill a person if it exhales directly on them.

The ch'ing shih feeds off the blood of men, but with its voracious sexual appetite, it is well known to first rape and then devour the bodies of women.

After it rises from the dead, the ch'ing shih will have the ability to theriomorph into a CORPSE CANDLE, and, once it reaches maturity, it will have the ability to fly, track its prey by scent, and shape-shift into the form of a wolf.

The ch'ing shih is blind, and, although able to do so, it has difficulty crossing running water. Its supernatural power is derived from the moon; during the day and on moonless nights it stays in its underground lair. Although it is afraid of thunder and loud noises, the only thing it is truly fearful of is the White Emperor, to whose court it must pay homage.

To destroy an adolescent ch'ing shih, there are two proven methods. The first is to trap it in a magical circle that is made by encircling the vampire with iron filings, red peas, or rice. The other method is to throw handfuls of grain on the ground as soon as one is spotted. An adolescent ch'ing shih is mystically compelled to count these grains and will cease its attack. Then, using a broom, a person can begin to sweep the grain back to the creature's resting place. It will follow, if for no other reason than to begin to recount the grains as soon as the sweeping stops.

Once an adolescent ch'ing shih has been captured, it can be destroyed by taking Buddhist or Taoist death blessings written on a piece of paper and slapping it against the vampire's forehead. Another method is to take the captured ch'ing shih to an ancestral burial ground and after a proper burial rite is given for the creature, Buddhist or Taoist magic spells are used to bind the vampire to its new grave.

A mature adult ch'ing shih can only be destroyed by the noise of a bullet being fired, a modern belief, or the sound of a large thunderclap. As soon as it falls over, the body must be burned to ash to it will rise again.

Sources: Maberry, *They Bite!*, 64; MacDougall, *Vampire Slayers' Field Guide to the Undead*, 655; New York Folklore Society, *New York Folklore Quarterly*, vol. 29–30, 195; Redfern, *The Zombie Book*, 52; Summers, *Vampire: His Kith and Kin*, 237; Thompson, *Studies of Chinese Religion*, 91; *Atenea*, 93

choorail

The choorail is the ghost of a woman who died while pregnant, according to the beliefs of the Muslims of India. To prevent a choorail from haunting its remaining family, which according to folklore is typically a cruel mother-in-law, mustard seeds are scattered at various points throughout the funeral trail in the graveyard; iron tacks are also driven into the ground as a means of deflecting the ghost. Unlike a vampire who would be compelled to count the seeds, the choorail is captivated by the loveliness of the plant's blossoms and will remain in the graveyard throughout the night admiring its beauty.

Sources: Bonnerjea, *Allborough New Age Guide*, 58; Oman, *Cults, Customs and Superstitions of India*, 280–1

chuiaels (CHEW-ee-ales)

Variation: cijurreyls

A vampiric energy demon from Hindu lore, a chuiaels is created when a woman dies in childbirth; it manifests as a beautiful woman and, like a succubus, lures men to bed. This vampire has the reputation for being an excellent lover, and the few men who survived the experience claim that during fellatio, it literally drained away their life.

Sources: DePierre, *A Brief History of Oral Sex*, 72; Masters, *Eros and Evil*, n.p.

churel (CHUR-el)

Variations: ALVANTIN, CHEDIPE, churail, churreyls, MUKAI, nahulai

In India, when a woman dies an unnatural death or during childbirth, she will return as a type of undead. If, however, she should do so during the five-day Festival of Diwali, she returns specifically as the vampiric REVENANT known as a churel.

Churels are an extremely ugly species of vampire in their true form, having backward-facing feet; a black tongue; sagging breasts; thick, rough lips; and wild hair. The churel is a theriomorph, however, and will shape-shift into a beautiful woman carrying a lantern.

Bitter and carrying the anger of her early and tragic death, the churel starts its vampiric life by attacking the male members of its family. Beginning with the youngest and most handsome in its family line, it will seduce him, drain him of his blood, and leave him as a shriveled husk. Once the men of its family are used up, it will move on to others, stalking the roadways and luring lone male travelers astray. Sometimes it captures a man and takes him back to its lair in a graveyard, keeping him prisoner and feeding off him for as long as it can.

In the south, there is the practice of making a Stonehenge-like structure at the entryway to the village that is blessed in order to keep a churel from entering.

Sources: Briggs, *The Chamars*, 129–31; Crooke, *An Introduction to the Popular Religion*, 69–70, 72, 168–71; Kiev, *Magic*, 135, 136; Maberry, *They Bite!*, 66; MacDougall, *Vampire Slayers' Field Guide to the Undead*, 655; Taylor, *Death and the Afterlife*, 67

cihuateteo (chee-who-ta-TAY-oh)

Variations: ciuatateo, ciuateteo, civapipltin, civatateo

A type of vampiric, demonic demigoddess of the Aztec people of ancient Mexico, a cihuateteo is created when a mother dies in childbirth or when a child is stillborn. Cihuateteo, a name meaning "right honorable mother," fall under the dominion of the goddess of evil, lust, and sorcery, Tlazolteotl, and all of the cihuateteo are considered to be her followers. They are depicted as having arms, faces, and hands white as chalk, and they live in the jungle, keeping to the dark places, as they were susceptible to sunlight; long-term exposure to it will destroy them. Although cihuateteo will feed off lone travelers whom they happen upon as they fly on their brooms through the jungle, they prefer the blood of infants. Their bite has a paralytic effect, which enables the cihuateteo to feed in silence.

Fending off this vampire is difficult, as only powerful Aztec apotropes and charm work against them, and even then not against the cihuateteo who were stillborn. Because they did not live to learn the culture and customs of its people, these cihuateteo are immune to their effects. Fire will drive both types of these vampires off, but only so long as it is present.

Sources: Aguilar-Moreno, *Handbook to Life*, 147, 199, 258; Kanellos, *Handbook of Hispanic Cultures*, 227; Maberry, *They Bite!*, 66–7; MacDougall, *Vampire Slayers' Field Guide to the Undead*, 655; Salas, *Soldaderas*, 5–6, 34, 95; Stefoff, *Vampires, Zombies, and Shape-Shifters*, 17; Turner, *Dictionary of Ancient Deities*, 129

co-hon

In Vietnamese mythology, the co-hon ("forsaken spirits" or "wandering souls") are the ghosts or returned spirits of people who died a violent death or died without having any family to see to their needs in the afterlife. Offerings of dried rice, fresh water, gruel, and popcorn are left for these piteous spirits near temple doors and in the graveyards. It is especially important to leave offerings in the summer when cholera and floods take many lives.

Sources: Kendall, *Vietnam*, 261; Lung, *Lost Fighting Arts of Vietnam*, 37; Tang, *Death and Remembrance*, 30

con tinh

This type of vampiric REVENANT of southern Vietnamese lore is created when a woman's death is involved in an illicit love affair or if she is a virgin who died a violent death.

Preying on travelers, it appears as a beautiful young woman dressed in the royal vestments of a princess carrying a fan and a basket of fruit. Usually, it has a pair of cranes or doves accompanying it. Travelers often mistake the birds for a good omen and follow them, ultimately coming upon the con tinh, who will be found standing beside a fruit tree, beckoning the traveler closer with the promise of a refreshing snack. Anyone who touches the fruit will wither and die on the spot, passing their life energy into the tree, which converts it into more fruit. The con tinh, desirous only of killing and consuming life, lives off the fruit of the tree and cannot leave its immediate area.

Sources: Do, *Vietnamese Supernaturalism*, 106–7; Fjelstad, *Possessed by the Spirits*, 65–6; Leach, *Funk and Wagnalls Standard Dictionary of Folklore*, 284; Stein, *The World in Miniature*, 84, 97, 300, 302

corpse candle

Variations: brunnlig, buchelmannle, corpse sans ame, dichepot, draulicht, droglicht, druckfackel, dwallicht, dwerlicht, earthlights, erlwischen, feu-follet ("foolish fire"), flackerfur, flammstirn, follet, friar's lantern, fuchtel-mannlein, FUERSTEIN-MANNLI, ghost lights, heerwisch, huckepot, ignis fatuus ("foolish fire"), irdflammken, irdlicht, irrluchte, irrwisch, jack-o'-lantern, lichtkedrager, lidercfeny, lopend fur, luchtemannchen, putzhupfer, quadlicht, schauble, schwidnikes, spoklecht, spooky lights, stauble, stolten, stoltenlicht, tuckebold, tuckebote, tummelding, will o' the wisp, willy wisp, wipplotsche, zunselwible

A spectral vampiric light whose origins are most likely German, a corpse candle appears to those who travel at night and lures them into danger. Appearing as a glowing ball of light is oftentimes one of the forms a vampire can assume when flying. Many sources claim a corpse candle is created when a child dies unbaptized and acts as a psychopomp (death omen). Some corpse candles are also guardian spirits of treasure.

Sources: Ellis, *Mainly Victorian*, 305–6; Folklore Society of Great Britain, *Folklore*, Volume 6, 293–4; Masters, *Natural History of the Vampire*, n.p.; Radford, *Encyclopedia of Superstitions*, 58–60

craqueuhhe (crack-COAL)

Variations: chan hook, craqueuhle, father toso, jean crochat, kaperman

In the Lorraine region of France, *craqueuhhe* is a word that is used when referring to a vampiric REVENANT, any sort of undead being that feeds off of human blood or life energy. Created when a person dies unbaptized, they return as an animated, rotting corpse that is strong and capable of movement no matter how mangled or decayed the body becomes. This anthropophagus is driven to consume human flesh and blood. Immune to pain and virtually unstoppable, the craqueuhhe can only be destroyed by several trained fighters holding it down while they burn the body to ash. If any part of the creature manages to escape, that part will continue to stalk and attack people. Additionally, if any part of this REVENANT is buried in a cemetery, it will contaminate the earth and spread to the surrounding graves, creating more monstrosities such as itself.

Sources: Maberry, *They Bite!*, 67; Maberry, *Vampire Universe*, 87; MacDougall, *Vampire Slayers' Field Guide to the Undead*, 655

creature of Pope Formosus, the

Variation: GOLEM of Pope Formosus

Pope Formosus (891–896 CE) had a troubled papacy; he had powerful political enemies and was brought up on charges of perjury, serving as a bishop while actually a layman, and transmigrating sees in violation of canon law, to name but a few. Most memorable of his alleged crimes was his practice of witchcraft; he created potions and kept small beings in jars. One of his alleged creations, said to have been created by use of semen, resembled a frog with overly large eyes that had "diabolical intelligence" and "brought terror to all who saw it."

It was seven months after his death in 896 that Pope Formosus was officially brought up on charges by his successor, Pope Stephen VI. His body was exhumed and set up on display for his trial; this became known as the Cadaver Synod of 897. The whereabouts of the creature were never revealed during the course of the interrogation, and yet, the cadaver was eventually found guilty. The three fingers he used to bless with were removed from his corpse and the remains were unceremoniously discarded in the Tiber River.

Sources: Curran, *Man-Made Monsters*, 100; D'Epiro, *The Book of Firsts*, 209

Croglin Grange vampire, the (CROG-lynn GRANGE)

In Cumberland, England, there is a vampire tale that began on the estate of Croglin Grange. Although the tale takes place in the early nineteenth century, it is believed the story originated in the seventeenth century because it was during that time that both a chapel and a burial vault were visible from the house. Both structures had long since been demolished by the time history shows that the Cranswells (or Cromwells, sources vary) rented the property; nevertheless, it is an enduring tale. Miss Amelia (or Anne, sources vary) Cranswell, a survivor of the vampire's attack, described it as a tall man smelling like death and decay, whose skin was nearly a translucent, dried-out brown. Its shriveled-up face had red eyes and lips. Its hands were clawed, long, and thin. Despite its appearance, it was fast and had the agility of a cat.

The Fisher family had owned and lived in the Croglin Grange estate up until the time it was rented out to the Cranswells: two brothers and a sister. One summer night as Miss Cranswell was preparing for bed, she noticed out of her bedroom window, which overlooked the ancient cemetery in the distance, two points of light moving between the stones. She could just make out a dark form. As the sighting left her feeling uneasy, she closed and locked the bedroom window before retiring to bed for the evening. Just as she was about to drift off to sleep, she opened her eyes to see a horrific face staring at her through the window, its eyes burning red, and instantly she somehow knew that the dots of light she had seen earlier were the eyes that were looking at her now.

She tried to scream but found that she was frozen with fear, unable to move. She lay there in her bed, helplessly, as she watched the creature use its clawed hands to pluck away at the lead window sealing and knock the glass out of place so that it could slip its arm inside and undo the latch. The window swung open, and the monster climbed in with startling ease. She was still unable to move as it crossed the room, grabbed her up by her hair, and pulled her face close to its own as if it were preparing to kiss her. Only when it bit down into the flesh of her neck was she able to scream.

Her brothers awoke and immediately dashed to her room. Finding the door locked, they had to waste precious time smashing it down. When they finally broke through, their sister lay sprawled on her bed, blood pumping from a severe neck wound. The smell of mold and decay filled the room; one of the brothers just caught a glimpse of something flitting out the window. He raced to it in time to see a form dashing across the cemetery grounds off in the distance. The rest of the long night was spent bandaging their sister's neck; they barely managed to save her life.

As soon as Miss Cranswell was well enough to travel, the brothers whisked her away to Switzerland to recover. There she told them of the events that had occurred, and, believing her, the brothers swore revenge on the monster. The three siblings returned to Croglin Grange and laid a trap for the vampire. The sister insisted that she act as bait while her brothers laid in wait. Not long after their trap was set, the vampire returned. The brothers were prepared for battle and shot it several times. With a howling wail, the vampire fled back out the window and into the night. The brothers waited until morning to try to track it.

At first light, they took their sister to a safe place and rounded up some of the local residents to help them search the graveyard for evidence of their sister's attacker. After a thorough search, they noticed that one of the crypt doors was ajar. Looking inside they came upon a grisly sight. Within, all the coffins, save one, were smashed to bits. Bones were scattered everywhere and showed signs of having been gnawed upon. They opened the one coffin that remained intact and found the corpse of a tall man who was sporting what they considered to be several fresh gunshot wounds. Assuming that this had to be the vampire and their sister's assailant, the coffin and the body within were taken outside of the crypt and moved to the churchyard. There, the coffin was set ablaze and watched carefully as it burned, making sure it was rendered down to ash.

Sources: Copper, *Vampire in Legend*, 51–4; Farson, *Man Who Wrote Dracula*, 108; Masters, *Natural History of the Vampire*, 132–5; Summers, *Vampire in Lore and Legend*, 112–5

dakhuls

Among the Buryat people of the Buryat Republic, Siberia, the dakhuls are the souls of destitute men and women who have returned to haunt the living; every hamlet has at least one. Dakhuls are only injurious to children.

The dakhuls and all the other souls of the dead have an unnamed one-eyed chief who rules over them. This overseer of wandering souls can be killed only if shot in the eye. Once dead, he will transform into a pelvis bone which must then be burned.

Sources: Czaplicka, *Shamanism in Siberia*, n.p.; Hastings, *Encyclopædia of Religion and Ethics*, Volumes 3–4, 8, 9

darklings

In Vodou folklore of New Orleans, Louisiana, in the 1800s, darklings were believed to be creatures that prowled the city looking for innocent people to possess. The Vodou queen Marie Laveau (1801–1881) said they are malevolent entities formed when good churchgoers have evil thoughts they do not act upon.

The lore says that darklings enter their victim through their mouth and that, once possessed, the person acts as if they were a zombie. Children between the ages of three and nine years old can see them. Darklings are fearful of any source of light and spend daylight hours hiding from it; their favorite places are inside cracks, dolls, stuffed animals, and toy chests. There is a magical apotrope powder that will ward them off said to be created by the vodun queen consisting of ground-up monkey and rooster statue, red brick dust, and an unnamed secret ingredient.

Sources: Redfern, *The Zombie Book*, 72; Steiger, *Real Zombies*, 144

dearg-due (DEER-rig DUEL)

Variations: deamhain fhola, deamhan fola, dearg-dililat, dearg-diulai, dearg-dul, dearg dulai, derrick-dally, headless coach ("coach a bower"), marbh bheo ("night walking dead")

The dearg-due ("blood drinker") is a type of vampiric REVENANT from Ireland that has been feared since the days before the introduction of Christianity. These ancient creatures are described as looking like beautiful yet pale women who can be seen strolling aimlessly through graveyards at night. A dearg-due uses its beauty to lure men to it and then kisses them on the mouth. When it does so, it drains them of their blood.

To stop a dearg-due from continued assaults, one must find its grave and erect a cairn on top of it, trapping it beneath. Ireland's most famous dearg-due is said to be buried beneath a strongbow tree. About four times a year it is able to escape from its grave and feed.

Sources: Jones, *On the Nightmare*, 123; Harris, *Folklore and the Fantastic*, 135; Stuart, *Stage Blood*, 15

deildegast

In Norwegian folklore, a deildegast ("derelict guest") is a very specific type of ghost; it is created when, in life, a person moves boundary stones to give themselves more and better property. Now, returned as ghosts, they must haunt the area of the stones, compelled to pick them up and return them to their proper location. This task is impossible, however, as the ghost is intangible and unable to interact with the mortal world. Each time the deildegast attempts and fails to achieve a peaceful afterlife, it lets loose with a loud and mournful wail.

The deildegast has the ability to transform into a bird, usually an owl. When it appears, it is usually described as looking like an old man and dressed in clothing appropriate for the time period the man is believed to be from.

Source: Bringsvaerd, *Phantoms and Fairies*, 52

devil baby of Hull House, the

In the city of Chicago, Illinois, the folktale of the devil baby of Hull House came into being. Constructed in what was then the southwestern suburbs of Chicago in 1856 as the home and residence of James J. Hull, Hull House was eventually surrounded by factories and mills and tenant housing that served the employees who worked in them. Jane Addams (1860–1935) and Ellen Gates Starr (1859–1940), social workers, founded the first welfare center in America in the late 1800s; they were able to provide many services to the immigrants who lived in the area. Operating out of Hull House, the women were so successful in their undertaking that they were able to add a third story to the original building and, over time, 12 additional buildings.

Suddenly, in 1913, rumors began to rapidly spread in the immigrant communities about a demonic child dwelling within Hull House. For nearly two months, crowds massed outside the building, demanding to see the devil; their insistence continued even after Jane Addams herself assured them there was no devil baby. Addams spoke with many of the women present to try to discover the cause of their beliefs and concerns. The story varies depending on the ethnic group telling the tale.

For instance, according to Italian immigrants, a young and pious woman, against her family's wishes, married an atheist and quickly became pregnant. A few weeks into the marriage, the wife hung a painting of the Virgin Mother on the wall; this enraged the husband, who, in a fit of anger, destroyed it, yelling that he'd rather have the devil in his home. When the child was born, it had all the telltale marks of Satan: cloven hooves for feet, pointed ears, a hideous laugh, scales covering its body, and a small tail. It learned to talk and walk remarkably quickly and spent much of its days running around the house, smoking cigars, and threatening the life of its father. In church, it danced on the pews and fled the church when the mother attempted to have it baptized. Finally, the father had had enough of the devil baby and took it to Hull House, demanding Addams take and keep it.

The only true variation in the story between the different ethnic groups was the type of sin committed that brought about the monstrous birth.

In the Irish telling the bride-to-be neglected to mention to her priest that she had familiar relations with another man prior to her wedding day.

In the Jewish community, a young woman married a Gentile man; her father told everyone he would rather have a devil for a grandchild than a Gentile for a son-in-law. In another story from this community, a father who already had many daughters told his pregnant wife he'd rather a devil for a son than another daughter. In some variations, the child is said to smoke cigars and drive a red car.

In the Orthodox community, the story said a pregnant woman attended a play of Faust and stared too intently at the devil character. Another story said an Orthodox wife was hiding the fact that her child was illegitimate, claiming her firstborn child—who was actually her second born—was her first.

No matter the reason or logic applied, Addams was never able to convince anyone the devil baby was not being kept in the third-story attic, as the rumors claimed. Visitors to Hull House always asked to see it, even offering money for a look. She was made an offer by a Milwaukee businessman to take the child off her hands so he could take it on a tour.

It took years, but, eventually, the rumors ceased. Addams even wrote about it in her book, *The Second 20 Years at Hull-House*. To this day, there are stories of the devil baby looking out from the upstairs window. There was also said to be the ghost of a woman who committed suicide on the third floor, which is mentioned in the Addams's book, but there is no other evidence to prove this took place.

In 1963 the headquarters were moved to a new location and Hull House was preserved as a museum.

Sources: Addams, *The Long Road of a Woman's Memory*, 3–5, 25–54; Guiley, *Encyclopedia of Ghosts and Spirits*, 240–1

dodelecker (Doe-DE-lic-er)

Variations: dodeleker, NACHZEHRER

The dodelecker of German vampire lore is a highly aggressive REVENANT; however, it lacks the manual dexterity, physical coordination, and speed to catch prey. As it lies in its grave, its cries of hunger can be heard from above, as well as the gnashing sounds it makes as it chews on its own body and burial shroud attempting to sate its hunger. Its cries of anguish and frustration as it tries to free itself from its grave can also be heard.

Should it ever free itself, the dodelecker will harmlessly shamble about, moaning and whimpering as it attempts to hunt for food—human flesh and blood. As much as it craves this food, it will never capture a person, so it must satisfy itself and live a ghoul-like existence, consuming rotting corpses of anything it can scavenge. Were it not a plague carrier, it would otherwise be a completely harmless vampire.

After nine years of a miserable existence, wandering aimlessly and eating rotten offal, it will return to its grave and rise no more.

Sources: Barber, *Vampires, Burial, and Death*, 95; Conway, *Demonology and Devil-lore*, 51–2; Guiley, *Complete Vampire Companion*, 25; Lindahl, *Medieval Folklore*, 1017

doppelsauger (DOP-ool-saug-er)

Variations: doppelganger, double auger, doppelssauger, dubblesuger, dubbelsuger

In eastern Germany, the Wends, who occupied the land between the Elbe and Oder Rivers, used the word *doppelsauger* ("double sucker") to describe a vampire (see

German vampire). Later the word was applied to the Germanic imagery of what was a vampire.

A doppelsauger is created upon the death of a person whose mother allows them to breastfeed long after it should have been weaned. In the Hanoverian version, this occurs when a child who had stopped breastfeeding is allowed to begin again.

The only way to prevent the recently deceased from rising as one of the undead is to place a gold coin between their teeth before they die. If the coin is not placed in time, then some sort of propping device must be employed to keep the chin from resting against the chest, such as blocks or a semicircular wooden collar. This preventative method must be taken to ensure the deceased does not feed on itself in order to gain the strength required to actually rise from its grave. If the mouth is not blocked, it will somehow manage to chew off its own chest to gain strength. Some sources say the hands are tightly bound to prevent the vampire from using its hands while still buried.

In either event, after the body has been removed from the home, the sill of the doorway must be removed and immediately replaced. Should the person rise as a vampire, this will prevent it from being able to return to its old home.

If every preventative method is taken and the deceased still manages to return as a doppelsauger, it will drain the life of its victims, starting first with its own family before moving on to others, without ever leaving its grave. When the vampire does leave its grave, it will look like a bloated corpse whose lips have not decomposed. When it physically attacks a person, it drains their life energy through their nipples, occasionally biting them off.

The only way to destroy a doppelsauger is to strike it in the back of the neck with a spade. The creature will cry out in pain just before it falls over, finally at rest.

Sources: Barber, *Vampires, Burial, and Death*, 37; Maberry, *They Bite!*, 68–9; MacDougall, *Vampire Slayers' Field Guide to the Undead*, 655; McClelland, *Slayers and Their Vampires*, 197; Perkowski, *The Darkling*, 106; Voigt, *Folk Narrative and Cultural Identity*, 300

drakul (DRA-cool)

Variation: dracul

In the Moldovan and Romanian languages, the word *drakul* translates as "the dragon" or "demon nearly"; it is used to describe a type of demon that possesses the body of a deceased person and animates it. Once situated in the remains, the demon has control of the corpse; usually, it has the body walk around naked while carrying its coffin on its head. It does this all the while hunting for humans to prey upon. Fortunately, if the burial shroud of the person is destroyed, the demon will lose its hold on the body.

Sources: Andreescu, *Vlad the Impaler*, 183; MacDougall, *Vampire Slayers' Field Guide to the Undead*, 655; McNally, *In Search of Dracula*, 21; Twitchell, *Living Dead*, 16

drauge (DRAW-ged)

Variation: GIENGANGER

In the lore of the ancient Norse people, a drauge was created when a powerful necromancer died and returned as a vampiric REVENANT. This new form was exceptionally physically strong, enabling the vampire to kill anyone who entered its tomb with a single blow to the head. It was also said that eye contact with a drauge must be avoided at all costs, as it would steal vital *ond* ("breath") and kill the viewer.

Once a drauge comes into being, it is harmless so long as it is not encountered, as it does not leave its crypt. It is very rare to hear a tale of a drauge wandering the countryside hunting prey. Nevertheless, to be safe, runes of protection can be carved onto its gravestone to keep it entrapped.

After the introduction of Christianity, the drauge was able to be destroyed if it was reburied in a Christian cemetery or had a mass said for it. Eventually, it was replaced altogether and merged with the DRAUGR, an evil undead corpse of someone who had drowned at sea (see UNDEATH).

Sources: Crabb, *Crabb's English Synonymes*, 287; Curran, *Vampires*, 93; Henderson, *Norse Influence on Celtic Scotland*, 106; Vicary, *An American in Norway*, 119

Draugr, sea (DAW-gr, See)

Variations: sea trow, trowis

According to Icelandic lore, a draugr of the sea is created whenever a person drowns in the ocean. They have been described as being "black as hell and bloated to the size of a bull," their bodies covered with curly hair and seaweed. The penis and testicles of these beings are also noted as being overly large. They no longer have a head, it having been replaced with a facsimile made of seaweed, sporting evil, red eyes. It is also told that no matter the clothes they were wearing at the time of their death, the return wearing oil-skin coats.

This draugr, a vampiric REVENANT, preys on seamen using an array of supernatural abilities. It can shape-shift into rocks along a shoreline, is impervious to mundane weaponry, and has supernatural strength. Like the draugr of the land that it thoroughly hates, it too retains its personality and all of its memories. Usually, it only makes itself visible to its victims as it sails the sea in half a boat.

There is a draugr story that takes place on Christmas Eve of 1857. On the Norwegian isle of Lurøya, all the farmhands were celebrating the holiday. When they ran out of drink, everyone was too afraid to go out to the boathouse to retrieve more alcohol for fear of encountering a draugr—except for a young boy. He made it there, filled his jug, and on the way back to the celebration, a headless draugr confronted him. The boy attacked the draugr, knocking it off balance, which gave him just enough time to escape. As the boy ran for his life, he looked back over his shoulder and saw that not one, but a great number of draugr were rising from the sea behind him, ready to give chase. The boy pressed on and jumped over the churchyard wall, hollering as loudly as he could, "Up, up, every Christian soul, save me!" As he landed in the churchyard, the church bell tolled the midnight hour and draugr began to rise from the earth. Within moments the two species of draugr were engaged in battle. The land draugr clutched the wood from their coffins to use as weapons; the sea draugr made whips of their seaweed. The boy fled to the servant quarters and told the tale of what had happened. On Christmas morning, everyone went to the graveyard to see what had transpired. It looked like a battlefield; bits of broken coffins, seaweed, jellyfish, and slime were everywhere.

Sources: Grimm, *Teutonic Mythology*, 916; Marwick, *An Orkney Anthology*, 261–2; McKinnell, *Runes, Magic and Religion*; Redfern, *The Zombie Book*, 95; Shipley, *Dictionary of Early English*, 686

draugr (DAW-gr), plural draugar

Variations: aptgangr ("one who walks after death"), APTRGANGR, barrow dweller, gronnskjegg, haubui, HAUGBUI ("sleeper in the mound")

The draugr is a type of vampiric REVENANT from Iceland. Its name is derived from the Indo-European root word *dreugh*, which means "to deceive" or "to damage." The more modern and literal translation means "after-goer" or "one who walks in death," but the word is usually taken to mean a type of undead, not a ghost but a physical being. There are two types of draugr, those of the land and those of the sea (see DRAUGR, SEA).

A draugr of the land is created when a very greedy and wealthy man is buried in a barrow with all of his possessions. To prevent his resurrection as a REVENANT, traditional lore says to place a pair of iron scissors on his chest or straw crosswise under the burial shroud. As an additional precaution, the big toes of the deceased are tied together, preventing the legs from moving. As a final measure, pins were driven partway into the bottom of the corpse's feet to prevent him from getting up and walking anywhere, as it would be too painful to do so.

Christian traditions demanded that the body of the deceased, as it was carried out of its home for the final time, be raised and lowered three times in different directions, an action taken to symbolize the holy cross. Then, all glasses, pans, pots, and stone jars were to be turned upside down as well as any chairs or tables the body may have rested on. It was then also believed the draugr could only reenter the home it once lived in by the door the body was removed from. It was for this reason homes were sometimes built with what was called a coffin door, an opening big enough for a coffin to pass through. After the body was removed, the coffin door was bricked over to prevent entry.

A draugr will jealously guard its treasures and viciously attack anyone who enters its tomb. It uses its supernatural strength to crush them to death or strangle them with its bare hands. It is impervious to all mundane weaponry, and a few stories say that it can even increase its body size by two to three times. Some draugr are able to leave their tombs and wander off into the night with the intent of crushing anyone they happen upon. If one should be encountered, an elderly woman must throw a bowl of her own urine at it to drive it away.

In addition to its physical abilities, a draugr has an array of magical abilities as well. It can control the weather, move freely through stone and earth, and see into the future. It can also shape-shift into a cat, a great flayed bull, a gray broken-back horse with no ears or tail, or a seal. In its cat form, it will sit on a person's chest, growing heavier and heavier until the victim suffocates to death, much like the ALP of Germany.

The draugr's skin is described as being either *hel-blar* ("death-blue") or *na foir* ("corpse pale"). It smells like a rotting corpse, although even after many years it may show no real signs of decay. It retains the personality and all the memories of the person it once was, longing for the things it had in life—food, loved ones, and warmth—but can no longer have. Enraged with its lot, it destroys property and kills livestock and people. The only pleasure it has in death is taken through acts of violence.

Destruction of a draugr must be undertaken by a hero, who defeats it in hand-to-hand combat, wrestling it into submission and then beheading it. Some of the traditional tales say that after the beheading, the hero must then walk three times around the head or body. Other stories say that a stake must also be driven into the headless corpse. Additionally, the sword that is used in the beheading must be some sort of ancestral, special, or magical sword; typically, this sword is already in the tomb somewhere in the draugr's treasure hoard. Stabbing it with iron will weaken the draugr's powers but not kill it.

After the introduction of Christianity, a draugr could be destroyed if it was exhumed and given a Christian burial in a churchyard or if a mass was said for it. Burning the body to ash was also said to destroy it.

It has been speculated by some scholars that the monster GRENDEL from the heroic epic poem *Beowulf* was a draugr, an opinion that goes in and out of vogue. Also, there is speculation that dragons and draugrs may well be interchangeable opponents in some stories, as they are both greedy guardians of treasure that is kept in an underground chamber; they act violently when motivated by greed or envy; they are shape-shifters; and they were both important enough to be Christianized when times changed.

The oldest, best-known story of a draugr is that of Glam from the *Grettis Saga*. In it, after Glam died he became a draugr, killing many men and cattle. He was defeated by the outlaw hero Grettir Asmundarson in a wrestling match. Grettir promptly beheaded the creature with his sword, Jokulsnaut. He placed the head between the knees of the draugr and burned the body to ash.

Sources: Chadwick, "Norse Ghosts"; Cohen, *Prismatic Ecology*, n.p.; Grimm, *Teutonic Mythology*, 915; Houran, *From Shaman to Scientist*, 103; Marwick, *Folklore of Orkney and Shetland*, 40; Redfern, *The Zombie Book*, 93, 94, 95, 126

drekavac

Variations: drek, drekalo, krekavac, zdrekavac, zrikavac

The description of the drekavac ("one that cries while yelling"), a nursery bogie from Serbian folklore, varies widely; it can appear as a bird, child, a dapple-colored foal, dog, dog with kangaroo-like hind legs, fox with oversize hind legs, a ghostly soldier, a long-neck and long-legged animal with a catlike head, a one-legged humanoid with glowing red eyes, an undead man, or werewolf-like creature.

What is consistent is the bloodcurdling BANSHEE-like scream it emits. Some stories say it sits in the graveyard it was buried in crying out into the night, begging for someone to come and baptize it.

In its child guise, its appearance is seen as a death omen; in its many canine-like appearances, it foretells cattle blight.

Folklore says a drekavac is created whenever an unbaptized child dies.

Sources: Maberry, *Cryptopedia*, 232; Zell-Ravenheart, *Wizard's Bestiary*, 36

dullahan (DAH-hool)

Variations: dubhlachan, dulachan ("dark man"), dullaghan, far dorocha, gan ceann, gan geann ("without a head"), headless horseman

Stories of this REVENANT, a dullahan ("dark, angry, sullen, fierce" or "malicious being"), existed throughout the Irish countryside for years, but it was not until the potato famine of 1845 that sightings of a headless man astride a horse began to appear and were reported by reliable witnesses. People claimed that on some occasions, such as midnight on feast days, the BANSHEE appeared with it. The stories described a man carrying his own severed head, which was smiling from ear to ear; it was the color and texture of moldy cheese, but there are some instances where the head was tied to his saddle.

As the story evolved, the dullahan would sometimes opt to leave his horse behind and drive a coach made of human thigh bones at madcap speeds down the country roads. This was known as a "coach-a-bower" or *coiste gan cheann* ("headless coach"); occasionally it was called a *coiste bodhar* ("soundless coach"), as it was reported to move like a shadow and make not a sound. The coach, or hearse, was pulled by six black skull-headed horses, their eyes ablaze with lit candles in the empty sockets.

Whether on horseback or by coach, wherever the dullahan traveled, he spread disease; entire households would fall ill after his passing. He would also use a long bullwhip to lash out at the eyes of anyone he passed on the roads; they say this is because he has terrible eyesight or is completely blind and angry about it. Some versions of his tale describe the whip being made from the bones of a human spine. The lucky miss the whipping but are instead doused with a bucket of rank blood.

It was believed the dullahan was the REVENANT of some avarice-fueled aristocrat and the only way to avoid being assaulted by him was to throw money, no matter how small an offering, at it. Filled with greed, the dullahan would accept the bribe and gallop off into the night.

The character of the Headless Horseman was popularized in 1820 by Washington Irving's American retelling of a German folktale in a short story called "The Legend of Sleepy Hollow." The title character has all the telltale attributes of a dullahan, although he is not referred to as such in the story.

Sources: Curran, *Vampires*, 57; Fee, *American Myths, Legends, and Tall Tales*, 285–296; Burgess, *Indian Antiquary*, 300; Leatherdale, *Dracula: The Novel and the Legend*, 79; Ray, *Fairy Tale Films*, 207

Earl of Desmond

Variations: Gearoid Larla Fitzgerald, Gerald Oge Fitzgerald, the Great Earl, the Wizard Earl

In Limerick County, Ireland, there once stood a castle overlooking Lough Gur (Loch Gair). It was the home to the Earl of Desmond, Gearoid Larla Fitzgerald, the 14th Earl of Desmond and Kildare, a professed scholar and user of magic.

The story goes that the earl always conducted his magical ceremonies and rites behind closed doors, never permitting anyone to witness his activities. His wife would always begged him to let her watch, and one day in a moment of weakness, he agreed on the one condition that she swear to him that, no matter what she saw or heard, she would remain absolutely silent. It was only after soliciting her solemn promise that he permitted her entry into his forbidden chambers.

The earl began his magical ceremonies and soon began to assume various shapes and forms as his wife bore witness. Soon, his appearance became distorted, ugly, and then horrific. It was not long before he took on an appearance so ghastly and revolting the wife could not contain herself and let out a primal scream of terror. With the silence shattered, the castle began to shake and tremble, and before anyone could escape it, sank directly into the nearby lake.

This was not the end of the earl, for he returned as a REVENANT; on occasion, he would leave his watery grave and travel the surrounding countryside searching for attractive young men and women to bring back to his sunken castle with him. It is said that he uses them, draining away their life energy through sexual intercourse.

Legend tells us the earl is forced to live such an existence until such a time as he can figure out a way to "restore all to as it was."

Sources: Curran, *Explore Vampires*, 98; Ellis, *Dictionary of Irish Mythology*, 135; McCormack, *Earldom of Desmond*, 20, 32, 39, 40, 46, 54; Spence, *Encyclopædia of Occultism*, 299; Summers, *Geography of Witchcraft*, 92

edimmu

Variations: ekimmu, ekimmu

An edimmu ("the seizer") is a species of ghost from Sumerian mythology; invisible and incorporeal, they are created when a person does not receive proper burial rites. Because of the conditions of their UNDEATH, edimmu hate the living and are well known for attacking the "middle part" of men, draining away the life of children while they sleep, inspiring criminal behavior, and spreading disease. They also have the ability to possess a person, but only those who have broken specific taboos, such as eating the meat of an ox.

Fortunately, the destruction of this type of undead is as easy as performing a proper funeral rite for the body of the deceased; this will dissolve the entity.

When not in the earthly realm, the edimmu live in the underworld kingdom of Ereshkigal, the goddess of death and gloom, where they are her favored subjects.

Sources: Jastrow, *Religion of Babylonia and Assyria*, 260; Pivarcsi, *Just a Bite*, 257; Thompson, *Semitic Magic*, 3, 26, 3; Turner, *Dictionary of Ancient Deities*, 4879

ekimmou (ECK-ay-moo)

Variations: edimmu ("hollow"), ekimmu ("robber") or ("that which is snatched away"), ekimu, "evil wind gusts," lamassu ("bullgod"), shedu

Dating as far back as 4000 BCE in the writing of the ancient Assyrians, the vengeful ekimmou is one of the oldest vampiric myths. Its lore and belief spread to the ancient Babylonians, Egyptians, and Inuit—all of which developed this same type of entity in parallel evolution.

Usually, an ekimmou is created when a woman dies giving birth, while still pregnant, or, if she was never in love. A person can also become one if they die of heat exhaustion or starvation or if they leave behind no surviving family.

One can also be created when burial procedures are not followed correctly, such as when the family of the deceased does not make the proper burial offerings, when the funeral offerings are not plentiful enough, or when the body is simply not buried at all. The returned ekimmou is bitter and angry, now doomed to walk the world forever, unable to find peace, desperate to live again.

They are described as being ghostlike in appearance, keen to relentlessly attack someone until they are dead and then possess the body to use as their own. Sometimes the entity will pause the attack, stalking their victim, letting years pass before returning to finish the assault.

Sources: Guiley, *Encyclopedia of Vampires, Werewolves, and Other Monsters*, 117;

Kallen, *Vampire History and Lore*, 12–9; Maberry, *They Bite!*, 69–70; Mew, *Traditional Aspects of Hell*, 12; Muss-Arnolt, *Concise Dictionary of the Assyrian Language*, 20, 36, 489; Perrot, *A History of Art in Chaldæa and Assyria*, 345; Thompson, *Semitic Magic*, 9, 39

eloko

A ghost or returned spirit of a person who died an unfortunate death and is unable to move forward, the eloko ("bogeyman") from the folklore of the Nkundo people of Zaire is said to rise from the grave appearing as an ugly dwarf covered in coarse grass and leaves, eyes alive with fire. The eloko also has claws, a doglike snout giving it an incredible sense of smell, and sharp teeth.

Once one has risen, it moves into the woods, where it will live in the hollow of a tree. Preying on unwary travelers, the eloko uses its near-perfect camouflage to gain a surprise advantage on its prey. It can unhinge its jaw, allowing it to swallow a human whole. It also has a magical bell whose chime is said to paralyze a man, and against which there is no known protection. Protective charms and apotropes can ward off an eloko, but if otherwise confronted, it can be physically overpowered with raw strength. Fortunately, they can be slain with ordinary weapons; the entity must be decapitated and the parts buried in separate graves.

Sources: Knappert, *Bantu Myths and Other Tales*, 139–43; Maberry, *Vampire Universe*, 109–10

emere

Variation: ogbanjeaie

The returned spirits of children, the emere from the Yoruba mythology are evil, petty, powerful, and seductive. Created when a young person dies on a day of great happiness, such as the birth of a child, graduation day, or day of someone's wedding, they have the ability to travel freely between the physical world and the spiritual one; they linger at crossroads, where they seek out someone to possess, preferably a pregnant woman so they can possess her unborn child.

Source: Falola, *Mouth Sweeter than Salt*, 73–5

enfant diabolic

An enfant diabolic is a specific type of ZOMBIE created by a Vodou midwife. While the child is in the process of being birthed, partially emerged but still within the woman's body, the vodun midwife bites off the tip of the infant's tongue and then snaps its neck. The child's soul, not yet truly born into the world, will linger between life and death, never dying but also never truly alive. Because of their unique condition, it may take up to 30 years for the zombie to grow into a handsome boy or beautiful girl who only looks to be in their teens.

Sources: Redfern, *The Zombie Book*, 85; Steiger, *Real Zombies*, 7

epheles (eff-ee-YAHL-teas)

Variations: ephialte, ephialtes ("leaper")

Originally an entity from the mythology of the ancient Greeks that was later adopted by the ancient Romans, an epheles ("one who leaps upon") was a type of demonic vampire created whenever a person dies before their time; murder victims were especially susceptible to this misfortune. A bringer of nightmares, an epheles had hooks in place of hands; it would leap upon the chest of a sleeping person, securing itself firmly there, and then proceed to send the sleeper nightmares.

The epheles were identified with the gods Artemis and Pan (Diana and Faunus in Roman times) as well as the satyrs, sirens, and Silvani. During the reign of Augustine, the epheles were directly tied to the incubus, succubus, and the god Pan, who, apart from having dominion over flocks and shepherds, was also the giver of bad dreams.

Sources: Hufford, *Terror That Comes in the Night*, 131, 229; Roscher, *Pan and the Nightmare*, 97; Rose, *Handbook of Greek Mythology*, 62; *Man*, 134

eretik

Variations: elatomsk, erestan, erestun, erestuny, eretica, eretich, ereticy, eretiku, eretitsa, eretnica, eretnik, eretnitsa (female), xioptuny, xloptuny

In Russian folklore, an eretik ("heretic") is created when a dying person is possessed by an entity, passes away, and is then animated by a sorcerer or witch. One can also become an eretik by having been a blasphemer, made inappropriate noises in a bathhouse, practiced black magic, sold one's soul to the devil, or slept on a grave in life. No matter how the REVENANT was created, once it rises, it will immediately set out to consume human flesh and drink blood. It always starts with its family members.

These beings also have the ability to cause a person to wither away and die; its glare is so full of hate, that it can literally stare at a person and cause their death. The eretik is said to be most active at night during the spring and fall. They can be found sleeping in dry riverbeds, where they will also perform black masses.

To be slain, an eretik must be staked through the heart with a wooden stake, then beheaded, and all remains burned to ash.

Sources: Dundes, *Vampire Casebook*, 53; Maberry, *They Bite!*, 71; McClelland, *Slayers and Their Vampires*, 81; Oinas, *Essays on Russian Folklore and Mythology*, 121; Ryan, *Russian Magic at the British Library*, 34

fantasma malo, el

In El Salvadoran folklore, a specific type of spectral entity known as el fantasma malo ("the evil ghost") is a poltergeist that haunts home. It is believed that this entity comes into existence when a homeowner dies within a self-built abode and is reluctant to relinquish their dwelling to another inhabitant. This spectral figure manifests itself as a mist and is known to carry out acts of violence against the new occupants; these include hovering above individuals during their sleep to remove their blankets, relocating items within the house without apparent reason, and causing disarray by hurling objects across the room. It is also believed to endanger infants by hovering over them while they sleep, causing respiratory difficulty by stealing their breath. Continued exposure to such a situation could potentially lead to fatal consequences for the child.

Source: Maberry, *Vampire Universe*, 116–7

farkaskoldus (far-KISS-ole-dis)

In Hungary, tales of werewolves and vampires are frequently encountered, and, occasionally, these narratives intersect. One such instance is the emergence of a unique creature known as the farkaskoldus, which is essentially a werewolf transformed into a vampire. The transformation occurs when a werewolf consumes the flesh of an executed person. After its demise, the werewolf reanimates as a farkaskoldus. Equipped with the ability to metamorphose into various animals such as cats, dogs, or goats, it stealthily navigates the town under the cover of night, seeking its next prey. It feeds on the blood of its victim before returning to its grave before dawn. Furthermore, an individual who has been wronged and died without exacting revenge can also turn into such a creature. The farkaskoldus seeks justice, and, once it is served, it may end its nightly hunts or expand its hunting scope.

A suspected farkaskoldus's grave may be unearthed, revealing a corpse showing no decomposition or smell of death; instead, it appears to be filled with fresh blood. There are various methods to vanquish a farkaskoldus. The most straightforward approach is to incinerate the body or immerse it in holy water. If more drastic measures are deemed necessary, however, a stake may be thrust through the heart or a nail driven through the head before burning the body. An even more severe method involves dismembering and decapitating the corpse, removing the heart from the back, and then burning the entirety to ashes. The ashes are then gathered and discarded in a deep river.

Sources: Heinze, *Proceedings*, 270; Kenyon, *Witches Still Live*, 39, 52; Maberry, *They Bite!*, 180–1; MacDougall, *Vampire Slayers' Field Guide to the Undead*, 655; Volta, *The Vampire*, 144

forso

In New Guinea and the adjacent islands off the northern coast of Australia, they speak of a vampiric ghost known as a forso. This spectral entity is classified by many folklorists as an energy vampire, as it draws sustenance from the emotional, vital, and sexual energies of its victims. Additionally, it is believed to afflict its victims with misfortune and feelings of despondency.

Despite being intangible and invisible, the forso rarely travels too far from its burial site. It does not hesitate, however, to exploit any opportunity to attack individuals who venture near its resting place. Protective measures, such as charms and prayers, are considered effective in repelling its assaults, but only under the condition that the forso, during its mortal existence, led an immoral yet religious life.

The Papuan communities perceive the forso as a pitiable entity, a solitary spirit craving attention. Therefore, as soon as the presence of a forso is identified and confirmed, they locate its burial mound, exhume its skeletal remains, and incorporate them into a household. The rationale behind this practice is the belief that by welcoming the forso into their homes and accepting it as part of their family, the spirit no longer feels compelled to drain or hex individuals.

Sources: Frazer, *Belief in Immortality*, 152, 164, 174, 451; Maberry, *Vampire Universe*, 121

fuersteinmannli

In Swiss folklore, there exists a male, vampiric, spectral entity referred to as a fuersteinmannli. Fundamentally, this entity is similar to what is known in general parlance as a CORPSE CANDLE, which is a luminescent, spectral orb of light typically observed in graveyards or at near-death scenes.

Source: Meyer, *Mythologie der Germanen*, 75

funayūrei (foo-nah-yoo-ray)

Variations: AYAKASHI, funa YŪREI

Japanese folklore narrates the tale of the funayūrei ("boat spirits" or "mariner's spirits"), vengeful apparitions of those who drowned at sea and whose bodies were never recovered. Like many other vengeful spirits, they lash out at humanity because they did not receive a proper burial. These tales were prevalent during the Edo period (1603–1867) and continue to be popular.

Funayūrei are linked with erratic weather patterns, such as an abrupt shift from a warm, sunny day to a chilly, overcast one or the sudden appearance of whitecap waves on a calm sea. They are most often spotted on nights with a full moon and during the Obon festival for the departed.

These spirits manifest as sailors or fishermen treading water in the ocean or clinging to some flotsam, crying out for help at passing ships. If they are brought onboard, they mimic the behavior expected of their situation until they request a bailing ladle, known as a *hishaku*. Once they acquire it, it is used to sink the ship. For a large vessel, they invert the hishaku, causing it to spill water onto the deck in an endless flow. For smaller boats, like fishing vessels, they ladle water into the boat, pouring an improbably large volume of water with each scoop.

If the spirit is denied the hishaku or if there is none onboard, it reacts violently, capsizing the boat. If it does receive a hishaku, however, the only way to save the ship from sinking is to return the funayūrei to the ocean; most often it must be forcibly thrown overboard.

Funayūrei are not always solitary encounters; sometimes they are met in groups. As they sail the ocean in a ghost ship, they will pull alongside another vessel and demand to be given a hishaku. If they were to gain possession of it, they would have the ability to sink the ship and take the souls of the drowned men, making them crew on the ghost ship. It is for this reason that a second hishaku is often kept on many ships; this spare will have holes drilled into it so that, should the ship encounter funayūrei, they will not be able to sink them, no matter how much they try. Eventually, the angry spirits will give up and sail away.

Sources: Brown, *The Complete Idiot's Guide to the Paranormal*, n.p.; Murakami, *Strange Japanese Yokai*, 93–5; Yoda, *Yokai Attack!*, 48–9

fyglia (FIG-lee-ah)

In the cultural lore of Iceland, there exists a form of flesh-eating, supernatural REVENANT referred to as a fyglia ("following spirit"). This entity is distinguished by its peculiar tendency to ascend rooftops and displace roof tiles in its quest for its prey. In order to neutralize this vampiric being, it is necessary to apprehend and decapitate it. Then, the creature must be reinterred with its head placed beneath its body.

Source: Dillon, *Winter in Iceland*, 272

Gabriel hounds

Variations: cron annwn, cwn annwn, Dogs of Hell, Gabble Retchets, Gabriel Ratchets, Gabriel Ratchet's hounds, Gobble-ratches, Gytrash, heath hounds, hell hounds, sky yelpers, wish hounds, wisk, yell hounds, yesk, yeth hounds

According to the lore of fairy mythology originating from Wales, the Gabriel hounds are depicted as a spectral pack of dogs that prowl the regions of Durham, Lancashire, North Devon, Staffordshire, and Yorkshire in England. They are under the command of the archangel Gabriel during an event known as the Wild Hunt—a procession of supernatural beings racing across the countryside. The addition of a new member to this spectral pack is reportedly linked to the unfortunate occurrence of an unbaptized infant passing away.

These phantom canines are described as being extraordinarily large, possessing red ears and eyes. Their bodies are said to emit an uncanny green or white luminescence as they journey through the night sky. In some instances, these hounds are reported to bear a human head. Folk belief holds that the sight of a Gabriel hound floating over a residence signifies an impending death amongst the inhabitants of that particular dwelling.

Sources: Allardice, *Myths, Gods, and Fantasy*, 88; Briggs, *Encyclopedia of Fairies*, 183; Chambers, *Book of Days*, 430; Wright, *English Dialect Dictionary*, 530

gaki (GA-key)

Gaki are persistent vampiric spirits originating from Japan, said to be created when an excessively greedy individual passes away. These spirits are believed to be condemned to a life on earth with a perpetual and unquenchable thirst for blood. Characteristically, gaki are described as having cold bodies, hollow facial features, and pale skin. The stomach of a gaki is believed to be large, but its neck is slender, preventing it from sating its thirst. Despite their theriomorphic ability to transform into mist, gaki are known to prefer launching attacks on humans in one of their physical forms, typically that of a nonhuman animal, a humanoid with red skin and horns, or a specific person.

It's noteworthy that gaki do not necessarily need to physically harm their victims to feed from them; their mere proximity is sufficient to drain individuals of blood. Their communication is mostly incomprehensible chatter until they initiate an attack. Once the assault begins, gaki are known to enter into a vicious feeding frenzy, completely focused on their target.

In terms of their invulnerability, gaki are believed to be immune to damage in their mist form, unless assaulted by weapons specifically designed to combat ghosts. Even such a specialized weapon, however, would only inflict harm upon it and not destroy it. The only known method of destroying these spirits is when they are in one of their physical forms, with the optimal opportunity being while they are feeding, as they are less likely to defend themselves.

Interestingly, there are multiple types of gaki, each with a unique diet. The most lethal type is known for consuming flesh, human blood, and souls. Another dangerous variety feeds on a person's thoughts during meditation. Other types of gaki are believed to consume samurai topknots or tattoos, while some feed on incense, paper, sweat, or tea. The less dangerous gaki are known to be sated by Zen monasteries that offer them small food donations.

Sources: Ashley, *Complete Book of Vampires*; Covey, *Beasts*, 96; Davis, *Myths and Legends*, 388; Smith, *Ancestor Worship*, 41

gashadokuro

Variation: odokuro ("rattling skull")

In Japanese mythology, the gashadokuro (literally translated means "starving SKELETON") is the physical reconstruction and animation of the wrath of numerous deceased individuals who were not given proper burial rites. Most often, these angry spirits are individuals who died of starvation, soldiers who perished on the battlefield and were left there, or victims of plague who were buried in communal graves. Their collective anger pools together and causes their bones to merge into a massive skeletal structure that can be up to 15 times larger than an average human. This conglomeration is almost indestructible and has the ability to become invisible.

The enormous skeletal figure emerges from the vicinity of graveyards and battlefields during the darkest hours of the night, preying on solitary humans. Upon locating a target, it launches its attack either by crushing its prey or severing the victim's head. *Gashadokuro* is sometimes translated as "rattling skull" due to the distinctive rattling sound produced by teeth, which resonates as *"gachi gachi."* There are reports of this sound causing a ringing sensation in a person's ears.

One of the most terrifying aspects of a gashadokuro is its invulnerability, as it is composed of the bones of the deceased. It will continue to hunt random and innocent people until the energy binding its bones dissipates, leading to the separation of the bones and the collapse of the entity.

According to the myth, the first gashadokuro dates back to the tenth century, and it was borne out of a unique form of retribution. During this period, a violent rebellion against Japan's central government in Kyōto was led by Taira No Masakado (903–940), a samurai from the Kantō region. The rebellion was ruthlessly suppressed by the government, which placed a bounty on Masakado. In the end, he was assassinated, and his severed head was presented to Kyōto to claim the reward. Then, his entire family was deemed to be enemies to the imperial court, and their executions were also ordered. His daughter, Takiyasha-hime ("waterfall demon princess"), a formidable sorcerer, was filled with rage. To punish the government for disgracing her father, she summoned the first gashadokuro and unleashed it onto Kyōto.

Sources: Boutland, *Gashadokuro the Giant Skeleton and Other Legendary Creatures of Japan*, 6–12; Markowitz, *Robots that Kill*, 4, 17–8; Murakami, *Strange Japanese Yokai*, 117

gayal

Originating from India, the entity known as gayal ("simple") is a type of vampiric spirit. The creation of this entity is linked to two specific circumstances: firstly, when a man passes away without any sons to conduct his funeral rites appropriately; and secondly, when an individual dies whilst having suffered a significant injustice that has gone unanswered.

Upon its return, the gayal manifests its aggression towards the male offspring of those it was familiar with during its lifetime. This hostility takes the form of physical attacks, culminating in the consumption of their flesh and blood. However, it exhibits a particular delight in targeting expectant mothers. The gayal manages to infiltrate a woman's body when she opens her mouth to eat. Once inside, it gradually depletes both the mother and the unborn child's vital energy, leading to the eventual demise of both.

In periods of nonaggression, the gayal can be located in graveyards, where it feeds on the flesh of the deceased under the cover of darkness; it retreats to its own grave during daylight hours. A potential safeguard against a gayal attack for young boys is to have them wear a necklace composed of coins.

While the gayal cannot be completely annihilated, its aggression can be mitigated if the correct burial rites are performed for its body. This procedure involves cremation. To prevent the gayal from being resurrected from its grave, one may place containers filled with a mixture of milk and water sourced from the Ganges River around its resting place. Additionally, the placement of lit lamps around the grave during nightfall could potentially deceive the gayal into believing it is daytime, thus confining it to its grave.

Sources: Asiatic Society of Bengal, *Bibliotheca Indica*, 415; Briggs, *The Chamars*, 131; Crooke, *Introduction to the Popular Religion*, 69–70, 72, 168–71; MacDougall, *Vampire Slayers' Field Guide to the Undead*, 655

genderuwa

Variations: gandaruwo, genderuwo, gendruwo, setan

Originating in Persian mythology, the genderuwa is perceived as a spectral entity or ghost, believed to be formed when an individual meets a violent end. This concept transitioned into Javanese folklore, where the genderuwa was depicted as a benign supernatural creature that often remained unseen.

The physical manifestation of the genderuwa varies; sometimes it is portrayed as an oversize primate with a distinctive red and black fur coat. There have been rare instances, however, where it has been described as an elderly gentleman, dressed entirely in white, who will attempt to seduce women. Regardless of its guise or form, the genderuwa possesses the ability to manipulate its size, shrinking to as small as a few centimeters.

In daylight hours, the genderuwa may assume the form of various carnivorous creatures, such as crocodiles, raptors, serpents, or tigers. It is known to inhabit areas surrounding large trees, antiquated damp structures, and bodies of water. The males of the species are referred to as memedis, while the females are known as wewe gombel.

Sources: Bruun, *Asian Perceptions of Nature*, 51–2; Geertz, *Religion of Java*, 16, 18

German vampires

Germany is home to approximately 50 known vampire species, the majority of which are revenants; the sheer number of species is notable. These German vampires display characteristics that align with many people's conventional understanding of what a "vampire" is. They are repelled by garlic and hawthorn, and their destruction necessitates either a stake through the heart or decapitation. This, however, is where the similarities end.

The capacity of German vampires to multiply or produce others of their kind is not straightforward or even wholly within their own power. In fact, there is scant evidence to suggest that these revenants possess anything beyond rudimentary animal instincts. If a German vampire were to endeavor to create another REVENANT such as itself, however, there would be only three possible methods.

Firstly, they could instruct an individual in the ways of witchcraft, thereby enabling them to live their life as a witch. Secondly, they could choose a person and guide them towards leading an immoral lifestyle. Lastly, they could push someone to the point of taking their own life. Only through these approaches can an individual possibly become a vampire after their death. All other means of creation are uncontrollable, such as being born with a red caul, dying prematurely or during childbirth, or dying unbaptized. These people also have a chance of rising as one of the undead.

Regardless of its origin, the German vampire is a creature of the night, prowling populated areas under the cover of darkness. During daylight hours, it gnaws voraciously on its burial shroud within its grave.

Interestingly, it is relatively straightforward to prevent a German vampire from causing harm. Upon a person's death, if there's even a slight suspicion for the potential of an undead resurrection, preventative measures can be taken. Simply placing a stone or brick in the deceased's mouth or fastening their mouth shut before burial can effectively ensure their eternal rest.

Sources: Dundes, *Vampire Casebook*, 5; Leatherdale, *Dracula: The Novel and the Legend*, 41, 52, 95; Taberner, *German Culture*, 121, 126

ghost

Variations: aave (Finnish), ahma (Gothic), aitu (Samoan), andi (male, Old Norse), apparition, arvoh (Uzbek), bhutas, chipoko (Shona), cirfiid (Somali), con ma (Vietnamese), dab (Hmong), draugur (Icelandic), duch (Czechoslovakian), duch widmo (Polish), duh (Bosnian, Croatian, and Slovenian), exspiravit (Latin), fantasma (Catalan, Italian, Portuguese, and Spanish), fantazme (Albanian), fantom (Haitian Creole), fantoma (Romanian), fantôme (French), fantomo (Esperanto), fatalwa (Hausa), gaist ("spirit," Saterland Frisian), gast ("ghost," Old English, Frisian, and Swedish), geast ("spirit," West Frisian), geescht (Luxembourgish), geest ("spirit, mind, ghost," Dutch), geisa ("to rage," Old Norse), geiskafullr ("full of fear"), geiski ("fear"), geist ("spirit, mind, intellect," German), gest (Old Dutch and Saxon), ghaist ("ghost," Scots), ghois-d-oz ("fury, anger," pre–Germanic), ghost (Corsican and Maltese), haint, hantu (Indonesian and Sundanese), hayalet (Turkish), heda ("anger, hatred," Sanskrit), hedas ("anger," Sanskrit), imprint, isipoki (Zulu), isiporho (Xhosa), iwin (Yoruba), kehua (Maori), kummitus (Estonian and Finnish), larvae (ancient Roman), mamua (Basque), manifestation, masina (Malagasy), memedi (Javanese), mmuo (Igbo), MULTO (Cebuano and Filipino), mzuka (Swahili), mzukwa (Nyanja), ond (female, Old Norse), pantasma (Galician), phantom, poltergeist, puca (Irish), ruh (Kurdish), schatten, sepoko (Sesotho), shade, shiryo ("spirit of a deceased person"), specter, spirit, spogelse

(Danish), spoke (Swedish), spokelse (Norwegian), spoks (Latvian), spook (Afrikaans and Dutch), szellem (Hungarian), taibhse (Scot Gaelic), taidhbhse, tais, ʻuhane (Hawaiian), usgaisjan ("to terrify," Gothic), usgaisnan ("to be terrified," Gothic), vaiduoklis (Lithuanian), wraith, xeyal (Azerbaijani), ysbryd (Welsh), zest ("ugly, hateful, disgusting," Persian), zois (Avestan), zoisnu ("shivering, trembling," Avestan), zoizda ("terrible, ugly," Avestan)

A common concept in nearly every culture, the idea of a ghost is nearly universal, although the definitive definition of what a ghost is or may be is uncertain. These spectral entities incite conjecture, fear, and inquiry into the unknown, by both the religious and secular.

Necromancy is a deliberate act aimed at initiating contact with the soul of a deceased person. A necromancer, the individual who performs this act, seeks to resurrect the spirits of the dead and inquire about aspects typically related to the future. The underlying belief here is that the departed, akin to a divine entity, exist beyond the constraints of earthly time. This transcendence, theoretically, enables the necromancer to access information from any point in time, be it past, present, or future.

In the practice of spiritism, this connection between the seen and unseen worlds is facilitated through a ritual known as a séance. Through these séances, communication with "those on the other side" is attempted by mediums who serve as conduits. The afterlife, within this context, does not conform to traditional notions of heaven or hell. Instead, it bears similarity to a form of purgatory where the soul can persist in its quest for knowledge beyond death. This acquired wisdom is often relayed back to the living world through the mediums participating in these séances.

The concept of the soul, an alternate self, distinct from the physical body, implies the existence of an invisible world separate from our sensory reality. This unseen realm is perceived as an ethereal community of the deceased, inhabited by entities possessing knowledge inaccessible or forbidden to those living in their bodily forms.

There are those individuals who will explain a ghost as an imprint or shadow, the non-conscious manifestation of a person who is deceased.

Other individuals will explain a ghost as the disembodied energy of a deceased human; when it appears, it is not only self-aware but also capable of interacting with the world we live in. These interactions may take the form of being able to communicate audibly or telepathically; being able to manifest odors associated with it in life, such as aftershave, perfume, or tobacco; being visible to the human eye; and being capable of touching an object or individual. Ghosts of this sort may or may not be aware they are no longer among the living because they have the ability to utilize and affect all five of the human senses.

The self-directed or independent spirit frequently has a defined objective, irrespective of the religious setting in which it manifests. Whether in Christian, Shinto, or Islamic contexts, these spirits often emerge with the intent of retribution or to accomplish unresolved matters. They symbolize a violation, an alert that appropriate rituals have not been conducted. Consequently, the spirit functions as a guardian of religious compliance, pursuing vengeance on the living due to neglect of the proper practices. For such reasons, spirits are often associated with specific locations; places that have a ghost attached to them are called haunted.

Since the dawn of human civilization, the concept of ghosts has been widely accepted. Evidence of such beliefs can be found in the ancient religions of Assyria,

Babylon, Sumer, and other early Mesopotamian civilizations. Vestiges of these beliefs persist within contemporary faiths such as Christianity, Islam, and Judaism.

Broadly speaking, these early societies held that a person's death led to the creation of their ghost, which retained the deceased's memory and personality. This spectral entity was thought to journey to another realm, where they would lead an existence similar to their previous life. It was customary for surviving family members to present offerings of food and drink to appease the deceased, thereby ensuring a pleasant afterlife. Failure to provide satisfactory offerings incited the wrath of the ghosts, potentially resulting in various illnesses as a form of retribution.

The ancient Egyptians harbored a profound belief in the afterlife and the potential influence of the departed. Despite their religion undergoing continuous evolution, the conviction that the deceased continued to exist post-death, possessing the power to aid or afflict the living, remained constant.

Turning to the classical Greeks of the fifth century BCE, they too perceived ghosts as frightening entities capable of either benevolent or malevolent actions. The spirit of the deceased was thought to linger near the burial site, thereby turning cemeteries into areas generally avoided by the living. There was a belief that without ritualistic mourning, which included public ceremonies, sacrifices, and libations, the dead might return to haunt their families. Consequently, the ancient Greeks organized annual feasts dedicated to honoring and pacifying the spirits of the dead. Family ghosts were welcomed to these feasts and subsequently requested to depart until the arrival of the festival in the following year.

During the medieval era in Europe (476–1450), beliefs around ghosts were typically categorized into two types: the returning soul of a deceased individual or a demon seeking to deceive, tempt, and torment the living. It was believed that a returning soul would disclose the reason for its reappearance if commanded to do so in Jesus Christ's name, whereas a demon would retreat at the mere mention of His name.

Ghosts during this period were thought to cross over into our world from Purgatory, a place where they were repenting for their earthly sins. Often, these spirits would implore the living to pray for their suffering to cease and urge them to confess their sins while they still had the opportunity.

Up until now, descriptions said ghosts were mist-like, ethereal, and fragile entities. During this era, however, they began to be depicted as more substantial, albeit never solid. The majority of reported apparitions were male, and accounts of spectral armies engaging in combat were not uncommon.

During the Renaissance, which spanned from the early fourteenth to the late sixteenth century, there was a resurgence in interest in and study of magic and the occult, including necromancy. This revival did not occur without intermittent periods of resistance or backlash, however. Additionally, it was during this era that the concept emerged suggesting that the creation of a ghost could be attributed to the immense grief experienced by the living. The continuous mourning generated by a bereaved loved one was believed to prevent the souls of the departed from achieving peaceful rest.

In both Western and Eastern traditions, particularly in the folklore of China and Japan, there is a common belief that spirits can emerge from their graves in a state of intense anger. This rage can stem from various factors, such as their discovery about being dead, resentment about the circumstances of their death, or bitterness about being forgotten by friends and family. Often, this anger is targeted at a specific individual. In numerous Japanese ghost stories, however, it is frequently a woman wronged by society who returns as an onryou, a vengeful spirit. This spirit's rage represents a cultural environment where personal anger, particularly among women, is often suppressed.

Ghosts in Japanese folklore are the returned soul of a human and are always described as being human in appearance, even if it is as a macabre SKELETON wearing ethereal garments.

During the initial centuries of the Christian church, the existence of ghosts was typically dismissed by religious scholars. This was primarily because the idea of an abundant and complex spiritual world with numerous ghosts, spirits, and ethereal beings seemed to contradict the principles of a religion that believed in a single God with an eternal afterlife from which there was no return.

Sources: Braudy, *Haunted*, 37, 38, 39–40, 61; Danelek, *Case for Ghosts*, 25–7; Goss, *Lost at Sea*, 91; Kroonen, *Etymological Dictionary of Proto-Germanic, 163*; Nesbitt, *Civil War Ghost Trails*, 6; Orel, *A Handbook of Germanic Etymology*, 262

ghoul (gool)

Variations: ghole, ghul, ghuul, KASHA

The narratives of the *ghole* from Arabic culture spread eastward and were assimilated by Oriental societies. The concept transformed into a form of vampiric entity referred to as a ghoul ("grabber"), which takes possession of deceased bodies. When a corpse is claimed, it is reanimated by the ghoul to devour other corpses within its cemetery residence, displaying a notable preference for livers. In artistic depictions, the ghoul is portrayed as a three-year-old boy with reddish-brown hair, a mouth filled with black teeth and blood, and eyes suggesting insanity.

To deter a ghoul from claiming a corpse, an ongoing watch is necessitated, accompanied by the continuous sounds of bells, drums, and gongs. Ghouls exhibit a pronounced aversion to loud noises, facilitating their expulsion. Talismans intricately woven from crimson thread can also be employed for protection, along with Passover bread and metallic plates inscribed with the tetragrammaton (the four-letter Hebrew name of God, typically represented as JHVH for Jehovah or YHWH for Yahweh). If a ghoul successfully seizes a body, removal becomes impossible. The ghoul must be apprehended and incinerated to ash to ensure its destruction.

The ghul (male) and ghulah (female) in Muslim folklore are predominantly depicted as desert demons. They frequent secluded locations such as ancient battlefields, desert oases, graveyards, ruins, and other remote settings conducive to ambushing fatigued travelers. These entities often masquerade as prostitutes, luring their victims into slumber before murdering them and subsequently consuming them. Posing as a water bearer or nurse on a battlefield, the ghul or ghulah would dispatch wounded soldiers. It is believed that they possess the capacity to transform into diverse animal and bird forms. If living prey is scarce, they satisfy their hunger by exhuming corpses and consuming the residual flesh.

In Muslim folklore, it is an infrequent occurrence for a person to transform into a ghoul postmortem, and this only transpires as a result of a curse inflicted during their lifetime. If such an event occurs, the REVENANT will haunt a particular location for multiple generations. The sole method of eliminating it involves a holy man invoking Allah for seven consecutive days at the haunted site to perform an exorcism on the REVENANT.

Sources: Curran, *Man-Made Monsters*, 76; Guiley, *Encyclopedia of Ghosts and Spirits*, 200; MacDougall, *Vampire Slayers' Field Guide to the Undead*, 64, 547; Redfern, *The Zombie Book*, 121; Scarborough, *Supernatural in Modern English*, 158–9; Steiger, *Real Zombies*, 17; Summers, *Vampire: His Kith and Kin*, 204; Thompson, *Devils and Evil Spirits of Babylonia*, 35–7

giang shi (gang gwa)

Variations: chang kuei, chiang-shih, jiangshi, jiang shi, kiang-shi, kuang-shii, xianh-shi

Historical records dating back to 600 BCE document the existence of a Chinese vampiric entity known as the giang shi. This creature is reputed to inhabit the freshly deceased bodies of individuals who met violent ends or committed suicide. Upon possession, it is said to spring forth from the grave and assault unsuspecting travelers.

The giang shi is characterized by two distinct forms. Its first manifestation is that of a towering corpse with hair that is either green or white. It possesses red eyes, jagged teeth, and elongated claws at the ends of its fingers. The second form is indistinguishable from a human until it reveals its true nature, such as displaying an evident aversion to garlic or transforming into a wolf.

The breath of the giang shi is reputedly so repugnant that it can physically repel a person to a distance of 20 feet. As the creature ages and its hair grows long and turns white, it acquires the ability to fly. At this point of maturity, it is invulnerable to most forms of destruction, save for the sound of an extraordinarily loud thunderclap.

Preventing a giang shi from possessing a corpse is not possible according to folklore. Therefore, its destruction becomes the sole viable course of action. It is believed that the vampire is unable to traverse running water, and on nights when the moon is visible, it can be ensnared within a circle comprised of rice grains. Once captured, the creature must be reinterred and subjected to appropriate burial rites to ensure its permanent neutralization.

Sources: Bush, *Asian Horror Encyclopedia*, 96; Glut, *Dracula Book*, 25; Groot, *Religion of the Chinese*, 76–7; Summers, *Vampire: His Kith and Kin*, 213

gienganger

Variation: gienfard

Originating from Denmark, the term *gienganger* refers to a REVENANT, traditionally understood as the unsettled spirit of an individual who, despite being buried, does not find peace. This spectral entity is known to revisit its family, causing them distress and anxiety. It is believed that the gienganger sustains itself by drawing upon the fear it induces in its living relatives.

Sources: Gaster, *Thespis*, 334; Grimm, *Teutonic Mythology*, 915; Palgrave, *Collected Historical Works*, 193; *The Quarterly Review*, vol. 29, 460–74

gierach (GEAR-ruck)

Variations: gierrach, girrach, givach, stryz

In what is now northern Poland, the gierach is very similar to the UPIER of Poland and the VIESCZY of Russia. A REVENANT with long teeth and red eyes, it smells like death and decay. Hunting between noon and midnight, the gierach is easily distracted and confused fairly easily.

This particular vampire, distinguished by its unique method of execution, operates through the power of its voice. It ascends to the top of a structure, such as a bell tower, residential building, or steeple, and calls out the name of its intended victim. Afterwards, the named individual succumbs within a span of hours or days. The majority of the village population hears the vampire's call as nothing more than the nocturnal song of a bird. However, the targeted victim distinctly hears their own name. This association has led many to view owls with suspicion, considering them either malevolent creatures, vampires in disguise, or at the very least, harbingers of misfortune. This vampire feeds on the despair experienced by its predestined victims.

To prevent a gierach from rising from its grave, place a fishing net over its coffin. The vampire will busy itself trying to untie all of the knots. Another method is to put poppy seeds into its grave, as the gierach will be compelled to count them, but will eventually drift off to sleep before it finishes. When it awakes, it will start over. Even a simple sock placed in the grave will occupy its attention. The gierach will not leave the grave as long as the sock is intact, but it will not undo more than a single stitch a year.

Preventing a gierach from rising is a safer method than trying to destroy one. As with many vampires, it can only be destroyed if burned to ash, but with a gierach one must be very careful. Every single piece of the vampire must be completely destroyed. If so much as one bit survives the fire, the gierach will return, focused and vengeful.

Sources: Aristotle, *Aristotle's History of Animals*, 45; Barber, *Vampires, Burial and Death*, 151; Maberry, *They Bite!*, 73; Maberry, *Vampire Universe*, 138

gierfrass (GEAR-firss)

In German folklore, specific circumstances surrounding death and burial can potentially result in the deceased returning as a vampiric REVENANT known as a gierfrass ("greed eater"). Such scenarios include instances where an individual has committed suicide or when they are interred in clothing that bears their name. This type of REVENANT is believed to carry and spread disease. The gierfrass primarily targets its kin and acquaintances before extending its attacks to unfamiliar individuals.

Sources: Briggs, *Encyclopedia of Fairies*, 206; Curtin, *Hero-Tales of Ireland*, 482; *Transactions of the Gaelic Society*, 236; Lecouteux, *History of Vampire*; O'Donnell, *Confessions of a Ghost Hunter*, 124, 132

gjakpires

In Albanian folklore, a reanimated corpse belonging to an individual of Turkish-Albanian heritage is referred to as a gjakpires; this can be loosely translated as "blood feeder." The conditions that create this REVENANT, beyond being of Turkish-Albanian descent, are not specified in the lore. The gjakpires is easily identifiable as a particular type of vampiric REVENANT due to its distinctive attire: it dons both its funeral shroud and high-heeled shoes while seeking human blood.

Given their distinctive appearance, gjakpires rely heavily on cunning during their hunts. They often feign helplessness by the side of a road, attacking well-intentioned passersby who stop to assist. Alternatively, they may opt to attack sleeping individuals, taking care to only draw a small quantity of blood. This cautious approach stems from the knowledge that excessive greed could alert the community to the presence of a vampire, potentially leading to their demise.

In instances where a gjakpires is suspected to be active within a community, one can visit the local cemetery and search for a phenomenon known as a CORPSE CANDLE. The grave over which this spectral light hovers is believed to be occupied by the gjakpires. It is generally accepted that this vampire is inherently cowardly due to its vulnerability; a simple stake or nail driven into its chest can either immobilize it by pinning it to the ground or completely obliterate it.

Sources: Drizari, *Albanian-English Dictionary*, 38; Maberry, *Vampire Universe*, 138; Maberry, *They Bite!*, 74; MacDougall, *Vampire Slayers' Field Guide to the Undead*, 655

gjenganger

Variations: attergangar, genfaerd, gengangare, genganger, gjenferd

In the realm of Scandinavian folklore, the gjenganger is a notable REVENANT, akin to the HAUGBUI. The word *gjenganger* can be translated to mean a person who has returned from death with the express purpose of haunting the living. They are not a spectral form but the returned corpse of an individual capable of interacting with the material world. According to tradition, a gjenganger could return for several reasons. One common belief is that these entities are often the revenants of individuals who left something unresolved or unfinished in their lives.

This entity bears resemblance to what contemporary culture would categorize as a ZOMBIE. Its predatory behavior is characterized by the pursuit and assault of living humans. Individuals fortunate enough to evade immediate death following an encounter with a gjenganger are, nevertheless, not spared from subsequent affliction. They fall prey to a necrotic condition that progressively consumes their flesh.

Sources: Astonishing Legends, "Gjenganger," n.p.; Webley, *The Playful Undead and Video Games*, 9–10; Wikipedia, "Gjenganger"

golem

The golem, a fascinating figure originating from Hebrew folklore, is often linked to the esoteric tradition of kabbalah. The term *golem* signifies a humanoid or shape, suggesting a being molded from clay and brought to life through the intricate manipulation of Hebrew alphabets. This legend is thought to have stemmed from the *Sefer Yetzirah* (*Book of Formations*), one of the earliest kabbalistic texts. The ability to create is seen as part of what it means for humans to be made "in the image of God"; this is why fashioning a golem is not considered to be against God's will.

Typically, a kabbalist shapes a humanoid using soil from an untouched or unploughed mountain and water from a pure spring. The creator then inscribes the Hebrew word for truth, *emet*, on its forehead. When the first letter of the word for truth, aleph, is erased, the remaining word is death, *met*, causing the creature's demise. The golem gains life through a process known as *tzeruf*, which involves combining the tetragrammaton (the four-letter Hebrew name of God, typically represented as JHVH for Jehovah or YHWH for Yahweh) with various permutations of the Hebrew alphabet, as mentioned in the *Sefer Yetzirah*. It remains uncertain, however, whether these combinations should be spoken aloud or written on the golem's body.

Inherently, the golem lacks both free will and the ability to speak, although there are occasional accounts of it expressing divine warnings; in these instances, it is being used as an instrument and it is not speaking for itself or because it has the will or capability to do so. Historical narratives tell of figures like Rabbi Zera, who, upon recognizing he was interacting with a golem, returned it to its inanimate state. Another notable story involves Rabbi Loew of Prague, who created a golem to safeguard his community from anti–Semitic violence. When the golem becomes uncontrollable and overly powerful, however, the rabbi is forced to destroy his creation, learning a lesson in humility.

Creating a golem is seen as a significant spiritual accomplishment, reserved for those who have advanced in kabbalah and alchemy practices. After undergoing ritual purification, the creator must blend the collected soil and water into mud and then shape it into a humanlike figure. This process is mystical and is more like summoning than creating. Once formed, the golem is brought to life either by placing a piece of paper inscribed with the tetragrammaton under its tongue or by writing the Hebrew letters *aleph*, *mem*, and *tav* on its forehead.

Once the golem has completed the task it was created for, it can be returned to its inert state by reversing the creation process. This involves reciting the letters and words backward and circling the golem in the opposite direction. Caution is advised when creating a golem, as improper handling can lead to the creation of a destructive entity.

The term *golem*, appearing once in Psalms 139:16 within the Bible, is identified as a "shapeless mass." This connotation is further enforced in Talmudic teachings, which depict the golem as an "unformed" or an "imperfect" entity. Interestingly, these teachings suggest that Adam, in his initial phase of creation, was essentially a golem—a body devoid of a soul—for a period of 12 hours. This process of golem creation underscores the profound spiritual dimensions and potential perils associated with manipulating life forces.

Simultaneously, the Hebrew Talmud put forward the human capacity for creation as an aspect of their divine image, thereby not considering the act of crafting a humanoid from clay as violating God's will. Although the term *golem* appears solely in the Old Testament's Psalm, typically interpreted as an unformed mass, the golem that later surfaces in Jewish mythology and biblical commentaries is far from being unformed. It bears a striking resemblance to a human, yet it lacks the quintessential qualities that constitute a human. The Sanhedrin, ancient commentaries on the Old Testament narratives, delineate the difference between golems and humans by referencing the day God created Adam.

The day consisted of 12 hours. In the first hour, Adam's dust was gathered; in the second, it was kneaded into a shapeless mass. In the third, his limbs were shaped; in the fourth, a soul was infused into him. A golem is what Adam was before the fourth hour, a soulless being. By the fourth century, the golem had changed. It is still made from dust or clay but isn't created by God. It is made by a rabbi or other scholar who gives it life by chanting mystical incantations and writing the word *emet*, truth, on its forehead or on a piece of paper that is put into the golem's mouth.

The rabbi cannot give the golem a soul. Nor can the rabbi give it the ability to speak because, in the Jewish tradition, language—the word—is what distinguishes humans from all other living things, including golems. The earliest golems were usually made to be servants because they were obedient, placid, and not very intelligent. The golem was then reinvented after the Crusades (1100–1300). This next generation of golems was made to protect the Jewish community. These golems were almost always male, and physically they were large, powerful creatures. The most well-known of this new breed of golem is the golem of Prague. It was introduced to the world by Yudl Rosenberg in his book *The Golem and the Wondrous Deeds of the Maharal of Prague*, recounting how Rabbi Yehuda Loew ben Bezalel and his golem repeatedly saved Prague's Jewish community from powerful anti–Semites.

Sources: Braudy, *Haunted*, 115, 116; Curran, *Man-Made Monsters*, 54, 57, 58, 75; Dennis, *Encyclopedia of Jewish Myth, Magic, and Mysticism*, 110–1; Markowitz, *Robots That Kill*, 43, 75, 76, 77; McCoy, *Witch's Guide to Faery Folk*, 236; Pivarcsi, *Just a Bite*, 5, 150, 153–4, 259; Schwartz, *Tree of Souls*, 251, 279–80

goryō

In Japan, throughout the early Heian era, spanning from 794 to 857, a certain belief permeated society regarding the goryō. These were perceived as spirits that had returned from the afterlife, fueled by vengeance. These spirits were thought to originate from individuals who had met untimely deaths due to political conspiracies, such as dying in exile or being executed by royal decree. It was widely held that these spirits carried with them a host of calamities, including diseases, natural disasters, and war. Techniques such as divination and necromancy, prevalent in ancient times, were employed to discern the identity of these spirits. Subsequently, these spirits were placated and transformed into *goryō-shin*, or ("goryō deities").

As the ninth and tenth centuries unfolded, the belief system around goryō took a significant turn. It was now believed that any individual had the potential to transform into a goryō after their death. This change could be a result of the individual's will at the moment of death or due to an unfortunate or peculiar circumstance leading to their death. In order to ward off a goryō, various methods were adopted. One such practice involved the recitation of the Buddhist nembutsu, an invocation of Buddha Amida, which was said to guide the spirit towards Amida's heaven. The application of Shugendō (a tradition combining Buddhism with folkloric beliefs, philosophies, and rituals) was used to perform an exorcism on the goryō. Alternatively, the practice of *in-yo* magic, derived from Daoism and Shinto, was also utilized for this purpose.

Sources: Doniger, *Merriam-Webster's Encyclopedia of World Religions*, 385; Hori, *Folk Religion in Japan*, 43, 51

grateful dead, the

The literary motif known as the grateful dead is a venerable theme with origins traceable to the Hebrew narrative of Tobit, between 225 and 175 BCE. This motif chiefly involves the interaction of the protagonist with spirits or apparitions, which are typically portrayed in a benevolent light. These entities often assume various forms such as an elderly man, a fox, or even a servant.

The crux of this motif lies in the reciprocal relationship between the protagonist and the returned. The ghost or spirit seeks the assistance of the protagonist, often requesting the respectful and proper interment of their remains; sometimes they ask for the execution of a specific task. The protagonist, by fulfilling these requests, earns the gratitude of the spirit.

Their thankfulness is expressed in the form of guidance or by bestowing critical information to the protagonist. This advice or information invariably plays a pivotal role in the successful accomplishment of the hero's mission.

This motif, therefore, underscores the themes of reciprocity, gratitude, and the instrumental role of supernatural intervention in human affairs. It is a testament to the rich tapestry of human folklore and storytelling, offering a unique lens through which to explore the complex interplay between the living and the dead, as well as the profound influence of the unseen on the tangible world. Because the grateful dead are not a specific species of ghost, REVENANT, or spirit, they can be whatever type of undead the narrator needs.

Sources: Garry, *Archetypes and Motifs in Folklore and Literature*, 186; Yassif, *Hebrew Folktale*, 66–7

Greek vampires

The Greek language contains more than a dozen terms that can be translated as "vampire," and Greek mythology boasts nearly 30 vampire species, celebrated for their rich diversity and unique characteristics, surpassing the variety found in any other country.

Similar to the great white shark, which has undergone minimal evolutionary changes over millennia, the Greek vampire has also remained largely consistent in its mythological representation. This stability persisted until the advent of Christianity, after which there was a minor modification in the vampire narrative to align it with the new faith. Since then, the Greek vampire's depiction has remained steadfast. Minor regional variations do exist, however, concerning the process of becoming a vampire, the appearance of the vampire, preventive measures against vampirism, and methods for destroying the creature.

The spelling of a particular vampire's name often has multiple variants, likely attributable to Greece's geographic configuration as an island nation. As inhabitants freely moved between islands, each developed its own linguistic nuances, leading to slight variations in spellings.

Greek vampires are predominantly revenants, individuals who return from the dead as animated corpses. Typically, this results from evil deeds committed throughout a person's life or from a person having been excommunicated by the Church. Suicide was also considered a cause for returning as undead. Per Catholic beliefs, suicide precludes a person from receiving a mass for their soul or being buried in consecrated ground, effectively barring them from heaven. Other factors contributing to vampirism include being a murder victim, consuming meat killed by a wolf, or allowing an animal to leap over a corpse.

Revenant Greek vampires are consistently described as corpses with tanned skin stretched taut over their bodies, producing a drumlike sound when struck. This condition is known as timpanios. Apart from occasional bloating, these vampires show no signs of decay.

According to the Church of Saint Sophia in Thessalonica, Greece, four types of bodies do not decay. The first type, where the front remains preserved while the back shows decay, is associated with individuals who die under a curse or fail to fulfill their parents' specific request. The second type, characterized by yellowing and wrinkled fingers but otherwise preserved, occurs in those who die amidst scandal. The third type, appearing pale but preserved, happens to those excommunicated from the Church. The final type pertains to individuals excommunicated at a local level, such as by a bishop, where the body remains intact, but the skin turns black.

These Greek revenants can hunt for human prey at any time, often knocking loudly on doors in the middle of the day. If unanswered after the first knock, they do not persist. They have the inexplicable ability to rise and return to their graves without disturbing the earth. Merely sighting a Greek vampire can be fatal, and their sheer presence can harm nearby humans. They do not require human blood for survival, meaning their hunting and killing only amplify their inherent evil.

Despite their fearsome reputation, Greek vampires can be avoided and defeated due to their predictable behavior and well-known characteristics. They have no physical weaknesses or vulnerabilities to exploit. Simply refraining from answering the door when they knock or having the Church revoke the excommunication can effectively neutralize these vampires.

Sources: Melton, *Vampire Book*; Summers, *Vampire in Lore and Legend*, 18, 43, 217–20; Szigethy, *Vampires*, 4, 6, 59

Grendel

In the epic saga *Beowulf*, written between 700 and 750 CE, Grendel, one of the three antagonists, is a character often overlooked in vampire lore, although he exhibits traits commonly associated with vampiric creatures from that culture. While the text does not explicitly categorize Grendel as a REVENANT, it is reasonable to infer such a classification given the similarities.

According to the narrative, Grendel is a descendant of Cain and is portrayed as a colossal entity that embodies both human and water troll characteristics. During the night, he would depart from his aquatic dwelling in Dark Lake to mount attacks on King Hrot's courtiers and servants. His method of attack involved tearing his victims apart by hand, followed by the consumption of their blood and flesh. A formidable warrior, Grendel was rendered invulnerable to swords due to a spell cast on him by his witch mother. His only source of satisfaction came from the act of killing. The narrative culminates in Beowulf, the hero, being requested by the king to eliminate the beast, a task the hero accomplishes by severing one of Grendel's arms in a wrestling match.

The narrative of Beowulf's encounter with Grendel bears similarities to numerous ancient Norse tales concerning vampiric revenants referred to as DRAUGE and DRAUGR. These entities, like Grendel, are depicted as being large and exceptionally powerful, capable of killing a man in a single stroke. The DRAUGE was created through magic, and Grendel was shielded by the witchcraft his mother bestowed upon him.

The narrative of the DRAUGE underwent a transformation with the advent of Christianity. Coincidentally, the story of Beowulf was also penned during this transitional period, when the old religion was gradually being replaced. DRAUGR, similar to Grendel, craved the comforts they had in life such as warmth, sustenance, and family. Being denied these pleasures, they sought satisfaction through acts of death and destruction. Neither Grendel nor a DRAUGR could be harmed by conventional weapons. The defeat of a DRAUGR could only be achieved by a hero in a wrestling match, mirroring the manner in which Grendel was vanquished.

Sources: Hoops, *Kommentar zum Beowulf*, 163; Olsen, *Monsters and the Monstrous*, 79; Perkowski, *Vampires of the Slavs*; Robinson, *Tomb of Beowulf*, 185–218; Tolkien, *Beowulf*, 278

Grey Lady

Variation: White Lady

In the British folklore tradition, the apparition known as the Grey Lady is typically understood to be the spectral manifestation of a woman who has met her end due to complications arising from a tragic love affair. This unfortunate circumstance often entails either an act of murder or suicide. The "Grey Lady" moniker, despite its explicit color reference, does not strictly dictate the attire of this spectral entity, which has been reported to appear in garments of varying colors, including black, brown, and white.

The Grey Lady, while not considered harmful, is associated with certain peculiar phenomena. There are stories that recount instances where this ghostly figure has been observed hovering over individuals in slumber, whispering the narrative of its sorrowful existence into their ears. The potency of this tale is so tragic that it reportedly compels the awakened individual, still garbed in their nightwear, to walk towards the closest cliff and leap off it immediately. This is, of course, according to folklore.

Sources: Maberry, *Vampire Universe*, 142; Ogden, *Complete Idiot's Guide to Ghosts and Hauntings*, 153–4

Grim Reaper, the

Variation: Angel of Death

The Grim Reaper, as a symbol of death, is often classified as an undead entity in literature and popular culture. The term *undead* in this instance likens it to beings that are deceased and yet behave as if they are alive. As with many undead beings, it takes human lives, although in this instance it does not devour individuals. Despite its skeletal form, the Grim Reaper exhibits sentient characteristics, such as movement and speech.

From an academic perspective, the concept of the undead has been prevalent in folklore, mythology, and religious beliefs across various cultures and historical periods. This concept challenges our understanding of life and death, blurring the boundary between the two states.

The Grim Reaper, with its skeletal appearance, cloaked in a dark, hooded robe, and wielding a large scythe, is often depicted as a male figure who appears to individuals to collect their souls at the moment of their death. The scythe, a tool traditionally used by peasants to reap crops, symbolizes the Reaper's role in "cutting down" lives, just as a farmer would harvest grain. The skeletal form represents the physical decay that follows death. The cloak, often black or deep purple, adds an element of mystery and fear.

Its horrific image exemplifies the notion of the undead. While its physical form represents death and decay, it performs tasks akin to those of the living—namely, the collection of souls at the moment of death. This dichotomy enhances the Grim Reaper's eerie and ominous aura, contributing to its enduring cultural significance.

The figure of the Grim Reaper finds its roots in ancient cultures. In Greek mythology, for instance, the god Thanatos was often portrayed as a winged spirit or a bearded man carrying an inverted torch, symbolizing the extinguishing of life. The image of the Grim Reaper as we know it today—a SKELETON carrying a scythe—seems to have emerged during the Middle Ages, influenced by the widespread devastation caused by plagues like the Black Death. It's important to clarify, however, that while the Grim Reaper is depicted as an undead entity in popular culture, this does not necessarily align with all cultural or religious interpretations of death. Additionally, it is not always portrayed as a malevolent being. In some interpretations, it is seen as a neutral figure performing a necessary task. In either version, the figure serves as a personification of death rather than a literal embodiment of an undead being. Its portrayal varies widely depending on cultural context and individual interpretation.

Sources: Barber, *Vampires, Burial, and Death*, 51; Caciola, *Past & Present*, 3–45; Laderman, *Rest in Peace*, 170–5, 193–4

Groa

Groa, a figure known as a *volva*, features prominently in the poem *Grógaldr* (*Groa's Magical Chant* or *The Incantation of Groa*). This work is part of the *Poetic Edda*, a manuscript originally transcribed in the thirteenth century. Notably, *Grógaldr* is one of six poems from this era that explores the theme of necromancy. Often, it is presented alongside another poem, *Fjölsvinnsmál*, forming a combined work known as *Svipdagsmál* (*The Lay of Svipdagr*).

The narrative of *Grógaldr* centers on Svipdagr, who employs necromancy to resurrect his deceased mother, Groa. The opening stanza depicts Svipdagr at his mother's burial mound, urging her to return from the beyond. The text further reveals that during her lifetime, she had made her son vow to summon her from the dead if he ever required her assistance. When she was alive, she was well known as a powerful *volva* (or *vala*, that is "prophetess," "sorceress," or "wise woman," "witch").

Upon being summoned, Groa rises from the dead and learns from her son that he requires her help to complete a mission imposed on him by his crafty stepmother. Additionally, Svipdagr seeks to acquire magical charms that would guarantee him a prosperous life.

Before she died, Groa was the *volva* who almost succeeded in extracting a whetstone lodged in the head of the god of thunder, Thor. While she was in the midst of performing the removal spell, however, she discovered that Thor had saved her husband Aurvandil's life. This joyful news disrupted her focus, causing the spell to fail and leaving the whetstone embedded in Thor's head.

Sources: Lecouteux, *The Return of the Dead*, n.p.; McKinnell, *Meeting the Other in Old Norse Myth and Legend*, 202; Olsen, *Germanic Texts and Latin Models*, 209

grobnik

In the geographical districts of Kukush, Ohrid, and Struga within Bulgaria, a particular type of vampiric entity known as a grobnik ("of a grave") is said to roam. This entity is created under two very specific conditions: either when an individual is strangled to death or when a person has an inherent predisposition towards becoming such a creature.

Following its burial, the grobnik remains as an invisible spirit for an initial period of nine days, during which it can only execute minor mischief. After a span of 40 days, however, it gains the ability to leave its grave, adopting the appearance of a human being. The distinctive features that set it apart from a regular human are a single nostril and a shadow that contains sparks.

This entity, noted for its exceptional density and strength, sustains itself by feeding on cattle, specifically by draining their blood and consuming the remains of any available animal carcasses. Protective amulets can be utilized to fend off the grobnik, but the best and surest solution is its capture and destruction, as, if left to its own devices, it can decimate all the cattle in a village.

To eliminate the grobnik, it must be securely tied to a pyre made from thornbushes and incinerated until it is reduced to ashes. In situations where the grobnik is identified within its initial nine-day phase of existence, a professional vampire hunter known as a *djadadjii* can be employed to contain it within a bottle.

These hunters specialize in the destruction of a specific type of vampire known as the KRVOIJAC, but they can slay other species as well. The hunter uses a distinctive method known as bottling to capture and then kill the vampire. They begin by baiting a bottle with blood and carrying it while searching for the vampire. They employ religious symbols such as images of Jesus, the Virgin Mary, a saint, or even a holy relic to lure the vampire to the bottle. The hand holding the bottle will begin to shake and move violently as the hunter approaches the—usually invisible—vampire. The icon is waved about to herd the vampire into the bottle, and once it is within, the container is corked and thrown into a roaring fire. The resulting explosion is sufficient to obliterate the vampire.

In instances where the djadadjii fails to entrap the vampire in the bottle, or the vampire is not an invisible spirit but a REVENANT, they must then exhume the corpse, penetrate its heart with thorns, and incinerate the remains in a fire fueled by hawthorn branches.

Sources: Georgieva, *Bulgarian Mythology*, 95; *Journal of the Gypsy Lore Society*, 131; Perkowski, *Vampires of the Slavs*, 206

gui po

In Chinese folklore, there exists a particular kind of ghost known as a gui po ("devil aunties"). These entities are generally considered to be benign spirits and are typically believed to be the returned spirits of former servants. The unique characteristic of these spirits is their manifestation in the form of amiable elderly women. This transformation serves the purpose of allowing them to maintain their roles of service among the living.

Source: Dupler, *Death Explained*, 42

gui xian

Variation: xuanwu

Gui xian ("first ghost"), a term originating from Chinese mythology, denotes a particular type of demonic entity. These entities are believed to be the restless souls of individuals who have ended their lives through suicide or have perished by drowning. The specific nature of their deaths renders them ineligible for the cycle of reincarnation, a core belief in many Eastern religions and philosophies. As a result, these souls, unable to transition to the next stage of existence, continue to persist in our physical world in a spectral form, haunting it.

Further, in Chinese culture and religious practices, such spirits are often associated with hungry ghosts, another category of beings that are often the subject of rituals, particularly during the Hungry Ghost Festival. This festival, held in August, is a traditional Buddhist and Taoist event celebrated in certain Asian countries; offerings are made to appease restless spirits and provide them with a chance for salvation.

It is worth pointing out that the concept of the gui xian aligns with the folklore and myths about water-related spirits or entities from around the world. Many cultures have similar tales about spirits tied to bodies of water due to tragic ends, further emphasizing the universality of such themes in human storytelling and mythmaking.

Sources: Kelly, *Who in Hell*, 102; Lurker, *Dictionary of Gods and Goddesses, Devils and Demons*, 71; Redfern, *The Zombie Book*, 19; Teiser, *The Ghost Festival in Medieval China*, 125–9; Zell-Ravenheart, *Wizard's Bestiary*, 45

haltia (hal-TEA-ah)

The haltia ("governor" or "ruler") is a returned spirit that originates from Baltic, Estonian, and Finnish folklore, functioning as a guardian for the household. This entity is typically understood as the spectral manifestation or reincarnated spirit of the individual who first claimed ownership of the land, built a residence, ignited a fire, or was the initial person to pass away there. The spirit is believed to mirror its original in all aspects, including attire, behaviors, and mannerisms. In fact, up until the mid–nineteenth century, it was believed that every flower, forest, heath, stream, swamp, and tree had a guardian haltia.

If a family wished to relocate or transfer a haltia from one place to another, they would light a torch from the hearth fire and carry it to the new dwelling, effectively transporting the haltia's presence. Another method involved moving the ashes from one location to another.

The haltia is described as having certain behavioral preferences. They are said to disapprove of brawling, cursing, drinking, and any form of socially inappropriate conduct. Despite its primary role as the protector of the home and its inhabitants, the haltia are also believed to collaborate and work in tandem with other spirits. These partner spirits usually reside in the barn, safeguarding the welfare of the livestock, and in the millhouse if such a structure exists on the property.

The word *haltia* has lent itself to other spirits; for instance, in the historical province of Angermanland, Sweden, a *huoneenhaltis* is the spirit of the living room.

Sources: Abercromby, *Pre- and Proto-historic Finns*, 272; Doniger, *Merriam-Webster's Encyclopedia of World Religions*, 408–9; Lecouteux, *The Tradition of Household Spirits*, n.p.

hameh

The hameh is a mythical bird from Arabian folklore, characterized by its striking green or purple plumage. This creature is said to rise up from the blood that spills from a murder victim. The hameh's call is a repetitive utterance of "*iskoonee*," a phrase that translates to "give me blood." Its incessant call serves as a constant reminder of the crime committed upon it, signifying the societal expectation for justice to be served. It is also known to emit this same cry upon witnessing an impending act of murder.

According to mythology, the hameh is said to be relentless in its pursuit of its own murderer, never resting until it has consumed their blood; it is thus often portrayed as being a symbol of justice and retribution. Its dogged determination embodies the cultural value of holding individuals accountable for their actions, regardless of the passage of time.

Once the hameh locates and exacts revenge on its killer, it then journeys to the realm of spirits, where it proclaims with satisfaction that its death has been avenged. This transition to the afterlife shows a belief in spirits being able to find peace in a realm beyond our physical world.

Sources: Hulme, *Myth-land*, 140–1; Lane, *Selections from the Kur-an*, 35; Muir, *Songs and Other Fancies*, 157–9; Nozedar, *The Secret Language of Birds*, 40–1; Reddall, *Fact, Fancy, and Fable*, 250

han-ridden ghost

Variation: haan-ridden ghost

In the study of Korean folklore, one learns of the han-ridden ghost, an entity that is the returned spirit of an individual who cannot achieve tranquility in death. The inability to find peace is attributed to severe injustices that were inflicted upon them during their lifetime and remained unresolved at their death.

The term *han* itself, central to understanding this concept, is deeply rooted in Korean culture and psychology. It represents a unique emotional state or collective sentiment arising from experiences of injustice, oppression, or profound sorrow. Despite the absence of a direct English equivalent, *han* can be best described as a blend of deep lamentation, resentment, and longing for resolution, particularly stemming from unresolved injustices or grievances.

Thus, a han-ridden ghost is a figure burdened by this intense, unresolved anguish from its past life. The only means to assuage such a spirit, according to the lore, is to rectify the injustice that was originally done to it. This rectification serves not only as a means of pacifying the disturbed REVENANT or spirit but also as a symbolic representation of the resolution of the deep-seated *han*.

Sources: Bush, *Asian Horror Encyclopedia*, 66; Son, *Haan*, ix, xi, 56, 129

hanako-san

Variations: hanako of the lavatory, toilet hanako, toire-no-hanako-san ("hanako of the toilet")

The origin of the hanako-san folklore is not definitively established, with some accounts suggesting its roots lay in urban legend while others propose it began in mainstream media. Regardless of its inception, it is clear that the stories associated with hanako-san predate contemporary educational institutions.

According to the legends, hanako-san is believed to be a REVENANT or the spirit of a young girl who tragically lost her life. The exact details of her demise vary across different versions of the story, adding to the mystery and intrigue surrounding her existence.

Some tales describe her as a victim of a heinous crime, while others depict her as a victim of a tragic accident; suicide is never mentioned.

These spectral apparitions are said to predominantly haunt school bathrooms, specifically those used by boys in recent times. The chilling presence of hanako-san is often held responsible for unexplained phenomena, such as doors closing and opening on their own, strange noises echoing through the halls, and sudden drops in temperature.

One popular belief is that invoking the name of the deceased by knocking on the designated stall it is said to favor or haunt elicits an array of frightful responses. The brave few who dare to perform this ritual claim to have experienced hair-raising encounters, ranging from eerie whispers and cold gusts of wind to seeing glimpses of a pale figure in the mirror.

Sources: Drazen, *Gathering of Spirits*, 175; Foster, *Pandemonium and Parade*, 205; Yoda, *Yokai Attack*, 174–8

hannya (HAN-ya)

Variations: akeru, hannya-shin-kyo ("emptiness of forms")

The hannya, a supernatural entity from Japanese folklore, is depicted as a vampiric and demonic creature that primarily preys on beautiful women and infants. Its distinctive physical traits include an enlarged chin, elongated fangs and horns, green scales, a forked tongue akin to a snake's, and eyes that seem to burn with an intense flame.

These creatures are often featured in Noh plays, a form of theater that originated in the fourteenth century and remains prevalent in Japan today, relatively unaltered. Noh plays typically revolve around a central character who experiences a potent emotion, expressed through various artistic mediums such as dance, gesture, poetry, and music. A crucial moment in these plays occurs when the actor takes on a demonic mask, signifying the character's complete transformation. These masks, crafted from cypress wood, are painted in symbolic colors, heavily lacquered, and designed to embody the specific emotion that has overtaken the character. Despite variations in the emotional context, the masks share common features: fangs, a square jaw, a melancholic smile, and a disheveled black mane indicative of madness.

One notable play narrates the story of Hannya, a beautiful woman deeply in love. After being betrayed and spurned by her lover, she is consumed by grief, anger, and sorrow, ultimately transforming into an *oni* demon (which will come to be known as a hannya) in her quest for revenge.

Hannya are typically found near the sea or in wells, but they maintain proximity to human dwellings, capable of silently infiltrating houses harboring potential victims (sleeping women). Prior to an attack, the hannya emits a terrifying shriek, startling the woman before possessing her. This possession gradually drives the woman to madness, physically mutating her into a monstrous form. Ultimately, it compels her to assault a child, consuming its blood and flesh.

While there is no explicit vulnerability attributed to the hannya, a particular Buddhist sutra is known to render humans invisible to spirits and demons. In Noh theater, young men are often portrayed as the preferred victims of particularly malevolent and vengeful hannya.

Sources: Frédéric, *Japan Encyclopedia*, 287–8; MacDougall, *Vampire Slayers' Field Guide to the Undead*, 655; Pollack, *Reading Against Culture*, 50; Toki, *Japanese No Plays*, 40; Williamson, *Women of Myth*, 219–22

Harppe (HARP)

Variation: The Vampire of Milos

In his extensive exploration of the Greek Church, Chevalier Ricaut had the privilege of rediscovering the remarkable tale of a vampiric REVENANT as related by the admired and respected monk, Sophrones. This captivating account, originating from Sophrones's parish in the Turkish town of Smyrna, forms the foundation of the legendary vampire of Milos tale. While the exact timeline of these extraordinary events remains unknown, the story itself was meticulously documented by the scholar Dom Augustin Calmet in his renowned 1751 publication, *Dissertation on Revenants, the Excommunicated, and the Ghosts of Vampires.*

At the heart of this tale lies the character known only by the name Harppe, a man from Smyrna who had been tragically excommunicated by the Church for reasons not given in the story. Following Harppe's untimely demise, his lifeless remains were laid to rest in an unhallowed ground. It wasn't long, however, before rumors began to circulate, suggesting that Harppe had risen from the grave as a bloodthirsty vampire. Faced with this horrible turn of events, the local inhabitants initially contemplated following the conventional method of disposing of a vampire—by beheading and quartering the body, and then boiling the severed parts in wine. Yet, Harppe's grieving parents, desperate to save their son's soul, implored the compassionate monks to refrain from such drastic measures, at least until they could undertake a pilgrimage to Constantinople in search of absolution for their beloved child. Moved by the parents' pleas, the monks agreed to honor their request, albeit with a cautious approach. They decided to relocate the dormant vampire to the sanctity of the church, where it would be kept under constant vigilance within its coffin. The devoted monks, unwavering in their dedication, conducted their daily morning mass over the dormant vampire and offered prayers throughout the day, beseeching for the redemption and restoration of Harppe's tormented soul.

It was during one such morning mass that a sudden, thunderous noise reverberated from within the confines of the coffin, sending shivers down the spines of all those present. Anticipating a ghastly spectacle of Harppe's bloated, blood-filled body showing no signs of decay, the monks, with a mix of trepidation and awe, cautiously opened the coffin. To their astonishment, the sight that greeted them was far from what they had expected. Harppe's body had undergone a remarkable transformation, rapidly shriveling and decaying at a rate consistent with the time elapsed since his demise. When Harppe's parents finally returned from their pilgrimage, the truth behind the peculiar noise was revealed. It was at the precise moment when the monks heard the thunderous sound over the chants of their unwavering prayers that Harppe's tormented soul was granted absolution, allowing him to lie in eternal peace at last.

Sources: de Plancy, *Dictionary of Demonology*, 101; Dundes, *Vampire Casebook*, 65; Masters, *Natural History of the Vampire*, 184–6; Summers, *Vampire: His Kith and Kin*, 304, 344, 410

haugbui, plural haugbuar

In the mythology of Scandinavia, a specific type of REVENANT known as the haugbui ("barrow," or "howe") exists. This REVENANT is unique in its preference to remain within its *draughus* ("burial mound" or "grave hill"); it only emerges if an individual ventures too close. Its response to such intrusion is primarily defensive, as it attempts to deter trespassers by chasing them to an extent sufficient to instill fear. If the person is caught, however, they will suffer the same fate as if they dared to enter into the burial mound.

The haugbui maintains its innocuous solitude within the mound, and if undisturbed, it will not exit its dwelling. Furthermore, its presence does not negatively impact the surrounding land, nor does it induce disease or illness in animals. This potent undead entity possesses a violent stance towards those it manages to apprehend, however, consuming their flesh and drinking their blood. It exhibits particular aggression towards grave robbers attempting to pilfer its funerary possessions.

Sources: Brodman, *The Universal Vampire*, 4; Houran, *From Shaman to Scientist*, 103–4; Redfern, *The Zombie Book*, 94

Headless Horseman

The Headless Horseman is a legendary figure whose origins trace back to the folklore from the Middle Ages. This character is traditionally represented as a headless rider astride a spirited black horse.

In some versions of the tale, the Horseman is depicted carrying his severed head or has it tied to his saddle, while in others, he is in active pursuit of his missing head. The Headless Horseman gained considerable recognition through Washington Irving's 1820 short story "The Legend of Sleepy Hollow," part of his collection, *The Sketch Book of Geoffrey Crayon, Gent*. This popular narrative has since been integrated and fully adopted into both American folklore and legend.

Irving's tale begins in Sleepy Hollow, New York, during the American Revolutionary War. The folklore asserts that the Headless Horseman, also known as the Headless Hessian of the Hollow, was a Hessian trooper who lost both his life and his head to an American cannonball during the battle of White Plains on October 28, 1776. His comrades hastily retrieved his body from the battlefield, leaving his shattered head and skull fragments behind. His remains were interred in the cemetery of the Old Dutch Church of Sleepy Hollow. From this resting place, the Horseman is said to rise, seeking his lost head and brandishing a jack-o'-lantern as a temporary replacement and weapon.

In Irish mythology, the DULLAHAN is another headless REVENANT. He rides a horse, carrying his head under his arm, and wields a whip crafted from a human spine. Another version of the myth presents him as the headless driver of a black carriage, the *coiste bodhar* ("soundless coach") as it never made a sound as it traveled. A similar figure, the *gan ceann* ("without a head"), can be warded off by wearing or placing a gold object in his path.

Scottish folklore features a prominent tale of a headless horseman named Ewen, who was decapitated during a clan battle at Glen Cainnir on the Isle of Mull. His untimely death denied him the opportunity to become a chieftain, and both he and his horse are described as headless in accounts of his spectral appearances in the area.

In Germany, particularly in the Rhineland, stories tell of headless horsemen who cause death merely by touch. These horsemen are described as revenants, forced to roam the earth until they atone for their sins, often through acts of kindness towards strangers. Instead of expressing gratitude through a would-be-fatal handshake, the horseman extends to the stranger a tree branch, which withers and dies, sparing the person's life.

hija

In Albanian folklore, there is a type of female ghost called the hija ("shade shadow"). Believed to be the soul of a deceased person or an unspecified entity or demon, the hija is considered independent of the body and not responsible for its sins. After spending the first night with the body, the hija is free to leave its grave and often returns to places it frequented in life.

Interestingly, dogs possess a natural ability to perceive the hija and will bark when in their presence. It is believed that when dogs bark without apparent reason, it may be due to the presence of a hija delivering a message to nearby living souls. Additionally, it is customary to place flat stones beneath shade trees along the roadside for the hijas to sit upon.

In central Albania, hijas are associated with nightmares, while in Tomor they are described as wearing a golden crown covered with jewels. If a hija embraces a person, and they manage to touch one of the gems, it is believed that they will become one of the richest and most powerful people on earth. If the hija returns and commits evil acts, however, it is referred to as *hija e lige* ("evil shadow").

Source: Elsie, *Dictionary of Albanian Religion, Mythology, and Folk Culture*, 113–4

hikiko

According to Japanese folklore, a hikiko is the ghost of an adolescent girl who experienced bullying by her peers and mistreatment from her parents. She may also be a social recluse or pariah. In life, she may even be referred to as a hikikomori, someone who has withdrawn from society and may suffer from depression. Although this can be experienced by adolescent boys, the ghost is always described as being female.

Hikikos are believed to be vengeful spirits that haunt those who have wronged them in life. They are said to possess supernatural powers and can cause harm to those around them.

It is important to note that the concept of hikikos is deeply rooted in Japanese culture and reflects societal issues, specifically the high rate of suicide among young people in Japan. The existence of these supernatural entities reflects the psychological trauma that some individuals may experience and provides insight into the cultural attitudes toward mental health and social isolation.

While hikikos are often sensationalized in popular culture, it is crucial to acknowledge and respect the cultural significance and historical context of these folkloric beliefs.

Sources: Joly, *Scary Monsters and Super Creeps*, n.p.; Whaley, *Toward a Gameic World*, 109–11

hminza tase (MENS-za TAY)

According to Burmese folklore, a hminza tase is created when an individual experiences extreme suffering and trauma during their life, often as a result of mistreatment by others. The intense emotions and negative energy that build up as a result of this mistreatment can manifest after death as a vengeful spirit seeking revenge on those who wronged it in life.

Once the spirit has been created, it is said to haunt the village where it lived, targeting and attacking those who caused it the most harm. In some cases, the hminza tase takes possession of the body of an animal, such as a crocodile or tiger, to carry out its attacks.

There are various beliefs and rituals associated with preventing the creation of hminza tase, including treating others with kindness and respect and avoiding causing harm to those around you. For those already affected by this vengeful spirit, however, there are limited remedies, such as performing death dance rituals or removing the spirit's grave marker to prevent its return.

Sources: Burma Research Society, *Journal of Burma*, Volume 46–7, 4; Hastings, *Encyclopædia of Religion*, 30; Jobes, *Dictionary of Mythology*, 1537; Leach, *Funk and Wagnalls Standard Dictionary of Folklore, Mythology, and Legend*, 1104; Maberry, *They Bite!*, 113–4

homunculus, plural homunculi

Variation: anthroparion

The homunculus is an artificial human being that was said to be the greatest achievement obtainable for an alchemist through the use of alchemy. The term *homunculus* was perhaps first used by the Swiss-German physician, botanist, alchemist, and astrologer Paracelsus (1493–1541), who is credited as the first systematic botanist.

The process of creating a homunculus involved placing human semen into a sealed flask and gently heating it over a flame for 40 days until it began to move and resemble a human being in form. The creature was then fed a specially prepared chemical diet consisting largely of human blood for 40 weeks, after which it would be a fully formed homunculus.

Despite looking like a human child, the homunculus was believed to possess innate knowledge and powers, such as knowing all of the arts required to create itself. This was, according to legend, because it was not created with the taint of the female element. It was believed that using menstrual blood instead of semen in the same experiment would produce a creature known as a basilisk.

The concept of a tiny, fully developed human body, whether made by those who once believed that human sperm or eggs were complete little people from the outset or referring to creatures made of lifeless material to serve their creators, has a long history. The first mention of the homunculus in alchemical lore appeared in the writings of an early Greek Christian mystic Zosimos of Panopolis around 300 BCE. He referred to it as an anthroparion, a being not unlike a GOLEM but possessing more intelligence and guile. This being undergoes some sort of chemical change that involves self-mutilation and self-destruction to be borne against another entity.

The term *homunculus* has been used broadly in various disciplines to refer to the representation of a human being. Its manifestation in Jewish folklore is the tiny, fully developed person at the core of GOLEM legends. In Akkadian mythology, the son of Ea mixed the blood of Kingu with clay to create the first human being to serve the gods, Marduk. These genderless beings of early archetypes, Galaturra and Kurgarra, were created from mud to guard food and water and later resuscitate Inannam, the goddess of fertility and warfare. They are what came to be known in medieval Europe as GOLEM.

The process of homunculus creation, as described in historical texts, necessitates two crucial elements: blood and mandrake. The latter, a member of the nightshade family, bears roots that occasionally mimic the human form, thus earning it the nickname "little man." In German folklore, it is suggested that mandrake only sprouts in locations where human semen has been deposited on the ground, leading to the belief that the plant possesses human characteristics. This is further supported by the notion that when uprooted, the plant emits a distressing cry, a sound so horrifying that it is said to possess the capacity to end the life of a robust adult male.

In the context of alchemical practices, the inclusion of the mandrake root, also known as mandragora, is indispensable in the vessel designated for homunculus creation. In instances where mandrake root cannot be obtained, an acceptable alternative can be found in the form of a bryony sprig. This is contingent, however, upon it being planted on the grave of a recently deceased individual and being nourished with blood and milk for 30 days. Furthermore, the harvesting of the bryony must occur between two full moon cycles.

Doctor David Christianus, a scholar at the German University of Giessen in the eighteenth century, documented an alternate methodology for homunculus production. He emphasized the necessity of an egg procured from a black hen as the cornerstone of the procedure. The egg was to be delicately perforated using a silver pin, creating a small hole. Then, a small amount of the egg white was extracted and an equivalent volume of semen substituted. The puncture was then sealed, and the egg was interred in the earth on the first day of the March lunar cycle.

Exactly one lunar month later, the homunculus would make its appearance, emerging from the egg, burrowing through the soil, and surfacing. Were it regularly nourished with a diet of worms and seeds, the homunculus would remain a steadfast guardian to its creator.

Sources: Curran, *Man-Made Monsters*, 85, 98, 118–9; Draaisma, *Metaphors of Memory*, 212; Pivarcsi, *Just a Bite*, 149, 150, 260–1; Principe, *Secrets of Alchemy*, 131–2; Redfern, *The Zombie Book*, 235

homunculus of Tsou Yen, the

Tsou Yen was a wise man from ancient China who lived between the third and fourth centuries. He was born in Shantung, which is now called Shandong province, around 305 BCE. Tsou Yen became an advisor to the king of Wei, named Hui, who ruled from 370 to 319 BCE. During his time at the king's summer palace, Tsou Yen created a small creature that could move, speak, and even show signs of intelligence. Although the creature did not live very long and turned into dust right after it died, it is considered one of the early versions of what we now know as a homunculus.

Source: Curran, *Man-Made Monsters*, 98

Hone-onna

Hone-onna is a REVENANT from Japanese folklore. She has returned to the living world after death and appears as a woman made entirely of bones. As a species of

REVENANT, a Hone-onna is typically a woman who has been abandoned by her spouse and spends her days waiting for his return, wasting away in the process, dying, and transforming into this type of REVENANT.

Hone-onna is specifically depicted in the work *Konjaku Gazu Zoku Hyakki* (*The Illustrated One Hundred Demons from the Present and the Past*), written by artist Toriyama Sekien in 1779. This book is a bestiary of ghosts, monsters, spirits, and other supernatural creatures, each with an accompanying picture.

In *Konjaku Gazu Zoku Hyakki*, the entry for Hone-onna is called *Otogi Boko*; it tells the story of an old woman made completely of bones who carries a *chōchin* (a traditional lantern) as she travels to visit a man she loved when she was alive, hoping to rekindle their romance.

Sources: Mizuki, *Kitaro's Yokai Battles*, n.p.; Sekien, *Japandemonium*, 124, 126

hopping corpse

Variations: jiangshi ("stiff corpse"), jiang-shi, pinyin, XI XIE GUI ("blood-sucking ghost")

The Chinese myth of the hopping corpse is based on a story called "The Corpse Who Traveled a Thousand Miles." It tells the tale of a wizard who enchants corpses to hop home so that they can receive a proper burial and their soul can be laid to rest. Some people speculate that smugglers invented this myth or at least capitalized on it by dressing up as these hopping corpses to scare away local law enforcement who may have been superstitious.

According to the myth, a corpse that has had its yin shocked and its P'o (soul) disrupted will become a vampiric REVENANT. Various events can cause this to happen, such as a cat jumping over the corpse, moonlight falling on it, or the body not receiving a proper burial. If the soul cannot be laid to rest, the P'o will not leave the body.

A hopping corpse is described as wearing burial clothes from the Qing Dynasty and is accompanied by monks, mourners, and Taoist priests. The corpse's eyes bulge out of its sockets, its tongue lolls from its mouth, and its arms are outstretched. Furthermore, it emits a horrible smell that can make people fall unconscious.

The hopping corpse hunts by using its sense of smell. When it finds a victim, it goes straight for the throat, either biting them in the jugular or strangling them to death. Its touch can kill a person instantly, and it never gets tired. In dire situations, it can even fly.

Yellow and red Chinese death blessings placed on the hopping corpse's forehead can slow it down, as can throwing long-grain rice at it since it is compelled to count each grain. While the hopping corpse is afraid of chicken blood, straw brooms, and Taoist eight-sided mirrors, only long-term exposure to dawn's light or burning the corpse and its coffin to ash can destroy it.

Overall, the myth of the hopping corpse is a unique and fascinating aspect of Chinese folklore. It highlights the importance of proper burial customs and the belief that the soul cannot rest until the body has been laid to rest.

Sources: Chiang, *Collecting the Self*, 57, 98–101, 106, 113, 169–70, 173, 250; Hauck, *International Directory of Haunted Places*; Redfern, *The Zombie Book*, 52; Yashinsky, *Tales for an Unknown City*, 142, 145

hsi-hsue-kue

Variation: hsi-hsue-keui

The hsi-hsue-kue is a vampire-like demon from China. As the name implies, this creature is known for its ability to suck blood from its victims.

Sources: Bunson, *Vampire Encyclopedia*, 126; Colloquium on Violence and Religion, *Contagion*, 32; Crowell, *Farewell, My Colony*, 182; Maberry, *Vampire Universe*, 152

huitranalwe (Hoot-TRA-nal-we)

Variation: piguechen ("vampire")

The huitranalwe is a vampiric REVENANT that originates from Chilean folklore. The huitranalwe is believed to be created when a wizard enchants an old SKELETON to come to life and terrorize the living. This creature is described as having the ability to hunt by night, with its sense of smell guiding it towards prey.

Sources: Darwin, *Naturalist's Voyage Round the World*, 22; Summers, *The Vampire*, 124; Tierney, *Highest Altar*, 146

Iannic-ann-od

Variation: Yanning an Aod

In Brenton folklore the Iannic-ann-od ("Little John of the shore") is a type of ghost. It is a collection of lost souls presented as a single ghost; it is the very embodiment of the unsettled spirits of those who met their end at sea and whose remains were never brought back for proper interment. These entities are known for their distinctive lament, "*Iou! Iou!*," which is reported to be audible during nocturnal hours.

Although these spirits are not inherently malicious or harmful, they do exhibit a particular behavior when provoked. If a living individual echoes their cry, the Iannic-ann-od will halve the space between itself and its tormentor. Upon a second mocking, the spirit advances again, this time bringing itself face-to-face with the instigator. A third provocation will result in the Iannic-ann-od losing its patience and responding with lethal force, specifically by breaking the caller's neck.

While there are parallels between the Iannic-ann-od and other globally recognized spectral entities, like vampires and werewolves, this REVENANT holds a unique place within Breton culture. It symbolizes the convergence of natural calamities and spiritual convictions in the region's folklore. This portrayal is significant as it informs us in part about how they interpret and make sense of tragic events such as drownings at sea.

Source: Le Braz, *Celtic Legends of the Beyond*, 72–3

iara (EE-yara)

Variations: mboiacu, yara

The iara is a figure rooted in Brazilian mythology that can be classified as either a vampiric spirit or a vampiric witch, contingent upon the circumstances of its creation. In instances where an individual experiences a violent death, dies prematurely, passes away outside the Catholic Church, is not provided a proper Catholic burial, or is interred within the jungle, they are believed to transform into the vampiric spirit variant of the iara. Contrarily, if a living person willingly surrenders their soul to the devil in exchange for power, they are said to become the vampiric witch version of the iara.

Regardless of the manner in which it was formed, the iara possesses the ability to assume human form and lure men into the jungle through the allure of its enchanting, siren-like song. Following the ensnarement of its victim, the iara undergoes a metamorphosis into a serpent with red eyes. It then employs a type of mesmerism to hypnotize its prey before proceeding to drain their blood and semen. The remains of its victims are typically found in proximity to bodies of water.

There exists a protective chant that can be invoked upon hearing the iara's melody, although the individual must act swiftly to avoid succumbing to its hypnotic effect.

Sources: Bryant, *Handbook of Death*, 99; de Magalhaes, *Folk-Lore in Brazil*, 75, 81; Prahlad, *Greenwood Encyclopedia of African American Folklore: A–F*, 160

ino, plural inua

Within the cultural beliefs of the Ihalmiut (Ahiarmiut) people, indigenous to the Keewatin region of Northern Canada, there exists a category of spectral entities referred to as ino. This class of ghost is bifurcated into two distinct sizes: inua mikikuni ("little ghosts") and inua angkuni ("great ghosts"). Additionally, an ino can also symbolize the spirit or essence of an inanimate entity such as a plant, river, or stone to a certain extent.

The behavior of these spectral entities is not predetermined, and they may exhibit either benevolent or hostile tendencies toward humans. The inua considered dangerous are believed to be the reanimated spirits of the deceased, who have turned malevolent due to perceived neglect from the living, particularly in relation to the death rites they feel their mortal remains were entitled to. It is also possible that their return is driven by malicious intent present at the time of their demise or as a consequence of a crime they committed and were penalized for.

Generally, these angry inua tend to inhabit rugged, hilly terrains, though they have been reportedly encountered in open plains on occasion. These malevolent spirits are in search of a human host they can possess through intimidation or deceit, striving to regain a semblance of their previous mortal existence.

Sources: Merkur, *Becoming Half Hidden*, 309; Mowat, *People of the Deer*, 255–6; Rose, *Spirits, Fairies, Leprechauns, and Goblins*, 163

inovercy (in-o-VER-see)

In the Russian language, the word *inovercy* is utilized to denote a "nonbeliever," specifically referring to an individual who does not believe in or actively participate in the practices of the Russian Orthodox Church. Such individuals, often marginalized within their communities, may, upon their death, rise from their graves as undead beings, frequently as some species of vampiric revenants.

Sources: Jackson, *Compleat Vampyre*; Oinas, *Essays on Russian Folklore*, 127–8; Senf, *Vampire in Nineteenth-Century*, 21

inugami

In the realm of Japanese mythology, inugami ("dog gods") are potent guardian spirits that can be invoked for the purpose of retribution. These formidable entities are believed to have autonomous capabilities, including the ability to possess humans. Their creation involves a cruel process that combines the starvation of a dog and the application of dark magic, resulting in the manifestation of an entity characterized by fear, anger, and immense power. Only those proficient in magic are considered capable of harnessing these creatures.

Within the Awa region, in Tokushima Prefecture, it is customary to refer to all the female members of a family maintaining an inherited inugami as inugami themselves. The men in this region often express embarrassment over having intimate relations with these women. The families possessing an inugami are frequently associated with poverty and mental instability, leading their neighbors to suspect that they are being coerced into providing them with food through the use of the inugami.

Conversely, there is a documented instance from the village of Takada where a bride was reputed to be of such extraordinary beauty that it was presumed she was possessed by an inugami. As news of her beauty and alleged possession spread, it incited such fear among some villagers that they relocated to other settlements. When a relative of the groom confronted her about the rumors, the situation escalated, and the family member began to speak in an unintelligible manner, reduced to mere babbling thereafter. Similar afflictions were observed in other members of the groom's family, seemingly corroborating the theory of the bride's possession by an inugami. This type of assault is colloquially referred to as *inugami ni kui tsukaretari* ("being bitten by a dog-god").

Sources: de Visser, *The Dog and the Cat in Japanese Superstition*, 66, 67, 68; Joya, *Mock Joya's Things Japanese*, 408; Plutschow, *Reader in Edo Period Travel*, 16

isithfuntela (EYES-it-von-tel-la)

In West Africa, it is believed that witches exhume the corpses of individuals who have taken their own lives, and then, through a ritualistic process imbued with magic, the witch extracts the deceased person's tongue and implants a wooden peg into their head. This act results in the creation of a subservient entity, referred to as an isithfuntela; it exhibits characteristics akin to a REVENANT vampire or a zombie.

Despite its lack of physical strength, the isithfuntela is endowed with a variety of abilities, including shape-shifting into bats or rats and exercising powers of hypnosis. Its most potent ability, however, is its capacity to resurrect the dead and control them until dawn, at which point the reanimated bodies disintegrate into dust.

The survival of the isithfuntela is contingent upon its consumption of human blood. Its greatly reduced physical strength prevents it from overpowering a healthy individual, however. Instead, it utilizes its hypnotic abilities to immobilize a person, subsequently driving a wooden peg into their brain, thereby causing their death. It then feeds on the deceased body at its convenience.

Wolves are known to harbor a profound hatred towards the isithfuntela, and a pack of wolves will likely tear one apart if encountered. Alternatively, the isithfuntela can be eliminated by driving a stake through its heart or via decapitation.

Sources: Hammond-Tooke, *Bhaca Society*, 287; Melton, *The Vampire Book*, 7

istral (its-TRILL)

Variation: USTREL

In Bulgarian cultural beliefs, a child who is born on a Saturday and dies prior to receiving baptism is thought to reanimate as a vampiric REVENANT, referred to as an *istral* ("lost heart"). This reanimation is believed to occur nine days following the child's burial. Such entities are known to target livestock, purportedly killing five or more animals per night by draining their blood.

The destruction of the istral is considered possible only at the hands of a *vampirdzhija*, a term that translates to "vampire hunter." These individuals specialize in the hunting and destruction of both istral and USTREL but can be called upon to destroy any species of vampire.

Sources: Bryant, *Handbook of Death*, 99; Frazer, *Leaves from the Golden Bough*, 37; Keyworth, *Troublesome Corpses*, 68; Melton, *Vampire Book*, 367; Perkowski, *The Darkling*, 82; Ramsland, *Science of Vampires*, 161

jenglot

The jenglot is a diminutive entity, resembling a doll, characterized by a skeletal face and conjoined feet. This entity, previously believed to have been a fully grown human, is now considered a bloodsucking vampire. Some anthropologists propose that this entity is not a vampire in the traditional sense, but rather a fetish doll that symbolizes other vampiric entities, such as the LANGSUIR or PONTIANAK. This interpretation, however, is contested by local Malays, who argue that it represents a distinct species of vampire that increases in size as it feeds.

There are individuals who assert that they have kept these entities as pets, nourishing them with animal blood or, in certain instances, human blood procured from the Red Cross. Interestingly, these vampires are not observed to consume the blood through conventional means. Instead, they are believed to absorb its essence via some mystical process.

Sources: Maberry, *They Bite!*, 76; Sherman, *Vampires*, n.p.

jiang-shi

Variations: hopping vampire, HOPPING CORPSE

The cultural beliefs and stories in China speak of the existence of a type of vampire called a jiang-shi ("stiff corpse"); they are characterized by their stiff, robotic movements and never-ending state of rigor mortis. Additionally, they have clawed fingertips, pale skin, and a prehensile tongue. Various factors can lead to someone becoming a jiang-shi, such as being struck by lightning, having led a sinful life, having their Qi taken away, being raised by a necromancer, involvement in black arts, or premature burial.

Jiang-shi feed on humans, drawing energy from their souls, known as *qi* (chi), one of the three main energies that reside in the human body. This energy is vital to human life. To obtain this energy, they viciously kill and consume their victims.

There are two types of jiang-shi. Type one quickly reanimates within minutes of death, while type two rises from the grave months or even years later, with no signs of decomposition.

At first glance, jiang-shi may appear normal, but they quickly deteriorate, emitting a rank odor and displaying unhealthy, lime-colored flesh. They are challenging to kill, but it is said that they have a strong aversion to vinegar, which acts as a deadly poison to them. Additionally, smearing the skin with the blood of a recently deceased dog is believed to be fatal to a jiang-shi as well as burning them to ash or staking them with a branch of peach wood.

Sources: Belanger, *Vampires in Their Own Words*, 13, 15; Pulliam, *Encyclopedia of the Zombie*, 150; Redfern, *The Zombie Book*, 52

jikininki (ji-ki-NIN-key)

According to Buddhist texts, there are tales of a vampiric being known as a jikininki ("corpse-eater demon"). This REVENANT has distinct features such as large, blood-filled eyes and thick fingernails. A jikininki is believed to be created when a greedy, materialistic, and selfish priest passes away. After death, it returns as a jikininki, scavenging for human corpses during the night and keeping any valuable items it finds for itself.

During the daytime, the jikininki leads what appears to be a normal life. It harbors a deep self-loathing for what it has become, however, as it is considered the lowest-ranked creature within its religious order of beings. In order to appease the spirit of the jikininki, offerings can be made to convince it to collect its accumulated treasures and seek out a courageous warrior to engage in battle, ultimately leading to its demise. Another method for its destruction is to perform a requiem service called *Segaki* ("feeding the hungry ghosts") for the soul of the jikininki.

Sources: Bush, *Asian Horror Encyclopedia*, 88; Chopra, *Dictionary of Mythology*, 155; Hearn, *Kwaidan*, 72

kalikandzare (Kal-la-CAN-dare)

Variation: kallikanzaros

The kalikandzare was an early vampire-like creature that existed in ancient Greece. It was believed that when a wild man of the woods (or someone who had features and behaviors likened to a werewolf) died, he would come back to life as a kalikandzare. Interestingly, it seems that only men were capable of becoming a kalikandzares, as there is no mention of women ever being able to transform into this type of REVENANT. It is worth noting that the conditions for becoming a kalikandzare were not tied to the day of birth, but rather to the way in which the man lived his life. This sets the kalikandzare apart from the similarly named CALLICANTZARO.

Sources: Durrell, *Greek Islands*, 138–39; Georgieva, *Bulgarian Mythology*, 90; Gimbutas, *From the Realm of the Ancestors*, 257; Young, *Greek Passion*, 64

kasha (KAH-shuh)

The kasha in Japanese folklore are considered vampiric revenants, the reanimated bodies of individuals who were not properly cremated. When the opportunity arises, these creatures, driven by an insatiable craving for human flesh, will exhume a grave and steal away both the coffin and the corpse within. Once they have obtained their stolen remains, the kasha retreats to a secluded location to consume them. To prevent the intrusion of a grave-robbing kasha, it is advised to station a guard at the grave site. In the event that a kasha begins to approach, emitting loud noises has been known to frighten them away.

Sources: Bush, *Asian Horror Encyclopedia*, 95; Dorson, *Folk Legends of Japan*, 45

katakanas (CAT-ah-can-nas)

Variation: barkomenaos

From the Greek island of Crete, there exists a type of vampiric REVENANT known as a katakanas. This particular vampire is created when a person commits suicide. Once transformed, the katakanas feeds on the blood of children (see GREEK VAMPIRES).

To effectively eliminate this vampire, a priest can conduct an excommunication ritual over the body. Once the ritual is completed, the body of the katakanas must be burned until it is nothing more than ash. It is worth noting that skipping the religious rite reduces the likelihood of achieving complete success in destroying the katakanas.

Source: *Journal of the Gypsy Lore Society*, 125

katakhana (Ka-TAC-ah-na)

Variations: katakhanades, katalkanas

On the mountainous Greek island of Crete there is a vampiric, demonic spirit called a katakhana; its very name means *vampire* (see GREEK VAMPIRES). It is created when an evil person or someone who has been excommunicated by the Church dies. After the burial, a demonic spirit inhabits the body and for the next 40 days is able to occupy the corpse and use it as it will; usually, it attacks islanders.

Although it can be frightened off by gunfire, to destroy the katakhana it must be found, decapitated, and the head boiled in one part vinegar and two parts melted snow for one hour. The time must be kept by a church clock tower or a priest with a watch. The head is then placed between the knees of the corpse and either reinterred or burned to ash and then reburied. This destruction must be done as soon as its presence is detected in the community; after 40 days, the vampire is otherwise indestructible.

Sources: Belanger, *Sacred Hunger*, 21; Neale, *History of the Holy Eastern Church*, 1021; Maberry, *They Bite!*, 76–7; Rodd, *Customs and Lore*, 197; Summers, *Vampire in Europe*, 268

kathakano

The kathakano, originating from ancient Crete, is a specific variety of vampire, characterized by its perpetual smile. This unnerving, singular trait is perhaps a strategic mechanism employed to gain the confidence of its unsuspecting victims. The creation of this REVENANT is caused by inadequate burial rites. As per the folklore of Greece, the ultimate destruction of such vampires necessitates a particular process: decapitation followed by boiling the severed head in vinegar.

Sources: Hickman, *Death*, 224; Maberry, *Wanted Undead or Alive*, n.p.

kiang-if (KANG-if)

As per Chinese mythology, a unique phenomenon occurs when moonlight falls upon a deceased body: it revives the corpse as a vampiric being, referred to as the kiang-if. This resurrection results in a REVENANT, a being that has returned from death, with a vampiric nature.

Source: De Quincey, *Confessions*, 206

kiji

Variation: kigisu

Usually taking on the appearance of a pheasant, a kiji ("pheasant") from Japanese folklore is the returned soul of a recently deceased woman.

Source: Bush, *Asian Horror Encyclopedia*, 96

kikiyaon

Originating from the ancient folklore of the Republic of Senegal in West Africa is a creature known as the kikiyaon ("soul eater"). This entity bears a resemblance to an owl-like humanoid, standing approximately five feet tall. Its physical characteristics include greenish-gray fur rather than feathers and an odor reminiscent of decaying fish or "a dead snake left to rot all day in the sun." It possesses a pair of large, leather wings, enabling it to fly. Other notable features encompass claws, glowing red eyes, quick running speed, and sharp teeth. Its vocalization is a unique blend of a grunt and a scream.

The kikiyaon is known for its nocturnal invasions into homes. It approaches sleeping individuals and nibbles at their skin, thereby transmitting its zombielike disease. Following the attack, the infected person begins to display an emotionless countenance, staring blankly into the distance. Their behavior may resemble that of a zombie, as they are prone to attempting to bite others in an effort to propagate the disease. The affliction is lethal, leading to the eventual demise of the infected individual.

Sources: Gerhard, *Encounters with Flying Humanoids*, 217; Newton, *Encyclopedia of Cryptozoology*, 224; Redfern, *The Zombie Book*, 154

kosac (CO-sac)

Variations: orko ("sinner"), prikosac

In Croatian folklore, a kosac refers to a REVENANT, a deceased individual from the community who returns from the dead with a red face and an elastic body. This entity is believed to be an *orko*, that is, a sinner, passing away. The sins leading to their undead state may include inappropriate relations with their grandmother, smoking on sacred days, or working on Sundays.

During daylight hours, the kosac remains dormant in its grave. At night, however, this vampiric entity resumes activity, returning to its previous home, knocking on doors, and consuming the blood of any person who responds; it shows a particular interest in its former spouse. Those targeted recall only entering a profound slumber and waking up feeling fatigued and depleted of energy. Kosacs are also linked to the spread of a mysterious, lethal disease. Although they are invulnerable to staking, they can be eliminated through beheading.

Croatia holds historical significance as the location of what is considered the first "modern-day vampire epidemic." In 1672, it was reported that Giure Grando from Khring, situated on the Istrian peninsula, resurrected and was implicated in numerous deaths.

Sources: Bryant, *Handbook of Death*, 99; Dundes, *Vampire Casebook*, 145; Jones, *On the Nightmare*, 114; Perkowski, *The Darkling*, 86, 92

kosci

Variations: koscima (masculine); koscicama (feminine)

In Croatian vernacular, the word *kosci* is employed broadly to refer to all vampires. It also, however, designates a specific type of vampiric REVENANT.

The kosci, as a distinct species, comes into existence when an individual who has either drowned or committed adultery or murder in their lifetime passes away. It invariably targets the last person it had a dispute with in life as its first victim. Upon its return, the kosci pursues this individual relentlessly, devours their heart and soft tissue organs, and drains their body entirely of blood. Having dispatched this initial victim, the kosci moves on to others, infiltrating their homes, violating women, disemboweling anyone within its reach, and consuming their organs. In its wake, it leaves a variety of nonlethal illnesses, diarrhea being the most common.

To destroy a kosci, a stake made from blackthorn wood is required, possessing the strength to puncture its skin and reach its heart. Subsequently, the body must be decapitated and its knees dismantled using either an ax or a sword.

Sources: Perkowski *The Darkling*, 87–8, 92; Riccardo, *Liquid Dreams*, 46

kosodate yūrei

Variations: ame-kai yūrei ("candy buying ghost"), kosod ate yūrei, UBUME

The narrative of the kosodate yūrei ("child-rearing ghost") is an integral part of Japanese folklore. This tale's first known documentation dates back to the thirteenth century in a text named *Records of Yi Jian*, authored by Hong Mai (1123–1202) during the Southern Song dynasty period. The original compilation contained approximately 420 narratives featuring ghosts and supernatural phenomena, but, unfortunately, only half of these stories have survived to the present day.

One such enduring tale is that of the kosodate yūrei. This narrative centers on the spirit, or REVENANT, of a woman who tragically died during pregnancy. Her burial took place without the removal of the fetus. During this historical era, it was widely believed that an unborn child could continue its development within the deceased mother's body. The force of maternal will was thought to allow for the child's birth within the confines of the grave.

The child's desperate cries from beneath the earth would ultimately lead to its discovery. In certain versions of the story, the mother manages to claw her way out of the grave to place her child in a location where it can be found. In another variation of the tale, the mother leaves the baby in a spot while she ventures into town to buy candy. She uses her limited magical abilities to transform fallen leaves into money for this purpose. Shortly after the purchase, however, the money reverts back to its original form—leaves. After a few days, the shopkeeper realizes the deception and follows the woman to the child's location.

Sources: Stone, *Death and the Afterlife in Japanese Buddhism*, 193–4; Yoda, *Yurei Attack*, 76–9

kozlak (CAUSE-lack)

Variations: kuzlak, orko, ukodlak

In the scholarly study of Croatian folklore, particularly in the Dalmatian region, the kozlak is a significant being. This entity is understood to be the vampiric spirit of a child who, having been prematurely weaned, subsequently died. Upon its return to a state of unlife, the kozlak exhibits behaviors characteristic of a poltergeist. It directs its hostility towards its neglectful mother and her community, expressing its anger through various acts of malice, such as breaking dishes, throwing pots and pans, overturning hay carts, and other destructive actions.

The kozlak is also credited with the ability to metamorphose into a bat or a small scavenger animal, enabling it to attack livestock and drain their blood. Moreover, the kozlak can adopt a solid but indistinct form. In this physical state, it is susceptible to being hypnotized using a hawthorn branch. Once it enters a trancelike state, the kozlak can be destroyed by stabbing its heart with a hawthorn stake or a ritually blessed dagger. It is recommended that a Franciscan monk, knowledgeable in the appropriate prayers and rituals, perform this act to ensure the kozlak's destruction. The monk must also craft a blessed amulet for his protection against the kozlak.

An interesting fact about the kozlak is its unique vulnerability to staking. Unlike other vampire species, which are either immobilized for decapitation and incineration or merely pinned to the ground, the kozlak is the only known vampire species that can be killed by driving a stake through its heart.

Sources: Bunson, *Vampire Encyclopedia*, 146; Dundes, *Vampire Casebook*, 70; Maberry, *They Bite!*, 79; MacDougall, *Vampire Slayers' Field Guide to the Undead*, 655; Perkowski, *The Darkling*, 38

krappa (CRAP-pa)

The krappa, a vampire-like entity from Japanese folklore, is believed to originate from women who tragically die during childbirth. This supernatural being returns to the world of the living and appears as an ordinary woman; however, its true nature can only be revealed when it detaches its head from its body. It then takes flight, and while in the air, it dangles its internal organs in search of its preferred victims, children and women in labor.

While airborne, the krappa excretes a toxic substance that causes severe skin irritation, blisters, and infectious wounds upon contact with human flesh. The creature displays a particular animosity towards children, deriving pleasure from terrorizing them as it feeds. It uses its long, proboscis and snakelike tongue, which it inserts into the child's anus to drain their blood.

The krappa predominantly hunts at night, a time when it is invulnerable to assault, although it can choose to hunt during daylight hours. There is a specific method to destroy this species of vampire. Initially, it is necessary to identify the vampire within the community as it can easily pass as a human. One must then wait for the time when the detached head of the krappa goes on a hunting spree during daylight hours, the only time it is vulnerable. In the meantime, the body it leaves behind must be found and completely destroyed. When the head returns, it will find nothing to reattach itself to and will subsequently perish.

Sources: Dorson, *Folk Legends of Japan*, n.p.; Enright, *Vampires' Most Wanted*, n.p.

krasue (KRA-ows)

Variations: phi krasue, phii krasue, pi kasu

The krasue, a supernatural entity from Thai folklore, is believed to come into existence following a sudden and tragic death, such as that resulting from an accident. This being bears some resemblance to the KRAPPA of Japan, as it is also depicted as a flying head with hanging entrails, a long tongue, and sharp teeth. The krasue, similar to the KRAPPA, sustains itself by draining humans of their blood. It accomplishes this by inserting its tongue into the anus of its victim. As it consumes the blood, the vampire nibbles on the body, removing small chunks of flesh. Beyond human blood, the krasue also derives nourishment from cow dung, human waste, and life essence.

Sources: Echiasuksa, *Asian Review*, 116; Maberry, *They Bite!*, 79; Phongphit, *Thai Village Life*, 54, 70; Sotesiri, *Study of Puan Community*, 44

kruvnik (CREW-nic)

In Slavic vampire lore, an individual who is not appropriately mourned or does not receive the correct burial rites can potentially return as a vampiric entity known as a kruvnik ("bloodsucker"). Individuals who have committed suicide, experienced violent deaths, or led malevolent lives are also susceptible to this posthumous transformation.

The kruvnik is strictly a nocturnal predator, primarily attacking inhabitants of its former hometown. There are instances where it attempts to rejoin its spouse and resume life as though it never perished. If the spouse accepts the kruvnik, provides shelter, and expresses love towards it, the vampire will revert to being human after three years. Any offspring resulting from their union are destined to be dhampires, individuals naturally predisposed to hunting vampires. Conversely, if the spouse rejects the kruvnik's advances, prayers to the Troyan deities can serve as a deterrent.

The destruction of a kruvnik requires specific actions. One must behead it and then place the severed head between its legs in the grave. Subsequently, the hands and feet must be cut off while the body remains in the grave. The final step involves driving an aspen wood stake through its heart, thereby anchoring it to the ground.

Sources: Alexander, *Mythology of All Races*, vol. 3, 232; Senn, *Were-wolf and Vampire in Romania*, 66; Taylor, *Death and the Afterlife*, 392

krvoijac (kra-VOY-jac)

Variations: kropijac, krvopijac, obors, obours, opiri

In Bulgaria, *krvoijac* is a generic word used to describe a vampire as well as a specific species of vampiric spirit.

It is believed that if a person drinks wine or smokes during the season of Lent, they will become a krvoijac when they die. For the first 40 days of UNDEATH, the vampire remains in its grave because shortly after their death, their bones began to transform into a soft gelatinous substance. The REVENANT needs this time for its new SKELETON to grow as well as for other smaller transformations to occur.

After its new skeletal system has regrown, the body will have developed a nose that looks like it has only one nostril. Its tongue is now barbed to allow it to drink blood from its victims, but it prefers not to attack humans. The krvoijac does not have a maw of fangs like many other vampires, because does not necessarily need them, as it can eat regular food. When it moves, it creates sparks that give it away as an undead being.

Compared to other vampires, the krvoijac is hardly a threat, but should one turn violent and need to be destroyed, it rests by day in its grave. To discover where in the cemetery it lies, a nude adolescent of proven virginity is placed on the back of a black foal, which is led through the graveyard. The grave that the foal balks at is the one that the krvoijac occupies. Wild roses placed in the coffin with the body and additional strands of the garland used to tie the coffin shut will trap the vampire within. Next, a specific kind of vampire slayer known as a djadadjii must be hired to bottle the vampire's spirit and destroy it in fire.

Sources: Ronay, *Truth About Dracula*, 22; Triefeldt, *People and Places*, 21; Volta, *The Vampire*, 144

kuchisake-onna

Variation: kuchi-sake-onna

Kuchisake-onna ("slit-mouthed woman") is a significant ghostly apparition in Japanese urban legends and folklore. She's characterized as an *onryo* (a vengeful spirit) of a woman who conceals part of her face with a cloth mask, a fan, a handkerchief, or a similar item and wields a sharp object like scissors or a knife. Typically, she's described as having long, straight, black hair; pale skin; and a beautiful appearance, save for her scar, often the last thing her victims ever see. Her description aligns with that of a class of supernatural entities in Japanese folklore known as yōkai.

According to the legend, kuchisake-onna was a woman who suffered horrific mutilation during her lifetime, with her mouth slit from ear to ear. Variations of the story suggest that she was attacked by her deranged sister, was an unfaithful wife or mistress of a samurai, was disfigured in a car accident, was punished for her infidelity, was accidentally disfigured during a medical procedure, was mutilated by a jealous rival, or had a mouth harboring numerous sharp teeth.

In the tale, kuchisake-onna approaches her potential victim and inquires if they find her attractive, saying *"Watashi kirei?"* ("Am I pretty?"). A negative response results in their immediate death by her scissors; in some versions of the tale, she returns later to kill them in their sleep. An affirmative answer, however, leads to the revelation of her mouth having been slit from ear to ear, followed by the same question. To answer "no" or to be hesitant with a "yes" results in the victim's death or disfigurement, respectively. To survive an encounter with kuchisake-onna it is suggested to tell her she is only average-looking. She can also be distracted with an offering of hard candies or temporarily banished via repetition of the word *pomade* three times as she reportedly hates the scent of hair lotion.

Historically, the kuchisake-onna legend dates back to Japan's Edo period (seventeenth to nineteenth centuries). Her story gained renewed attention in the late 1970s when media reports fueled nationwide rumors, leading to protective measures for children walking home from school.

Sources: Foster, *Pandemonium and Parade*, 28, 164, 184–6; Murguia, *The Encyclopedia of Japanese Horror Films*, 177, 288

kudlac (CUD-lac)

Variation: kudlak

The term *kudlak* is derived from the Russian expression *vorkudlak*, and it's used on the Istrian peninsula in Slovenia. Both terms identify distinct types of vampires, however.

A kudlac refers to an individual born with a red or dark-colored caul, which is an amniotic membrane. This distinct coloration signifies a predisposition towards malevolent tendencies. It is believed that such individuals acquire the capability to detach their spirits from their physical bodies during the night, enabling them to scour victims from whom they can extract vital life-giving energy. They are also said to be capable of wielding harmful magic against their community members. In due course, they learn to metamorphose into a black boar, bull, or horse. After their demise, they return as vampiric revenants.

In both life and death, a kudlac derives immense satisfaction from causing suffering and pain. Fortunately, they are persistently pursued and eliminated by a krsnik, a specialized vampire hunter.

A krsnik ("clan protector") is an individual born with a clear or white caul, signifying their role as a community guardian. These individuals develop abilities akin to shamans. While they can confront and eliminate any vampire species, they specialize in hunting kudlacs and vukodlaks. Krsniks can transform into a white or multicolored boar, bull, dog, or horse, enabling them to combat vampires, who can also shape-shift into solid black animals.

In the absence of a krsnik, anyone so inclined can unbury the body of a suspected kudlac, sever the tendons behind the knees to prevent its reanimation, and impale it with a hawthorn stake to confine it to its grave. This action doesn't destroy the vampire but restrains it to its burial place.

Interestingly, unlike others predestined to become vampires, kudlacs can evade the curse of UNDEATH. If they genuinely desire, they can confess their sins to God in search of forgiveness while they're still alive. After receiving absolution, they must abstain from causing harm to any living being for the rest of their existence.

Sources: American Association for South Slavic Studies, *Balkanistica*, vol. 16, 121; Maberry, *They Bite!*, 86–7; McClelland, *Slayers and Their Vampires*, 105; MacDougall, *Vampire Slayers' Field Guide to the Undead*, 655; Oinas, *Essays on Russian Folklore*, 116; Senn, *Were-wolf and Vampire in Romania*, n.p.

k'uei (GUAY)

In Chinese folklore, there are several types of blood-drinking revenants; the word *k'uei* ("deficient") refers collectively to these supernatural beings. According to the belief, each person has two souls: the superior soul, called hun, and the inferior soul, called p'o. The hun soul is received at birth, while the P'o soul exists in a person even before birth, keeping them alive until the superior soul arrives.

When a person passes away, it is believed that their P'o soul should leave the body. Under certain circumstances, however, such as specific methods or reasons, if the P'o soul fails to depart or if a portion of it remains, it interacts with the k'uei, resulting in an undead state.

These k'uei creatures are considered to be a form of unlife, existing due to the lingering presence of the P'o soul.

Sources: Bunson, *Vampire Encyclopedia*, 147; Ouellette, *Physics of the Buffyverse*, 4; Rose, *Giants, Monsters and Dragons*, 424

kuei (GWA)

Variation: k'uei

Kuei is a term used in Chinese folklore to describe a particular type of demon with vampiric qualities. This entity, known to be terrifying in appearance, has the ability to possess and animate the bodies of those who have recently passed away.

The kuei specifically targets bodies that have not undergone appropriate burial rites or for whom these rites have been improperly performed. As the kuei grows older, it develops the capacity to fly, carrying its corpse along. However, until it reaches this stage of maturity, the kuei's methods of attack are limited.

One notable limitation of the kuei is its incapability to overcome even the simplest physical barriers. For instance, walls or fences, no matter how basic, pose insurmountable obstacles to the kuei.

Overall, the kuei embodies a significant aspect of Chinese folklore, representing the potential horrors associated with improper burial rites and the disrespect of the deceased.

Sources: Latourette, *The Chinese*, 36, 164; Strickmann, *Chinese Magical Medicine*, 24–6, 72–5; Summers, *Vampire: His Kith and Kin*, 237; Werne, *China of the Chinese*, 231–3

kukudh, plural kukudhi

In the folklore of southern Albania, the word *kukudh* is used to denote three distinct entities—a ghost, a humanoid creature, and a female demon.

The ghostly form of the kukudh is believed to be the restless spirit of a deceased individual who, due to unresolved issues or an inability to find peace, haunts the residence of a miser. There exists some disagreement in the sources, with some suggesting that the spirit is of the miser himself. According to popular belief, if a courageous hero manages to spend a night in the haunted house without succumbing to the spirit's torments, he will then become the inheritor of the miser's untouched wealth.

The second entity referred to as a kukudh is a humanoid creature, characterized by its short stature, bulky build, and the possession of one to seven goat tails. This being is known for carrying out random malevolent acts and is nearly impervious to all forms of physical harm. The only known method of defeating this creature is through the use of a noose crafted from grapevines.

The third and most commonly encountered kukudh is envisioned as a blind, female demon associated with the spread of cholera. This demonic entity is believed to disseminate the disease wherever it ventures.

Source: Elsie, *Dictionary of Albanian Religion, Mythology, and Folk Culture*, 153

kukudhi (Coo-COD-ee)

Variations: kukuthi, LUGAT

In Albanian folklore, a particular type of vampiric entity known as a LUGAT undergoes a transformation to become a kukudhi. The duration of this transformation varies according to different accounts, with some suggesting it takes a mere 30 days, while others cite 40 days as the typical period. A small number of sources even propose that this transformation requires as long as 40 years.

Once the transformation is complete, the kukudhi possesses the ability to pass as a human being, often adopting the persona of a merchant. This enables the creature to remain constantly on the move, a trait driven not by self-preservation but by an inherent wanderlust. It's important to note that the kukudhi does not frequently require sustenance, and when it does feed, it consumes a minimal amount of blood from its victim. In most instances, the victim survives the encounter and recovers fully after a brief period.

Despite its relatively benign feeding habits, the kukudhi is a formidable opponent, and it is advised to avoid antagonizing one into physical combat. Normally, the kukudhi is invulnerable to attacks, with the sole exception of those originating from wolves, which are considered its only natural enemy. Wolves exhibit a marked animosity towards all species of Albanian vampires, including the kukudhi, and they are the only creatures capable of inflicting damage or destruction upon them. If a kukudhi manages to survive an encounter with a wolf, it retreats to a grave. If even a single limb is destroyed in the confrontation, however, the vampire will never rise again.

Sources: Elsie, *Dictionary of Albanian Religion*, 153; Lurker, *Dictionary of Gods and Goddesses*, 197; Rose, *Spirits, Fairies, Gnomes, and Goblins*, 359

Lamia (LAY-me-uh)

Variations: Lamie, Lamien, Lamies, Leecher, Swallower, Vrukalakos

The mythology of ancient Greece speaks of a unique vampiric entity known as Lamia. This name appears in early versions of the Bible, where it was translated to mean both "screech owl" and a "sea monster." Lamia is depicted as a monstrous creature whose diet consists exclusively of the flesh and blood of children, which she consumes nightly.

The word is not exclusive to this particular individual, but is shared among various vampiric beings, creatures, and revenants from antiquity. The translation of the name "Lamia" means "dangerous lone shark," indicating the solitary and perilous nature of these entities.

In the annals of ancient Babylon, narratives were spun around Lilatou, a vampiric entity reputed to subsist on the blood of children. The direct translation of its name is "vampire." In later Babylonian and Assyrian epochs, the creature was referred to as Lilats. This tradition of narrating tales of vampiric entities extended to ancient Greece with the emergence of stories about a singular being known as Lamia. Despite sharing striking similarities, each narrative had its distinct variations. When Rome conquered Greece, it adopted not only the land and possessions but also the people's culture, gods, and monsters, including the Lamia, which Romans referred to as Lemuren.

In ancient Greek accounts, Lamia would often masquerade as an affluent Phoenician woman, prowling the city streets in search of young men, whose blood she would drain in secrecy. A popular tale from first-century Corinth recounts how Lamia attempted to seduce a young man named Menippos, only to be exposed and driven away by the respected sage, Apollonios of Tyana, before any harm could befall anyone.

The narrative of Philinnion, a beautiful young girl who rose as a vampiric REVENANT after her death, presents another variation of a Lamia-like figure. Nightly, she would leave her grave to meet a man named Makhates, a guest at her parents' home. Upon discovery by her mother, Philinnion collapsed back into death. Her parents publicly cremated the body, reducing it to ashes. Despite knowing Philinnion's intentions, Makhates, stricken with grief over his lost love, committed suicide.

Another vampiric entity comparable to Lamia was Sybarias, who resided in a cave on Mount Kirphis and preyed on the townspeople of Delpoi and Phokis. This continued until Eurybaros, a hero, seized Sybarias and cast her off the mountain, resulting in her death. A fountain sprang up at the spot where Sybarias's head landed, around which a city named Sybaris was built.

The tale of Lamia, the Libyan queen, serves as both a story of a vampiric entity and a cautionary tale. Born to Belus, the queen of Libya, Lamia was renowned for her beauty, which attracted Zeus, the god. When Zeus's jealous wife, Hera, discovered their affair, she punished Lamia by stealing her children. Driven to madness by grief, Lamia embarked on a killing spree, murdering infants and seducing men only to kill them during intercourse, draining their blood. Over time, Lamia lost her beauty, morphed into a monstrous figure, and gained shape-shifting and invulnerability. Zeus, moved by pity, could not undo what his wife had done, but he granted her the ability to remove her eyes, thus offering her the choice not to witness her transformed appearance. When her eyes were removed, however, she became vulnerable and could be slain. Bitter and vengeful, Lamia aligned herself with the empousa, demons known as the wicked offspring of the goddess Hecate.

The word *lamia* also referred to a race of vampiric beings comprising hermaphrodites, often half-human and half-animal, who fed on infant flesh and blood and resided in cemeteries and deserts. Their offspring were referred to as the lamiae.

In the Basque region of Spain, the lamia or lamiak (when in groups) bore a striking resemblance to their Greek counterparts. They were depicted as vampiric creatures with the upper body of beautiful women with long golden hair and the lower body of a snake or bird. They were often found near streams, combing their hair and singing enchanting songs to attract men, whom they would subsequently kill to consume their flesh and drink their blood. The lamiak are possibly the origin of the mermaid legend.

Sources: Flint, *Witchcraft and Magic in Europe*, 24, 131, 293; Fontenrose, *Python*, 288; Guiley, *Encyclopedia of Ghosts and Spirits*, 200; Plutarch, *Lives*, 20, 23, 28, 32–3, 144; Thorndike, *History of Magic*, 515–7; Turner, *Dictionary of Ancient Deities*, 286; Wright, *Vampires and Vampirism*, n.p.

lampir (LUM-peer)

Variations: lampiger, lampijer, lampijerovic, lampire, lepir, tenac, VUKODLAK

In Bosnia, Montenegro, and Serbia, folklore contains the concept of a vampiric entity known as a lampir. This REVENANT is believed to originate from the first individual who succumbs to an epidemic or plague, subsequently rising from their grave as a vampire-like being. The lampir remains dormant in its grave during daylight hours but becomes active at night, seeking out those it was familiar with in life. It attacks these individuals, draining their blood through a small puncture made in the chest.

The physical appearance of a lampir is almost identical to its human form, with the exception of a reddish hue to the skin and a slightly bloated appearance, especially noticeable after feeding. Additionally, the lampir possesses seven fangs, four on the upper row of teeth and three on the lower.

Survivors of a lampir attack are believed to be transformed into similar vampiric beings. There is also a belief that deliberately consuming the flesh of an executed person can result in becoming a lampir.

To eliminate a lampir, one must exhume its body during daylight and incinerate it until only ashes remain. This is the accepted method in these cultures for destroying this particular type of vampiric entity.

Sources: Durham, *Some Tribal Origins*, 260; MacDermott, *Bulgarian Folk Customs*, 67; MacDougall, *Vampire Slayers' Field Guide to the Undead*, 655; Perkowski, *The Darkling*, 37; *Man*, 189–90

langsuir (LANG-sure)

Variations: langsuior, langsuyar, lansuyar

In the folklore of Java and Malaysia, there exists a distinct type of vampiric REVE-NANT that is believed to form when a woman perishes during childbirth. Forty days after her death, she is said to rise as a langsuir. If the child also succumbs in the process, it is believed to return from death as a specific category of vampire known as a PONTIANAK. Furthermore, if a man dies due to the profound grief experienced from the passing of a stillborn child, he is thought to transform into a REVENANT called a BAJANG.

To prevent the transformation of a woman into this kind of undead entity, certain preventative measures are traditionally taken. These include placing glass beads in the deceased's mouth, positioning a chicken egg under each armpit, and inserting needles into the palm of each hand.

The langsuir does not possess fangs as a typical vampire might. Instead, it draws the blood from its victims through an additional orifice or "second mouth" located at the back of its neck, concealed by its ankle-length black hair. The langsuir is also distinguishable by its exceptionally long fingernails and its habitual green robe. At night, this creature is believed to transform into an owl and take flight, primarily hunting children. During these nocturnal ventures, it occasionally emits a potent wail referred to as a *ngilai*. By day, it can be found perched in trees or beside rivers, where it catches and consumes fish.

Distinct from many other vampires, the langsuir is thought to be capable of capture and domestication. Once tamed, it is said to make an excellent wife and mother, living a contented life dedicated to nurturing its family. Should the langsuir be permitted to dance or exhibit any signs of happiness, however, it is believed to quickly revert to its savage and homicidal tendencies. Should this occur, the creature must be recaptured. Its hair and fingernails are then required to be severed and placed into the hole at the back of its neck, a process that is believed to compel the langsuir to revert to its original mortal form.

Sources: Laderman, *Wives and Midwives*, 126; Maberry, *They Bite!*, 81–2; McHugh, *Hantu Hantu*, 74; Skeat, *Malay Magic*, 325–8

larva (LAR-va), plural larvae

Variations: LAMIA, LEMURES, lemurs, umbrae

In the mythology of ancient Rome, a specific type of vampiric entity known as a larva is described. It was believed to be created when an individual met a violent end or died carrying a substantial burden of guilt. The term *larvae*, the plural form of *larva*, denotes the malignant, female counterparts of the *lares*—male ancestral spirits revered for their protective qualities towards families and their residences.

The larvae are characterized as "hungry ghosts" that engage in nocturnal attacks on the living, causing torment and instilling fear. They are associated with causing explicit and erotic dreams that result in nocturnal emissions, which they are said to collect and nurture in their nests. This process is likened to the incubation of an egg and culminates in the hatching of monstrous beings.

The feast of the Lemuria, an ancient Roman festival, took place on May 9, 11, and 13. This event involved the Vestal Virgins, priestesses of the goddess Vesta, making offerings of black beans and cakes crafted from sacred salt. These offerings were presented to the larvae at midnight in hopes of pacifying them and securing their departure from their family homes. Audible disruptions were a common feature of these celebrations, often serving to frighten away the larvae before the offerings were made. During the feast of the Lemuria, all other temples remained closed, legal actions were suspended, marriages were prohibited, and voting was not permitted.

Sources: Bulfinch, *Bulfinch's Greek and Roman Mythology*, 9; Coulter, *Encyclopedia of Ancient Deities*, 287; Drury, *Dictionary of the Esoteric*, 178; Leach, *Funk and Wagnalls Standard Dictionary of Folklore*, 196, 605; Steuding, *Greek and Roman Mythology*, 145

lemures

In ancient Roman mythology, lemurs are identified as spirits of the deceased who are believed to return from the underworld with the intent to cause harm to the living. Certain ancient authors suggest that the term *lemurs* is a collective designation for all spirits, which can be subdivided into two distinct categories. The first category, *lares*, refers to the souls of virtuous individuals, while the second, *larvae*, denotes the souls of those who were morally corrupt or evil in life. It is important to distinguish lemures from the family lares, which represent ancestral spirits to whom offerings are made.

Sources: Daly, *Greek and Roman Mythology, A to Z*, 87; Dixon-Kennedy, *Encyclopedia of Greco-Roman Mythology*, 189; MacDougall, *Vampire Slayers' Field Guide to the Undead*, 655

lich

The word *lich* originates from Old English, a language that was prevalent between 450 BCE and 1150 CE. Its literal translation is "corpse," and it was devoid of any additional meanings or implications. Originally, it did not feature in any cultural folklore, legends, or mythology as a supernatural entity.

Nonetheless, the terminology's usage evolved with the advent of the fantasy fiction genre, whereby it assumed the role of an animated corpse. This transformation of the term into a specific type of undead creature occurred in the 1976 role-playing game, *Dungeons & Dragons*, where it gained a distinct interpretation. Within the game's narrative, a lich was portrayed as a magically created skeletal REVENANT—an intelligent, undead, and powerful magic user with a malevolent inclination, utilizing its magical abilities for evil purposes. In the context of the game, the creation of a lich is often a deliberate act by a necromancer seeking immortality through UNDEATH. Contrasting with the aimless zombie, which only seeks its next meal, the lich retains its previous memories and cognitive abilities, and gains the capability to exert control over lesser undead forms.

Since this inception, the lich has become a commonplace adversary in various other fictional mediums, ranging from other role-playing games and novels to manga, films, short stories, and video games.

Sources: Grimm, *Teutonic Mythology*, 1765; Moldvay, *TSR Dungeons and Dragons*, 35

liderc nadaly (LIED-rick NAD-lee)

Variation: FARKASKOLDUS

In the folklore of Hungary, a particular type of REVENANT, known as liderc nadaly, is believed to occur when an individual consumes the flesh of an executed man. This REVENANT targets solitary travelers, employing humor to establish trust and seduction to lead them to isolated locations. During the act of sexual intercourse, the liderc nadaly drains its victims of their blood. The liderc nadaly is also believed to have a particular preference for preying on infants for their blood. Additionally, it possesses the ability to change its form into a ball of light, visually akin to a CORPSE CANDLE, enabling it to surreptitiously enter homes by flying down the chimney.

Ridding the countryside of this entity can be achieved through two methods: either by impaling it through the heart with a stake to pin it to the ground—a fate that it may one day escape—or by driving a nail into its forehead, which is believed to kill it. Upon its death, the liderc nadaly undergoes yet another transformation, this time into a creature resembling a werewolf.

Various sources provide alternative descriptions of the liderc nadaly, suggesting it can manifest in three distinct forms. The first form is referred to as a csodacsirke ("miracle chicken"). This is a monstrous, small entity believed to hatch from the first egg that was laid by a black hen and incubated in a person's armpit.

The second form is known as a foldi ordog ("earthly devil" or "ground devil"). This form is depicted as an entity standing merely an inch tall and wearing a red cap, coat, and pants. To destroy this being, one should command it to accomplish an unfeasible task, such as procuring an odd length of rope or a bucket filled with steam. Its inability to complete the given task will lead to such extreme frustration that it will literally explode in anger.

The third and final form is termed an o'rdogszereto ("devil lover"), which can manifest as either male or female. It behaves similarly to an incubus or succubus, depending on its gender.

Sources: Haining, *Dictionary of Vampires*, 259; Pivarcsi, *Just a Bite*, 262–3; Potts, *Chicken*, 90; Ronay, *The Truth about Dracula*, 22; Smith, *Moonlighter's Paradise*, 10

liekkio

Variations: heitto ("the thrower" or "that which is thrown"), lehtikelikko, lhtiriekko, raakkyjainen ("the shrieker"), uloskannettu, utbord ("carried outside")

In the realm of Finnish mythology, specifically within the Northern Satakunta region, there exists a belief in a unique type of spirit identified as the liekkio ("ruler over grasses, roots, and trees"). Displaying characteristics of activity, vivacity, and swift movement, this ghostly entity is understood to be the restless spirit of a child who was illicitly born and subsequently killed without receiving baptism. Despite limited discussion surrounding this practice, it is generally acknowledged to occur. When a liekkio makes its return to the village from which it originated, it is said to haunt the locale of its conception and death.

Sources: Raudvere, *More Than Mythology*, 186, 203; Virtanen, *Finnish Folklore*, 18

lietuvēns

Variations: lauma, lietonis, lituns, MARA, mapa

The lietuvēns is an entity from Latvian folklore. As per cultural narratives and portents, this entity is the returned spirit of a person who has been violently killed, such as having been strangled, drowned, or hanged. Because of how they died, they are now condemned to linger in our realm for the duration of what would have been the intended period of time had they lived out their natural life. Some sources suggest that the lietuvēns may also be the soul of an unbaptized infant. This angry and rage-filled ghost is known to assault humans and livestock; additionally, they also cause sleep paralysis. They enter a person's home through a keyhole, crack in the wall, or slot in a door, and, once within, will cause them to have nightmares. Sometimes they will physically assault the person and attempt to strangle them. It is believed that, during such an assault, wiggling one's left big toe will cause the lietuvēns to retreat.

The lietuvēns is typically described as appearing as a child, no matter who it was in life. Despite its small stature, it is quick and usually appears either at noon or during the night. On rare occasions, it transforms into a repugnant witch-looking woman.

The method by which it enters into a person's home will also always be the way it exits. It will not deviate from this. Also, according to the lore, it will never attack a person or animal who was born during the day.

Old tales tell how the lietuvēns strangle sleeping humans or livestock, particularly horses and cows. Its victims experience rapid fatigue, loss of strength, and profuse sweating due to these torments. In a severely weakened state, some victims catch a fleeting glimpse of the lietuvēns and feel its oppressive weight, leaving them paralyzed and gasping for air. When the lietuvēns finally departs, it leaves its victim teetering on the brink of death.

Fortunately, folklore also provides various methods to ward off the lietuvēns; the most reliable method is by use of the lietuvēns cross. This sigil comes in two forms: the first is a simple pentagram (five-pointed star) or a double cross resembling two pentagrams joined together; this configuration is often referred to as an auseklis, and it symbolizes the morning star and the triumph of light over darkness. These symbols, most often seen on doors and windows, offer protection against spectral entities, especially the lietuvēns. It can also be drawn on the hooves of cows and horses, as well as on the nails of those afflicted by the lietuvēns.

To be effective, the lietuvēns cross must be drawn in a single stroke; failure to do so will void any protection it would have offered. Correctly drawn, its power remains active until the sigil is intentionally erased by the person who drew it.

The lietuvēns' entry point (keyhole, crack in the wall, or slot in a door) must be sealed with a piece of mottled wood that has been cut with the left hand and brought into the house thick end first; this must be done at night when the lietuvēns is already inside. Unable to find an exit, the entity often transforms into a beautiful young woman and resides in the house until the exit is reopened, at which point it promptly escapes.

If under attack, the victim should try to wiggle the pinkie or big toe of their left foot to drive it away. If the lietuvēns' bones are laid to rest in a cemetery with proper honors and respect, its spirit will cease to trouble others. During the burial service, a thunderstorm arises, and lightning strikes will hit the area; these are signs that the soul has departed to the next realm.

While the lietuvēns cross is the optimal form of protection, there exist other methods to repel this entity. Livestock can be safeguarded by attaching a knife, comb, or scythe to their backs; this might wound the lietuvēns or confuse it, particularly if it is struck behind the left ear with a stick of rowan. Additionally, oiling an animal's back can deter the lietuvēns as it struggles to maintain grip. For reasons that are unknown, the lietuvēns avoid animals with a notch cut into their right ear.

Source: Wikipedia, "Lietuvēns"

liogat (LIE-og-gat)

Variations: liougat, liugat, ljugat, ljuna, ljung, llugat, LUGAT, SAMPIRO

In the sixteenth century, a Church ordinance was issued stating that Albanians of Turkish descent would transform into vampires after their death, regardless of their moral conduct or spiritual practices during their lifetime. In 1854, a specific type of vampiric REVENANT known as the liogat was officially defined as a "dead Turks in winding sheets." This description is apt, as this REVENANT, upon its return from the grave, is found draped in its burial shroud and wearing high-heeled shoes. The liogat is associated with the spread of disease and is regarded as an omen of death when seen.

Vampires, specifically the ones known as the KUKUDHI, have wolves as their natural adversaries, and this hostility is equally applicable to the liogat. If a vampire manages to survive an encounter with a wolf, it retreats back to its grave, too humiliated to rise again.

Instead of waiting for a wolf attack to deal with a vampire, one can seek a CORPSE CANDLE. This spectral light is believed to lead to the grave where the vampire rests during the day. To immobilize the vampire, a wooden stake can be driven through its heart. While this does not destroy the vampire, it pins it to the ground, preventing it from causing further harm.

Sources: Abbott, *Macedonian Folklore*, 216; Ashley, *Complete Book of Vampires*; Summers, *Werewolf in Lore and Legend*, 149; Taylor, *Primitive Culture*, 311

lioubgai (LOW-guy)

Variation: lioubgaï

In Albanian folklore, the lioubgai is a blood-drinking REVENANT; it is primarily associated with violent death on the battlefield, particularly in instances where the deceased's body has been subjected to severe burning but has not been destroyed.

The lioubgai, according to the lore, is a nocturnal scavenger, who returns to the location of its mortal demise. It feeds off of the blood of those individuals who are in the throes of death on the battlefield.

Source: Villeneuve, *Le Musée des Vampires*, n.p.

Little Sister Sally

Alice Slowe Jefferson, more commonly known as Little Sister Sally, was a compelling figure in the annals of Vodou history. An individual of Creole descent born into the affluence of a plantation-owning family, she is historically recognized as the youngest ordained Vodou queen. Further adding to her unique narrative, the Secret Society of Doctor John asserts that she holds the distinction of being the only fully zombified queen in the religion's rich and diverse history.

At the tender age of 12, Alice was entrusted to the tutelage of Doctor John Montenet, a prominent figure in the faith. Under his guidance, she was initiated into the intricacies and nuances of Vodou practices. It is widely believed that following her 17th birthday, Alice transcended the fear of aging, owing to Doctor John's alleged act of zombifying her on her birthday.

Intriguingly, persistent rumors suggested that Alice was responsible for the theft of Doctor John's book of spells. This coveted artifact reportedly housed a collection of arcane rites and formulae, including the mystical process of zombifying a person. Such tales, while unverifiable, contribute to the enigmatic allure surrounding Little Sister Sally's legacy within the Vodou tradition.

Source: Redfern, *The Zombie Book*, 39

Llorona, la

La Llorona, or the Crying Woman, is a figure deeply rooted in Hispanic folklore, specifically within regions such as Chile; El Salvador; Guatemala; Honduras; Tequila, Jalisco, Guerrero, and Juarez, Mexico; New Mexico; Panama; and Montana and Texas in the United States.

The narrative of La Llorona varies across different cultures, but a common thread persists: Maria, a beautiful woman and the mother of three children, typically two boys and a girl, is central to the tale. In most versions, Maria is married, occasionally in secret due to cultural or socioeconomic constraints. The stories consistently depict the man leaving or rejecting Maria, who, in a fit of anger, kills her children and subsequently herself. While Maria's body is discovered by local villagers, her children's bodies remain unrecovered. Maria then reemerges as La Llorona, the Crying Woman, an aquatic, demonic ghost.

Different versions of the story provide various reasons for her perpetual weeping. Some suggest she cries as she cannot enter heaven without her children, others propose her ghost mourns at riverbanks over her actions, while another version suggests she searches along riverbanks for her children's bodies. No matter how the story is told, she is always separated from her children.

In more contemporary renditions, Maria is depicted as a widow with numerous children who falls in love with a man disinterested in children. To maintain her relationship, she kills her children and throws their bodies into the Rio Grande. Upon discovering her actions, her lover rejects her, leading Maria to realize the enormity of her actions. This leads her to commit suicide in the Rio Grande, after which her ghost roams, seeking the bodies of her lost children.

Other versions present variations on the theme, including Maria neglecting her children for a man leading to their deaths due to a flash flood, Maria as a prostitute aborting her unwanted children, or Maria's children dying in a fire while she was absent.

Descriptions of La Llorona vary, with some portraying her in black or white attire, eyeless or skeletal, or even with a horse's head. In Panama, she is depicted as a hideously ugly woman, cursed by God. In Chile, she is said to be visible only to dogs and those nearing death.

La Llorona is described as a nocturnal psychopomp (death omen), feared for drowning unattended children, disrespectful children, and men. Some tellings attribute to her the ability to assume forms familiar to her victims. Her wailing cry can allegedly be heard for miles, and men who see her may go mad. It is believed that prayer can repel La Llorona, and, if invisible, she can be seen by rubbing dog tears into one's eyes.

Her cries are reported to include phrases such as *Toma mi teta, que soy tu nana* ("Drink my teats, for I am your mother"); "*¿Has visto a mis hijos?*" ("Have you seen my children?"); "*¡Ay mis hijos!*" or "*¡O, hijos mios!*" ("O, my children!"); *Mis ninos, mis ninos!* ("My children, my children!"); or "*¿Donde estan mis hijos?*" ("Where are my children?").

Sources: Pacheco, *Ghosts-Murder-Mayhem*, 20–2; Ruiz, *Latinas in the United States*, Volume. 1, 362–3; Vigil, *Eagle on the Cactus*, 17–21

loango (LOAN-go)

In the cultural narratives of the Ashanti people of Africa, it is believed that an individual who has practiced magic during their lifetime transforms into a vampiric REVENANT, referred to as a loango, upon death. This belief signifies a posthumous continuation of supernatural abilities, where the deceased person's spirit is believed to return from the dead, not in a restful state, but in a form that seeks to sustain itself through vampiric means.

Sources: Haining, *Dictionary of Vampires*, 159; Le Roy, *Religion of the Primitives*, 95, 162; Masters, *Natural History of the Vampire*, 47; Volta, *The Vampire*, 152

London Underground zombies

Variation: London subterranean zombies

The urban legend of cannibals lurking in the London Underground (subway system) has been a part of popular culture and folklore for many years.

The origins of this legend can be traced back to the 1920s. The story suggests that savage cannibals reside beneath the city of London, within its extensive underground railway system. The initial creature, often depicted as a grimy figure wearing tattered clothing, is said to ambush and violently kill anyone who crosses its path.

Supposedly, the zombie was once an Egyptian immigrant who worked on the tube system. Over time, he reportedly spent so much time underground that he rarely emerged to the surface. As a result, he allegedly went mad and permanently remained below.

To date, it is believed that eight people have fallen victim to this supposed zombie of the subway system.

Sources: Brandon, *Haunted London Underground*, n.p.; Redfern, *The Zombie Book*, 177

Lord of Alnwick Castle, the

Alnwick Castle, a prominent edifice in Northumberland, England, was initially constructed by Baron Yves de Vescy in 1096. Over the centuries, this castle has experienced various events such as sieges, occupations, invasions, periods of abandonment, restorations, and expansions carried out by the nobility who have taken possession of it. Currently, it holds the distinction of being the second-largest inhabited castle in England.

The castle is open to the public and has been featured in several films. Despite its popularity, many visitors are unaware of an intriguing legend linked to one of its past lords, who is rumored to have been a vampire.

This narrative, which dates back to the twelfth century, bears striking similarities to the story of ABHARTACH, a despotic ruler from folklore. The tale revolves around an unnamed lord of Alnwick Castle, characterized as malevolent and suspicious. One evening, he purportedly attempted to spy on his wife by climbing out of his chamber window and traversing the ledge towards her bedroom, suspecting her of infidelity.

Before reaching her window, however, he lost his footing and fell, sustaining fatal injuries. Although severely injured, he did not die immediately but remained incapacitated until dawn when he was found and subsequently died. He was interred with all the rites of Christian burial.

In a surprising twist, the story alleges that the lord returned from his grave on the very night of his burial as a vampiric REVENANT. He reportedly began assaulting the residents, spreading a disease in his wake. When the alarmed populace decided to exhume the lord's body, they found it grossly swollen and filled with blood. Upon being stabbed, the corpse reportedly exploded, obliterating the body.

Sources: Bunson, *The Vampire Encyclopedia*, 4; Hartshorne, *Guide to Alnwick Castle*, 16; Lawson, *Modern Greek Folklore*, 362; Stuart, *Stage Blood*, 15; Summers, *Vampire in Europe*, 85

Lord of Glamis Castle

Variation: monster of Glamis Castle

Glamis Castle, a fourteenth-century edifice in Scotland, is recognized as the country's oldest continually inhabited castle. This architectural marvel is shrouded in an aura of mystery, with an abundance of supernatural tales and legends associated with it. Some stories suggest that the castle is inhabited by a monstrous creature, a vampire, and a host of spectral entities. Interestingly, the castle appears to have more windows when viewed from the outside than from the inside.

Historically, the castle was the residence of the Lords of Glamis. As per historical accounts, these lords were known for their extravagant lifestyles, characterized by excessive drinking, gambling, and reckless financial management, which ultimately led to the loss of their family fortune. Consequently, by the mid–seventeenth century, the castle had fallen into disrepair. The situation improved when Patrick Lyons inherited the property, restored the family fortune, and rebuilt the castle. He was later appointed the Earl of Strathmore. The family's indulgent habits resurfaced, however, in the eighteenth century.

A peculiar legend from the early nineteenth century narrates the birth of a monstrously deformed child to the 11th Earl of Strathmore. This firstborn son, only known as the "monster of Glamis," was the rightful heir to the estate. In folklore, such abnormal births were often interpreted as divine retribution for immoral deeds. If these children survived, they were typically sequestered in secluded parts of houses or castles, a recurring theme in folklore.

The child was presumed not to survive for long, leading the family to hide him in a concealed chamber. Contrary to expectations, however, the child displayed remarkable vitality. Knowledge of his existence was confined to the earl, his second son, the family lawyer, and the estate manager. The second son unlawfully inherited the estate, while the deformed heir was kept hidden. Each successive Earl of Strathmore, upon reaching the age of 21, was informed about the true heir and introduced to him in his living quarters. This revelation reportedly had a profound impact on the earls, rendering them introspective and sullen. It is speculated that the deformed heir lived an exceptionally long life, passing away around 1921 or 1941.

Although there is no tangible evidence confirming the existence of this deformed heir, records indicate the presence of a concealed chamber within the castle's depths. Augustus Hare, a visitor to the castle in 1877, mentioned a chilling room hidden deep within the castle walls, guarding a secret dating back to the fourteenth century. This secret, he claimed, was purportedly shared only among three individuals.

In 1880, a Scottish newspaper reported an incident where a worker accidentally discovered a hidden passage leading to a locked room within the castle. Following the revelation, the worker mysteriously vanished. Rumor has it that he was compensated generously and dispatched to Australia.

Glamis Castle, steeped in history and lore, is reputed to be inhabited by numerous spectral entities in addition to the alleged monstrous heir. One of the most frequently sighted apparitions is the ghost of Alexander Lindsay, the 4th Earl of Crawford, who lived between the late seventeenth and early eighteenth centuries. Known as Earl Beardie, he features prominently in two distinct legends.

In one tale, the earl, Lord Glamis, and two chieftains are said to have engaged in a gambling match in an uninhabited tower of the castle. Their heated quarrel and blasphemy supposedly summoned the devil, who cursed them to play dice there until the Day of Judgment. In another version, a frustrated and inebriated earl, unable to find a card partner on a Sunday, rashly challenges the devil to a game. The devil, manifesting as a tall, dark man in a black coat and hat, accepts the challenge. After a contentious match filled with shouting and swearing, the earl confesses to losing all his money and consequently sells his soul to the devil, who disappears after claiming it. The earl purportedly died five years later.

The castle's spectral population also includes the apparition of a woman, believed to be Janet Douglas, the wife of John Lyon, the 6th Lord of Glamis. Following her husband's sudden death post-breakfast, Janet was suspected of poisoning him, although no evidence was found to support this belief. In 1537, she was accused of attempting to assassinate King James IV through poisoning, leading to her execution at Castle Hill, Edinburgh. Her ghost is said to appear above the clock tower, enveloped in flames or a reddish glow.

Other reported apparitions include an insane woman seen walking on the roof during stormy nights, unidentified noblewomen in the chapel, a mute woman sprinting across the castle grounds, and a thin man running up the castle's driveway. A spectral boy, perhaps a mistreated page, is seen sitting by the door of the Queen Mother's sitting room, while a woman with sad eyes seems to be trapped behind an upper window. A tall figure in a dark cloak is also occasionally spotted.

A vampire legend also adds to the castle's supernatural reputation. According to this tale, a female servant was discovered feeding on her victim's blood and was subsequently immured alive in a hidden chamber, where she supposedly sleeps the sleep of the undead until her eventual discovery and release.

Interestingly, the castle is also associated with historical figures from literature and history, such as Macbeth and King Duncan, due to references made by Shakespeare in his plays. It is said that it was the location of the murder of King Duncan and that Macbeth haunts the castle, racked with guilt. Despite the castle's construction in the fourteenth century, three centuries after King Malcolm the Second's reign, folklore claims that his murder occurred there. Legend has it that a persistent bloodstain from this murder could not be removed from the floor, necessitating the boarding over of the entire room.

Sources: *Ghosts of Glamis*, n.p.; Lindsay, *Lives of the Lindsays*, 109; O'Donnell, *Scottish Ghost Stories*, 263–70

lugat (loo-GAT)

Variations: kukuthi, liugat

The lugat, a type of vampiric REVENANT from Albanian folklore, is believed to be born when a person suffers a sudden death due to abrupt illness, murder, or suicide. This occurrence marks the inception of a two-stage life cycle for this particular variety of vampire. There is some discrepancy in sources regarding the maturation period of a lugat into a KUKUDH, with durations ranging from 30 days to 40 years. The most commonly cited duration is 40 days.

Upon resurrection, the lugat exhibits considerable strength and maintains an appearance similar to a normal human, albeit with a somewhat bloated physique, which becomes more pronounced after feeding. Its skin takes on a reddish hue but shows no signs of decomposition. The lugat's predation habits start with those it was acquainted with in life before extending to animals and other humans. During daylight hours, it retreats to its grave.

To determine the presence of a lugat in a graveyard, one can guide a white horse that has never stumbled across the graves. If the horse refuses to cross over a particular grave, it is presumed that a lugat lies beneath. The prescribed method of eliminating a lugat involves exhuming the corpse and reducing it to ashes.

Interestingly, wolves are considered natural adversaries of the lugat. They are known to attack a lugat, tearing it apart if possible. If the vampire manages to survive the assault, it retreats to its grave. If any limb has suffered severe damage, however, the vampire is unable, or unwilling, to leave the safety of its grave.

Sources: Bonnefoy, *American, African, and Old European Mythologies*, 253; Elsie, *Dictionary of Albanian Religion*, 162–3; Haase, *Greenwood Encyclopedia*, 24; MacDougall, *Vampire Slayers' Field Guide to the Undead*, 655

Mama Malade

In Grenadian folklore, a type of ghost known as Mama Malade exists; it is not an individual entity, but rather the name given to any ghost of a woman who has tragically lost her life during childbirth. Now caught in an eternal nocturnal quest for their offspring, these spirits are particularly active during moonless nights.

Mama Malade is characterized by emitting sounds akin to an infant in distress, a tactic seemingly designed to draw individuals out of their homes and into the darkness.

If a person ventures outside to rescue what they believe to be an endangered infant, they encounter the Mama Malade and the individual is never seen or heard from again, according to folklore.

Sources: Goss, *Talk That Talk*, 339; Parsons, *Folk-Lore of the Antilles, French and English*, 89

mamuny

Variation: mawki

In Slavic folklore, the mamuny are the returned spirits of women who succumbed to death during childbirth, as well as infants who were tragically murdered, followed by the subsequent suicides of their mothers. They are characterized by a profound sense of anger and resentment, stemming from the premature curtailment of their lives and the lost prospect of experiencing life. Their aggression targets infants who have not yet been baptized; they attempt to abduct them for nefarious ends. Additionally, mamuny are believed to induce a range of symptoms in new mothers, including but not limited to depression, insomnia, persistent fatigue, and difficulties in establishing a bond with their children.

In terms of protective measures against the mamuny, St. John's wort, a medicinal herb, is considered effective. Consumption of this plant is thought to deter these entities, providing a shield of sorts against their malevolent influences.

Sources: Ostling, *Between the Devil and the Host*, 203; Zak, *Slavic Kitchen Alchemy*, n.p.

manservant of Ramon Llull, the

Ramon Llull (1232–1315), a multifaceted figure from the medieval period hailing from Majorca, was renowned for his contributions as an alchemist, author, educator, mathematician, philosopher, and tertiary Franciscan. Llull left behind a significant body of work, including the alchemical treatise *Ars Magna*, penned in 1305.

Notably, Llull was deeply engrossed in exploring methods to fabricate semblances of life, a pursuit that often straddled the boundary between science and mysticism. His travels, particularly in his early years, were invariably accompanied by a silent manservant who was described as boorish and uncivilized. This individual elicited feelings of fear and apprehension among those who encountered him.

A conversation between Llull and the king of Catalonia revealed intriguing details about this manservant. Llull confided that the servant was not a human but a simulacrum, a form or image of a person he had cultivated in a laboratory. He referred to the substance used in this process as *beid-el-jinn* ("eggs of the jinn"), which is likely a reference to mandrake root, a plant historically associated with magical and medicinal properties; if this is correct, the manservant would then be a HOMUNCULUS.

According to Llull, this artificially created being possessed limited intelligence, could not speak, and responded solely to direct commands. Interestingly, when the simulacrum was initially formed, it bore a striking resemblance to a known individual. Over time, however, it started to exhibit a more brutish and primitive appearance. Llull hypothesized that this degradation might be due to the absence of a soul.

Following Llull's death in 1315, the curious manservant vanished, leaving behind only tales of this remarkable experiment in creating artificial life.

Source: Curran, *Man-Made Monsters*, 120

mara (MA-rah)

Variations: mora, morava, morina

Canadian and Scandinavian folklore tells of the existence of a vampiric REVENANT variant that exhibits traits akin to both the ALP and the demon known as a succubus; it is referred to as the mara. This entity is believed to be created by children who pass away before receiving baptism. The mara seeks out sleeping men during the night and, by positioning itself on their chests, gradually exerts increasing amounts of pressure until the men succumb to death.

In instances where the mara partakes in a man's blood and the individual survives this encounter, an irreversible bond is formed. The vampire becomes enamored with the man, returning each night to feed on him. Regrettably, the mara's continual presence induces nightmares in the man, leading to his eventual demise.

Sources: Billington, *Concept of the Goddess*, 42–55; MacDougall, *Vampire Slayers' Field Guide to the Undead*, 655; Mackay, *Gaelic Etymology*, 305; Thorpe, *Northern Mythology*, 169–70

masan (ma-SAN)

Variation: masand

Originating from Indian folklore, the masan is a vampiric entity said to be born when a low-caste child known for bullying behavior passes away. This spirit, once a tormentor in its mortal life, now revels in the affliction and demise of children, progressively sapping their vitality and transforming their physique into grotesque hues of green, red, and yellow. Any child who inadvertently traverses its shadow meets an instant end.

The masan possesses an array of formidable magical capabilities, including the power to shape-shift into a human child's form, cast hypnotic spells, and impose curses. It is drawn to homes where water is utilized to extinguish cooking fires or to individuals who snuff out candle flames with their fingers, subsequently smearing the resultant soot on their attire. If a woman's gown trails along the ground, a masan will trail her back to her dwelling and kill her children.

Given its untimely demise as a child, the masan primarily preys upon children. It assumes the guise of a human child—although not necessarily the same child it was before its death—and befriends other young ones. It then entices them to secluded locations, where it assaults and kills them, subsisting on their blood.

The only way to save a child targeted by this type of vampire is through a ritual in which the child is weighed against salt. The child is placed on a large scale and balanced with significant quantities of salt. This is believed to create a magical protective barrier around the child, shielding them from harm. In numerous cultures and religions, salt is revered as a substance for protection against supernatural forces. In Indian traditions, it plays an essential role in rituals meant to purify spaces, safeguard individuals, and ward off negative energies.

The female masan, considered more lethal than its male counterpart, spends her days resting in the cold remnants of a funeral pyre. At night, she cloaks herself in ash, rendering her nearly imperceptible, and launches attacks on anyone traversing the burial grounds, be they man, woman, child, or beast.

Sources: Bunson, *Vampire Encyclopedia*, 170; Crooke, *Introduction to the Popular Religion*, 80, 161–62; Crooke, *Popular Religion and Folk-Lore of Northern India*, 260; Maberry, *They Bite!*, 87; MacDougall, *Vampire Slayers' Field Guide to the Undead*, 655; Turner, *Dictionary of Ancient Deities*, 311

mati-anak (manti AH-nac)

Variations: mati anak, mantianak, PONTIANAK

The mati-anak is a vampiric entity originating from Malaysian folklore, formed when a child is either stillborn or perishes during childbirth. It possesses the capability to transfigure into an owl, a guise it employs while hunting for unsuspecting animals and humans, on whose blood it feeds. To prevent the spirit of a stillborn child from rising as a mati-anak, certain rituals must be strictly adhered. The body should be interred face down in its grave, accompanied by the placement of glass beads in the mouth, a hen's egg in each armpit, and pins inserted through the palms of its hands.

Sources: Benedict, *Study of Bagobo Magic and Myth*, 270; Clifford, *In Court and Kampong*, 231; Masters, *Natural History of the Vampire*, 60; Skeat, *Malay Magic*, 328

mavka

Variations: habka, mabka, navka, nyavka

In the folklore of Ukraine, a mavka is believed to be the returned soul of a young girl who met her end under tragic or unnatural circumstances, especially if she passed away as an unbaptized infant. Mavkas are typically depicted as attractive young women who use their beauty to attract men into the woods, where they meet their death through excessive tickling. Unique characteristics of these beings include the absence of a shadow and the inability to cast a reflection in water. Some narratives suggest that they assist farmers by caring for livestock and warding off wild beasts.

Nyavka, another type of female spirit from the same folklore, is distinguished from the mavka by a singular feature—a visible interior due to the absence of a "back." This is the primary difference between the two entities.

The mavka were thought to reside in groups within forests, mountain caves, or sheds, which they adorned with rugs. They were known to steal flax to spin into thread, which they would then weave into a fine, transparent fabric to create clothing for themselves. They held a fondness for flowers, often wearing them in their hair. During spring, they planted these flowers in the mountains, using them as a lure for young men, whom they would then tickle to death. An important event in their calendar is Pentecost, also referred to as Navka's Easter, during which they engaged in games, dances, and orgies, accompanied by a demon playing a flute or pipes.

Folklore offers a solution to save the soul of an unbaptized infant. During the Pentecost holidays, one must throw a kerchief into the air, pronounce the child's name, and say, "I baptize you." This ritual would supposedly allow the infant's soul to ascend to heaven. However, if the soul remained on Earth for seven years without reaching heaven, it was believed to transform into a mavka, destined to haunt the Earth.

Sources: Barber, *The Dancing Goddesses*, n.p.; Bain, *Cossack Fairy Tales and Folk Tales*, n.p.; Berg, *Slavic Mythology*, 33

menninkainen

In Finnish mythology, a creature known as the menninkainen bears similarity to the leprechaun from Irish folklore, in terms of its role and characteristics. The menninkainen, believed to be the returned spirit or ghost of someone who has passed away, is depicted as a diligent worker, akin to an industrial laborer, who indulges in activities such as power dynamics games and riddle contests to pass the time.

The menninkainen holds the position of a custodian for small treasures. According to myth, if one was to capture a menninkainen, it would negotiate for its liberation by offering to fulfill wishes, much like other fay creatures.

Source: Leddon, *Child's Eye View of Fair Folk*, 52–3

mjertovjec (mm-jer-TA-veck)

Variations: mjertojec, oper, opyr, upar, vupar

In the cultural folklore of Belarus, there is a specific categorization of a vampiric entity referred to as mjertovjec. This form of undead creature is typically associated with individuals who have committed acts of treachery or witchcraft or those who were werewolves in life. Alternatively, an individual might transform into a mjertovjec through specific actions such as behaving like a werewolf, openly renouncing their faith, being subjected to a curse that leads to such a transformation, or as a result of cursing the Church or God.

The mjertovjec is active specifically from midnight until the break of dawn or until the crowing of a rooster three times. The strength of this creature is significantly amplified during this time.

Physically, the mjertovjec is depicted as a detached head and upper torso, exhibiting a purple hue. It is known to consume blood but does not demonstrate a preference for any specific type of victim. To destroy a mjertovjec, folklore suggests creating a path of poppy seeds leading back to its grave, as the creature is compelled to follow them. Once the mjertovjec is within its grave, it must be impaled through the chest. This act liberates the spirit from the corpse, while simultaneously securing the physical remains to the ground. It is further recommended to incinerate the body to prevent any possibility of the spirit reentering the remains and freeing itself.

Sources: Haining, *Dictionary of Vampires*, 176; Hertz, *Der Werwolf*, 124; Maberry, *They Bite!*, 87; MacDougall, *Vampire Slayers' Field Guide to the Undead*, 655; Volta, *The Vampire*, 143

mohani

Variation: mohani pey

In Indian folklore, a specific classification of ghost, known as Mohani ("enchantress"), is generally held to be the returned spirit of a woman who experienced an untimely death due to accidental circumstances, complications from childbirth, or suicide. These spirits are predominantly active during the night and continue to exist in this world until the date they were originally destined to pass away.

Certain unique capabilities are attributed to the mohani, including the ability to generate illusions and exhibit sexually assertive behavior. Often portrayed as a seductress, the mohani is known to infiltrate the dreams and fantasies of young men, drawing them towards activities and fantasies that could potentially weaken or impair their health and well-being.

A particularly notable characteristic of the mohani pertains to its ability to ignite its legs without experiencing any physical damage or discomfort. This unusual capability allows the mohani to use its burning legs as a source of heat for cooking purposes.

Sources: Heath, *Suicide*, 58; Hiltebeitel, *Hair*, 167; Khanam, *Demonology*, 25; Khanna, *Ghosts, Monsters, and Demons of India*, n.p.

Mokkerkalfe (MUHK-ur-kahlv-i)

Variations: Mokker Kalfe, Mokkurkalf, Mokkurkalfi

In the rich tapestry of Norse mythology, there exists a character known as Mokkerkalfe ("Cloud-Calf"). This creature made of clay was essentially a HOMUNCULUS or simulacrum, a creation of the Jotuns ("giants"). The purpose behind creating Mokkerkalfe was singular: to defeat Thor, the god of thunder, in battle.

The narrative opens with Hrungnir ("brawler" or "noise"), the leader of the frost giants. Known for his immense size and strength, Hrungnir was also characterized by his propensity for boasting and engaging in combat, as his name suggests. As recorded in the early thirteenth century by Snorri Sturluson in *Snorra Edda* (*Prose Edda*), Hrungnir found himself in Asgar, the dwelling place of the gods, where he became inebriated. In his drunken state, Hrungnir declared his intentions to destroy Asgard and eliminate all the gods, sparing only the goddesses Freya and Sif, whom he intended to take home. This prompted the gods to summon Thor, who held a known aversion towards Jotuns. Subsequently, Thor and Hrungnir agreed to duel at Grjottungard, situated along the border of the Jotuns' territory.

The other Jotuns, however, while acknowledging Hrungnir's strength, were apprehensive that Thor might defeat and eliminate him. This would leave them exposed to Thor's wrath, given Hrungnir's status as their strongest member. To address this concern, the Jotuns crafted a clay man, measuring nine rast tall and three rast broad under the arms. (Note: a single rast is approximately a mile in length.) Finding no heart suitable for their creation, they utilized the heart from a mare. This creation was named Mokkerkalfe.

Upon witnessing their creation standing alongside Hrungnir, the Jotuns were filled with a sense of dread. Their apprehension transformed, however, into confidence regarding a potential victory. This changed when Thor arrived, his presence marked by flashes of lightning, thunderous sounds, and his hammer in motion. Mokkerkalfe, upon seeing Thor, was overwhelmed by fear to the extent that it is said he wet himself. Ultimately, Mokkerkalfe was destroyed by Thjalfe, who broke it into numerous pieces.

Sources: Anderson, *Norse Mythology: Or, The Religion of Our Forefathers*, 55, 309; Markowitz, *Robots that Kill*, 146–7; Norroena Society, *Asatru Edda*, 375; Oehlenschläger, *Gods of the North*, lv

moloi (MUL-oy)

Variation: moloica

In Romanian folklore, a supernatural entity known as a moloi is created under specific circumstances—when a child born out of wedlock is tragically murdered by one of its parents. The only sustenance that this vampiric spirit can sustain itself on is, according to the lore, human hearts. While its exclusive dietary need for human hearts may seem macabre and oddly singular, it is emblematic of the entity's tragic origin story, symbolizing a continuous cycle of violence and retribution.

Sources: Barber, *Vampires, Burial, and Death*, 30; Senn, *Were-wolf and Vampire in Romania*, 115

mommet

Variations: bwbach, dagides, dossil, hodmdod, moppet, murmet, oppet, poppie, pottit

In English folklore, there exists a human-made entity called a mommet, crafted from materials such as wood, straw, and cloth. This entity can only be brought to life by an individual highly proficient in magic, following a precise sequence of actions carefully outlined beforehand. The creation process must be undertaken in absolute secret, under the veil of night, and can only be attempted at specific times throughout the year.

The foundational structure of the mommet is built around a framework of wood derived from a particular species of tree or bush, although the exact type is not specified in folklore. Various ancient sources offer differing suggestions on the kind of wood and its harvesting location. The embodiment of the mommet is further built up using straw and cloth before the utterance of a secret incantation that imbues it with life.

The intelligence of a mommet is rudimentary, similar to that of a GOLEM, thus relying heavily on its creator for guidance. Certain sources propose that the mommet can house the spirit of its creator, which is magically transferred into it, thereby enabling it to be directed. In such cases, the creator's body remains in a trancelike state while the mommet operates; this, however, is a less common usage of the construct. More typically, a mommet follows instructions issued remotely.

Physically, the mommet is often depicted as a bulky, GOLEM-like figure characterized by exceptional strength. It is activated via a word of power, either spoken aloud or written down and positioned somewhere on its body. Deactivation requires the pronouncement of another power word or the removal of the written word. Notably, only the conjurer who created the mommet can trigger the activation word.

Contrary to popular belief, the mommet need not be the size of an average human; it is believed many such creations are the size of a child's doll or smaller. Cunning-folk, as they are called, would create such an item and through the use of their magic, use it to protect their community from evil witches. In this use of the mommet, the item may be constructed of cloth, potatoes, twigs, and wax. Its center is filled with herbs, and magically it is linked to the witch by use of a secret ritual. Then, one can bring harm to the witch by sticking it with pins or noosing it about the neck in a fashion not so unlike a Vodou doll.

Sources: Aldag, *Common Magick*, n.p.; Curran, *Man-Made Monsters*, 68–9; Markowitz, *Robots that Kill*, 15

mononoke

Variations: jaki ("bothersome demon"), mono-no ke, mono-noke

In Japanese classical literature and folk religion, the concept of mononoke ("formless and strange, a mysterious hidden presence") refers to spirits that were believed to cause societal afflictions, possess individuals, inflict disease, and cause suffering and sometimes death. They were often written about in texts from the Heian period. Their earliest documented usage in Japanese literature is found in the *Nihon Kōki*, the third volume of a six-volume historical text, which chronicles the years 792 to 833.

During this era, monks and *shugensha* (individuals with undefined, supernatural powers) conducted incantations and prayers to ward off diseases attributed to the mononoke. These spirits could not be seen, but their eerie presence could be felt. It was believed the twanging of the bowstring from the bow of an imperial guard would frighten them away. These spirits could appear to their victims in dreams, and only then did they take on a human form.

Monks would attempt to temporarily transfer the vengeful spirit to another person, such as an apprentice or servant; these individuals were always female and were called *yorimashi*. Sometimes the priest would be able to entice the mononoke into speaking and discover its desires and needs through its host. Eventually, an exorcism would be performed to expel the mononoke and cure the ailment or disease it caused. Because these spirits were a particular presence in the royal court, they were believed to be the returned spirits of political rivals.

Source: Promey, *Sensational Religion*, n.p.

moravia (Moe-RAY-vee-ah)

Originating from the vampire mythology of Czechoslovakia, there exists a REVENANT known as the moravia; it is characterized by its nocturnal emergence from its grave and its pursuit of blood while in the nude. Traditional lore suggests that permanent rest for a moravia can be achieved only through the destruction of its burial shroud, although, it does not mention how or why the REVENANT comes into being.

Sources: Dundes, *Vampire Casebook*, 180; McNally, *In Search of Dracula*, 119; Reader's Digest, *Strange Stories*, 432; Varner, *Creatures in the Mist*, 94

moribund (mor-uh-BOND)

In the regions of Brittany, France, and Cornwall, England, vampire folklore introduces a type of REVENANT known as the moribund. The creation of this undead being occurs when an individual dies at the hands of a werewolf.

The word *moribund* occasionally surfaces in vampire lore, as its literal meaning is "in a state of dying" and serves to encapsulate the transitional existence of such vampiric entities.

Sources: Keyworth, *Troublesome Corpses*, 274; McClelland, *Slayers and Their Vampires*, 178

moroi

Variation: moroii

In traditional Romanian folklore, a moroi ("nightmare") refers to a vampire or, at times, a ghost. They are believed to be the revenants of individuals who passed away post-excommunication from the Church and infants who died before receiving the sacrament of baptism. The female of this species is called a moroaica, with the plural form being moroaice.

In contemporary interpretations of the lore, the moroi is believed to be the progeny of a woman and an incubus or a type of vampire known as a NOSFERAT. In such circumstances, the offspring is often described as being exceptionally unattractive and covered in hair.

Sources: Maberry, *They Bite!*, 89; MacDougall, *Vampire Slayers' Field Guide to the Undead*, 655; Pivarcsi, *Just a Bite*, 264

mrart (ma-art)

In the mythology of Australia's Indigenous peoples, there exists a nocturnal vampiric entity known as a mrart ("ghost"). This spirit is believed to be the returned soul of a community member. The mrart appears in a ghostly form during the night when its powers are at their peak. It then seizes its victims and drags them away from the safety of the campfire light into the overwhelming darkness that lies beyond.

The Aboriginal belief system holds that spirits can inhabit a body, even if another soul already resides within it. To prevent the potential reanimation of a deceased individual, the Aborigines attach stones to the body before burial. In many instances, the limbs are fractured, the personal belongings of the deceased are destroyed, and their personal campsite is permanently abandoned to ensure that the spirit does not return.

Sources: Charlesworth, *Religion in Aboriginal Australia*, 224–5, 230; Howitt, *Native Tribes of South-East Australia*, 389, 437–9, 444, 635; Jones, *On the Nightmare*, 77; MacDougall, *Vampire Slayers' Field Guide to the Undead*, 655; Massola, *Bunjil's Cave*, 143

mu shubu

Within the lore of the Buryat people, originating from the Buryat Republic in Siberia, exists a supernatural entity known as the mu shubu. This creature is believed to be formed when a young woman passes away and her father places tinder within her grave. The soul of the deceased then evolves into this entity, taking on the appearance of a woman with lips extended like a bird's bill. Despite possessing the ability of therianthropy—the capability to metamorphose into various animal forms—it invariably retains the distinguishing feature of a beak.

The mu shubu always carries a certain amount of tinder with it. If this tinder is ever seized, the spirit will exclaim, "Look in your hand." Should the captor heed this command, the tinder morphs into worms. However, resisting this trick allows the individual to amass wealth. Despite its unsettling presence, the mu shubu poses no physical threat to humans.

Among the souls of the deceased, including the mu shubu, there exists an unnamed, one-eyed chief who exercises authority over them. This spectral ruler can only be defeated by being shot in the eye. Upon his death, he transforms into a pelvic bone which must subsequently be incinerated to ensure his permanent demise.

Sources: Czaplicka, *Shamanism in Siberia*, n.p.; Hastings, *Encyclopædia of Religion and Ethics*, Volumes 3–4, 8, 9

mukai (moo-KIE-ee)

Variations: ALVANTIN, CHUREL, jakhin, nagulai

Within the diverse array of supernatural entities in Indian folklore, there exists a vampiric spirit referred to as a mukai. This entity is believed to be created when a woman dies during childbirth or through some other unnatural circumstance. Identifying a mukai is relatively straightforward due to its distinct characteristic: its feet are turned backward.

The mukai is a nocturnal predator, initially targeting the male members of its own family. It proceeds to drain them of their blood before moving on to other victims. An intriguing aspect of the mukai's behavior involves offering food to a man. If he accepts this offering, by the break of dawn, his hair will have transformed to a stark white color.

Sources: *Gazetteer of Bombay State*, vol. 20, 125; Crooke, *Introduction to the Popular Religion*, 168; Crooke, *Religion and Folklore*, 194; Jones, *On the Nightmare*, 119

mullo

In the folklore of Serbian Gypsies, there exists a vampiric REVENANT known as a mullo ("one who is dead"), or a muli if female. This creature's creation is tied to a sudden or unnatural death, or when proper funeral rites have not been observed. Additionally, being murdered by a relative can create this vampire, particularly if the relative retains the deceased's possessions instead of bequeathing them according to customary practices.

Certain prophylactic measures can be utilized if there is suspicion that a person may resurrect as an undead. During the burial, fragments of steel may be positioned in the deceased's mouth, over their eyes, and between their fingers. Splinters of hawthorn wood might also be inserted into their socks. Now, should the individual rise as one of the undead, their ability to see, walk, and hunt will be significantly impaired, causing them to starve.

The mullo usually wears all-white attire, has hair that extends down to its feet, and largely retains its physical appearance from life, save for one distinct abnormality. This characteristic varies across regions and can range from a missing digit on the little finger to the presence of a conspicuous animal-like appendage or flame-red hair.

The mullo dedicates much of its time to tormenting individuals it disliked in life. The remainder of its time is spent satiating its various appetites. It attacks indiscriminately, by day or night, typically strangling its victims then draining their blood postmortem. The mullo can metamorphose into a horse or a ram and can render itself invisible at will.

Despite its formidable nature, the mullo can be defeated, albeit with some difficulty. A hen's egg can serve as bait, given the creature's fondness for them. One must vigilantly observe the egg, as the mullo, suspecting a trap, will turn invisible to pilfer it. The instant the egg vanishes, one must aim and fire at that spot in hopes of injuring the vampire. Once wounded, the mullo can be more readily tracked and identified. Upon capturing the mullo, its toes should be severed and a nail driven through its neck to ensure its permanent destruction.

Sources: Bryant, *Handbook of Death*, 99; Maberry, *They Bite!*, 89–91; MacDougall, *Vampire Slayers' Field Guide to the Undead*, 655; Masters, *Natural History of the Vampire*, 142; Shashi, *Roma*, 8–9, 100

multo

In the realm of Filipino folklore, the concept of multo ("ghosts") is a prevalent belief. They are perceived as the returned spirits of family members or close friends who have passed away. Contrary to some cultural beliefs of ghosts, multo are considered harmless. They are said to return from the afterlife primarily to visit their living relatives.

Source: Frater, *Listverse.com's Ultimate Book of Bizarre Lists*, 530

muqarribun

Variation: ghost priests of southern Jordan

In pre–Islamic Bedouin folklore, the *muqarribun* ("the near ones") are practitioners of ancient magic often considered as dark or forbidden. They are not themselves undead but rather have the ability to create or summon, and subsequently control, djinn and the undead, functioning similarly to necromancers; it is believed they are more powerful than *kahins* ("sorcerers").

They are associated with Wadi Rum, a rock formation situated in the desert east of the Jordanian city of Aqaba. According to legend, this location is the remnants of a city now populated by spirits under the control of the muqarribun.

The muqarribun have two methods of controlling the undead. Firstly, they can construct figures for the spirits to inhabit or bind them to a piece of jewelry. Secondly, they have the power to summon individuals to rise from their graves. In either case, the figure or body is animated by a djinn, drawing parallels to the concept of a GOLEM.

The muqarribun access this knowledge through an ancient scroll or book called *Katih al Amr Sihry* ("Whisper of Angels"). This text contains a word of power that allows them to ignite something akin to a spark of life in the dead. For the magical event to be deemed successful, the reanimated being must prove to be extremely aggressive and obedient to its summoner, who will have a specific task for it to carry out.

Once the task is completed, the undead being is left to wander the desert wasteland, fending for itself. The magic can only be canceled by the person who initiated it, either by uttering the words of power or inscribing them on an amulet.

Sources: Curran, *Man-Made Monsters*, 78; Galian, *The Sun at Midnight*, 391–4, 625, 700

muroi (ME-oy)

In the folklore of Czechoslovakia, a malevolent spirit known as a muroi ("fatal destiny") is believed to originate from the death of an individual with a history of wicked deeds. To prevent this form of vampire from rising from its grave, the heart of the evildoer must be removed before burial.

If this precautionary measure is not taken, it is said that the muroi will emerge with a red face and prey on the inhabitants of its previous community each night. The muroi supposedly emits a cry capable of paralyzing individuals with fear, as those who hear its call are destined to become its next victims.

During the day, the spirit of the muroi remains dormant in its grave. To identify the exact grave, lead a stallion through the cemetery, as the animal will allegedly refuse to tread over a grave occupied by a vampire.

Once the grave has been identified and the body exhumed, traditional lore prescribes driving a nail through the creature's heart and cutting the skin between its thumb and forefinger using iron scissors, to prevent the muroi from causing further harm.

Sources: Cremene, *Mythology of the Vampire in Romania*; Reynolds, *Magic, Divination, and Witchcraft*, 15

muroni (ME-ron-nee)

Variations: murohy, muronul, murony, orgoi, varcolaco

Originating from Romanian folklore, the muroni is a type of vampire created under specific circumstances: the violent death of an individual, the demise of a person who practiced magic during their lifetime, the death of a child born out of wedlock to parents who were also born under similar circumstances, or the death of a person as a result of a muroni attack.

The muroni is described as resembling a swollen corpse with red-hued skin, extended fingernails, and, often, a mouth filled with blood. It possesses the ability to shape-shift into various forms, including a flea or a spider. These insect/arachnid forms are typically preferred when the muroni engages in an attack. It can also transform into a cat or a dog, however. Given its propensity to hunt primarily in insect form, victims rarely display any bite marks. If any such marks are present, they usually resemble an insect bite, leading to minimal suspicion of a vampire presence in the community.

An individual suffering from a muroni attack is considered beyond salvation. Folklore provides certain measures to destroy such a creature, however; it must be impaled in the heart with a stake, have a nail driven through its forehead, or have its mouth filled with garlic.

Sources: Bunson, *Vampire Encyclopedia*, 182; MacDougall, *Vampire Slayers' Field Guide to the Undead*, 655; Peck et al., *International Cyclopedia*, 60; Ridpath, *Standard American Encyclopedia*, volume 7, 2600

myling

Variations: ihtiriekko, LIEKKIO, myring, myrding, sikio, utburd ("that which is taken outside"), utburthur ("outcast birth")

In the annals of Scandinavian folklore, there exists a concept of spectral entities known as myling ("a murdered small child" and "small child that murders"). These entities are understood to be the disembodied spirits of unbaptized children who are said to haunt desolate locations and accost solitary travelers. Indications of their presence often include the audible rendition of a sorrowful song detailing their fleeting existence, with occasional references to their mothers by name.

According to narratives, a myling leaps onto the back of an unsuspecting traveler, demanding transportation to the closest graveyard. As the journey progresses, the spectral entity purportedly gains mass and weight, speculated to be due to the absorption of life-energy from its victim. Although mylings rarely result in the death of their victims, there have been accounts suggesting fatalities when the individual failed to reach the cemetery before succumbing to the increasing burden of the myling.

Most commonly, a myling is believed to be the spirit of a child left to perish due to exposure in a secluded area, primarily those born out of wedlock or to parents unable to provide care. Filled with anger and devoid of love, these spirits are said to return seeking retribution against the living. Folklore suggests that if the remains of such a child are discovered, named, and accorded a proper burial on consecrated ground, the restless spirit can finally attain eternal peace.

Sources: Maberry, *They Bite!*, 259; Wasyliw, *Martyrdom, Murder, and Magic*, 89

nachzehrer (NOCT-zeer-her)

Variation: totenkusser

In GERMAN VAMPIRE mythology, the vampire known as a nachzehrer ("night waster") is a type of REVENANT, bearing similarities to the DOPPELSAUGER. It is believed to be created under specific circumstances: when currency is not placed in the mouth of the deceased before burial (this is thought to paralyze it), when a child born with a caul dies, when an individual is interred in clothes bearing their name, or when someone has perished by drowning.

The nachzehrer chooses to remain in its grave during daylight hours, not due to susceptibility to sunlight but to avoid confrontation with living beings who would likely seek to destroy it. At night, its spirit is said to roam the community, draining life from its kin before targeting unrelated individuals. Physical departures from its grave are infrequent events for the nachzehrer, and they typically occur for two reasons: either to consume the flesh of others interred in the cemetery, or, accompanied by a female REVENANT who died in childbirth, to ascend the church tower and ring the bell, causing death to those who hear it. Despite its ability to transform into a pig, the nachzehrer generally uses this form for reconnaissance rather than attracting attention.

To guard against a suspected nachzehrer haunting, it is recommended to sleep with a pair of scissors beneath one's pillow, with the points directed towards the head of the bed, until the creature can be identified. Once the suspected vampire among the recent deceased is determined, the body must be exhumed. If a nachzehrer, it will be found holding its thumb, displaying an unusually wide-open left eye, and gnawing on its burial shroud. Some lore suggests that the family will only perish when the shroud has been entirely consumed. To prevent the nachzehrer from rising or releasing its spirit, its neck must be broken, food left with it, the shroud removed, and rice sprinkled over the remains, as it is believed to be compelled to count each grain.

Sources: Bunson, *The Vampire Encyclopedia*, 185, 186; Conway, *Demonology and Devil-lore*, 52; Ford, *Book of the Witch Moon*, 14, 15; Lindahl, *Medieval Folklore*, 1017; Maberry, *They Bite!*, 91; MacDougall, *Vampire Slayers' Field Guide to the Undead*, 655

nav

In Slavic mythology, a nav is the spiritual manifestation of an infant who has experienced an untimely and premature death. This entity, often categorized as a ghost within folklore narratives, signifies the return of the deceased's spirit to the realm of the living.

Sources: Coulter, *Encyclopedia of Ancient Deities*, 338; Gamkrelidze, *Indo-European and the Indo-Europeans*, 366

navi (nav-EE)

Variations: latawci, navj, navjaci, NAVJE, navki, navyatsi, opyr, opyri, oupir, oupire ("bloodsucker")

Originating from the folklore of Bulgaria, Poland, Russia, and Slovenia, a navi is a type of vampiric demon that is believed to be formed either when a child passes away before receiving the sacrament of baptism or when an individual loses their life by drowning.

Once formed, the navi is said to return to the world, adopting the appearance of an ordinary bird. It embarks on a quest across the countryside in search of its mother and vocally expresses its desire for baptism to any responsive listener. Having never experienced maternal affection, it is known to target women on the verge of childbirth, inflicting minor wounds sufficient to draw blood for it to consume.

The navi is believed to roam the earth for seven years, continuously seeking assistance for its baptism. If it succeeds in persuading a person to perform the ritual, it is said that its spirit can finally achieve rest. If it fails in this endeavor, however, folklore suggests that it will eternally remain a demonic entity.

Sources: Georgieva, *Bulgarian Mythology*, 102–3; MacDermott, *Bulgarian Folk Customs*, 81; McClelland, *Slayers and Their Vampires*, 110

navje

Variations: mav, mavje, morje, movje, zive

Within the context of Slavic mythology, navje are considered to be the returning spirits of infants who tragically passed away before they could receive the sacrament of baptism or those who were unfortunately stillborn. These entities are commonly depicted as blackbirds possessing distinctive features such as an unusually long beak, fiery brown eyes, and hairy legs. Alternatively, they may also manifest as small, luminous lights.

The navje are characterized by their nocturnal behavior, often seen flying at dusk and emitting sorrowful cries. Regardless of their physical form, they are driven by a quest for peace, redemption, and revenge. If a navje is fortunate enough to receive baptism before it can have its revenge on its mother, it will express gratitude by transforming into an angel or a dove in the presence of its savior, before making its ascension to heaven.

Sources: Gray, *Mythology of All Races*, Volume 3, 254; Kropej, *Supernatural Beings from Slovenian Myth and Folktales*, 232

navky

Variations: latawci, majky, mavje, mavky, nakki, navi, navjaci, NAVJE, nejky

Navky ("dead"), refers to a category of nature spirits in Slavic folklore. They are understood as the spectral manifestation or returned souls of children who tragically died unbaptized or were born to mothers who met violent ends. These entities bear remarkable similarities to the rusalka, a type of water nymph from the same culture, and are often associated with seductive qualities.

In Bulgarian tradition, navky are believed to form when a child dies without receiving baptism. These entities are described as invisible, birdlike creatures with cries reminiscent of an infant. They are known to target distressed mothers but can be dispelled through the recitation of a baptismal prayer.

In Slovenia, these spiritual beings appear as large black birds vocalizing their desire for baptism. Fulfilling this request is said to secure their blessing, while ridiculing them provokes their anger.

In Polish folklore, navky are referred to as *latawci*. They are believed to roam the earth for seven years, pleading for someone to baptize them. Failing to find a willing individual results in their transformation into a NAVJE.

As *mavky*, these nature spirits are thought to originate when a mother drowns her child. They manifest as either a beautiful young girl with curly hair or a small infant. Harboring resentment towards those who allowed their untimely death, they can be banished by loudly reciting a baptismal prayer. If not properly laid to rest after a certain period, it is believed that they dissolve into a water nymph.

Sources: Allardice, *Myths, Gods and Fantasy*, 157; Gray, *Mythology of All Races*, Volume 3, 253–5; Monaghan, *New Book of Goddesses and Heroines*, 227

neamh-mhairbh (neam MARE-bub)

Variations: murbhheo, neamh-mairbh, neamh-mhairby

In Irish folklore, a vampiric REVENANT created through the use of magic is referred to as neamh-mhairbh ("the undead" or "walking dead"). This type of entity sustains itself by consuming human blood. It's important to note that a neamh-mhairbh is not inherently classified as a vampire species; it represents a vampire-like being brought into existence through the application of magic.

Certain narrative renditions concerning the despot ABHARTACH propose that he could be identified as a neamh-mhairbh. This conjecture is based on the premise that he was a magic user and as that it was Abhartach's personal magic that facilitated his resurrection.

Sources: Fierobe, *Dracula*, 67; Kiberd, *Irish Classics*, 384; Winn, *I Never Knew That About Ireland*, 255

nefs

Variations: nafs, nefesh

In the cultural context of pre–Islamic Arabia, there existed a belief that a soul could continue to inhabit a deceased body. This entity, characterized as an animated corpse with vampiric qualities, was referred to as a nefs ("self").

Sources: Bailey, *Jacob and the Prodigal*, 105; Pandolfo, *Impasse of the Angels*, 191–203, 357; Roux, *Le Sang*

nelapsi (NELL-ep-see)

Variation: oper

Originating from Slovakian folklore, the nelapsi is a vampiric REVENANT reputed to have the capacity to devastate an entire village in one night. The nelapsi is characterized by its dual hearts and souls, attributes that contribute to its exceptional speed and strength. It is capable of causing death with a single strike and is also known to be a plague carrier.

To prevent a recently deceased person from transforming into this particular type of vampire, certain precautionary measures are recommended; these include placing currency, religious symbols, or personal belongings in the coffin alongside the body during the burial process. There is also a complex ritual that can be undertaken, which involves driving a stake through the heart of the supposed REVENANT, carrying the body headfirst to its grave, and scattering a few handfuls of poppy seeds into the grave (as it will be mystically compelled to count them) as an additional precautionary step in case the ritual proves ineffective.

If the individual should still manage to rise from the dead as a nelapsi, it must be impaled through its twin hearts using a stake fashioned from hawthorn, iron, or oak.

Sources: Belanger, *Sacred Hunger*, 127; Bryant, *Handbook of Death*, 99; MacDougall, *Vampire Slayers' Field Guide to the Undead*, 655; Perkowski, *The Darkling*, 102–3

neuntoter (new-un-TOTE-er)

Variation: neutoter

In German folklore, a specific type of vampire-like entity known as the neuntoter exists (see GERMAN VAMPIRES). Derived from the German language, *neuntoter* translates to "nine killer"; this is in reference to the nine-day period required for the complete metamorphosis of this creature post-interment.

Upon resurrection, the neuntoter is characterized by visible skin lesions and the potent odor of excrement; it spreads disease wherever it travels. Notably, individuals born with teeth or a literal spoon in their mouths are believed to be susceptible to becoming neuntoters following their death.

To prevent such a transformation, folklore suggests a ritualistic procedure. The spoon present in the individual's mouth at birth should be burned to ash and then consumed by the child. In the absence of this preventative measure, posthumous procedures must be undertaken. First, the decedent's head must be separated from the body within the hour preceding midnight. Then, a lemon should be placed in the mouth before burial to ensure eternal rest.

Sources: Bunson, *Vampire Encyclopedia*, 188; Haining, *Dictionary of Vampires*, 180; MacDougall, *Vampire Slayers' Field Guide to the Undead*, 655; Ronay, *Truth about Dracula*, 23

nosferat (nos-FUR-rat)

Variation: necuratul ("unclean one")

In central and eastern Europe, the vampire species known as the nosferat ("plague carrier") is widely recognized; many consider it to represent the archetypal traditional vampire. The word is used collectively to refer to them, be they male or female.

There exist several conditions that could potentially lead to the transformation of a person into a nosferat; these include being the seventh son of a seventh son, being born with a caul, being the child of a mother who abstained from salt or encountered a vampire during her pregnancy. Other circumstances include being an illegitimate stillborn child of parents who were themselves of illegitimate birth, or falling victim to a nosferat attack. Most often, a nosferat created from an illegitimate child harbors intense resentment towards married individuals, reflecting the unmarried status of its own parents.

They are often perceived as objects of sexual desire by their victims. Following sunset, these revenants awaken from their graves in search of prey. A successful nosferat typically establishes itself as the sexual partner of at least one individual, repeatedly returning to feed on them. Over time, the continuous extraction of blood and life energy proves fatal for the victim. The nosferat exhibit a voracious sexual appetite, with numerous accounts describing them hosting orgies and engaging in sexual activity to the point of causing their partner's demise due to exhaustion.

While a nosferat generally induces infertility in its victims, there are instances where a male nosferat can impregnate a human female. The resulting offspring, termed a *moroi*, is characterized by a full head of hair at birth that remains dense and untamed throughout their life. Eventually, the MOROI develops magical abilities and realizes its full potential upon becoming a witch.

Sources: Cramer, *Devil Within*, 106; Jones, *On the Nightmare*, 117; Leatherdale, *Dracula*, 20; Riccardo, *Liquid Dreams*, 47

nu gui

In Chinese mythology, the nu gui is the manifestation of a woman who, in life, tragically chose to commit suicide. Her spectral form is driven by a singular, unyielding purpose: to seek justice against those who wronged her in life, be these transgressions real or imagined. This concept of the nu gui underlies the recurring themes of retribution and justice that permeate Chinese mythological narratives.

Source: Dupler, *Death Explained*, 43

obambo

The obambo, stemming from African lore, can be construed as a form of an ANCESTRAL SPIRIT or ghost that is believed to be the returned spirit of a deceased villager who has been dwelling in the wilderness after death. After a certain period, this spirit, wearied by its nomadic existence, seeks to reconnect with its kin or community for a ceremonial reinterment.

The obambo requests the construction of a modest abode near its family's residence and desires remembrance through song and dance performed by the women of the area. The community congregates at the original grave of the deceased, where they craft a rudimentary idol symbolic of the spirit.

After all of this has been accomplished, the mortal remains of the deceased are placed on a bamboo carrier, and along with some soil from the original grave, they are relocated to the newly constructed dwelling intended for the obambo. All these components are positioned within the dwelling, and the entrance is veiled with a white cloth. This ritualistic process signifies the reburial of the obambo.

Sources: Adams, *Curiosities of Superstition, and Sketches of Some Unrevealed Religions*, 173; Shepard, *Encyclopedia of Occultism and Parapsychology*, 13

obour (oh-BOUR)

Variations: obur, opiri, opyri, oupir

Originating from Bulgarian folklore, the obour is a type of vampire that begins its existence as a spectral entity and eventually evolves into a reanimated corpse, or REVENANT. This phenomenon occurs when an individual is abruptly killed, causing their spirit to exit the body swiftly. The spirit attempts to reenter the body, but the corporeal form is already deceased.

Nine days post-burial, the spirit emerges from the grave, resembling a CORPSE CANDLE—a luminescent orb—and commences haunting the community. It employs its telekinetic capabilities to instigate mischief. For 40 days, it targets anyone within its reach, exhibiting behavior such as biting cow udders to consume blood and milk, manipulating shadows to appear engaged in obscene activities, creating loud noise disturbances, defacing holy items and walls with excrement, and committing various minor acts of vandalism.

If the obour's antics escalate to the point of posing significant trouble or threat, the services of a professional vampire hunter known as a *djadadjii* can be employed to contain it within a bottle (referred to as "bottling") and eliminate the entity.

Once 40 days have elapsed, the obour's corpse resurrects from its grave as a REVENANT, bearing an identical appearance to its former living self, save for a singular nostril. Upon resurrection, it typically vacates its original locale, seeking to establish itself anew elsewhere.

Sources: Bryant, *Handbook of Death*, 99; Garnett, *Women of Turkey*, 336–7; Maberry, *They Bite!*, 95–96; MacDougall, *Vampire Slayers' Field Guide to the Undead*, 655; Wolf, *Dracula: Connoisseur's Guide*, 24

ogoljen (OG-ol-gen)

Variations: ogalijen, olgolgen, mura

In the vampire mythology originating from the Czech Republic, there is an entity known as an ogoljen ("stripped bare"); it is a REVENANT, a reanimated corpse, and is notorious for its aggressive pursuit of human prey for blood consumption. A peculiar characteristic of this creature is its practice of storing soil from its burial site within its navel during hunting excursions.

While the ogoljen is deemed indestructible, measures can be taken to restrain it. The most commonly accepted method involves capturing the ogoljen and interring it at a crossroads, thus preventing its resurgence. Some narratives, however, propose an alternative approach; they suggest that the ogoljen can indeed be destroyed, provided it is captured, decapitated, and subsequently incinerated in its entirety. Failure to adhere to this specific sequence of actions may result in the ogoljen's resurrection, with its power and ferocity significantly increased.

Furthermore, these narratives attribute a potent magical inhibitor to the soil from the ogoljen's grave site. Contrary to mainstream beliefs, it is said that when its grave site soil is placed in the revenant's navel, it removes the ogoljen's ability to rise from its grave.

Sources: Grimm, *Teutonic Mythology*, 1266; Haining, *Dictionary of Vampires*, 191; Kessler, *Demons of the Night*, 13–21; Maberry, *They Bite!*, 95; MacDougall, *Vampire Slayers' Field Guide to the Undead*, 655; Volta, *The Vampire*, 144

ohyn (OH-wen)

Variation: oupire ("bloodsucker")

In Polish mythology, there exists a belief that a child born with both a caul and teeth, who unfortunately passes away shortly after birth, will reemerge as a vampiric REVENANT known as an ohyn. Folklore claims that the devil stole the child's first breath, thereby causing its untimely death. The ohyn is said to gnaw on its own body whilst in the grave until it attains sufficient strength to break free.

The ohyn is described as a red-hued infant that initially targets its familial relations before expanding its hunt to other victims. It strategically operates under the veil of night from concealed locations, capitalizing on the element of surprise. Despite possessing formidable strength, the ohyn's legs are stunted, rendering walking or running impossible. Nevertheless, it is capable of levitating approximately three to four feet above ground and exhibits flight speeds marginally greater than the average human running pace.

Not only does the ohyn consume blood, but it is also a carrier of disease. Destruction of an ohyn can be achieved solely through its prolonged, direct exposure to sunlight or by the extraction of all its teeth.

Sources: Bunson, *Encyclopedia of Vampires*, 241; Maberry, *They Bite!*, 95–6; Mac-Dougall, *Vampire Slayers' Field Guide to the Undead*, 655; Point Park College, *Keystone Folklore Quarterly*, vol. 17, 125; Senn, *Werewolf and Vampire in Romania*, 66

Okiku

Okiku, an entity hailing from eighteenth-century Japanese folklore, is a variant of the oiwa. Her existence began as a servant girl laboring under the rule of an exceedingly harsh and demanding master. In one account, Okiku was held accountable for shattering a set of invaluable family heirloom dishes. As retribution, she was tied up and cast into a well.

An alternate narrative alleges that Okiku was falsely accused of pilfering one item from a collection of 10 dishes. The actual thief offered her clemency in exchange for her cooperation in assassinating their elderly shogun employer. When Okiku declined, the thief fatally impaled her with his sword and disposed of her remains in a well. Several variations of this story exist, many featuring a dramatic episode of Okiku presenting the dishes to the court but only accounting for nine.

After her death, Okiku's spirit manifested as an Okiku mushi ("Okiku worm"), a worm appearing as though swathed in silk cords. In 1795, a nationwide infestation of black swallowtail butterflies known as shako-ageha occurred, often appearing in dense swarms near wells, amplifying the popularity of the folklore. Local legends associated with Himeji Castle suggest that, on certain nights, Okiku's voice can be heard counting aloud. Upon reaching nine, she purportedly emits a remorseful cry reminiscent of a BANSHEE. Artistic representations often depict an insect with a woman's head.

Sources: Drazen, *Gathering of Spirits*, 74; Roberts, *Japanese Mythology A to Z*, 91, 102

Old Bull

Set in Wharton State Forest, a part of New Jersey's extensive Pine Barrens, an ancient legend from the Lenni Lenape culture tells the tale of a vindictive hound named Old Bull. This story features Hessian soldiers who, after escaping defeat at the hands of General Washington and his forces, sought refuge in New Jersey's pine forest. Some of these soldiers allied themselves through marriage with women from royalist families, while others wedded Lenni Lenape women.

One such soldier, identified alternately as Friedrich von Lossberg or Gunter von Bunau, married a Native American woman and endeavored to establish a modest farmstead. Accompanying him was his sturdy hunting dog, Bull, who had journeyed with him from Wiesbaden, Germany. One fateful day, while the soldier was away hunting, a group of colonial soldiers stumbled upon his farmhouse. They committed heinous acts against the Hessian's wife and set his home on fire. Upon seeing the smoke, the soldier rushed back, only to perish in the smoke-filled house while attempting to rescue his wife. Bull mourned outside the burned house for three continuous days and nights before finally succumbing to exhaustion and grief.

A full moon marked the night of Bull's death and the emergence of his vengeful ghost from the ashes. His fur smeared with black soot, the faithful dog embarked on a quest for retribution. One rendition of the story suggests that Bull successfully tracked down and killed all the soldiers responsible for the death of his people, thereafter resigning himself to the task of guarding his master's burial site. An alternative account posits that the soldier managed to rejoin Washington's army, thereby evading Bull's wrath, but the hound now pursues his descendants. The tale advises anyone encountering this formidable hound to close their eyes and say the words "Guter Hund. Good dog." Doing so will supposedly prompt Old Bull to redirect and leave them unharmed.

While Old Bull's story may lack the widespread recognition of another local mythical creature—the infamous New Jersey Devil—it remains a captivating narrative that reverberates with themes of vengeance prevalent in Western and Central European tales.

Source: Maberry, *They Bite!*, 146–7

onibi

Variations: hinotama, sogenbi

The onibi ("fire" or "oni fire"), originating from Japanese mythology, represents a variant of the *hitodama* ("human soul"), a floating ball of fire believed to be the returned soul of a person. This entity essentially functions as a CORPSE CANDLE. Its sighting typically signifies the proximity of a supernatural entity. When an onibi is observed in the vicinity of a graveyard, it is traditionally interpreted as the soul of a departed individual making a return.

Source: Yoda, *Yurei Attack*, 179

onryo

Variation: goryō ("honorable ghost")

The onryo, a form of yōkai from Japanese folklore, is created when an individual succumbs to an untimely or unnatural death, such as dying in an accident, falling victim to treachery, or losing their life in warfare. If the deceased experienced intense anger or fury due to their abruptly shortened existence, their spirit does not transition into the afterlife. Instead, it continues to dwell at the site of their death, seeking retribution on unsuspecting individuals who happen to pass by if the entity responsible for their untimely death remains inaccessible. Onryo are single-minded entities that persist until their wrath has been appeased and revenge has been exacted.

Assisting an onryo instills a sense of *on*, or indebtedness, within the spirit, subsequently rendering it harmless. The spirit then endeavors to reciprocate the benevolence shown to it. Under certain conditions, the onryo may become reliant on its human benefactor, evolving into a source of annoyance.

Sources: Brown, *Complete Idiot's Guide to the Paranormal*, 33–4; Kalland, *Facing the Spirits*, 7

otgiruru (ot-GOO-roo)

Variation: OWENGA

According to the folkloric beliefs of the Herero community in Namibia, Africa, an evil sorcerer can, upon death, reincarnate as a vampiric entity known as an otgiruru. This being, bearing resemblance to an ordinary dog, wanders harmlessly in the village until it finds itself unobserved. At this point, it calls out, and any individual responding to this summons meets a fatal end at the hands of the otgiruru, who consumes their blood and soft tissue organs.

Additional sources suggest that the sorcerer reemerges as a ghost or spirit due to their refusal to acknowledge their death. Using their indomitable will, they create a new form for themselves, utilizing dirt and offal, with the form taking the shape of a dog, although, on rare occasions, they will create a human form. This entity targets solitary individuals and steers clear of gatherings comprising two or more people. By feigning injury and limping whimpering to a shadowy or lonely place, it tricks compassionate individuals into following it to secluded locations; there the unsuspecting helper becomes the next victim of the otgiruru. The only method to destroy this horrific creation involves immobilizing it with a spear and subsequently dismembering it into countless fragments, thereby destroying the constructed body and shattering the sorcerer's soul.

Sources: Maberry, *They Bite!*, 96–7; MacDougall, *Vampire Slayers' Field Guide to the Undead*, 655; Masters, *Natural History of the Vampire*, 48; Silver, *Vampire Film*, 18; Volta, *The Vampire*, 152

ovengua (ov-in-GUAY)

Variations: owang, oweng, OWENGA

Originating from Guinea, Africa, the vampiric spirit known as the ovengua is deeply rooted in local folklore. It is believed that upon the death of a malevolent sorcerer, his skeletal remains escape from their burial site one by one, collecting in a secluded location. Once all bones have gathered, they undergo a process of self-assembly, resulting in the formation of an ovengua—a skeletal, spectral entity equipped with large hooks instead of hands.

The ovengua adopts a nocturnal lifestyle, taking refuge in caves during daylight hours and roaming through forests under the cover of darkness. It targets solitary travelers, attempting to possess them. In the event of a successful possession, the ovengua kills its prey and then reanimates the corpse for its personal use. The only known method to destroy the ovengua requires first waiting until it has claimed a body. Once this occurs, the possessed body must be captured and incinerated, reducing it to ashes.

Sources: Du Chaillu, *King Mombo*, 79–83; Wood, *Natural History of Man*, 572; Wood, *Uncivilized Races of Men*, 513

owenga (oh-WING-ah)

Variation: owang

In Guinea, Africa, a particular kind of vampiric entity, known as an owenga, is believed to originate from individuals who died due to profound heartbreak. This REVENANT will remain confined in its grave, meticulously plotting and strategizing out its revenge. It only emerges once a comprehensive plan has been devised and decided upon. Upon its rise, the owenga presents itself as a humanoid figure with a singular, bloodshot eye. Every action it takes is solely focused on exacting revenge, causing harm only to those who are integral to fulfilling its vengeful intentions. It remains undeterred in its mission and can only be destroyed if captured and incinerated in its grave.

It is further suggested that an owenga may also arise from the death of a sorcerer or an individual who led a morally reprehensible life. These individuals arise from their grave as vampiric revenants, preying upon the inhabitants of their former village. This variant of owenga is considered indestructible but can potentially be pacified through blood offerings. The blood of female animals, particularly those that have never given birth, is typically employed for this purpose. This offering is usually placed in a wooden bowl and left outside dwellings during the night.

On occasion, the vampire accepts the blood offering, leaving the village undisturbed. If it is displeased by the quality or quantity of the offering, however, it retaliates by unleashing lethal diseases throughout the village. If the blood offered is accidentally spilled and not promptly cleaned up, the vampire returns with increased strength. Consequently, the local inhabitants of Guinea have developed the practice of immediately sanitizing any spilled blood and incinerating objects stained with blood. Adherence to this custom often results in generations of a village remaining free from vampire attacks.

Sources: Maberry, *Vampire Universe*, 244; Maberry, *They Bite!*, 97; MacDougall, *Vampire Slayers' Field Guide to the Undead*, 655; Masters, *Natural History of Vampires*, 48; Volta, *The Vampire*, 152

pacu pati (PA-coo PA-tee)

Variations: Lords of Herds, Lords of Mischief Making, Masters of Human Cattle, mmbyu, pacupati, PISACHA

Originating from Indian folklore, the pacu pati ("masters of the herd") represents a category of vampiric revenants; they are typically found in cemeteries and at the sites of executions. These entities exhibit characteristics akin to GHOULS as they partake in the consumption of human flesh. Their creation is attributed to the death and resurrection of immoral men.

The pacu pati are by nature malevolent and lack all amicability. They assault their victims through possession, subsequently animating the corpses. Despite their reputation as instigators of mischief, leading to their designation as the Lords of Mischief Making, there are instances where the pacu pati can be persuaded to heal individuals of ailments.

Sources: Clothey, *Many Faces of Murukan*, 92–4; Cuppiramaniyan, Philosophical Heritage of the Tamils, 16–17; Forlong, *Faiths of Man*, 401

p'ai (PIE)

Variation: P'O

Per Japanese spiritual doctrine, the p'ai represents one of the two souls believed to inhabit every living individual. This soul is present from the fetal stage and remains until the final moments following death, being the last soul to depart the deceased body. Typically, this soul becomes active in circumstances where an individual meets a violent end, such as by suicide or drowning.

Should the p'ai of an individual possess significant strength, it can utilize the body to realize its desires, thereby reanimating the corpse. When this occurs, the entity is referred to as a CH'ING SHIH, distinguished from a p'ai by its serrated teeth, elongated claws, and luminescent glow. The energy of the p'ai is insufficient to enable the animated corpse to extricate itself from its grave, however. Therefore, even in cases of possession, conducting proper burial rites and ensuring the body's interment will maintain its state of rest and confinement within the ground.

Sources: Davis, *Myths and Legends of Japan*, 226; Heinze, *Tham Khwan*, 37–40; Kuhn, *Soulstealers*, 96–7; Rivière, *Tantrik Yoga*, 92

palasik

In the folklore that originates from the Minangkabau people of Sumatra Island, there exists a particular species of creature known as the palasik. This entity is imbued with vampiric qualities and primarily targets children and infants.

Appearances can be deceiving, as the palasik has the capability to blend in with ordinary individuals. It possesses, however, an extraordinary ability to detach its head from its body, facilitating nocturnal flights in search of its next victim.

A palasik assault on a child manifests in several distinct symptoms. The child may experience diarrhea and exhibit an abnormal enlargement of the stomach. A noticeable odor may emanate from the fontanel, which is the membrane-covered gap in the cranium often referred to as the "soft spot." Additional signs include an overall appearance of frailty and eyes that appear watery.

To shield their offspring from the potential harm inflicted by a palasik, mothers are required to procure a specific set of amulets, referred to as *tangka palasik*. These amulets are crafted by a specialist known as a *dukun tangka palasik*. Both the mother and child must wear these amulets as a protective measure.

Source: Sanday, *Women at the Center*, 111, 258

pelesit (pa-LIS-it)

In the folklore originating from Malaysia, there exists a vampiric entity known as the pelesit ("spirit devil"). This creature is not naturally occurring but is rather a product of magic, conjured by a witch to serve as her familiar.

The creation process of the pelesit is intricate and often requires multiple attempts. The witch must venture into the forest on a night with a full moon, position herself with her back towards the moon, face a hill, and then vocalize the necessary incantations to capture her own shadow. Upon successful completion of this ritual, an apparition of a child materializes and protrudes its tongue. The witch must swiftly seize the tongue, causing the disappearance of the child. Subsequently, the tongue undergoes a transformation into a small imp, the pelesit. An alternative version of the spell involves the witch extracting the tongue from the corpse of a firstborn child, whose mother was also a firstborn and was interred at a crossroads upon her death.

Like many familiars, the pelesit necessitates a particular diet to sustain its existence. The witch must feed it a mixture of blood from her fourth finger and saffron rice. The pelesit is endowed with the ability to morph into the form of a commonplace house cricket. This disguise is employed when the pelesit is commanded by its witch to afflict the children of a woman suspected by the witch of engaging in an extramarital affair with her husband. The pelesit derives considerable pleasure from this task. It infiltrates the child's body and induces a mysterious illness from within, causing the child to experience seizures and rant incessantly about cats.

While there exists a specific charm that can repel a pelesit, it is rendered ineffective once the individual is already under attack. It is common for a witch who possesses a pelesit familiar to also have a second familiar, known as a *polong* (a type of vampiric creature). These two entities often collaborate in their efforts to torment an individual.

Sources: Folklore Society of Great Britain, *Folklore*, Volume 13, 150–1, 157; Masters, *Natural History of the Vampire*, n.p.; Skeat, *Malay Magic*, 321, 328–30

penangglan (PEN-non-gwen)

Variations: pananggaln, panangglan, penangal, penanggalan, pennanggalan, PONTIANAK

According to Malaysian folklore, there exists a particular type of vampiric entity known as the penangglan; this creature is believed to be created when a woman perishes during childbirth. Another scenario suggests that a penangglan can materialize if a woman engaged in religious prayer is startled by a man to such an extent that she is literally startled to death.

The penangglan exhibits a dual nature. During the day, it can successfully masquerade as an ordinary woman. Come nightfall, however, it undergoes a grotesque transformation where its head detaches from its body and takes flight, with all its internal organs, from the esophagus to the rectum, dangling below. As it embarks on its hunt, it secretes bile so virulent that it causes open sores upon contact with human skin.

The penangglan's preferred victims are children and women in labor. It harbors an intense dislike towards children and derives immense satisfaction from their demise. Upon the birth of a child, the penangglan utters the cry, "*Mangilai!*" In the absence of its preferred prey and driven by extreme hunger, it will reluctantly consume the blood of a man.

Upon returning to its dwelling after a hunt, the penangglan's intestines, bloated with the blood of its victims, are immersed in a vat of vinegar. This process serves to contract the expanded organs, enabling them to fit back into its body.

To deter a penangglan from approaching one's home, it is advised to position the thorny branches of the jeruju plant on the roof. The thorns ensnare the creature's dangling organs, effectively trapping it. Although no confirmed method exists for the destruction of a penangglan, potential strategies involve identifying the penangglan's human guise within the village. Once it leaves its body to hunt, one can intrude into its home and destroy both its body and its vat of vinegar. Consequently, upon its return, the penangglan is unable to resume its human facade as its body no longer exists and the vinegar required to shrink its organs is unavailable.

Sources: Laderman, *Wives and Midwives*, 126–7; Skeat, *Malay Magic*, 325–8; Wright, *Vampires and Vampirism*

phi (PIE)

Variations: phii, phis

In Thailand, the term *phi* is used to collectively refer to spirits or ghosts. The range and diversity of these entities are vast and varied, much like the categories of ghosts, undead, and fay. Among these spirits, a certain, specific vampiric entity known as phi has been documented since pre–Buddhist times in Thailand. This entity is believed to emerge when an individual experiences a sudden death, such as in an accident.

The phi, typically invisible to the human eye, is often found residing in secluded areas in rural locales. It is known to assault people by scratching them to draw blood, which it then laps up. The bite of a phi can induce illness and disease. Certain individuals known as *maw du*, who possess extensive knowledge in occult matters, can provide and create charms that offer protection against attacks from a phi.

In cases where there is an infestation of phi or a particularly dangerous one that proves resistant to these protective charms, the hunting services of a maw du can be sought. They have the ability to either banish or destroy the offending spirit.

Sources: Bastian, *A Journey in Siam*, 158; Blanchard, *Thailand*, 97; Lewis, *Peoples of the Golden Triangle*, 260; Maberry, *Vampire Universe*, 247

phi song nang (pei song nang)

In the cultural context of pre–Buddhist Thailand, there existed a specific type of vampiric spirit known as phi song nang. This spirit is believed to materialize when a woman passes away before she has had the opportunity to marry. The phi song nang presents itself as an attractive woman and embarks on nocturnal hunts seeking handsome men as its prey. It attempts to entice the man to a secluded location with the allure and promise of a sexual indiscretion; once isolated, the being transforms and attacks, draining his blood.

Interestingly, there have been instances where men have employed unconventional tactics such as applying nail polish and wearing women's night attire to bed in an attempt to deceive the phi song nang into mistaking them for women. In a notable incident from the 1980s in Thailand, a phi song nang was held accountable for the proliferation of a mysterious disease that claimed the lives of approximately 230 migrant workers. This disease was referred to as Sudden Unexplained Nocturnal Death Syndrome.

Individuals who professed to have survived these attacks reported experiencing a sudden onset of fear while they were asleep. Upon awakening, they felt a distinct presence in the room. They also described mounting pressure on their chests and found themselves unable to move or vocalize. These symptoms are remarkably similar to those associated with an anomalous licking phenomenon (ALP) attack.

Sources: Bryant, *Handbook of Death*, 99; Graham, *Siam*, 544; Maberry, *Vampire Universe*, 247; MacDougall, *Vampire Slayers' Field Guide to the Undead*, 655; Melton, *Vampire Book*, 602

pijavica (pie-java-CA)

Variations: pijawica, pijawika

In Croatia and Yugoslavia, there exists a type of vampiric REVENANT known as a pijavica ("drinker"); this vampire is typically male and is believed to be created when an individual who has committed an act of incest with his mother passes away. However, this form of vampire can also arise from an individual who was notably malevolent during their lifetime.

The pijavica primarily targets its own family members and descendants, methodically eliminating every individual linked to its family tree until it is stopped. Only after annihilating its entire lineage will it shift its attention to others. Remarkably, the pijavica possesses the ability to identify its own kin, irrespective of the degree of relation.

Characterized by its exceptional speed and strength, the pijavica is also capable of reading minds and possesses the power of suggestion. Unless eradicated through a deliberate act, the pijavica is essentially immortal.

Continuous exposure to direct sunlight or impalement through the chest with hawthorn can lead to the demise of a pijavica, as can incineration. The most effective method to eliminate a pijavica involves decapitation, however, followed by the reburial of the body with the head positioned between its legs.

Sources: Maberry, *They Bite!*, 99–100; MacDougall, *Vampire Slayers' Field Guide to the Undead*, 655; Ralston, *Songs of the Russian People*, 410; Ronay, *Truth about Dracula*, 22; Senn, *Were-wolf and Vampire in Romania*, 66

pisacas

Variations: kravyad, picacas, pisachi (feminine form), pisac, pisakas, pishachas, pishashas

In the folklore of the Himalayas, pisacas are perceived as the ghosts of individuals who have met a tragic end, like being caught in a landslide.

In the context of Hindu mythology, pisacas are interpreted as remnants of elementary or human spirits, and they materialize as a phenomenon known as a will-o'-the-wisp (see CORPSE CANDLE). They exhibit heightened activity on full moon nights.

If pisacas inhabit a residence, such as a home, it necessitates their forceful eviction by an exorcist. When they possess an individual, it is believed that they start to consume the person's body from the inside, causing gradual deterioration.

Sources: Oldenberg, *Religion of the Veda*, 132, 133, 288; Sidky, *Haunted by the Archaic Shaman*, 128

pisacha (pa-SITCH-ah)

Variations: hatu-dhana, kravyad, pischca, pishacas, yaksha, yatu-dhana

In India, the word *pisacha* ("bloodthirsty savages" and "eaters of raw flesh") is a collective term used to describe all ghosts and vampires. There exists a vampiric entity known as a pisacha, which is believed to originate from human vice or as a result of Brahma's anger.

This being is characterized by its grotesque appearance and its preference for feeding on human corpses. The pisacha has been known to prey on inebriated women, an act that is typically fatal due to its swift and formidable nature; additionally, its blood contains a contact poison. Pisachas are typically found in cemeteries and at crossroads, and unless they wish to be discovered, they remain undetectable. Interestingly, they can sometimes be persuaded to cure individuals suffering from leprosy, a disease they are known to propagate. They are particularly drawn to engaging conversations, as they are intelligent and generally courteous entities, when not attacking individuals.

In the event of a pisacha attack, it can be temporarily deterred by dousing it with holy water, but this measure is short-lived, as the pisacha is likely to return once it dries off. In the meantime, the victim should presume that they have contracted leprosy or some other severe disease. The individual must then proceed to the crossroads with offerings of rice and conduct a ceremony each night until the pisacha appears. Despite the pisacha's desire to consume the rice, the victim should only offer it in return for the pisacha curing them of their disease. The definitive method to permanently destroy a pisacha involves burning it to ash.

Sources: Agrawala, *India as Known to Panini*, 447–8; Bkah-Hgyur, *Tibetan Tales*, 23–5; Crooke, *Introduction to the Popular Religion*, 153; Wright, *Vampires and Vampirism*

plakavac

The plakavac is a creature of vampiric nature, originating from the Slavic folklore in the Herzegovina region. It's described as being roughly the size of a frog, and, traditionally, it is believed to be created when a mother murders her child by strangulation. This creature, the plakavac, is said to crawl about, condemning its mother who brought it into existence, only to later end its life in such a brutal manner.

Furthermore, the word *plakavac* has additional meanings; it can be used to denote a child who passes away without receiving baptism or when a mother terminates the life of her own illegitimate child. The latter scenario carries a superstition within the folklore that such an act would cause the village to experience a devastating hailstorm, resulting in the destruction of their crops.

Source: Filipovic, *Among the People*, 176

platnik (PLAT-nic)

Variations: platenki ("fleshed out"), plotenik, plutenik, plutnik

The platnik, hailing from Bulgarian folklore, is a vampiric entity with a distinct life cycle. Following burial, the spirit remains in the grave for the initial nine days of its spectral existence. During this period, as the spirit matures, the ground above its grave begins to sink in. After this phase, the platnik ascends from its grave as a spirit and initiates a 40-day assault against its kin. In its spectral form, it appears as the silhouette of a dog, hen, or human. The platnik's attacks are varied, spanning from dish-breaking to livestock scattering at night, property defacement, and physical assaults.

To deter a platnik while it's still in its spectral state, one must utilize the objects it fears, namely animal skulls, fire, iron, light, and wolves. The presence of these items will frighten it enough to compel the platnik to vacate the area. Unfortunately, only a lightning strike can destroy it, which is an unlikely occurrence. An alternative strategy, which has been said to work on occasion, involves exhuming the body on a Saturday and piercing the cadaver with a red-hot poker.

If the spectral vampire succeeds in consuming sufficient blood without being destroyed, it transforms into a full-fledged, corporeal vampire REVENANT, known as a platnik, after its 40-day rampage. It now has the ability to blend in with normal humans, save for having red eyes and no fingernails. Moreover, it gains the theriomorphic capability to shape-shift into a dog or wolf. Its new body doesn't possess bones but is composed of a substance akin to cartilage.

Upon acquiring its new body, the platnik's first act is to target its widow, murdering her in broad daylight. Once she has died, the platnik departs from its hometown to establish a new life as far away from its former community as possible. It will settle in a place where its true identity as a REVENANT remains unknown, marry, and have children. These offspring, known as *vampirdzhii*, are born vampires.

If the platnik's true nature is revealed, it can be easily destroyed. A simple cut will result in its death as it bleeds out, unable to staunch the flood of its blood. The blood, referred to as *pixtija*, is a thick, dark, jellylike substance.

Sources: Georgieva, *Bulgarian Mythology*, 98; Lecouteux, *History of Vampires*; Mac-Dermott, *Bulgarian Folk Customs*, 66, 67

p'o

Variation: P'AI

The Chinese concept of dual souls in human beings traces back to the Chou Dynasty (Zhou Dynasty), which existed from 1046 to 256 BCE. The first soul, called the p'o, is believed to enter a human during fetal development. It is associated with the yin and represents a person's physical existence. Usually, the p'o descends into the underworld, also known as the Yellow Springs, after death.

There are exceptions, however. If an individual has a particularly potent p'o or if a deceased body is exposed to sunlight or moonlight, the p'o might not descend as expected. Instead, it can remain, reanimate the body, and transform it into what is known as a REVENANT. This REVENANT is used by the p'o to satisfy its own needs. When this occurs, it results in the creation of a vampiric entity referred to as a CH'ING SHIH.

Sources: Heinze, *Tham Khwan*, 37–40; Kuhn, *Soulstealers*, 96–7; Watson, *Death Ritual*, 8–9, 56, 193; Werne, *China of the Chinese*, 231–3

pocong

Variations: kain kafan, hantu pochong, pochang

The pocong from Indonesian folklore is the manifestation of a deceased individual's soul, said to be trapped within their burial shroud. This REVENANT is identified by distinct auditory and olfactory cues—a ringing sound in one's ears coupled with the foul odor of decay. Dogs too, it is believed, react to the presence of a pocong.

As per traditional Indonesian customs pertaining to death and burial, the departed individual's body is wrapped in a precise length of white cotton cloth. The fabric is secured around the feet, head, and neck with knots. It is believed that as long as these knots remain intact, the soul is unable to depart from the body. These knots are usually untied just before the burial. If the knots remain, however, the body is said to rise from its grave after 40 days, signaling a plea for the release of its soul.

The appearance of a pocong is contingent on the extent of the corpse's decomposition. A recently deceased individual may manifest as a pocong with a pallid face and wide, open eyes, whereas a body that has been interred for a significant length of time may resemble a SKELETON. It is widely suggested that a pocong is bound to a hopping movement until the knots binding its feet are untied.

The behavior of a pocong is inconsistent across narratives. Some accounts portray them as benign spirits seeking liberation from their shroud or prayers for their peace, while others depict them as unpredictable and terrifying revenants. They are reported to primarily reveal themselves to family members responsible for untying their burial shroud knots and individuals with whom they have unfinished business.

A unique attribute of the pocong is their capacity to traverse through solid objects, and there are anecdotal references to their ability to teleport instantaneously between locations. They are predominantly encountered in their former residences and in close proximity to banana trees.

Unlike other undead entities, pocongs are said to congregate in colonies, varying in size from a dozen to thousands. Most narratives, however, typically recount encounters with a solitary REVENANT.

Sources: Bush, *Asian Horror Encyclopedia*, 151; Khairunnisa, *A Book of Indonesian Ghosts*, n.p.; Torchia, *Indonesian Idioms and Expressions*, 163

pontianak (PONT-ah-nook)

Variations: buo, kuntilanak, MATI-ANAK, matianak, pontipinnak

The pontianak, as depicted in the folklore of Bangladesh, Indonesia, Malaysia, and Pakistan, is a demon with vampiric attributes. The transformation into a pontianak is believed to occur when a woman passes away during childbirth, in her virgin state, or as a casualty of a pontianak assault. This unfortunate state of being can be circumvented, however, by adhering to specific burial rites that include placing glass beads in the deceased's mouth and an egg under each armpit and inserting needles into the palms of the hands and soles of the feet.

In its disguise as a human woman, a pontianak is discernible only by a hole at the back of its neck and its distinct frangipani-like fragrance. Its presence is usually signaled by a sound akin to a baby's cry.

Primarily nocturnal, the pontianak leaves its dwelling in a banana tree and assumes the form of a bird. In this avian guise, it embarks on its hunt for prey. While it is not particularly selective, it exhibits a preference for the blood of infants and expectant mothers, likely due to its resentment for never having experienced motherhood. Upon identifying a target, the pontianak reverts to its human form, detaches its head from its body, and flies back to its prey, leaving its organs to dangle below. It is known to violently extract unborn children from their mothers, consuming them immediately.

Interestingly, the pontianak exhibits a fear unique among vampire-like entities. It is said to retreat in fright from anyone who manages to extract a strand of hair from its head. Moreover, if a nail is inserted into the hole in its neck, it transforms into an attractive woman and remains so until the nail is removed. These vulnerabilities provide some solace given the absence of known methods to destroy a pontianak.

Sources: Laderman, *Wives and Midwives*, 126–7; MacDougall, *Vampire Slayers' Field Guide to the Undead*, 655; McHugh, *Hantu-Hantu*, 74; Skeat, *Malay Magic*, 326–8

porcelnik (pour-SELL-nick)

In the folklore of Russia, a specific category of human sorcerer exists known as a porcelnik ("harmer"); they engage in activities associated with vampires. Upon the demise of a porcelnik, it is of the utmost importance that their body be incinerated until it is reduced to ashes. The pyre used for this purpose must be constructed from aspen wood. Failure to adhere to this procedure will result in the body resurrecting as a type of vampire-like creature referred to as an ERETIK. This creature is a REVENANT.

Source: Melton, *Vampire Book*, 525

poroniec

The poroniec, originating from Slavic mythology, is an entity characterized by its malevolent and antagonistic nature. It is believed that the creation of a poroniec is linked to children who were stillborn. Additionally, it is also possible to inadvertently create one of these beings from the improperly interred remains of infants who tragically succumbed to death during their early years. This underlines the significance of appropriate burial rites in preventing the occurrence of such unfavorable entities.

Source: Instytut Historii Kultury Materialnej, *Ethnologia Polona*, Volumes 10–1, 91, 103, 105

preta (par-EE-ta)

Variation: hungry ghost

The preta ("morbid"), is a REVENANT spirit with vampiric attributes as described in Indian folklore. It manifests as a recently deceased body, characterized by a pendulous stomach paired incongruously with a small mouth that is only a tiny opening. This entity is believed to roam the earth in a constant state of disorientation and insatiable hunger for a specific substance, such as human blood.

In the perspective of the Buddhist faith, this condition of the preta is viewed as a just retribution for individuals who exhibited compulsive, corrupt, deceitful, false, greedy, or excessively desirous behavior while alive.

Despite being imperceptible to the human eye, these entities are thought to maintain their human form, albeit with protruding bellies, elongated thin necks, preserved skin akin to mummies, and slender limbs. They are typically said to be wandering in desolate environments like deserts and wastelands.

Sources: Crooke, *Popular Religion and Folk-Lore of Northern India*, 153; Danielou, *Myths and Gods of India*, 27, 213, 301, 311; Turner, *Dictionary of Ancient Deities*, 184

pricolic (PRAY-co-lic)

Hailing from Romania, a pricolic is a type of vampiric REVENANT; its creation occurs with the death of a child prior to baptism. Also, an individual who deliberately burns a porridge spoon or sweeps dust from their dwelling towards the setting sun will, upon death, join the collective of pricolici.

Upon its resurrection, a pricolic initially targets its own family members before proceeding to other victims. In instances where an individual is suspected of being this particular type of vampire, it becomes necessary to exhume their body. Confirmation of their vampiric nature is established if the corpse is discovered face-down in its grave with traces of blood on its lips.

While no established method exists to destroy this species of vampire, there is a preventative measure to halt its murderous spree. This involves extracting some of the blood from the vampire's lips and smearing it on the surviving family members, effectively shielding them from the pricolic's attacks.

Source: Melton, *The Vampire Book*, n.p.

pryccolitch

The pryccolitch, originating from the folklore of Romania, is a formidable creature, as it is a combination of the raw destructive force of a werewolf and the cunning of a vampire. During its life, the pryccolitch undergoes a gradual transformation into a werewolf, as it feeds on flesh. Then, upon its death, it resurrects from its grave as a REVENANT vampire that is bent on the consumption of human blood.

It is believed that a curse laid upon a person, even in jest—especially if laid by an aggrieved person or a witch—can transform a person into a vampire. This theme has been explored in many folktales where casual curses in jest have led to individuals turning into these lethal entities.

The metamorphosis into this vampire begins with the individual's soul either becoming frigid or entirely departing the body. This void allows for the occupation of malevolent spirits, who then serve as mentors to the newly transformed monster, educating it about its nature and assisting it in its reign of murder and terror. The spirits guide the pryccolitch in selecting its victims and constantly remind it to proceed cautiously and deliberately.

The pryccolitch can only morph into its monstrous form when concealed from human sight. Although the transformation process is rapid, it occurs with a considerable amount of pain. Once transmuted into a wolflike figure, the vampire has the liberty to hunt and kill without restraint.

Source: Maberry, *They Bite!*, 100–1

rabisu

In Akkadian mythology, vampiric spectral entities known as rabisu ("evil fiends") are believed to be malevolent spirits and are said to be predators lurking in the shadows. They prey on unassuming humans and leech off their vital, life-giving energy. It is said that individuals gifted with a heightened sense of the supernatural can discern the presence of a rabisu due to a sudden prickling sensation in their hair.

Intriguingly, the rabisu are not solitary hunters but tend to collaborate with other demonic species, such as the labartu, or various storm demons, participating in a form of cooperative predation.

The term *rabisu* also holds significance in another context, serving as the title for a high-ranking official—a preliminary court examining magistrate—which was second only to a judge in terms of authority. Over time, this title became demonized by the general populace, due to the immense power these officials wielded, which was almost akin to that of lesser divinities and therefore warranted serious regard.

A striking parallel exists between these officials and the spectral rabisu—the potential for both benevolent and malevolent actions. It was not an uncommon practice for many demons to have rabisu prefixed to their names, adding to this duality.

Sources: Barmash, *Homicide in the Biblical World*, 15–6; Ford, *Maskim Hul*, 107, 228–9

radiant boy

Variation: kindermorderinn

In European folklore, radiant boy is a spectral figure, characterized by its nocturnal appearance and luminescent quality; it is believed to be the ghost of a young boy who tragically met his end at the hands of his own mother. Encountering such a specter is traditionally associated with negative connotations, ranging from an impending streak of misfortune to serving as a psychopomp—an ominous signifier of an impending death akin to that of the radiant boy himself.

Certain narratives depict these apparitions as possessing a sinister disposition, pursuing individuals, or enticing them into hazardous marshlands. In the Germanic context, this particular class of phantoms is referred to as *kindermorderinn*.

Sources: Maberry, *Vampire Universe*, 253; Ogden, *Complete Idiot's Guide to Ghosts and Hauntings*, 39

rawa mugi

Variation: rawa ("spirit")

In the local lore of the Tsembaga community in New Guinea, there is reference to entities known as rawa mugi ("red spirits"). These are considered the returning spirits or ghosts of clan members who have lost their lives in tribal conflicts. Their presence is often described with terms like "cold" and "wet." In the ecosystem of Tsembaga, these spirits are associated with marsupials and other wildlife found in upland areas.

On the other hand, there are spirits from rival clans known as *tukump rakai* or *rawa awua* ("spirit other"). These spirits are believed to haunt and inflict harm and are thus viewed as highly dangerous. These entities are generally encountered in regions of higher altitudes.

Sources: Bayliss-Smith, *Subsistence and Survival*, 398, 399; Healey, *Maring Hunters and Traders*, 46; Jones, *Evil in Our Midst*, 211

rawa tukump (rh-wah too-kump)

Variation: rawa ("spirit")

In the traditional folklore of the Tsembaga community in New Guinea, entities known as rawa tukump ("spirit mold" or "spirits of rot") are believed to be malevolent spirits of individuals who tragically died due to accidents or illnesses.

Upon their return from death, these spirits are said to haunt the living, even going so far as to possess their bodies. This possession is associated with a specific type of illness that the host contracts, which can prove fatal unless an exorcism is successfully performed to rid the body of the spirit.

Sources: Bayliss-Smith, *Subsistence and Survival*, 398; Healey, *Maring Hunters and Traders*, 46; Jones, *Evil in Our Midst*, xiii, 211

revenant (rev-a-NINT)

The word *revenant* is derived from the French verb *revenir*, which translates to "to return." This label essentially refers to an entity that has made a return, perhaps after a prolonged period of absence or even post-death. Historically, the term was synonymous with the word *ghost*.

In the context of vampire folklore, a revenant denotes any creature or being that has experienced death, subsequently risen from its grave, and returned to an existence among the living, which is often characterized as *unlife* or UNDEATH. It's important to note, however, that while many types of vampires qualify as revenants, not all revenants are vampires. The category of revenants also includes zombies and certain types of ghosts, specifically those capable of assuming a solid form.

Revenants are typically depicted as undead human corpses in solid form, sporting pale complexions and visible signs of decay. They are often portrayed as possessing considerable strength and exhibiting a vicious nature. Interestingly, it is also possible for animals to transform into revenants.

Sources: Ashley, *Complete Book of Vampires*; Barber, *Vampires, Burial, and Death*, 85; Day, *Vampires*, 194; Guiley, *Encyclopedia of Ghosts and Spirits*, 417; MacDougall, *Vampire Slayers' Field Guide to the Undead*, 551

roaring bull of Bagbury, the

The roaring bull of Bagbury, a character from British folklore, is said to be a solid-form ghost. This entity was once an infamous squire who managed Bagbury Manor, a farm situated between the churches of Hyssington and Snead.

Different versions of the legend provide varying accounts of the squire's transformation into a bull. One rendition suggests that a member of the household staff wished for the squire to be turned into a bull for an unexplained reason. However, another version puts forth the idea that the squire, due to his extreme wickedness during his lifetime, returned from death as a massive, furious, REVENANT bull.

Regardless of the specifics of its origin, the story consistently portrays the bull as a menace that terrorizes the local countryside. It required several men and many days to finally capture the beast and confine it within the Hyssington church. There, 12 clergymen encircled the supernatural creature and performed a ritual known as "reading him down," perhaps a sort of exorcism, which resulted in the bull gradually reducing in physical size and mass.

Ultimately, the creature became small enough to be confined in a snuff box, which was then buried. The exact location where the snuff box was buried varies across different versions of the tale, with potential locations including the Red Sea and beneath the Bagbury Bridge.

Sources: Allardice, *Myths, Gods and Fantasy*, 184; Briggs, *Encyclopedia of Fairies*, 341; Jones, *Collections Historical and Archaeological*, Volume 34, 201

rolang (ROLL-ing)

Variation: ro-lang

In Tibetan mystic tradition, a practitioner known as a *ngagspa* can execute a highly specific and perilous spell ritual solely to obtain a magical artifact. This ritual's purpose is to create a vampiric REVENANT referred to as a rolang ("corpse who stands up"). The motivation for creating this dangerous species of vampire is to acquire its tongue, deemed a potent magical artifact.

To perform the ritual, the ngagspa secludes himself in a room with a corpse he has obtained. He positions himself on top of the corpse, focusing his mind solely on the continuous recitation of the magical incantation. Eventually, he places his lips onto the corpse's lips, securing the corpse's arms with his own.

At some point, the corpse, now transformed into a rolang, will attempt to rise and escape. The ngagspa must prevent this, maintaining lip contact with the rolang. Should even a brief separation occur, the spell would be disrupted, leading to the ngagspa losing control over the vampire. Consequently, the vampire would wreak havoc in the village, annihilating everyone in its path through brutal dismemberment. Its touch alone is lethal, so it would leave only a devastated village strewn with corpses in its wake.

It is believed that only a handful of lamas possess the knowledge of the magical rites required to subdue the rolang, compelling it to revert to its original state of a harmless corpse.

If the ngagspa can sustain the spell and physical contact long enough, however, the tongue of the rolang will extend out of its mouth into the mouth of the ngagspa, who then must bite down hard enough to sever the tongue. Upon success, the rolang falls dead, leaving the ngagspa in possession of a formidable and hard-earned magical artifact.

Sources: Cuevas, *Travels in the Netherworld*, 95–103; David-Neel, *With Mystics and Magicians in Tibet*, 127–9; Guiley, *Encyclopedia of Ghosts and Spirits*, 422; Knapp, *Women, Myth, and the Feminine Principle*, 9–10; Mead, *Primitive Heritage*, 441–3

rolling calf

In Jamaican folklore, there exists a creature known as a rolling calf. This entity is classified as a type of duppy, or ghost, which is said to frequent remote hillsides and secluded locations with the intention of instilling fear in travelers. The rolling calf is typically depicted as resembling a young bovine with glowing eyes, accompanied by the sound of clanking chains.

This creature is known to pursue its victims and, should it succeed in capturing them, the individual is killed and subsequently transformed into another rolling calf. Generally, a rolling calf is believed to be the result of the transformation of a man who, upon his death, was deemed too virtuous for hell but not sufficiently righteous for heaven.

In the event of being pursued by a rolling calf, the only known means of escape is to ascend a hill, as these creatures are incapable of uphill movement. Additionally, it's noted that rolling calves harbor a fear of the moon.

Sources: American Folklore Society, in *Journal of American Folklore*, Volume 7, 296–7; Spinner, *Living Age*, Volume 206, 161

rusalka (roo-SAW-ka)

Variations: mokosh, RUSALKY, samovily

In the Republic of Slovenia, folklore speaks of a vampiric entity known as a rusalka ("shore"). This creature is considered part of the Unseelie Court, believed to be a weaver of fate and a regulator of seasons. Its existence is said to result from the death of a child prior to baptism, or when an adolescent dies a virgin.

Descriptions of the rusalka exhibit regional variations. Some portrayals depict it as a young girl on the cusp of womanhood, adorned with long, green hair decorated with poppies, exuding an aura of beauty. In other regions, the rusalka is represented wearing an elegant gown or tunic, or barely covered by strategically placed leaves. Alternative accounts liken the rusalka to a drowned corpse or a mermaid. The male equivalent, known as a *vodyanik*, is described as a strikingly handsome young man, with the peculiar characteristic of the left side of his body always being wet. Regardless of region or gender, the rusalka consistently appears attractive and is typically found near bodies of water.

Rusalka are frequently sighted in ponds or rivers during full moon nights. They are known to kill cattle and horses that venture too close to the water's edge. Moreover, they are said to entice handsome men into the water, seeking a partner to spend the night with. These encounters rarely end well for the man, however, as the rusalka drains him of his youth and life, often forgetting in its fervor that humans require air to breathe. Yet, the few men who have survived such encounters claim that the rusalka's love is worth dying for. Occasionally, a rusalka may desire a child and will snatch one from the water's edge, leading to the child's inevitable drowning in the rusalka's underwater dwelling.

Rusalka are known to fiercely guard their water territories, doing everything in their power to drown anyone attempting to bathe in their waters or near their favored dancing spots. To avoid a rusalka's attack, it is suggested to tie ribbons and scarves to its sacred trees and offer eggs as gifts. It is believed that rusalka cannot bear the sight of a crucifix and will hastily retreat upon hearing prayers.

Prior to the arrival of Christianity in the region, it is likely that the rusalka was originally perceived as a singular entity named Mokosh, the goddess of bounty, fertility, and moisture, who provided protection for women during their work.

Sources: Hubbs, *Mother Russia*, 24–35; Ivanits, *Russian Folk Belief*, 75–80; Mack, *Field Guide to Demons*, 19; Willis, *World Mythology*, 211–3

sampiro (sam-PEER-oh)

Variation: LIOGAT

In Albanian folklore, there is a type of vampiric REVENANT known as a sampiro. Its origin is associated with individuals of Turkish descent, irrespective of their virtue or moral conduct during their lifetime. Furthermore, this fate could also befall any Albanian who had engaged in activities considered unnatural, such as bestiality, homosexuality, prostitution, transvestism, or heterosexual relations with a Turkish individual.

Other factors leading to this transformation include participating in Muslim religious services, consuming meat handled by a Turk, or exhibiting habitual dishonesty or professional thievery during life.

The sampiro is said to return from the grave three days after its burial, with its shroud enveloping its body and high-heeled shoes adorning its feet. Its eyes are large and exude a bright glow. Curiously, a small quantity of dirt from its grave is always found in its navel.

The sampiro emerges nightly from its grave, displaying a particular preference for foggy nights, which enhance the brightness of its eyes to an intensity comparable to car headlights. Upon identifying a victim, the sampiro follows behind them, making distinct "kissing" sounds that can be heard clearly over the clicking of its high-heeled shoes. When it eventually attacks, it extracts a survivable amount of blood from the person before hastily retreating on its heels. Victims experience fatigue and weakness, with repeated assaults potentially resulting in death.

On nights when the sampiro does not feed or has already done so, it ventures to the countryside, peering into homes. Its gaze alone can disseminate a disease to which infants are particularly vulnerable. Its time outside of town is limited, however, due to the animosity of wolves, which persistently pursue it upon detection. If the sampiro survives a wolf attack but sustains a mangled limb, it returns to its grave, never to rise again. Conversely, if an attempt on its life by humans fails, the sampiro becomes notably vengeful and seeks out those directly involved to kill them violently.

During the day, the sampiro rests in its grave, which is easily identifiable due to the perpetually loose soil resulting from its nocturnal activities and a hovering blue ball of light resembling a CORPSE CANDLE. The recommended method of extermination involves exhuming the body during the day when the sampiro is immobile and driving a yew wood stake through its heart with a single blow.

Sources: Abbott, *Macedonian Folklore*, 216; Ronay, *The Dracula Myth*, 22; Summers, *Werewolf in Lore and Legend*, 149; Taylor, *Primitive Culture*, 311

servant of Pope John XXI, the

Within the annals of papal history, Pope John XXI (1276–1277), the only individual of Portuguese origin to ascend to the papacy and the sole physician to do so, was reputed to have an interest in magic and alchemy. His intellectual pursuits extended beyond his ecclesiastical duties, as evidenced by his tenure at the University of Paris prior to his papal appointment. One particular anecdote attributed to Pope John XXI suggests that he constructed a small humanoid figure, which subsequently served him. This entity was believed to possess limited cognitive abilities and lacked the capacity for speech making it perhaps a GOLEM or HOMUNCULUS.

Source: Curran, *Man-Made Monsters*, 100–1

shui gui

In Chinese folklore, there exists a spectral entity known as a shui gui ("water ghost"). This entity is understood to be the disembodied spirit of an individual who died by drowning and continues to inhabit the site of their death. These water ghosts are notorious for their propensity to drag unsuspecting victims beneath the water's surface and take possession of their bodies.

This particular category of ghosts presents a significant threat due to the belief associated with their existence. It is held that individuals who meet their end by drowning or hanging are unable to achieve rebirth unless they secure a substitute, another person who undergoes a similar fate of either drowning or hanging in their stead.

Sources: Dupler, *Death Explained*, 43; Eberhard, *Dictionary of Chinese Symbols*, n.p.

shura

Within the Buddhist Japanese mythological framework, there exists a distinct category of spectral entities known as shura. These are understood to be the restless spirits of departed warriors. Manifesting as intimidating entities, these warrior spirits are believed to be condemned to an unending cycle of conflict and turmoil, reflecting their martial past in their spectral existence.

Sources: Drazen, *Gathering of Spirits*, 85; Mass, *Origins of Japan's Medieval World*, 206

shuten-doji (SHOE-tin dodge-EE)

According to Japanese mythology, there exists a frightful, grotesquely disfigured vampiric entity known as the shuten-doji ("sake-drinking lad"). This creature possesses elongated, clawed fingers that it uses to skillfully play the flute, producing a captivating melody that induces a trancelike state in anyone who hears it.

Under the influence of this hypnotic music, the individual falls prey to the shuten-doji, which then uses its long claws to kill them and consumes their blood. The shuten-doji is typically solitary, tending to avoid even the company of similar entities.

Despite its extraordinary ability to play the flute and its lethal claws, the physical strength and reflexes of the shuten-doji are equivalent to those of an average human being.

Sources: *Transactions of the Asiatic Society of Japan*, 67; Marra, *Japanese Hermeneutics*, 129–30, 140–1; Shirane, *Traditional Japanese Literature*, 1123; Tanaka, *New Times in Modern Japan*, 58–60

simulacrum

Variation: simulacra

The simulacrum ("likeness") is a creature that bears strong resemblance to the concept of the homunculus of medieval alchemy. Often depicted as devoid of independent thought or consciousness, the simulacrum is essentially a representation or imitation of another being. The simulacrum is seen as an artificial construct, but one that only imitates the appearance and attributes of another entity; it possesses no inherent essence or identity of its own and lacks the genuine substance, consciousness, and divine spark that would make it alive.

Source: Curran, *Man-Made Monsters*, 120

skeleton

The undead skeleton is a figure that has permeated mythology and folklore across countless cultures throughout history. As a symbol of death and the afterlife, skeletons are often portrayed as reanimated corpses, devoid of flesh and life yet somehow imbued with a semblance of their former consciousness and intent.

In ancient Roman mythology, reanimated skeletal figures were believed to serve a critical function as protectors of divine entities; specifically, they were considered the sentinels of Dis Pater, god of the underworld, and Hecate, the revered goddess of magic and lunar phenomena.

In Western culture, the image of the undead skeleton can be traced back to the Middle Ages, when it was commonly employed in memento mori artworks designed to remind viewers of their mortality. *Danse macabre* ("the dance of death"), a popular artistic genre during this period, often depicted skeletons dancing with the living, serving as a chilling reminder of the inevitability of death.

In Eastern mythology, particularly in Japanese folklore, there exists the figure of the GASHADOKURO, a giant skeleton formed from the bones of people who died from starvation.

Similarly, in Mexican culture, *Día de los Muertos* ("the Day of the Dead") celebrations prominently feature *calacas*, or skeleton figures, which are often depicted in a more jovial manner, embodying the belief in life after death and the ongoing connection between the living and the deceased.

Despite cultural variations, the common thread that binds these skeletal figures is their embodiment of death and the human fascination with what lies beyond the mortal coil. They serve as a stark reminder of our mortality, while also providing a window into the diverse ways cultures around the world perceive and interpret death.

Sources: Boutland, *Gashadokuro the Giant Skeleton and Other Legendary Creatures of Japan*, 6–12; Carmichael, *The Skeleton at the Feast*, 14–6; Murakami, *Strange Japanese Yokai*, 117; Wolf, *Britannica Concise Encyclopedia*, 509

snake zombies

Situated along the northern coastline of South America, bordering the Caribbean Sea, is the nation of Guyana. In the village of Taushida, the villagers were ruthlessly attacked and often raided by a neighboring tribe. Unable to protect themselves, they sought a solution by turning to their spiritual guide.

The shaman, believed to possess extraordinary powers, called upon a supernatural deity associated with serpents. To communicate with this divine entity, a series of animal sacrifices was conducted. Through these rituals, the shaman was granted the knowledge of how to stop the attacks from the neighboring village; he was advised to create a formidable army of oversize, killer snakes.

The process entailed capturing and killing many young anacondas, followed by arcane chants and spells over their remains. This magical process resulted in the reanimation of the snakes, which were now significantly larger in size and possessed an innate desire to annihilate the tribe's adversaries.

These serpentine soldiers, initially mere feet in length, reportedly grew to an astounding 40 feet. They were instrumental in overcoming the enemy tribe. Such power came at a considerable cost, however. To maintain control over these colossal creatures, it was deemed necessary by the shaman to offer a newborn child as a sacrifice to the snake god annually for two decades.

Source: Redfern, *The Zombie Book*, 270

stigoi (STEE-gway)

Originating from Romanian lore, a stigoi is a type of vampiric REVENANT. This entity is formed when the soul of a deceased person reenters its physical remains, thereby reanimating the corpse. The stigoi awakens twice daily, specifically at noon and midnight. During these periods, it ventures from its grave in pursuit of sustenance, driven by an unquenchable hunger. Its preferred food is human blood, which it drains from its victims.

When not actively hunting, the stigoi remains within its burial site, engaging in the peculiar activity of gnawing on its funeral shroud. The coffin that houses the stigoi bears evidence of its gruesome dietary habits, as it becomes filled with the blood of those unfortunate enough to fall prey to this creature.

Sources: Masters, *Natural History of the Vampire*, 44; Senf, *Vampire in Nineteenth-Century English Literature*, 18

strige (STREE-gee)

In the folklore of Macedonia and Romania, there exists a creature known as a strige, which is a type of vampiric bird. The creation of a strige involves the soul of a witch, post-death, returning to the realm of the living with malevolent intent. This bird possesses a beak of considerable length and sharpness, capable of effortlessly piercing human skin to access the blood it craves. The strige may choose to launch its attack singularly or as part of a collective, demonstrating its capacity for both solitary and communal hunting.

Sources: Bryant, *Handbook of Death*, 99; Cremene, *Mythology of the Vampire in Romania*; Gaster, *Myth, Legend and Custom*, 579; Hurwitz, *Lilith, the First Eve*, 48

strigoi

Variations: STRIGON, strigun

In Romanian folklore, there is a particular emphasis on male witches, known for their practice in the dark arts and a preference for drinking blood. Following their death, these men are believed to transform into vampiric revenants, subsisting on the blood of both cattle and humans. Their supernatural abilities are said to include assuming the form of animals, extracting nutrients from wheat, inducing sterility in cows, instigating droughts, invisibility, and precipitating hailstorms.

Certain conditions of birth are thought to indicate a predisposition towards vampirism upon death. These include being born as the gender opposite to all other siblings, being the seventh child in a family, having a tail at birth, or possessing a third nipple.

Physical indicators of a *strigoi*, the Romanian term for such a vampire, are reported to include an aversion to garlic and onions, a sensitivity to incense smoke, baldness at the crown, and a fur-covered tail at the base of the spine.

Even without these inherent signs, an individual can still become a strigoi due to certain life events; these include committing suicide, dying as a result of a perjury conviction, succumbing to a witch's curse, dying unmarried, or living a sinful life.

Folklore suggests that the presence of a strigoi within a community can be inferred from environmental cues such as a drought. A simultaneous occurrence of rain and sunshine is interpreted as a sign of a strigoi's demise.

The process of eliminating a strigoi involves locating its grave, which contains a body showing no signs of decomposition. A priest must then recite funeral rites over the remains while a stake made of ash, oak, or yew is driven through its heart. The stake is then pierced with a nail or knife, effectively pinning the vampire to the earth and preventing its resurrection.

Sources: Florescu, *In Search of Dracula*, 8–9; Maberry, *They Bite!*, 108; MacDougall, *Vampire Slayers' Field Guide to the Undead*, 655; Melton, *The Vampire Book*, 584

strigoii morti (STREE-goy MOR-tea)

Variation: strigoii

In Romanian folklore, a strigoii morti is a male REVENANT with vampiric characteristics, who maintains amicable relations with the Romani groups. Its creation is caused by either an individual taking their own life or the death and subsequent resurrection of the seventh son born to a seventh son. The strigoii morti retains a physical appearance similar to its living state, characterized by red hair and blue eyes, along with the exceptional feature of possessing two hearts.

Its sustenance is derived from the consumption of blood, and its mere presence tends to evoke feelings of terror and revulsion. Despite this, it is relatively simple to ward off, as garlic is an effective deterrent. To destroy a strigoii morti one must destroy both of its hearts.

Sources: Konstantinos, *Vampires*, 30; Mackenzie, *Dracula Country*, 76, 87

strigoiul muronul (STREE-goy-ee-el moo-ron-OOL)

In Romanian folklore, a species of vampiric REVENANT known as a strigoiul muronul is created under the very specific circumstances of when a red-haired boy, born to parents who were themselves both born outside of wedlock, eventually passes away.

The methods to destroy a strigoiul muronul are distinctly limited. The body of the vampire must either be reduced to ashes through incineration or by driving a nail directly into its heart. These are the only means for effectively destroying this particular species of vampire.

Sources: Haining, *Dictionary of Vampires*, 179; Ronay, *Truth about Dracula*, 23

strigol (STRAY-goal)

In Romanian folklore, a unique type of vampire, known as the strigol, emerges following the death of an individual who practiced sorcery or magic. This supernatural entity is a theriomorph and can shape-shift into various animal forms, such as cats, dogs, frogs, and insects; this ability enables it to approach humans unsuspected and extract their life energy.

To prevent its resurrection from the grave, certain rituals must be performed on the sorcerer's mortal remains. First, the heart is extracted. Then, in a show of disrespect, it is spat upon, then nailed to the forehead using an iron nail. If the deceased sorcerer was female, the heart is nailed to her eye. The body is then transported to a mountainous area and left in a hidden location.

As part of the ritual, garlic is placed in the mouth of the corpse. If these proceedings coincide with St. Ignatius Day, an additional step is required: the body is covered in a layer of pig fat. The date of St. Ignatius Day varies according to different religious calendars: October 17 in the Roman Catholic and Anglican Churches, December 20 in the Greek Church, and January 2 in the Coptic Church.

Sources: Folklore Society, *Publications*, v. 79–80, 100; Senn, *Were-wolf and Vampire in Romania*, 10; Stratilesco, *From Carpathian to Pindus*, 250; Thigpen, *Folklore and the Ethnicity Factor*, 131

strigon (STRAY-gun)

Variation: vedavec

In the Istrian region, there exists a specific species of vampiric REVENANT known as the strigon. Its creation happens with the death of a sorcerer who had consumed the blood of children during his lifetime. The strigon is known to roam communities at the stroke of midnight, engaging in disruptive activities such as knocking on doors or shattering windows. A supernatural consequence of these actions is the death of an individual residing in the affected houses within three days.

The strigon displays a propensity for infiltrating residences to drain children's blood, and it also engages in intimate relations with sleeping women without disturbing their husbands. The destruction of a strigon demands a specific method: it must be impaled through its abdomen with a stake crafted from ash or hawthorn wood, but only after its midnight wanderings have ceased. Upon being staked, the strigon experiences violent convulsions, and blood is seen to spurt from its body. During this terminal phase, the strigon must be set ablaze until it is reduced to ashes.

Historically, the most recent known outbreak of strigons was documented in Larbach, Germany, in 1672. Nonetheless, it is not rare to discover recent corpses in the Istrian countryside even today, identifiable by the stakes embedded in them.

Sources: Oinas, *Essays on Russian Folklore and Mythology*, 116; Ralston, *Russian Folk-Tales*, 326; Summers, *Vampire: His Kith and Kin*, 185

sundal bolong (SUN-dil bal-LONG)

Variations: sundelbolong, sundel bolong

In Java, an Indigenous form of vampiric REVENANT called sundal bolong ("hollowed bitch") comes into existence under two specific circumstances: either when a woman takes her own life or when a child, conceived through an act of rape, passes away. The sundal bolong presents itself primarily to travelers and foreigners, appearing as an attractive woman with disheveled hair, clad in her burial garment.

The sundal bolong utilizes its physical allure as a strategic tool. It entices men by leading them to secluded areas under the guise of a potential intimate encounter. The true intention of this embittered and vengeful creature is far more sinister, however.

Instead of engaging in the promised act, the sundal bolong turns on the unsuspecting man, launching a violent attack to drain his blood.

Sources: Bunson, *Vampire Encyclopedia,* 250; Geertz, *Religion of Java*, 18; Koentjaraningrat, *Javanese Culture*, 342

taotao mona

In the folklore of the Chamorro people of the Mariana Islands there are entities known as taotao mona ("men of the before-time"). These are believed to be the reanimated spirits or ghosts of deceased *magas* ("chiefs"). These restless spirits, traditionally feared for their haunting presence in jungles, were once a significant source of dread.

To attempt to placate these spirits and keep them at a distance, stone monuments, known as *latte*, were constructed in their honor within the jungle. Each geographical region was associated with a different taotao mona, reflecting the fact that various chiefs had dominion over distinct territories. The temperament of these spirits varied widely; some were more forgiving or harsh than others.

The taotao mona possessed the ability to morph into various forms, including animals, humans, or even headless monsters, thereby exerting their influence over the people. According to tradition, one of the most straightforward ways to provoke their wrath was to relieve oneself in the jungle without obtaining their consent.

Sources: *Pacific Discovery*, 50; Carlson, *Folklore and Folktales Around the World*, 153

taraxippos, plural taraxippoi

Variation: equorum conturbator

In ancient Greek folklore, there existed an entity known as taraxippos ("horse disturber"). This entity was classified as a type of ghost that was believed to haunt hippodromes, or horse racing tracks, across the nation. The presence of a taraxippos was typically inferred when horses displayed signs of agitation and became difficult to control. It was suggested that some of these taraxippoi were the reanimated spirits of heroes.

Sources: Hard, *Routledge Handbook of Greek Mythology*, 432; Humphrey, *Roman Circuses*, 9

tase

In Burmese folklore, entities known as tase are considered to be a kind of ghost, characterized as the returned, demonic, and vampiric souls of the deceased. It is believed that their primary intention is to spread sickness and disease among humans.

A variety of tase species exist, each with its unique characteristics. This includes the HMINZA TASE, the succubus-like entity referred to as THABET TASE, and the vampiric REVENANT known as THAYE TASE.

To appease these spirits and keep them at bay, certain practices are observed, including offerings of death dances, festivals, and sacrifices, which may placate them temporarily. Additionally, creating loud noises is said to scare them away, albeit for a limited duration.

Sources: Burma Research Society, *Journal of Burma*, volume 46–7, 4; Hastings, *Encyclopædia of Religion and Ethics*, 25, 30; Jobes, *Dictionary of Mythology, Folklore and*

Symbols, 1537; Leach, *Funk and Wagnalls Standard Dictionary of Folklore, Mythology, and Legend*, 1104

taxim

The taxim, a vampiric REVENANT, is reported to populate various regions of Eastern Europe. This animate cadaver, driven solely by its quest for revenge, is associated with the spread of pestilence and the plague. It relentlessly pursues those who inflicted severe suffering upon it during its earthly existence, and its pursuit is undeterred until its objective is fulfilled.

Source: Bunson, *Encyclopedia of Vampires*, 252

tenatz (ten-ANTS)

Variations: tenac, tenec

In the regions of Bosnia and Montenegro, one may encounter a vampiric entity known as the tenatz. This ghostly entity is believed to commandeer a deceased body for its use. During nighttime, it is said to use its theriomorphic shape-shifting ability to transform into a rodent-like creature, typically a mouse, and infiltrate human residences. While the residents slumber, this cowardly vampire launches its attack, draining the victim of their blood.

The destruction of the tenatz comes through specific means. One such method involves incinerating the reanimated corpse in daylight, which purportedly annihilates the tenatz that is possessing the body. Alternatively, beheading the possessed body is also believed to be effective. Moreover, impaling the vampire in its resting place, its coffin, to pin it to the earth is sufficient to prevent any future resurrections.

Sources: Durham, *Some Tribal Origins*, 259; Petrovitch, *Hero Tales and Legends of the Serbians*, 21; *Man*, 189

thabet tase (thab-it say)

In Burmese folklore, there exists a variant of the succubus known as the thabet tase. This entity is believed to be created when a woman died during childbirth. Following its creation, the thabet tase is said to return to its original community and exploit the male populace. It does this by infiltrating their dreams during their nightly slumber.

Intriguingly, the thabet tase is perceived to derive particular satisfaction from inducing discord among newlyweds. Its interference is so disruptive that it can potentially prevent these couples from conceiving a child.

Sources: Hastings, *Encyclopædia of Religion and Ethics*, 25; Leach, *Funk and Wagnalls Standard Dictionary of Folklore*, 1104; Scott, *Gazetteer of Upper Burma*, 28

thaye tase (they say)

In Burma, there is a vampiric entity called a thaye tase. This being is created when an individual dies violently. Following this tragedy, the thaye tase reportedly reemerges as a grotesque giant.

The thaye tase is associated with the spread of severe diseases, specifically cholera and smallpox, in the communities it visits. An unsettling aspect of the thaye tase's behavior is its propensity to gravitate toward individuals on their deathbeds. It supposedly derives enjoyment from their suffering. Its presence is only perceptible to those nearing the end of their lives, however, as it is said to laugh and revel in their distress.

Sources: Bryant, *Handbook of Death*, 99; Hastings, *Encyclopædia of Religion and Ethics*, 25; Jobes, *Dictionary of Mythology*, 1537

three-month-old calf, the

Variations: third grown calf, three-year-old calf

Within the *Talmud Bavli* ("*Babylonian Talmud*"), there is an interesting narrative involving two disciples of Yehuda ha–Nasi, Rabbi Hanina, and Rabbi Hoshaiah (or Rabbi Oshaia, sources conflict). These individuals are said to have utilized the instructions and text from a preliminary version of the *Sefer Yetzirah* ("Book of Formations") to bring about the creation of a calf that was only three months old; this book was also known as *Hilkoth Yezirah* ("Laws of Creation"). The *Sefer Yetzirah* is the same kabbalistic text that gives the instructions on the creation of a GOLEM.

The calf they generated was not without its flaws, however. It was characterized by physical weakness and disease susceptibility. According to the story, they consumed it one Sunday evening. This story illustrates the complexities and potential limitations inherent in using ancient formulas and texts, even when wielded by knowledgeable practitioners.

Sources: Biggs, *The Case for Lilith*, 67; Curran, *Man-Made Monsters*, 52; Mordell, *The Origin of Letters and Numerals*, 47

uber (OO-bur)

In the country of Turkey, a supernatural entity known as an uber ("overlord," "vampire," or "witch") comes into existence under certain conditions. This REVENANT is created when someone died during an act of violence or when a foreigner who was not a Muslim died and is buried in Turkish soil.

Sources: de Vere, *Dragon Legacy*, 55–6; Jones, *On the Nightmare*, 124; Summers, *Vampire: His Kith and Kin*, 309

ubour (OO-bor)

Variation: OBOUR

In Bulgaria, the ubour ("undead") is a vampiric REVENANT that is created when a person dies a sudden and violent death and the spirit refuses or does not realize it needs to leave its body. After it has been buried for 40 days, the ubour digs itself free from its grave and begins its reign of terror as a vandal, smearing manure on the sides of a person's home and breaking the dishes in his house. It has been speculated that the ubour does this because it is grief-stricken and misses being with its family. It looks as it did in life, except that it has one nostril and creates sparks when it moves.

It is active only between noon and midnight, and only when all other food sources and options have been exhausted will the ubour seek out a human to attack for blood. It has a barb on the tip of its tongue that it uses to break a person's skin. If the would-be victim has the opportunity, however, he can offer the ubour something edible in exchange for his life; the vampire will not pass up the offer, no matter what the proffered "food" is, even if it is feces.

If an ubour must be destroyed, a trained vampire hunter called a vampirdzhija ("vampire hunter") must be employed, as he can detect an ubour while it is still unformed in its grave and knows how to destroy it at each stage of its unlife. The most common method employed is bottling.

Bottling transforms an ordinary glass bottle into a lethal vampire trap. The process begins with baiting the bottle with blood, an irresistible lure for a vampire. The hunter next searches for the vampire armed with his bottle and an array of various religious symbols, including depictions of revered figures such as Jesus or the Virgin Mary, representations of saints, or even sacred relics.

As the hunter nears the usually invisible vampire, the hand clutching the bottle begins to quiver and jerks more violently as he nears his prey. The religious icon is brandished, used like a shepherd's crook, to guide the entranced vampire towards and into the bottle. Once the vampire is inside, the bottle is sealed with a cork, trapping the vampire within. The last step is to cast the bottle into a raging fire. The intense heat causes the bottle to explode, and with it, the vampire is obliterated, effectively ending its reign of terror.

Sources: Belanger, *Sacred Hunger*, 134; Bunson, *Vampire Encyclopedia*, 259; Maberry, *Vampire Universe*, 240

ubume (oo-boo-may)

Ubume ("birthing woman") is a spectral entity originating from Japanese mythology; it is believed to be the returned and lingering spirit of a woman who tragically passed away during childbirth. There are varying narratives concerning this ghostly figure, each with its unique elements.

In one version of the lore, the ubume is described as patiently waiting on bridges, asking passersby to temporarily hold her infant. If the passerby agrees, the ghost promptly vanishes, leaving the individual with the child. The child gradually becomes increasingly heavy, to the extent that it becomes unbearable. When the child is unwrapped, it turns out to be a stone sculpture of Jizo, the deity of safeguarding children and travelers.

Another description describes the ubume drenched in blood from the waist downwards, aimlessly wandering whilst repeating the phrase "*Obareu, obareu!*" ("Be born, be born!"). A recurring theme across these stories is the ubume's relentless quest for a suitable protector for her child. On occasion, they continue to monitor their offspring diligently. It's important to note that these spectral entities maintain a peaceful demeanor unless their child is threatened or harmed.

Sources: Brown, *Complete Idiot's Guide to the Paranormal*, n.p.; Stone, *Death and the Afterlife in Japanese Buddhism*, 191

udug (OO-dug)

Variations: udu, uttuku, utuk

In the early civilizations of Mesopotamia and Sumer, there existed the belief in a vampiric entity referred to as an udug. This being was believed to be a divine creation, intended by the ancient deities as a form of retribution against humanity for their neglect in appropriately interring the deceased. Upon such transgressions, the udug would take possession of the unattended bodies, thereby reanimating them.

Once inhabited by the udug, these reanimated corpses developed an insatiable desire for human blood, subsequently exhibiting aggressive behavior and acting in their own volition. Initially, the udug was not categorized as inherently benevolent or malevolent but rather viewed as an instrument wielded by the gods.

Over time, individuals began to offer prayers to the udug, soliciting its aid in vanquishing their adversaries. Gradual shifts in perception and understanding led to the udug's evolution into a demonic figure.

The concept of divine entities crafting beings to serve as punitive agents upon their followers is not exclusive to Mesopotamian and Sumerian cultures. For instance, in ancient Egyptian mythology, the deity Sekhmet served a similar purpose.

Sources: Cunningham, *Deliver Me from Evil*, 34–8, 58–9; Emerton, *Congress Volume: Jerusalem*, 65; Lurker, *Dictionary of Gods and Goddesses*, 356

undeath (un-DETH)

Variations: undead, unlife

The concept of undeath pertains predominantly to the realm of vampire mythology. It characterizes a unique state of existence where an individual, although technically deceased, continues to exhibit characteristics associated with living beings.

The path to undeath necessitates an initial death. The manner in which this death occurs often plays a pivotal role in determining the likelihood of achieving an undead state. For example, various cultural beliefs propose that individuals who end their own lives or who perish during childbirth are likely candidates for returning to the world of the living as revenants. Despite their evident state of death, these entities remain active and mobile, pursuing specific objectives.

The factors that may precipitate the rise of a corpse to undeath can vary widely across different cultures. Similarly, the physical condition of the body and the mental state of the returned entity can also differ greatly. A majority of the undead entities are animated corpses that sustain their existence by consuming blood or vital human essences.

Entities in the state of undeath are immune to natural causes of death and continue to exist until they are destroyed in the precise manner dictated by their respective cultural or mythological norms.

Sources: Adams, *Slayer Slang*, 225; Auerbach, *Our Vampires, Ourselves*, 3–7; Russo, *Vampire Nation*, 14–6

upier (oo-PEER)

Variations: opyri, upeer, uperice, upi, upieri, upierz, upierzci, upierzhy, upior, upiorcsa, upiroy, upiry, UPOR, uppir, vieszcy, wampire, WIESZCZY, wrikodlaki

In the folklore of Poland, there exists a belief that a male infant who was born with teeth and subsequently dies will resurrect as a vampiric entity known as an upier; if the deceased is female it is known as an upiercsa. These revenants are active from midday until midnight, during which time they exit their tombs in search of human victims.

The upier attacks humans using a barb located at the end of its tongue, which it uses to puncture their skin and drain their blood. If given the chance, it will also extract and consume the person's heart, a delicacy it particularly enjoys. Upon returning to its grave, it regurgitates some of the consumed blood into its coffin, creating a pool in which it submerges itself.

Drawing parallels with the NACHZEHRER of German folklore, the upier ascends the bell tower and rings the bells, vocally identifying individuals in the community. Those who hear their names called out while the bells toll are believed destined to meet their demise soon.

To permanently destroy an upier, it must be incinerated to ashes. Caution is advised, however, as during this process the creature is said to explode into hundreds of small maggots at some point during the cremation. Each of these maggots must be located and destroyed to prevent the upier from resurrecting once more, this time with a vengeful intent.

Sources: Perkowski, *Vampires of the Slavs*, 163; *Sketches of Imposture*, 208–9; Summers, *Vampire in Lore and Legend*, 158

upierci (oo-PEER-see)

Variation: uppyr

In Russian folklore, there exists a vampiric REVENANT known as an upierci. This entity is believed to originate from individuals who end their own lives, experience violent demise, or engage in magical practices while living.

One of the significant attributes associated with the upierci is its capacity to induce extreme drought conditions. Such is the severity of this drought that it can deplete even the plants of their moisture.

Folklore provides two methods for the destruction of an upierci. One approach is to submerge the creature in a lake, effectively drowning it. The alternative method requires the use of an aspen wood stake. This stake must be driven into the upierci while it is in its grave. It is crucial to note that the stake must be driven in with a single strike; failure to do so may result in the revival of the upierci.

Sources: Bryant, *Handbook of Death*, 99; Davison, *Bram Stoker's Dracula*, 354

upierczi (oo-PEER-zee)

In Russian folklore, there exists a vampiric being known as an upierczi; it is believed to be the risen REVENANT of a deceased witch or heretic. Similar to the UPIER, the upierczi is active between the hours of noon and midnight, and it also possesses a stinger beneath its tongue. This stinger is used to puncture the skin of human victims, facilitating the process of blood consumption. Furthermore, the upierczi shares the UPIER's ability to induce substantial droughts.

The methods for destroying an upierczi mirror those applicable to the UPIERCI. One technique involves driving an aspen wood stake through its heart in a single blow while it is in its grave. Alternatively, the upierczi can be incinerated until only ashes remain. Just as with the UPIER, however, the upierczi will explode into maggots at some point during the process. Each of these maggots must also be destroyed, or the vampire is believed to return seeking revenge.

Source: Masters, *Natural History of the Vampire*, 101

upierzyca (oo-PEER-zee-ca)

In the folklore of the Ruthenian people of eastern Poland, there exists a vampiric REVENANT known as an upierzyca. This entity is consistently depicted as a young woman of striking beauty. According to tradition, the upierzyca embarks on a hunt for young men during the nights of the full moon. It attacks these individuals, using a barb located at the end of its tongue to puncture their skin and drain their blood.

In instances where a deceased woman is suspected of being an upierzyca, it is customary for her body to be exhumed for destruction. If the suspicions are correct, the body will exhibit no signs of decay. Moreover, the corpse's eyes, head, and mouth will continue to exhibit movement. The burial shroud may also display indications of partial consumption, further corroborating the suspicion of the deceased being an upierzyca.

Sources: Dundes, *Vampire Casebook*, 8; Haining, *Dictionary of Vampires*, 254; Masters, *Natural History of the Vampire*, 101; Perkowski, *The Darkling*, 113; Volta, *The Vampire*, 143

upir

Variation: vpir
In Russian folklore, there exist nocturnal, vampiric spirits known as upir. These entities are believed to inhabit the corpses of sorcerers or witches, using these bodies as vessels to pursue their malevolent intentions.

Predominantly, the upir targets individuals who journey alone. The spirit derives considerable satisfaction from the fear it induces in its victims, and it takes particular pleasure in consuming their blood.

Sources: Hunter, *Encyclopaedic Dictionary*, 404; Perkowski, *Vampires of the Slavs*, 164; Ralston, *Russian Folk-Tales*, 321

upor

In Russian folklore, there is a vampiric REVENANT known as the upor. This being feeds on the blood of children, demonstrating additional capabilities beyond those typically associated with vampiric beings. Notably, the upor is a theriomorph and can shape-shift into various forms, including chickens, dogs, insects, rats, and small birds.

Moreover, the upor possesses the ability to establish empathic and telepathic connections with a wide range of animals. Once this link is in place, the upor can employ the animal as its familiar, in addition to using it for surveillance purposes on potential victims.

The destruction of an upor requires a specific procedure. First, the grave of the upor must be located. Following this, an exorcism must be successfully performed on the corpse.

Sources: Indiana University, *Journal*, vol. 14, 255; Maberry, *Vampire Universe*, 285; Perkowski, *The Darkling*, 115

upyr (oo-PEER)

Variations: oupyr, uppyr
In Russian folklore, there exists a type of vampiric REVENANT known as an upyr. This entity is believed to originate from the death of socially undesirable individuals,

such as those who have been identified as heretics, sorcerers, or witches. Alternatively, an upyr can also be the offspring resulting from the union between a werewolf and a witch.

The upyr can pass as a regular human being and is typically active from noon until midnight. Its primary victims are families in their homes, targeting children initially before proceeding to the parents. The upyr drains each victim's blood, and, using its iron-like teeth, it gnaws into the victim's chest to consume the heart. These teeth serve a dual purpose, as they also enable the upyr to chew through the frozen ground during winter months, facilitating its escape from its grave.

To locate the upyr's grave, it is said the best method is for a hunter to attach a string to a button on the creature's clothing as it retreats from an attack. This allows the hunter to trace the string back to the upyr's grave. Once the grave is found, the ground surrounding it must be thoroughly doused with holy water. To ensure the upyr remains in its grave, a stake should be driven through its chest in one swift strike; any hesitation could result in the vampire rising again. An alternative method of destruction involves decapitating the vampire and incinerating its corpse until only ashes remain.

Sources: Indiana University, *Journal*, vol. 14, 255; Oinas, *Essays on Russian Folklore*, 126–7; Summers, *Vampire: His Kith and Kin*, 18

uruku (or-OO-koo)

Variation: UTUKKU

In ancient Mesopotamia, a type of vampiric REVENANT referred to as an uruku ("vampire which attacks man") was believed to exist. The emergence of an uruku was associated with disruptions to the appropriate burial rites of an individual.

The uruku, upon its return, assumed a translucent and specter-like form. Its presence was linked to the proliferation of disease, and it purportedly functioned as a malevolent muse, fostering criminal behavior among individuals.

Sources: Konstantinos, *Vampires*, 19; Rose, *Spirits, Fairies, Gnomes, and Goblins*, 192; Summers, *Vampire: His Kith and Kin*, 225

ustrel (oo-STRELL)

In Bulgarian folklore, a vampire known as an ustrel ("lost heart") is said to be created under a particular set of circumstances. Specifically, it is believed that if a child born on a Saturday passes away without receiving baptism, the child would rise from the grave as this type of vampire nine days post-burial.

The ustrel promptly commences its vampiric existence by seeking out cattle for sustenance, consuming the blood of up to five animals each night before returning to its grave. If the ustrel can survive for 10 days without falling prey to a professional vampire hunter, known as a vampirdzhija ("vampire hunter"), it no longer requires its grave for refuge. Instead, it adopts an invisible existence, residing in the space between the horns of a cow or ram. This location provides an ideal shelter for the ustrel due to the creature's aversion to wolves, its natural predator, which would tear it apart given the opportunity. A cow's or ram's horns offer protection as humans are inclined to keep wolves away from their livestock.

The vampirdzhija is specialized in the hunting and destruction of the ustrel. This process involves a highly ritualistic ceremony conducted on a Saturday morning. All fires within a community suspected of harboring a vampire are extinguished. Following this, the vampirdzhija constructs two bonfires at a crossroads, igniting them with "new fire," created via the friction of rubbing two sticks together. Subsequently, all cattle and sheep are gathered and herded to pass between the twin bonfires; the suspicion is that the mature ustrel is hiding between the animals' horns. Rather than risk being singed or worse, the ustrel will leap from the animal and flee into the countryside, where it is likely to be found and devoured by wolves. Once all the animals have traversed the bonfires, a fagot of new fire is brought into the community to relight all the extinguished fires.

Sources: Bryant, *Handbook of Death*, 99; Frazer, *Leaves from the Golden Bough*, 37; Keyworth, *Troublesome Corpses*, 68

ut (OOT)

In the folklore of India, there exists a belief related to the concept of vampiric revenants. Specifically, it is said that when an individual passes away without leaving behind a male descendant, they are destined to return from the grave. This returned entity, characterized by its vampiric nature, is referred to as an ut.

Sources: Bunson, *Vampire Encyclopedia*, 106; Daya, *Essay on Demonology*, 8

utukku (OO-too-coo)

In Mesopotamian literature, specifically in the *Epic of Gilgamesh*, a particular type of vampire known as an utukku is first introduced. The creation of an utukku is associated with instances where an individual passes away before fulfilling a specific obligation, resulting in the soul becoming tethered to its mortal remains and thus forming a REVENANT.

Typically, these entities are believed to inhabit deserted locations such as deserts, mountainous regions, and the vicinity of ocean shores. Their method of causing harm involves establishing direct eye contact with a person, which allows them to drain the individual's life-energy. As historical narratives evolved, this ancient form of vampire began to be increasingly perceived as a demonic entity.

Sources: Rogers, *The Religion of Babylonia and Assyria*, 147–8; Sayce, *Religions of Ancient Egypt and Babylonia*, 283–7; Thompson, *Semitic Magic*, 39–40; Wiggermann, *Mesopotamian Protective Spirits*, 113–4

vampir (vam-PEER)

Variations: PENANGGLAN, penangllaen, penanngallau, pernanggal, upeer, vampiir, vampyras, vrykolaka, vurkulaka, wamphyr, wampire, wukodalak

In German folklore, certain conditions in life are believed to lead to a vampiric afterlife; specifically, individuals who commit suicide, espouse heretical beliefs, fall victim to murder, or are werewolves or witches are said to rise from their graves as vampiric revenants (see GERMAN VAMPIRES).

This vampire is characterized by distinct physical features including a bloated body, elongated fingernails, reddened skin, and evidence of blood in and around its mouth. The creature is attributed with the capability to induce drought and illness in cattle; it also hunts humans for their blood. Interestingly, these vampires are deterred by garlic and silver and exhibit an inexplicable compulsion to count seeds scattered on the ground.

The destruction of these vampires necessitates specific measures. One method involves piercing its heart with a wooden stake crafted from mountain ash. This must be achieved in a single strike, however. Failure to do so would render the attempt to kill the REVENANT unsuccessful. An alternative procedure involves decapitating the vampire, extracting its heart, boiling the heart in wine, replacing it back within the body, and subsequently incinerating the entire corpse until reduced to ash.

Sources: Dundes, *Vampire Casebook*, 73; Indiana University, *Journal*, vol. 14, 266; Perkowski, *The Darkling*, 38; Stefoff, *Vampires, Zombies, and Shape-Shifters*, 17

vampire chair, the

In the mountainous region of East Tennessee, United States, specifically in Carter County, there were two chair-making brothers, Eli and Jacob Odom, who gained recognition for their distinctive style of chairs. These were characterized by hickory-split woven seats, mule-eared slat backs, and tight joints. From 1806 up until the late 1840s, their chairs were widely distributed across the state, numbering in the hundreds.

Among the numerous owners of these chairs was a woman residing near the Hiwassee River, close to Charleston, Tennessee. She was known as a self-proclaimed vampire. Although no documentation exists regarding her activities or demise, a body suspected to be hers was discovered in 1917 during a road widening project in the vicinity of her presumed residence. The body was found face-down, remarkably well preserved—a condition logically attributed to the high mineral content of the local groundwater. Notably, a stake, which was identified as a cradle-lathe support, a component from the type of chair manufactured by the Odom brothers, was found penetrating her chest, specifically her heart. It was inferred that this stake originated from one of the chairs in her possession, which was presumably stolen posthumously, repaired, and reintegrated into the community.

Following the unearthing of the petrified body, stories began to emerge regarding the so-called "vampire chair." According to these accounts, any individual who sat on this chair would become immobilized by an unseen force, which would then inflict scratches on their arms. These scratches would eventually bleed, and only when a droplet of blood fell onto the floor would the attack cease. The challenge lies in identifying this particular chair, as it bears a striking resemblance to hundreds of other chairs produced by the Odom brothers, making it virtually indistinguishable. As such, one can only discover the true nature of the chair once it is too late.

The chair is believed to still exist, as no one is willing to risk intensifying the alleged curse by attempting to destroy it. Over the years, the chair has purportedly been sighted in various locations, including an antique store, a garage sale, and even on the campus of Tusculum College.

Sources: Barnett, *Granny Curse*, 32–4; Burne, *Handbook of Folklore*, 64–5; Masters, *Natural History of the Vampire*, 140

vampire dog

The existence of vampiric dogs, as reported in various folklore, may have originated from observed cases of dogs suffering from rabies or canine leishmaniasis. The narratives about these monstrous canines continue to persist, however. These creatures, often described as revenants, are depicted as exceedingly aggressive and terrifying, exuding an aura of death, with eyes that radiate a sinister red or yellow glow. It is believed that these vampiric canines, much like the infamous *aufhocker* (a large, black vampiric dog, a subtype of the GERMAN VAMPIRE, known for targeting solitary travelers at crossroads, standing on its hind legs to viciously tear out its victim's throat), prey on both animals and humans, inflicting mortal wounds to their throats and draining their victims of blood.

The legend goes on to suggest that such a creature typically infiltrates a region, initially targeting smaller animals like rabbits and cats. Over time, it escalates its attacks to larger animals, including other dogs and sheep. The conventional methods of eliminating this vampire include beheading, shooting, or stabbing. These strategies are considered effective in halting the vampiric creature's reign of terror.

Sources: Barber, *Dictionary of Fabulous Beasts*, 134; Porter, *Folklore of East Anglia*, 89–91; Rose, *Giants, Monsters, and Dragons*, 419; Tongue, *Forgotten Folk Tales*, 70–2

vampire dog, Ennerdale

In the period spanning from 1810 to 1874, and again between 1905 and 1906, a total of 65 years, there were widespread reports of a predatory creature, believed to be a dog, that targeted sheep in England, Ireland, and Scotland. The initial account of this creature emerged in May 1810 from the town of Ennerdale, situated near the boundary between England and Scotland. Eyewitnesses characterized the animal as a large dog with long, deeply imprinted tracks. Reports indicated that this creature was responsible for the nightly deaths of six to eight sheep, which had their throats punctured and blood drained. Interestingly, none of the sheep carcasses exhibited signs of consumption.

In September of 1810, a large BLACK DOG was reportedly shot in a cornfield, temporarily halting the killings. The attacks soon resumed in Ireland, however. Despite suggestions of a wolf being the perpetrator, this was ruled out due to the last known sighting of a wolf in the region dating back to 1712. Instead, the mysterious vampire dog was blamed. By this stage, the creature's appetite appeared to have intensified, with reports indicating up to 30 sheep killed each night. The method of killing remained consistent—biting out the throat and draining the blood. The paw prints left behind matched previous descriptions—long tracks with evident claws.

The creature was reportedly shot on April 11, presumably by an archbishop, only to be sighted again 10 days later, 100 miles away from the previous location. This pattern repeated itself—sightings, sheep killings, shooting of the creature, and subsequent sightings at a new location. There were also reports of a man who had been bitten by the creature in Limerick, Ireland, subsequently developing mental health issues and being admitted to the Ennis insane asylum.

This cycle continued until 1874, when the creature was reportedly shot and did not reappear for nearly three decades. In 1905, reports of slaughtered sheep with drained blood resurfaced in Badminton, as reported by the *London Mail*. The creature was reportedly shot and killed near Gloucester on November 25, and then again on December 16, in Hinton. On March 19, 1906, 51 sheep were killed in a single night near Guildford. This marked the final reported sighting of the vampire dog.

Throughout this final phase of killings, theories circulated suggesting that a hyena or panther, potentially escaped from a menagerie, was responsible. There were no corroborating reports, however, of such animals escaping from zoos.

Over its active years, the so-called vampire dog of Ennerdale was implicated in the deaths of approximately 237,250 sheep, averaging 10 sheep per night. If these figures are accurate, it would suggest that the creature consumed approximately 1,594,320 liters of blood, equivalent to the volume of two Olympic-sized swimming pools.

Sources: Bradley, "The Wild Dog," 380–7; Forte, *Lo!*, 150; Hallam, *Ghosts of the North*, 36

vampire horse

On September 8, 1967, a startling discovery was made in San Luis Valley, Colorado, United States. The remains of Lady, a female Appaloosa pony, were found in a state that defied conventional explanations. The flesh extending from her shoulders to the muzzle was absent, exposing the underlying skeletal structure. The bones of the neck and skull were stark white, resembling those that had been exposed to the elements for an extended period, approximately a year. Intriguingly, the skull cavity was devoid of any organic material and was completely dry.

A powerful medicinal odor permeated the vicinity, and scorched patches were observed on the ground surrounding the cadaver. Despite the severity of the mutilation sustained by the pony, once a cherished companion of Nellie Lewis, there was a conspicuous lack of blood at the scene. Adding to the mystery were the hoofprints encircling the body, which did not belong to Lady. These footprints were notably large, with a reported width of 18 inches.

Lady's unfortunate demise marked the onset of a series of unexplained animal mutilations within the San Luis Valley over the subsequent three decades. These incidents gained significant attention due to their puzzling nature and consistent recurrence.

A postmortem examination of Lady's remains revealed an additional detail: she had been suffering from a severe leg infection at the time of her death. A later reexamination of the carcass uncovered two bullet holes in the pelvic bone, adding another layer of complexity to the already baffling case.

Sources: Keel, *Complete Guide to Mysterious Beings*, 84–5; Murphy, *Mysteries and Legends of Colorado*, 93–9; O'Brien, *Secrets of the Mysterious Valley*, 9–15; Randles, *World's Best "True" UFO Stories*, 83

vampire pumpkin

In the 1930s and '40s, Tatomir P. Vukavonić, a researcher, dedicated his time to studying the Lesani Gypsies of Serbia. His observations and insights culminated in a book titled *The Vampire*. Among the numerous facets of the Lesani culture that Vukavonić explored, one particular belief stood out, the concept of a vampiric pumpkin. This peculiar notion has been subject to much conjecture, with some suggesting that the Lesani might have fabricated the story as a playful jest at Vukavonić's expense. Whether the origins of this belief are rooted in humor or an obscure fragment of folklore, the notion of the vampire pumpkin has undeniably become part of vampire mythology.

According to the Lesani tradition, a pumpkin can transform into a vampire under certain conditions. These include keeping a pumpkin within a household for a period exceeding 10 days, using it as a receptacle that remains unopened for three or more years, or retaining it indoors past Christmas Day.

A pumpkin that has undergone this supernatural transformation will retain its original appearance, preserving its color, shape, and size. Unlike traditional depictions of vampires, a vampire pumpkin does not pose a physical threat to humans. Its actions are limited to extruding blood and moving around on the floor while producing a repetitive sound described as "brr, brr, brr." Despite this lack of aggression, there is a specific procedure for destroying a vampire pumpkin, indicating a degree of caution associated with its existence. The process involves boiling the pumpkin in water, which is then discarded. Subsequently, the vampire pumpkin is cleaned using a short whisk broom before being thrown away. The final step is burning the broom, thereby ensuring the complete destruction of the vampire pumpkin.

Sources: *Journal of the Gypsy Lore Society*, 25–7; Keyworth, *Troublesome Corpses*, 70; Perkowski, *Vampires of the Slavs*, 207; Shashi, *Roma*, 134

vampyre (vam-PIE-er)

Variations: upior (Polish), upir (Slownik), vampire, vampyre (Dutch), wampior (Polish), wampira (Servian)

In 1734, the word *vampire* was linguistically recognized in the English language, making its debut as *vampire*; its plural rendition was *vampyres*. This terminology was likely introduced into the English lexicon through the translation of a French newspaper article, which itself was a translation from a German report. At this time, the word *vampyre* was specifically used to denote an undead entity that preyed on both animals and humans for their blood, often causing illnesses or spreading diseases in the process.

This variant of the word remained prevalent even in 1819, when John William Polidori published his short story titled "The Vampyre" in the April edition of the *New Monthly Magazine*. His narrative, centered around the character of Lord Ruthven (RIV-inn), effectively established the archetype of an aristocratic vampire: affluent, cosmopolitan, ruthless, and with a penchant for seducing women before leading them to secluded locations to extract their blood.

By the time Bram Stoker's iconic novel *Dracula: The Dead Undead* was published in 1897, however, a linguistic shift had occurred. The "y" in "vampyre" had been replaced with an "i," resulting in the modern spelling of "vampire," which was already in common usage at that time.

Sources: Folklore Forum Society, *Folklore Forum*, vol. 10, 26–8; Hulme, *Myth-land*, 75–6; Polidori, *Vampyre: A Tale*; Senf, *Vampire in Nineteenth-Century English Literature*, 3, 21

vanpir (van-PEER)

Variations: VAMPYRE, vrykolaka

The word *vanpir*, synonymous with *werewolf*, is attributed to an anonymous German officer, although the reasons behind this linguistic creation remain unknown. In 1726, there was a surge in reports suggesting that a rampant plague in the southeast

Slavic regions was initiated by revenants. During their lifetime, these revenants were believed to have been werewolves. Following their death, however, they were perceived to have reincarnated as entities referred to locally as vrykolaka. The German officer opted to replace the word *vrykolaka* with his invented word—*vanpir*.

Subsequently, this story was adopted by German newspapers and disseminated widely. The story eventually reached France, where the foreign term underwent another transformation, evolving into the more familiar and equally ominous term—VAMPYRE. As the narrative continued to spread, it crossed the English Channel and reached England. Here, the term underwent further localization, adapting to its new linguistic environment as *vampire*.

Sources: Singh, *The Sun*, 276; Suckling, *Vampires*, 54; White, *Notes and Queries*, vol. 41, 522

vapir (va-PEER)

Variations: VEPIR, vipir

In Bulgarian folklore, a particular kind of REVENANT known as a vapir is believed to come into existence when a body does not receive its necessary burial rites, such as a final cleansing bath. Additionally, if a cat, dog, or shadow happens to cross over the deceased before burial, this too can result in the creation of a vapir.

Individuals who led morally questionable lives, such as those involved in excessive drinking or criminal activities like murder and theft, practitioners of witchcraft, and those excommunicated from the Church, are considered potential candidates for reanimation as vapirs. This could occur either through their own will or due to the absence of anyone to perform the appropriate burial rituals.

The destruction of a vapir involves the services of a specialist known as a *vampirdzhija* ("vampire hunter"). This individual is tasked with eliminating the vampire, employing either the bottling technique (see UBOUR) or using a wooden stake to pierce the creature.

Sources: Indiana University, *Journal of Slavic Linguistics*, 257–8, 265; MacDermott, *Bulgarian Folk Customs*, 66, 67; Summers, *Werewolf in Lore and Legend*, 15

varacolaci (va-ROC-o-loc-ee)

Variations: murohy, strigoii, varacolici, varcolac, velkudlaka, vercolac, vercolach, vircolac, vulcolaca, VUKODLAK, wercolac

In Romanian vampire lore, a being known as the varacolaci is created under specific circumstances, such as when an unbaptized infant passes away or if an individual takes their own life. Interestingly, the propensity to transform into a varacolaci could also be a hereditary trait, passing down familial lines over generations.

Upon its resurrection from the grave, the varacolaci maintains its human appearance, albeit with a noticeably pale complexion and desiccated skin. While it is active throughout the year, this being displays heightened activity on St. George's Day (April 23) and St. Andrew's Day (November 30). Its strength makes it a formidable creature among its vampiric counterparts. When it attacks, the varacolaci drains its victim's blood without leaving any visible wound. It possesses the theriomorphic ability to shape-shift into various forms, such as a cat, dog, flea, frog, or spider.

Furthermore, the varacolaci can enter a deep trance, during which it can cause lunar or solar eclipses or employ a form of astral projection known as "midnight spinning" for safe travel. In this state, its astral form resembles a dragon or a multi-mouthed, undefined monster. If the body of the varacolaci is moved during this trance, however, its spirit may lose its way back, resulting in perpetual sleep.

Preventative measures can be taken if a deceased person is suspected of potential transformation into a varacolaci. Planting a thorny bush atop their grave can prevent their undead resurrection. If the individual's death was self-inflicted, it is advised to dispose of the body in running water promptly.

The destruction of a varacolaci involves a series of intricate rituals. Once the creature rises from its grave and is captured, the subsequent steps depend on its gender. If male, its heart is removed and halved, a nail is driven into its forehead, and its mouth is filled with garlic or, in modern practices, quicklime. The body is then smeared with pig fat obtained from a pig slaughtered on St. Ignatius Day (July 31), wrapped in a shroud sprinkled with holy water, and abandoned in a secluded location. If the varacolaci is female, iron forks are driven through its heart and eyes before it is interred in an extremely deep grave.

Sources: Dundes, *Vampire Casebook*, 25; Mackenzie, *Dracula Country*, 87; McDonald, *Vampire as Numinous Experience*, 124; Taylor, *Buried Soul*, 240

vele (VEE-la)

Variations: veles, vile, vily, wila

In Lithuanian mythology, there exists a type of vampiric fay or nature spirit known as a vele. This entity is believed to originate from the spirit of a woman who has led a life characterized by frivolity or idleness. Upon her death, her spirit is reborn as a vele.

The vele typically manifests as an ethereal, cloudlike apparition, which can transform into the figure of an attractive young woman with long, flowing hair. Its voice is of such captivating beauty that it induces a state of enchantment in those who hear it, causing them to neglect their basic needs such as eating, drinking, and sleeping for several days. The vele's victims are usually men, whom it lures with its provocative appearance.

A vele attacks according to its whim, using its enchanting dance and song to draw its prey into the woods, where it drains their life force. Its dances leave behind a ring of lush grass; stepping on this is considered to bring misfortune.

Similar to the *samodiva* from Bulgarian folklore—a kind of wood nymph or nature spirit—the vele is a formidable warrior. It rides on deer or stags, wields a bow and arrow for hunting or combat, and possesses such strength that it can cause the ground to tremble during physical confrontations. Besides being a warrior, the vele also possesses prophetic abilities and can magically heal. It is also a theriomorph and can shape-shift into various forms, including a falcon, snake, swan, and wolf.

Veles reside in sacred caves, trees, and wells. They can be appeased with offerings of cakes, fresh fruits and vegetables, flowers, and ribbons, which may dissuade them from hunting. Occasionally, a vele might be persuaded to assist a human, but this depends solely on the creature's mood. Any promise made to a vele must be upheld, as breaking such a vow can result in death.

A vele can be weakened significantly if one of its feathers is stolen while it is in bird form. If it manages to retrieve the feather, it will promptly leave the area. If a single hair is pulled from its head, however, the vele will either revert to its true form or perish.

Sources: Alexander, *Mythology of All Races*, 299; Jakobson, *Selected Writings*, 36–9, 45–6; MacCulloch, *Celtic Mythology*, 300–1; MacDermott, *Bulgarian Folk Customs*, 14, 65, 184

vepir (vee-PEER)

Variations: VAPIR, vipir

In Bulgarian folklore, there exists a variant of a vampiric entity known as the vepir. The genesis of this creature is similar to that of the vapir. This transformation into a vepir occurs when certain funerary rites are not appropriately performed on a deceased individual. For instance, if the body does not receive a final ceremonial bath or if it is crossed over by a cat, dog, or even a shadow before its interment. Such circumstances typically befall individuals who lack societal support or care for their postmortem needs. This group can include those who led lives characterized by excessive drinking, criminal activities such as theft or murder, practicing witchcraft, or those who have been formally ostracized from the church.

The destruction of a vepir necessitates specific measures. The body must be exhumed and then reinterred in a face down position. The rationale behind this practice is to prevent the vepir from being able to dig its way to the surface and return to the world of the living.

Sources: Bryant, *Handbook of Death*, 99; *Journal of Slavic Linguistics*, 265; Perkowski, *The Darkling*, 38; Ronay, *Truth about Dracula*, 22; Summers, *Vampire: His Kith and Kin*, 22

vetala (vee-TA-la)

Variations: BAITAL, baitala, betail

In the cultural folklore of India, a vampiric entity known as a vetala is believed to originate each time a child's life prematurely ends and no appropriate funeral ceremonies are performed for it. This vetala, upon possession of a deceased body, induces a grotesque transformation: the extremities contort in a reverse orientation; the facial structure morphs to resemble a fruit bat with narrowed eyes; the skin alters its hue to either green, light brown, or white; and the nails elongate, secreting a toxic substance. The corpse, under the control of the vetala, animates, enabling it to seek human blood for consumption, which prevents the body from decomposition. It is also able to summon a green horse for transportation.

The vetala employs its magical abilities to infiltrate residences through an enchanted thread it passes down the home's chimney. Its victims are often unconscious due to intoxication or because they are asleep. It also targets women suffering from mental health disorders, preying on societal disbelief of their accounts. Children are its most favored victims, however. Regardless of the victim, the vetala primarily consumes intestinal matter and waste.

Vetalas are associated with causing severe mental disturbances and pregnancy losses. Survivors of a vetala attack frequently endure a debilitating illness before any signs of recovery manifest. Interestingly, vetalas possess the ability to perceive past, present, and future events and have a profound understanding of human nature. These characteristics make them valuable targets for sorcerers seeking to exploit these abilities for personal gain.

When not engaged in predatory activities, vetalas are found in repose, suspended upside down from trees located in cemeteries, dense forests, or other deserted locations. It is possible to placate them with gift offerings or repel them using magical incantations. In extreme circumstances, locating and performing the necessary funeral rites on the body of the child whose death resulted in the vetala's creation may be required to effectively eliminate the vetala.

Sources: Crooke, *Introduction to the Popular Religion*, 67, 97, 152; Cuevas, *Travels in the Netherworld*, 95–7; Saletore, *Indian Witchcraft*, 83

viesczy (VEETS-chee)

Variations: stryz, vieszcy, vieszy, vjescey, vjiesce

In Russian lore, a REVENANT known as the viesczy, an entity with a vampiric nature, is believed to originate under certain circumstances: birth with a caul or teeth, or as the offspring of a witch and a werewolf union. Upon death, this unfortunate person resurrects from its grave, manifesting as a vampire with a red-hued countenance. It primarily seeks out its kin or livestock to sustain itself.

The viesczy employs a unique method to feed—it punctures a hole in the chest of its prey, just above their heart, using a barb located at the end of its tongue. A preventative measure to keep the vampire from leaving its grave involves scattering a handful of poppy seeds or carrot seeds into the burial site. The viesczy is mystically compelled to count these seeds—a task it can never complete—thus eternally delaying its rise.

This vampire is active from noon until midnight, dedicating the remainder of its time to return to its grave. There, it gnaws on its burial shroud, feet, and hands. The destruction of a viesczy necessitates burning it until nothing remains but ashes. However, caution should be exercised during this process. Similar to the UPIER and UPIERCZI, the viesczy's body will undergo an explosive reaction, instead of maggots, the explosion is that of a swarm of rats. Each of these rodents must be located and killed, as any survivors could enable the vampire's resurrection, who would then seek vengeance.

Sources: Oinas, *Essays on Russian Folklore*, 124; Perkowski, *Vampires of the Slavs*, 162; Ralston, *Russian Folk-Tales*, 325

vjesci (va-JES-ee) or (vyeskee)

Variations: opji, vjeszczi, vjeszczi wupji

In Polish folklore, there exists a belief centered around individuals born with a caul or teeth. It is said that such individuals, upon their death, will renounce God with their last breath. Subsequently, their bodies take on peculiar characteristics: they retain heat longer than a typical corpse, maintain flexible limbs, and have red lips, and blood seeps from their cheeks and fingernails.

At the stroke of midnight following their burial, these individuals resurrect as a vjesci, a creature that preys on its kin. This entity, characterized by a ruddy brown complexion and immense strength, can pass for a human.

Fortunately, preventive measures exist to counteract the transformation of a child born with a caul into a vjesci upon its death. The caul must be preserved and, on the child's seventh birthday, ground up and ingested by them. Unfortunately, no such preventive measures are known for children born with teeth. It is possible, however, to hinder their resurrection as well.

The body is positioned face down in the coffin, ensuring that any escape attempts would lead the creature downward. A crucifix and a coin are placed in the corpse's mouth at the burial, providing the awakening vjesci something to chew upon. Additionally, a bag of seeds, typically poppy, is placed in the coffin. The vjesci is compelled to count these seeds before leaving its grave, but it can only count one seed every seven years. Finally, a net is wrapped around the coffin. Should the vjesci manage to count all the seeds, it must then untie all the knots in the net, succumbing to another irresistible urge.

Sources: Canadian Centre for Folk Culture Studies, *Paper* 1–4, 8, 21, 23, 25; Lorentz, *Cassubian Civilization*, 70, 132, 133; Perkowski, *Vampires of the Slavs*, 191, 195

vlkodlak (va-COD-lic)

Variations: volkodlak, volkoslak

The vlkodlak is a vampire-like creature originating from Serbia. There are two ways in which a vlkodlak is created; the first method involves the death of a man under the age of 20 who was either a murderer, perjurer, or engaged in sexual intercourse with his mother. The second method occurs when a young man is killed by a werewolf or consumes meat from an animal that was slain by a werewolf.

Regardless of its origin, the vlkodlak will rise from its grave as a blood-covered animated corpse, often behaving like a shameless drunkard. Additionally, it possesses the power to cause eclipses.

To prevent a corpse from transforming into a vlkodlak, it is believed that its thumbs and toes must be severed and a nail must be driven into its neck. A vlkodlak, unless it is killed, will wander the Earth for precisely seven years. At the end of this period, the vampire dies, and its soul is reborn into a human. The cycle then starts anew in a different region of the country.

To destroy a vlkodlak, it is necessary to stab it through the stomach with a stake made of hawthorn wood and cover the hair on its body with tar. Subsequently, the vampire must be set ablaze with a candle that was used during its wake. The fire must burn at a sufficiently high temperature and for a sufficient duration to reduce the corpse to ash.

Sources: Alexander, *Mythology of All Races*, 299; MacCulloch, *Celtic Mythology*, 229; MacDougall, *Vampire Slayers' Field Guide to the Undead*, 655; Mercatante, *Good and Evil*, 98; Turner, *Dictionary of Ancient Deities*, 500

volkolak (VOL-co-lac)

Variations: ukodlak, vuc, vuk ("wolf")

In Dalmatia, there exists a vampiric REVENANT known as a volkolak. The word *volkolak* encompasses several meanings, including "dead, but alive, resembling an ordinary man," "vampire in 40 days," and "werewolf's son."

The creation of a volkolak can occur through either of two distinct scenarios. Firstly, a man who also happens to be a werewolf cohabits with a woman as her partner without undergoing marriage rites, impregnates her, and subsequently passes away before the birth of their child. In such a situation, the child, upon its eventual demise, will rise again after 40 days as a volkolak.

Alternatively, a volkolak may be formed when an individual willingly exchanges their soul with the devil. Consequently, upon the death of this person, they too are transformed into this particular type of vampire.

Sources: Indiana University, *Journal*, vol. 14, 241; Perkowski, *The Darkling*, 53; Summers, *Werewolf in Lore and Legend*, 15

vompir (VOM-peer)

Variations: KRUVNIK, vonpir

In Bulgaria and Macedonia, there is a belief in a vampire-like spirit called a vompir. This type of entity is created when someone is not properly buried or mourned, dies in disgrace, or passes away unnaturally, such as through childbirth or suicide. During the night, the vompir enters the corpse and takes control of it. The possessed body then seeks out its prey, usually a sleeping person, suffocates them, and drains their blood.

If someone finds themselves under attack by a vompir, they are advised to pray to the god Troyan, associated with darkness and night, or the goddess Lada, associated with beauty and love, for deliverance.

In addition to possessing corpses, the vompir is believed to have the ability to cause nightmares, droughts, and alter the course of rivers.

A vompir can only be destroyed once it has taken over a corpse. To do so, the vompir must be captured and decapitated. Its hands and feet are then severed, and the body is tightly bound. The final steps involve either stabbing the vompir's heart with an aspen wood stake or driving a raven's claw into the skull from behind the right ear. Finally, the body is buried beneath a large millstone.

Sources: Indiana University, *Journal*, vol. 14, 265; Mayer, *Hungarian*, 174; Perkowski, *The Darkling*, 168

vpir (VA-peer)

Variation: Upir

In Russian folklore, there exists a vampiric spirit known as the vpir. This malevolent entity takes possession of the body of a sorcerer or witch who has passed away, animating it to serve its wicked intentions. The vpir prowls during the night, specifically targeting individuals who travel alone. It derives immense pleasure from instilling terror and feasting upon the blood of its victims.

Sources: Hunter, *Encyclopaedic Dictionary*, 404; Perkowski, *Vampires of the Slavs*, 164; Ralston, *Russian Folk-Tales*, 321

vrkolak

In Bulgaria's Haskov region, which borders Greece and Turkey, there exists a specific type of vampire known as a vrkolak. This vampire is characterized as resembling a shadow and is formed through a unique process. When the blood of an individual who has been fatally attacked with either a gun or a knife touches the ground, it transforms.

Fourteen days later, the spilled blood manifests into a vrkolak, which immediately embarks on a mission to infect the local livestock with diseases.

The eradication of a vrkolak can only be accomplished by a specialized vampire seer referred to as a sabotnik. The method employed to slay the vampire mirrors how it was created. For instance, if the vrkolak was formed as a result of a murder committed with a knife, the sabotnik must utilize a knife to bring about its demise. Notably, it is worth mentioning that a dog possessing the abilities of a sabotnik can also eliminate a vrkolak through a single bite.

Sources: Alexander, *Mythology of All Races*, 229; Baring-Gould, *Book of Were-Wolves*, 64; McClelland, *Slayers and Their Vampires*, 105; Summers, *Werewolf in Lore and Legend*, 16

vrukolak (vroo-co-lac)

Variation: ukodlak

The vrukolak is a REVENANT originating from northern Dalmatia, known for its vampiric nature. A vrukolak is formed under specific circumstances: when an individual dies as a victim of a vrukolak attack, when the person is murdered without any witnesses, or when a cat or dog crosses over the deceased before proper burial. Initially, the vrukolak preys upon its former family and friends before extending its malevolent influence on other unsuspecting victims.

Notably, the vrukolak possesses the unique abilities of having the power to create others of its kind. It can also mesmerize individuals by maintaining uninterrupted eye contact while emitting a disconcerting shriek.

While complete destruction of a vrukolak is not attainable, measures can be taken to render it permanently incapacitated, preventing it from rising again and posing a threat. The vampire's tendons must first be severed, rendering it unable to walk. Subsequently, it can be securely fastened within its coffin, with the final nail driven directly through its heart.

Sources: Alexander, *Mythology of All Races*, 229; Baring-Gould, *Book of Were-wolves*, 64; McClelland, *Slayers and Their Vampires*, 105

vrukolaka

In the northern regions of Greece, there exists a particularly savage species of vampire known as a vrukolaka. It is worth mentioning that the vrukolaka originally emerged from Slavic folklore. The genesis of this vampire occurs when the devil takes possession of a lifeless body, which subsequently rises from its grave. Once awakened, the vrukolaka embarks upon a systematic killing spree, starting with its kin before extending its malevolence to individuals outside its familial lineage.

To eliminate the vrukolaka, a specific course of action must be undertaken. The corpse needs to be exhumed, and a priest must conduct an exorcism ritual over the remains. If, by chance, this procedure fails to achieve the desired outcome, then the body must be dismembered into smaller fragments and incinerated until reduced to ash.

These practices, rooted in folklore, have been passed down through generations as a means of combating the vrukolaka menace.

Sources: Leake, *Travels in Northern Greece*, 216; Summers, *Vampire in Europe*, 253; Wright, *Book of Vampires*, 42

vryolakas (vree-oh-LAC-az)

In the Republic of Macedonia, there exists a vampiric REVENANT known as a vryolakas. Similar to other vampiric revenants in the neighboring regions of Albania, Bulgaria, Greece, and Serbia, vryolakas are formed under various yet specific circumstances including instances where an animal, such as a cat or dog, crosses over the deceased before burial, when a person dies as a result of murder or suicide, if an individual consumes meat from an animal killed by a werewolf, or when a malevolent individual who practiced magic passes away.

The vryolakas exhibits nocturnal activity, confined to the hours between 10 p.m. and the first crow of the rooster, as it is vulnerable to sunlight. During this time, it seeks out unsuspecting individuals to drain them of their blood. Notably, the vryolakas display a peculiar behavior that sets them apart even among vampires. They possess an inexplicable compulsion to pour wine over their face. Some sources suggest that this behavior stems from the vryolakas' untidy drinking habits during their mortal life and their inability as undead to consume liquid from a glass. Conversely, other accounts propose that the vryolakas is provoked into its vampiric resurrection when a person inadvertently spills or splashes wine over the face of the deceased.

Sources: Ronay, *Truth about Dracula*, 22; Stefoff, *Vampires, Zombies, and Shape-Shifters*, 17; Volta, *The Vampire*, 149

vudkolak (VUD-co-lac)

Variation: VUKODLAK

In the southern Slavic regions, there exists a vampiric REVENANT known as a vudkolak ("wolf's hair"). Interestingly, this word is also used to describe a werewolf. When a werewolf meets its demise, it is believed that on the night of the following full moon, it will reanimate as this particular type of vampire. It is worth noting, however, that if a bird were to fly over the body of an unburied individual, that person too would transform into a vudkolak. To prevent such a transformation, a customary honor guard comprised of family members and prominent community figures maintains a vigilant watch over the body throughout the night, ensuring its protection.

Should the honor guard fail in their duty, the vudkolak emerges from its grave during full moon nights and assumes the form of a werewolf. In this theriomorphic state, it hunts humans to satisfy its need for sustenance. Note that the burial site of a vudkolak can be identified by the absence of crows, as these birds are said to avoid such graves.

Sources: Guiley, *The Complete Vampire Companion*, 10; Perkowski, *The Darkling*, 38

vukodlak (VOO-cod-lac)

Variations: pricolici, triccolitch, tricolici, VRUKOLAK, vukodlack, vukodlaki, vukolak, vukozlak, vulkodlak, vulkolak

In Serbian folklore, there exists a vampiric REVENANT known as a vukodlak. The creation of this entity occurs upon the death of a heretic, magic practitioner, or werewolf, as well as in cases of suicide or murder. When the vukodlak awakens and arises from its grave, it assumes the appearance of a distended corpse, characterized by bloodstains around its mouth, elongated fingernails, and reddish skin. Initially, the vukodlak targets its surviving relatives and acquaintances, only moving on to other individuals once those connected to it in life have been eradicated. It is believed that wherever the vukodlak travels to, it brings with it diseases and acts as a carrier for cattle plague.

Traditional beliefs suggest employing the use of garlic and silver to safeguard against the vukodlak, as these substances are believed to possess vampiric warding properties. Additionally, it is said that throwing a handful of carrot or poppy seeds on the ground can create a distraction for the vukodlak, allowing potential victims to escape, as the vampire is mystically compelled to pick up and accurately count each seed. The destruction of a vukodlak requires adherence to a specific process. Firstly, it must be impaled with a stake made from mountain ash. Decapitation follows. Finally, the heart of the vukodlak must be removed from its body and boiled in wine.

Sources: Oinas, *Essays on Russian Folklore*, 116; Perkowski, *The Darkling*, 38; Wright, *Book of Vampires*, 90

vyrkolakas (vry-COO-low-casz)

Variation: tympaniaois

The vyrkolakas, a vampiric spirit mentioned in Greek folklore (refer to GREEK VAMPIRES), possesses unique characteristics. When a werewolf passes away, its spirit returns and takes possession of a corpse, animating it as its vessel. It is important to note that the spirit is distinct from the body it inhabits, differentiating it from a traditional REVENANT. Once the body becomes inhabited, a phenomenon known as *timpanios* occurs. This term describes the transformation of the bloated body, which becomes hardened, the skin tightening to such an extent that, when struck, it produces a drumlike sound. It is believed that at least one vyrkolakas exists within each Greek clan.

The vyrkolakas roams through the community it once inhabited, leaving a trail of disease in its wake. Additionally, it calls out the names of individuals whom it had known during its mortal existence. It is said that anyone who encounters the vyrkolakas and directly gazes upon it will face instantaneous death. Furthermore, individuals who respond to its calls are said to succumb to death within a span of 24 hours.

Sources: Guiley, *Complete Vampire Companion*, 26; Senn, *Were-wolf and Vampire in Romania*, 64; Summers, *Vampire in Lore and Legend*, 258

wanyūdō (wah-NEW-doh)

The wanyūdō, a notable yōkai from Japanese folklore, holds a prominent place in the annals of supernatural lore, with recorded accounts tracing back to the Heian period (794 to 1185 CE). It is described as a distinctive entity reminiscent of a flaming wagon wheel, featuring a human visage in place of the traditional hub. According to legendary tales, the wanyūdō's origin can be ascribed to the assassination of a tyrannical nobleman during his tour of the land, while seated in an ox-drawn cart. The restless and vengeful spirit of the nobleman subsequently returned to the city where his demise occurred, perpetually haunting residential areas within urban neighborhoods to this very day.

Encounters with the wanyūdō yield grim consequences, as unfortunate individuals who fall victim to its malevolence are relentlessly pursued and ultimately struck down by the flying, fiery wheel. Their bodies are tragically torn asunder, leaving behind charred remains that smolder upon the streets. Certain measures are said to be effective in safeguarding oneself from the wanyūdō's wrath. Swiftly averting one's gaze and assuming a posture of humility proves beneficial, as does seeking safety by hiding or even fainting; these actions are said to have saved the lives of those who have seen this yōkai.

Should one find oneself facing the wanyūdō in a death-defying chase, quickly seeking refuge indoors and affixing an *ofudia* (a sacred piece of paper bearing the inscription "kono-tokoro-shobo-no-sato") upon the doorway is believed to fend off the malevolent entity. As the hours approach dawn, the wanyūdō, being a nocturnal hunter, will eventually depart, providing respite from its pursuit.

Source: Yoda, *Yokai Attack*, 34–7

washerwomen of the night

Variations: clotha, kannerez-noz, les lavandières de la nuit, midnight washerwomen

In both England and France, there exists a peculiar kind of vampiric apparition known as the washerwomen of the night. These ethereal entities are believed to have been women during their earthly existence, who either neglected their religious duties or engaged in wicked deeds. They are frequently encountered near secluded bodies of flowing water. While the washerwomen in England manifest as ghostly figures, their counterparts in France possess a skeletal appearance. Regardless of their form, they are regarded as harbingers of death in both countries.

During the late hours of the night, should an individual find themselves in the presence of these washerwomen, they must assist in wringing out their laundry. Failure to do so will result in dire consequences, as the washerwomen will retaliate by inflicting severe harm upon the unfortunate traveler, breaking their limbs before casting them into the water. If the washerwomen successfully capture a victim, they compel them to wash their burial shroud. Survival hinges upon compliance with their instructions; failure to comply will result in immediate death.

The washerwomen are eternally bound to their task of laundering burial shrouds for unbaptized children, unless they can find a willing individual who will take their place. This grim duty serves as a perpetual penance for their past transgressions.

Sources: Curran, *Vampires*, 108–10; *The Gentleman's Magazine*, 150–1; Paulist Fathers, *The Catholic World*, 781; Summers, *Vampire in Lore and Legend*, 2

wewe gombel

Variations: wewegombel, wewe

The wewe gombel, a distinctive creature found in Indonesian and Malaysian folklore, holds a unique place among nursery bogies. Described as a fearsome hag with sagging breasts, she is believed to abduct children whose parents exhibit cruelty or negligence. Contrary to her ghastly appearance, however, the wewe gombel assumes a nurturing and grandmotherly role, caring for the captured children. Should the parents recognize their faults, undergo a genuine transformation, and sincerely yearn for the return of their offspring, the wewe gombel will relinquish the child from her abode atop the *Arenga pinnata* palm tree and ensure their safe reunion at home.

Legend suggests that the wewe gombel is the ghostly manifestation of a woman who was incapable of bearing children. Devastated by this news, her husband began to disregard her, ultimately casting her out and engaging in an extramarital affair. Overwhelmed by grief and anger, the wife succumbed to madness and murdered her husband. The community, lacking sympathy, relentlessly pursued her, eventually forcing her into a state of despair that led to her own tragic demise.

In Java, the wewe gombel belongs to the category of spirits known as "*memedis*." Within this classification, the male counterparts are referred to as "*gendruwo*," while the females adopt the name "*wewe*." Notably, the wewe are often depicted carrying small children upon their hips, reminiscent of human mothers cradling their offspring.

The intricate folklore surrounding the wewe gombel highlights the complex interplay of societal expectations, maternal instincts, and the consequences of human actions within the cultural context of Indonesian and Malaysian folklore.

Sources: Abdul, *Breast Ghost*, 1–11; Geertz, *Religion of Java*, 16; Muhaimin, *The Islamic Traditions of Cirebon*, 45

white ladies

Variations: die weisse frauen (Germany), grey ladies, ladies in white, les dames blanches (France), night ladies, white ladies of the fau

Throughout the British Isles and France, there exist vampiric entities known as white ladies. These spectral beings, considered harbingers of death, are believed to be the restless spirits of noblewomen who met tragic ends, either through murder or other unfortunate circumstances. Adorned in lavish period clothing, the white ladies often carry a ring of keys or chalices filled with poison.

Originating from the Jura lakes region, the white ladies of Fau, also known as dames blanches in their native France, exhibit a predilection for targeting young men. Through their captivating physical beauty and magical allure, they entice their victims to secluded areas, where they then turn and attack, draining their victims of their life-sustaining blood.

The apparitions of white ladies exclusively manifest on moonlit nights, particularly in the late hours. While sightings have been reported at bridges, cemeteries, and crossroads, they most commonly wander the halls and grounds of castles or manor houses where they once resided in their mortal lives. These ethereal beings call out with hypnotic voices, inviting those who can perceive them to partake in a dance, despite the absence of audible music. Notably, their touch emanates an icy chill, sapping the life energy from those unfortunate enough to come into contact with them. Tragically, anyone who succumbs to the white ladies' tempting invitation to dance will find their lifeblood drained, their lifeless bodies discovered by the roadside.

Opinions among scholars diverge regarding the classification of white ladies, with some positing that they belong to the realm of vampiric fairies rather than strictly being vampiric spirits, as they show vulnerability to weapons forged from iron. It is worth noting, however, that these beings can be repelled through the brandishing of a crucifix, invoking divine aid, or having recently received a priestly blessing.

Sources: Burne, *Shropshire Folk Lore*, 76–7; Curran, *Vampires*, 72, 184; Holland, *Haunted Wales*, 10, 69; Prince, *Remains of Folklore in Shropshire*, 15

White Lady of Stammheim, the

The "White Lady of Stammheim" is a popular ghost story relayed by Caesarius of Heisterbach, a Cistercian monk, scholar, teacher, and theologian who lived between 1180 and 1240. Caesarius authored numerous books, but two significant contributions stand out in history. The first one is his putting a name to the demon responsible for typographical errors, Titivillus. The second noteworthy aspect of Caesarius's legacy is his quotation of Arnaud Amalric, a leading figure in the Albigensian Crusade who passed away in 1225. When asked how to differentiate Cathars from Catholics, Amalric reportedly responded with the now-infamous phrase: "*Caedite eos. Novit enim Dominus qui sunt eius*" ("Slay them all, God will recognize his own"); it is better known as the ad hoc motto adopted by both the United States Green Berets and Marines, "Kill 'em all, and let God sort 'em out."

The tale of the White Lady is featured in Caesarius's work, *Dialogus miraculorum* (*Dialogue of Miracles*) written around 1219–1223. The White Ladies remain familiar even today, with a street in Fontenay-sous-Bois, near Paris, named after them. These spectral figures are often referred to as banshees in England and Ireland, traditionally associated with forewarning death.

The narrative revolves around two knights, Gunther and Hugo, who resided in the village of Stammheim under Bishop Ric of Cologne. On one occasion, as Gunther was traveling, a serving woman brought her children into the courtyard for their evening routine before bedtime. While waiting, she observed a female figure dressed in white with a pale face watching them from across a hedge. Without uttering a word, this apparition moved closer to Hugo's dwelling, gazed at it from the other side of the hedge, and then retreated to the cemetery from whence she came.

Soon after this incident, Gunther's eldest son fell ill. The boy prophesied his death within seven days and predicted that his sister Dirina would follow him to the grave seven days after his own demise. These tragic events unfolded exactly as foretold. After the deaths of their children, both the mother and the serving woman passed away. In the same period, Hugo and his son also met their untimely ends.

A significant detail in this story is that the White Lady never crosses the hedge. According to ancient German beliefs, hedges were considered protective borders against witches and harmful enchantments, safeguarded by a spirit known by the Latin name Dusius.

Source: Lecouteux, *The Return of the Dead*, 119–20

wiederganger

Variations: gengangers ("back-comers"), widerganger

In German folklore, wiedergangers ("one who walks again") are the ethereal manifestations or returned spirits of individuals who met their demise through criminal acts, execution, suicide, or other untimely and violent circumstances. It is worth noting that certain accounts depict them not as spiritual beings, but rather as revenants resembling zombies. These entities harbor a malevolent nature, intentionally inflicting misery upon the living.

According to tradition, the bodies of such individuals would be interred with specific measures taken to prevent their return. This involved mutilation of the corpse or, at the very least, covering the eyes, binding the hands, and shaving the head. These practices aimed to hinder the vengeful activities of the wiedergangers and protect the living from their wrath.

Source: Pringle, *Mummy Congress*, 128

wieszczy

Variation: wieszcy

In Polish folklore, there exists a belief regarding individuals born with a cleft palate, as well as the presence of either a caul or teeth. It is thought that such individuals will develop a vividly red complexion and experience heightened levels of hyperactivity throughout their lives. Upon their eventual death, they are said to transform into a particular type of vampiric REVENANT known as a wieszczy, characterized by a barbed tongue.

Apart from their insatiable thirst for human blood, wieszczys are believed to engage in certain behaviors. For instance, at the stroke of midnight, these revenants are said to ring the church bells and call out the names of local community members. Should an individual hear their name being called, it is believed that they will meet their untimely demise.

To prevent the transformation of an individual into a wieszczy, specific burial practices are prescribed. The deceased must be interred with several crosses made from willow wood, with one placed beneath each arm, beneath the chin, and upon the chest. Additionally, before the coffin is closed, a handful of soil from the deceased's doorstep is customarily sprinkled over their body.

Sources: Alexander, *Mythology of All Races*, 232; Lorentz, *Cassubian Civilization*, 276; Senn, *Were-wolf and Vampire in Romania*, 66; Taylor, *Death and the Afterlife*, 392

wili (VE-lee)

Variations: wiles, vila, vile

In Polish folklore, there exists a vampiric spirit known as a wili; one of these beings are created when a bride dies on her wedding day. Denied the life she was meant to live, the wili is condemned to eternal suffering and restlessness. In its spectral form, the wili takes on the appearance of a remarkably beautiful woman draped in a damp, white skirt.

The wili's haunting presence manifests itself on moonlit nights, particularly at midnight, along the roadside. With its seductive allure, it attempts to entice any man who crosses its path into engaging in a dance. Those who succumb to the wili's temptations become its unfortunate victims, as their life energy is gradually drained away. As dawn approaches, however, the wili vanishes, leaving no trace of its ethereal existence.

Sources: Beaumont, *Ballet Called Giselle*, 18–20; Creed, *Monstrous-Feminine*, 59; Perkowski, *Vampires of the Slavs*, 43; Summers, *Vampire in Europe*, 8

windigo (WIN-dee-go)

Variations: "He Who Lives Alone," upayokawitigo ("the hermit"), weendigo, wenbdigo, wendigo, wetikoo, wiendigo, wiitigo, windago, windigo, witiko, witko

The windigo, a malevolent creature deeply rooted in Ojibwa and Saulteaux

Manitoba folklore, holds a significant place within Algonquin culture. Its name, derived from the Algonquin language, translates to "cannibal" and "evil spirit."

According to tradition, the transformation into a windigo entails venturing into the creature's realm and presenting offerings of flesh and prayers. The windigo's response to these entreaties may result in either devouring the petitioner, thus terminating their plea, or adopting them. Once embraced by the creature, the individual's heart turns to ice, hair grows profusely across their body, and an insatiable desire for human flesh takes hold. In a desperate act to satisfy this craving, the afflicted will promptly chew off their lips. It is worth noting that windigos born through this process are typically not as towering in stature as their natural-born counterparts.

Descriptions of these cannibalistic giants predominantly depict them as male entities, characterized by simian facial features; bloodshot eyes; enormous, jagged teeth; and hearts composed of ice. Their height is said to rival that of pine trees, while their bodies are covered with long hair. Notably, their elongated and narrow feet possess a single toe each, alongside pointed heels. Furthermore, windigos emit a repugnant odor.

In their relentless pursuit of sustenance, windigos roam the subarctic forests in search of human prey. In the absence of viable victims, they resort to consuming their bodies. Once this source is depleted, they turn to carrion, moss, and decaying wood for sustenance. Tragically, windigos ultimately unleash their voracious appetites upon their own families, commencing with the consumption of their youngest offspring. As windigos traverse the land, blizzards accompany their every step. There are instances where these beings operate in packs, engaging in collective hunts. These malevolent creatures are known to traverse the woods in a frenzied state, unleashing cries of rage and displaying superhuman strength as they tear through the earth and trees.

Human weaponry and natural elements hold no power over windigos, rendering them impervious to harm. Speculation suggests that decapitation or melting of their icy hearts may prove fatal to these entities. Shamanistic conjurations are believed to serve as a deterrent against windigo assaults. In cases where an individual has succumbed to the windigo's influence, they must be captured, bound, and subjected to the intense heat and smoke of an open fire. This harsh treatment aims to drive away malevolence and melt their icy hearts. Should this method fail, regrettably, the afflicted individual is typically met with a grim fate.

Sources: Gilmore, *Monsters*, 75–90; Guiley, *Encyclopedia of Ghosts and Spirits*, 532; Jones, *Evil in Our Midst*, 43–6; Rose, *Giants, Monsters, and Dragons*, 119; Steiger, *Real Zombies*, 175

wulgaru

A HOMUNCULUS-like figure of great significance in the folklore of the Wardaman people, the wulgaru assumes the roles of judge, jury, and executioner for those who transgress tribal laws. Rooted in the traditions of the northern territories of Australia, this mythical creature was brought into existence by an elderly man named Djarapa, who embarked upon the creation of a humanlike entity.

With meticulous care, Djarapa fashioned a wooden frame from the bough of a young tree, meticulously shaping it to resemble a human body. The limbs of the construct were subsequently formed using sections of wood, while rounded stones sourced from a nearby riverbed served as joints for the knees and arms. Binding these components together with red ocher, Djarapa intoned an incantation infused with mystical power, passed down to him by a deceased tribal medicine man.

Days and nights merged as Djarapa relentlessly chanted, seeking to bestow life upon his creation. Eventually relinquishing hope, he departed for his home. As he ventured forth, however, a resounding symphony of clanking and crunching reverberated in the air, capturing his attention. Turning back, he was confronted by a towering monstrosity comprised of wood and stone, its lumbering gait instilling dread. This abomination, the embodiment of his handiwork, surged through the forest, its joints creaking, limbs flailing, and eyes shining like celestial orbs. Periodically, its monstrous maw opened wide, only to snap shut with an ominous finality. Djarapa's efforts to elude the creature's pursuit proved futile, and he inadvertently led it to the heart of the village.

Since that fateful encounter, the wulgaru has roamed the night, assuming the mantle of a self-appointed arbiter of tribal law and unpredictably materializing at the slightest infringement. Even the most trivial transgressions do not escape its attention, ensnaring both adults and children alike. Its unwavering commitment to enforcing tribal customs has earned the wulgaru a fearsome reputation, solidifying its status as one of the night's most dreaded entities.

Source: Markowitz, *Robots that Kill*, 84–5

wume (WOO-mee)

Located along the West African coast in the Gulf of Guinea, specifically near the Bight of Benin, resides a vampiric species known as a wume. The creation of a wume occurs upon the death of an unburied criminal or as a consequence of a cursed individual's transformation into an undead state. Possessing formidable power, cunning intelligence, and notorious resistance to termination, the wume represents a formidable adversary.

Traditionally, a contingent comprising ritualistically purified warriors and a priest embarks on a solemn mission to track down and exterminate a wume. Smart strategy dictates engaging the creature only after it has sated its thirst for blood, as this will induce a near-comatose slumber. At this time, the men, now on relatively equal footing with their foe, proceed to immobilize the wume by firmly restraining its limbs against its body. Multiple layers of rope are meticulously wound around its form until it is enveloped in a mummy-like fashion.

Once the wume is securely bound, resembling a tightly bound mummy, the surviving warriors transport the vampire to an undisclosed location, carefully selected for its seclusion. Here, the wume is interred in a deep and unmarked grave. The men must maintain strict silence regarding the burial site and refrain from revisiting the area, as the wume possesses the ability to compel anyone who ventures near its resting place to exhume it.

Sources: Jones, *Dawn of European Civilization*, 434; Pashley, *Travels in Crete*, 209; Wharton, *North American Review*, 95; Wright, *Book of Vampires*, 105

wurwolaka (vour-vah-LA-ka)

In Albania, a formidable variety of vampiric beings known as a wurwolaka can be found. Distinguished by its ruthless nature, the wurwolaka possesses a nearly unique ability among vampires: the power to propagate its own kind. Under the cover of darkness, this cunning predator lies in wait, launching ambush attacks on unsuspecting humans, tearing their bodies asunder and sating its thirst with their life-giving blood. One must exercise caution, however, for casting eyes upon the wurwolaka carries dire consequences, driving the unfortunate witness into the depths of madness.

When confronted with the task of destroying this vampire, only a single method prevails: reducing its corporeal form to ashes through the cleansing force of fire. This destructive act ensures the permanent eradication of the wurwolaka, severing its malevolent presence from the mortal realm.

Sources: Aylesworth, *The Story of Vampires*, 5; Wright, *The Book of Vampires*, 105

xi xie gui

In China, an entity known as a xi xie gui ("suck blood ghost") is classified as a vampiric apparition. Its existence arises when the second soul, known as p'o, fails to depart from the physical body upon the occurrence of death. The xi xie gui sustains itself by preying upon humans, specifically consuming their vital blood. While no specific method for eradicating this vampire has been recorded, it is believed that its entry into homes can be prevented by positioning a piece of wood measuring six inches in length beneath the front door of the dwelling.

Source: Schwarcz, *Place and Memory*, 146

xiang shi

In Chinese folklore, a vampiric REVENANT known as the xiang shi is created when an individual's second soul, referred to as the p'o, lingers within the physical vessel following the event of death. Notably, the sustenance of the xiang shi relies upon the consumption of human blood and flesh, as failure to acquire such sustenance triggers its gradual decomposition.

Source: Guiley, *The Complete Vampire Companion*, 26

you hun ye gui

In Chinese folklore, the you hun ye gui is a wandering ghost that is believed to be the spirit of a person who died while far away from home. These spirits are unable to find their way back to their rightful resting place. During festival times, people take precautions to avoid attracting these ghosts. For example, they may choose not to get married or move into a new home during these periods. It is believed that if a you hun ye gui attaches itself to such an event, it will bring continuous bad luck.

Source: Dupler, *Death Explained*, 42, 44

yuan gui

In Chinese folklore, the concept of a yuan gui represents the belief in the existence of ghosts or spirits that have returned from the afterlife. These spirits are believed to be individuals who died under unjust circumstances and are now seeking justice for the wrongs done to them.

It is important to note that yuan gui are perceived as entities that have not found peace due to unresolved grievances related to their untimely demise. According to folklore, these spirits may manifest themselves in various ways, sometimes appearing to individuals in dreams or other supernatural occurrences.

The notion of yuan gui reflects the cultural significance placed upon seeking justice and finding closure for those who have suffered wrongful deaths. By acknowledging the presence of these spirits, individuals aim to honor their memory and potentially assist them in finding the resolution they seek.

While the existence of yuan gui remains within the realm of folklore and superstition, the concept serves as a reminder of the importance of fairness and justice in Chinese culture. It is through such tales that traditional beliefs and values are passed down from generation to generation, shaping the collective understanding of morality and the pursuit of justice.

Source: Dupler, *Death Explained*, 43

yūrei

Yūrei are a type of supernatural entity from Japanese folklore. They are often mistaken for other supernatural creatures, such as bakemono or yōkai. Yūrei are human spirits that have not moved on to the afterlife, either because they are unable or unwilling to do so. While most yūrei are depicted as female, there are also male yūrei.

These spirits can haunt specific locations or individuals, or they may roam freely in pursuit of their objectives. They are most active during the summer months, particularly during the three-day festival known as Obon, which is dedicated to the spirits of the dead.

In traditional depictions, yūrei are portrayed as having a pale, ethereal appearance; floating bodies without clearly defined legs; and long, disheveled hair. Many stories about yūrei claim to be based on actual events or real people but often contain supernatural elements that have been added or embellished over time. The archetype of the wronged woman is often associated with powerful yūrei, with the belief that the more virtuous and unsuspecting the woman was in life, the stronger she becomes as a yūrei in death.

Yūrei are generally not friendly but are not necessarily dangerous. They can create various supernatural phenomena, including audible sounds, physical assaults, and visual manifestations. They are known for inducing fear, even in modern folklore and urban legends. Yūrei are driven by desire for revenge; intense emotions such as anger, devotion, rage, and sadness; and a refusal to accept their own deaths. This energy or power they wield, known as *onnen*, allows them to interact with and affect the physical world. As yūrei gain more power, they can become increasingly dangerous, sometimes losing focus, and causing harm to anyone or anything in their path, regardless of guilt or innocence, in order to achieve their goals.

Sources: Balmain, *Introduction to Japanese Horror Film*, 47, 141; Yoda, *Yurei Attack*, 7–11

zombie, modern

Variation: zombi

Zombies have a rich history in modern cultural folklore and popular culture. The modern version of the zombie, distinct from its representation in Haitian folklore, emerged during the latter half of the twentieth century.

In simple terms, a modern zombie can be described as an animated, lifeless, and soulless corpse. The modern zombie primarily exists as a concept in literature, movies, and other forms of media. The origins of these zombies, if discussed in their lore or stories, vary greatly and include explanations such as bacterial infections, curses, fungi, magic, mental illness, microorganisms, parasites, radiation, scientific experiments gone wrong, viruses, and more. Zombies cannot completely decompose; they show obvious signs of decomposition but never complete the process.

Zombies are typically portrayed as anonymous entities without individuality or personality. They are seen primarily as a collective, representing the dangers of a hostile natural world. They have lost their distinct human qualities and become part of a mindless group or swarm. It is rare to encounter a single zombie; they usually appear en masse.

Despite their aggressive nature, zombies lack cunning or strategic planning. They simply wander until they come into proximity with a human. Once aware of their potential food source, zombies relentlessly move towards it. Few zombies possess speed greater than that of an average walking human, however. They do not tire, give up, or respond to attempts at diversion or negotiation. When faced with obstacles, they persistently pound against barriers until they break through.

A common aspect of zombie lore is the belief that their bite is always lethal since the infectious agent that causes their undead state spreads through this attack. There is no known cure once someone has been bitten. Interestingly, the head of a zombie is believed to retain its desire to bite and consume even when separated from the rest of the zombie's body. It is widely accepted that penetrating the brain is the only guaranteed method of ensuring a zombie's destruction.

Sources: Braudy, *Haunted*, 105; Pivarcsi, *Just a Bite*, 273; Redfern, *The Zombie Book*, 27, 69

zombie, Vodou

Variations: gros bon ange, zombi (Haitian French), zonbi (Haitian Creole)

A Vodou zombie is a reanimated corpse that has been brought back to a semblance of life through magical means, often to serve as slave labor. It is not uncommon for recently deceased bodies to be taken from their graves for this purpose.

Unlike the popular portrayal of zombies in media, Vodou zombies do not possess independent consciousness or will. They obey the commands of the bocor, the person who created them, with robot-like precision.

According to Haitian Vodou beliefs, a supernatural power or essence can enter and animate a corpse. Interestingly, Haitian people do not fear zombies themselves, as they are not seen as inherently dangerous. Rather, they fear the possibility of becoming a zombie. Historically, zombification was used as a form of capital punishment by judicial tribunals, serving as a deterrent to maintain social order within the community.

Vodou originated in West Africa and was brought to Haiti and the southern United States. The word *zombie* likely has its roots in the Congolese word for the spirit of a deceased person, *nzambi*.

There is speculation that Vodou zombies may not actually be reanimated corpses but rather individuals who have been poisoned with a concoction of chemicals that induce a state of physical and mental impairment.

The ingredients of this magical potion or powder, although sources conflict, are said to include animals remains, bew pine (*Zanthoxylum martinicense*), bouga toad venom, cashews ground into a powder, desmembre plants (ground), dumbcane (*Dieffenbachia seguine*), leaves from the bresillet tree (*Comocladia dentata*), manman guêpes (*Urera baccifera*), mashasa (*Dalechampia scandens*), millipedes (ground), puffer fish poison, sugarcane, sweet potato, tarantulas (ground), tch-tch seeds from the *Albizia lebbeck* tree ground into a powder, toad (*Bufo marinus*), tremblador plant (ground), undisclosed powdered human remains, various unnamed toxic plants, white tree frogs skin (ground), and zombie cucumber (*Datura stramonium*). Additionally, belief in magic and faith in the existence of zombies is considered necessary for the efficacy of the potion.

It is believed that consuming salt can restore the ability of zombies to speak and taste, although this often results in their subsequent death. These temporarily restored zombies are referred to as *savanne*. Family members who witness their deceased loved ones in this state may try to feed them salt in an attempt to bring peace to their souls. Alternatively, stabbing the zombie in the heart or decapitating it is believed to release the soul, known as *ti bon ange* ("little good angel").

Salt does not always release a person from their zombified state, however. In some cases, administering a carefully measured tablespoon of white salt can induce a catatonic state in the zombie, keeping them inactive for years until called upon by the bocor.

These created zombies are primarily used as laborers in bakeries and on farms, particularly in agricultural fields. Some stories even suggest that they can be employed for bookkeeping or work in retail stores. These labor zombies are sometimes referred to as *jardin*.

Sources: Davis, *Passage of Darkness*, 300; Guiley, *Encyclopedia of Ghosts and Spirits*, 538–9; Pivarcsi, *Just a Bite*, 158, 159; Steiger, *Real Zombies*, 5–6, 8

Bibliography

Abbott, George Frederick. *Macedonian Folklore.* Cambridge University Press, 1903.

Abdul, Rahim. *Breast Ghost.* Trafford Publishing, 2013.

Abercromby, John. *The Pre- and Proto-Historic Finns: Both Eastern and Western, With the Magic Songs of the West Finns.* David Nutt, 1898.

Adams, Charles J. *The Encyclopedia of Religion.* Macmillan, 1987.

Adams, Michael. *Slayer Slang: A Buffy the Vampire Slayer Lexicon.* Sourcebooks, 2004.

Adams, William Henry Davenport. *Curiosities of Superstition, and Sketches of Some Unrevealed Religions.* J. Masters and Company, 1882.

Addams, Jane. *The Long Road of a Woman's Memory.* Macmillan, 1917.

Agrawala, Vasudeva Sharana. *India as Known to Panini, a Study of the Cultural Material in the Ashtadhyayi.* University of Lucknow, 1953.

Aguilar-Moreno, Manuel. *Handbook to Life in the Aztec World.* Oxford University Press, 2007.

Aldag, A.C. Fisher. *Common Magick: Origins and Practices of British Folk Magick.* Llewellyn Worldwide, 2020.

Alexander, Hartley Burr, Louis Herbert Gray, John Arnott MacCulloch, and George Foot Moore. *The Mythology of All Races*, Volume 6. Marshall Jones Company, 1917.

Allardice, Pamela. *Myths, Gods, and Fantasy: A Sourcebook.* Avery Publishing Group, Incorporated, 1990.

American Anthropologist, Volume 69. American Anthropological Association, 1998.

American Association for South Slavic Studies, American Association for Southeast European Studies, Southeast European Studies Association. *Balkanistica*, Volumes 1–3. Slavica Publishers, 2007.

Anderson, Rasmus Bjorn. *Norse Mythology: Or, The Religion of Our Forefathers, Containing All the Myths of the Eddas, Systematized and Interpreted. With an Introduction, Vocabulary and Index.* C.S. Criggs and Company, 1884.

Andreescu, Stefan. *Vlad the Impaler: Dracula.* The Romanian Cultural Foundation Publishing House, 1999.

Angell, Robert Cooley. *Principles of Sociology.* Overbeck Company, 1949.

Aristotle and Johann Gottlob Schneider. *Aristotle's History of Animals: In Ten Books.* Trans. Richard Cresswell. George Bell and Son, 1878.

Ashley, Leonard R.N. *The Complete Book of Vampires.* Barricade Books, 1998.

Asian Studies, Volumes 8–9. Philippine Center for Advanced Studies, 1970.

Asiatic Society of Calcutta, India, and the Asiatic Society of Bengal. *Bibliotheca Indica.* Baptist Mission Press, 1940.

Astonishing Legends. "Gjenganger." January 14, 2019. https://astonishinglegends.com/astonishing-legends/2019/1/14/gjenganger.

Atenea, Volumes 13–17. Facultad de Artes y Ciencias, Universidad de Puerto Rico, 1993.

Auerbach, Nina. *Our Vampires, Ourselves.* University of Chicago Press, 1997.

Avant, G. Rodney. *A Mythological Reference.* AuthorHouse, 2005.

Aylesworth, Thomas G. *The Story of Vampires.* McGraw-Hill, 1977.

Bailey, Gerry, and Karen Foster. *The Wright Brothers' Glider.* Crabtree Publishing Company, 2008.

Bailey, Kenneth E. *Jacob and the Prodigal: How Jesus Retold Israel's Story.* InterVarsity Press, 2003.

Bain, Robert Nisbet. *Cossack Fairy Tales and Folk Tales.* Kraus Reprint Company, 1975.

Balmain, Colette. *Introduction to Japanese Horror Film.* Edinburgh University Press, 2008.

Barber, Elizabeth Wayland. *The Dancing Goddesses: Folklore, Archaeology, and the Origins of European Dance.* W.W. Norton and Company, 2013.

Barber, Paul. *Vampires, Burial, and Death: Folklore and Reality.* Yale University Press, 1988.

Barber, Richard, and Anne Riches. *A Dictionary of Fabulous Beasts.* Boydell Press, 2000.

Baring-Gould, Sabine. *The Book of the Were-Wolf: Being an Account of a Terrible Superstition.* Smith, Elder, and Company, 1865.

Barmash, Pamela. *Homicide in the Biblical World.* Cambridge University Press, 2005.

Barnett, Janet, and Randy Russell. *The Granny Curse, and Other Legends from East Tennessee.* John F. Blair Publisher, 1999.

Bastian, Adolf, Christian Goodden, and Walter E.J. Tips. *A Journey in Siam* (1863). White Lotus Press, 2005.

Bayliss-Smith, Timothy P., ed. *Subsistence and*

Survival: Rural Ecology in the Pacific. Academic Press, 1977.

Beaumont, Cyril W. *A Ballet Called Giselle.* Cyril W. Beaumont, 1945.

Belanger, Jeff. *The World's Most Haunted Places: From the Secret Files of ghostvillage.com.* Career Press, 2004.

Belanger, Michelle A. *Sacred Hunger, the Vampire in Myth and Reality.* Dark Moon Press, 2005.

Belanger, Michelle A. *Vampires in Their Own Words: An Anthology of Vampire Voices.* Llewellyn Worldwide, 2011.

Bell, Michael E. *Food for the Dead—On the Trail of New England's Vampires.* Carroll and Graf, 2002.

Benedict, Laura Estelle Watson. *A Study of Bagobo Ceremonial, Magic and Myth.* E.J. Brill, Limited, 1916.

Berg, Sebastian. *Slavic Mythology: Folklore, Legends and Religious Beliefs.* Creek Ridge Publishing, 2023.

Beshir, Mohamed Omer. *The Nile Valley Countries, Continuity and Change.* University of Khartoum, 1984.

Besson, Gerard A., Stuart Hahn, and Avril Turner. *Folklore and Legends of Trinidad and Tobago.* Paria, 1989.

Biggs, Mark. *The Case for Lilith.* Lulu.com, 2010.

Billington, Sandra, and Miranda Green. *The Concept of the Goddess.* Routledge, 1999.

Bkah-Hgyur. *Tibetan Tales Derived from Indian Sources.* George Routledge and Sons, 1893.

Blair, Emma Helen, and James Alexander Robertson. *The Philippine Islands 1493–1803*, Volume V. The Arthur H. Clark Company, 1903.

Blanchard, Wendell. *Thailand: Its People, Its Society, Its Culture.* HRAF Press, 1958.

Boas, Franz, and Henry W. Tate. *Tsimshian Mythology.* Government Printing Office, 1916.

Bois, G.J.C. *A Comparative Study with the Traditions of the Gulf of St. Malo (The Channel Islands, Normandy and Brittany) with Reference to World Mythologies.* Vol. 2 of *Jersey Folklore and Superstitions.* AuthorHouse, 2010.

Bolle, Kees W. *The Freedom of Man in Myth.* Vanderbilt University Press, 1968.

Bonnefoy, Yves, Wendy Doniger, and Gerald Honigsblum. *American, African, and Old European Mythologies.* University of Chicago Press, 1993.

Bonnerjea, Biren. *The Allborough New Age Guide: Biren Bonnerjea's a Dictionary of Superstition and Mythology.* Allborough Publishing, 1992.

Bonnerjea, Biren. *L'Ethnologie du Bengale.* Paul Geuthnerl, 1927.

Borlase, William Copeland. *The Dolmens of Ireland: Their Distribution, Structural Characteristics, and Affinities in Other Countries; Together with the Folk-lore Attaching to Them; Supplemented by Considerations on the Anthropology, Ethnology, and Traditions of the Irish People.* Chapman and Hall, 1897.

Borrmann, Norbert. *Vampirismus oder die Sehnsucht nach Unsterblichkeit.* Diederichs, 1999.

Boutland, Craig. *Dullahan the Headless Horseman and Other Legendary Creatures of Ireland.* Gareth Stevens Publishing, 2018.

Boutland, Craig. *Gashadokuro the Giant Skeleton and Other Legendary Creatures of Japan.* Gareth Stevens Publishing, 2019.

Bradley, A.G. "The Wild Dog of Ennerdale." *The Badminton Magazine of Sports and Pastimes* 13, no. LXXV. Longmans, Green and Company, 1901.

Brandon, David, and Alan Brooke. *Haunted London Underground.* The History Press, 2009.

Braudy, Leo. *Haunted: On Ghosts, Witches, Vampires, Zombies, and Other Monsters of the Natural and Supernatural World.* Yale University Press, 2016.

Brennan, John T. *Ghosts of Newport: Spirits, Scoundrels, Legends and Lore.* The History Press, 2007.

Briggs, George Weston. *The Chamars.* Association Press, 1920.

Briggs, Katharine Mary. *An Encyclopedia of Fairies: Hobgoblins, Brownies, Bogies, and Other Supernatural Creatures*, Volume 1976. Pantheon Books, 1976.

Bringsvaerd, Tor Åge. *Phantoms and Fairies: From Norwegian Folklore.* Tanum, 1970.

Brodman, Barbara, and James E. Doan, eds. *The Universal Vampire: Origins and Evolution of a Legend.* Fairleigh Dickinson University Press,, 2013.

Broster, Joan A., and Herbert Bourn. *Amagqirha: Religion, Magic and Medicine in Transkei.* Via Afrika, 1982.

Brown, Nathan. *The Complete Idiot's Guide to the Paranormal: Indulge Your Fascination with the Mysterious and the Unexplained.* Penguin, 2010.

Brown, Nathan. *The Complete Idiot's Guide to Zombies.* Penguin, 2010.

Bruun, Ole, Arne Kalland, and the Nordic Institute of Asian Studies. *Asian Perceptions of Nature: A Critical Approach.* Psychology Press, 1995.

Bryant, Clifton D. *Handbook of Death and Dying.* Sage, 2003.

Buckland, Raymond. *The Weiser Field Guide to Ghosts: Apparitions, Spirits, Spectral Lights and Other Hauntings of History and Legend.* Weiser, 2009.

Budd, Deena West. *The Weiser Field Guide to Cryptozoology: Werewolves, Dragons, Skyfish, Lizard Men, and Other Fascinating Creatures Real and Mysterious.* Weiser Books, 2010.

Budge, Ernest Alfred Thompson Wallis. *Babylonian Life and History.* Barnes and Noble, 2005.

Bulfinch, Thomas. *Bulfinch's Greek and Roman Mythology.* Courier Dover, 2000.

Bunson, Matthew. *The Vampire Encyclopedia.* Three Rivers Press, 1993.

Burgess, James. *Indian Antiquary.* The Education Society's Press, 1872.

Burne, Charlotte Sophia. *Handbook of Folklore.* Sedgwick and Jackson Limited, 1914.

Burne, Charlotte Sophia. *Shropshire Folk Lore, a*

Sheaf of Gleaning, Volume 3 (1883). E.P. Publishing, 1973.

Burton, Richard Francis, Isabel Burton, and Ernest Henry Griset. *Vikram and the Vampire: Or, Tales of Hindu Devilry.* Tylston and Edwards, 1893.

Bush, Laurence C. *Asian Horror Encyclopedia: Asian Horror Culture in Literature, Manga and Folklore.* Writers Club Press, 2001.

Caciola, Nancy. "Wraiths, Revenants and Ritual in Medieval Culture." *Past & Present*, Volume 152. Cambridge University Press, 1996.

Calmet, Augustin. *Dissertation sur les apparitions des anges, des demons et des esprits. Et sur les revenans et vampires de Hongrie, de Boheme, de Modavie et de Silesie.* De Bure, l'aine, 1746.

Calmet, Augustin, and Henry Christmas. *The Phantom World: Or, The Philosophy of Spirits, Apparitions, Etc.* Richard Bentley, 1850.

Calmet, Augustin, Henry Christmas, and Clive Leatherdale. *Treatise on Vampires and Revenants: The Phantom World: Dissertation on those persons who return to earth bodily, the excommunicated, the oupires or vampires, vroucolacas, etc.* Desert Island Books, 1993.

Campbell, John Gregorson. *Superstitions of the Highlands and Islands of Scotland: Collected Entirely from Oral Sources.* James MacLehose and Sons, 1900.

Campbell, Joseph. *The Masks of Gods, Volume 1: Primitive Mythology.* Penguin, 1987.

Canadian Centre for Folk Culture Studies. *Paper: Dossier*, number 1–4. National Museums of Canada, 1972.

Cannell, Fenella. *Power and Intimacy in the Christian Philippines.* Cambridge University Press, 1999.

Carlson, Ruth Kearney, ed. *Folklore and Folktales Around the World.* International Reading Association, 1972.

Carmichael, Elizabeth, and Chloe Sayer. *The Skeleton at the Feast: The Day of the Dead in Mexico.* Trustees of the British Museum, 1991.

Cartey, Wilfred G. *The West Indies: Islands in the Sun.* Nelson, 1967.

Chadwick, Nora K. "Norse Ghosts: A Study in the Draugr and the Haugbui." *Folklore* 57, no. 2 (1946): 50–65.

Chambers, Robert, ed. *The Book of Days: A Miscellany of Popular Antiquities in Connection with the Calendar, Including Anecdote, Biography and History, Curiosities of Literature, and Oddities of Human Life and Character*, Volume 2. W. and R. Chambers, 1888.

Chan, Wing-Tsit, trans. *A Source Book in Chinese Philosophy.* Princeton University Press, 2008.

Charlesworth, Maxwell John, Diane Bell, Kenneth Maddock, and Howard Morphy. *Religion in Aboriginal Australia: An Anthology.* University of Queensland Press, 1984.

Chiang, Sing-chen Lydia, and Songling Pu. *Collecting the Self: Body and Identity in Strange Tale Collections of Late Imperial China.* Brill, 2005.

Chinese Literature, Essays, Articles, Reviews, Volume 24. Coda Press, 2002.

Chopra, Ramesh. *Academic Dictionary of Mythology.* Gyan Books, 2005.

Choron, Sandra, and Harry Choron. *Planet Dog: A Doglopedia.* Houghton Mifflin Company, 2005.

Clark, James. *Haunted London.* The History Press, 2007.

Clifford, Hugh Charles. *In Court and Kampong: Being Tales and Sketches of Native Life in the Malay Peninsula.* Grant Richards, 1897.

Clothey, Fred W., and A. K. Ramanujan. *The Many Faces of Murukan? The History and Meaning of a South Indian God.* Walter de Gruyter, 1978.

Cohen, Jeffrey Jerome, ed. *Prismatic Ecology: Ecotheory Beyond Green.* University of Minnesota Press, 2013.

Collins, Derek. *Magic in the Ancient Greek World.* Blackwell, 2008.

Conway, Moncure Daniel. *Demonology and Devil-lore.* H. Holt, 1879.

Copper, Basil. *The Vampire in Legend, Art and Fact.* Carol, 1989.

Cork Historical Society. *Journal of the Cork Historical and Archaeological Society.* Guy and Company, Limited, 1897.

Cotter, Charis. *A World Full of Ghosts.* Annick Press, 2009.

Coulter, Charles Russell, and Patricia Turner. *Encyclopedia of Ancient Deities.* McFarland, 2000.

Covey, Jacob. *Beasts!* Fantagraphics Books, 2007.

Cox, Marian Roalfe. *An Introduction to Folk-lore.* D. Nutt, 1895.

Crabb, George, and J.H. Finley. *Crabb's English Synonymes.* Harper and Brothers, 1917.

Cramer, Marc. *The Devil Within.* W.H. Allen, 1979.

Creed, Barbara. *The Monstrous-Feminine: Film, Feminism, Psychoanalysis.* Routledge, 1993.

Cremene, Adrien. *Mythologie du Vampire en Roumanie.* Rocher, 1981.

Crooke, William. *An Introduction to the Popular Religion and Folklore of Northern India.* Printed at the Government Press, North-Western Provinces and Oudh, 1894.

Crooke, William. *The Popular Religion and Folk-Lore of Northern India*, Volume 1. Archibald Constable and Company, 1896.

Crooke, William. *The Popular Religion and Folk-Lore of Northern India*, Volume 2. Archibald Constable and Company, 1896.

Crooke, William, and Reginald Edward Enthoven. *Religion and Folklore of Northern India.* Oxford University Press, 1926.

Crowell, Todd. *Farewell, My Colony: Last Days in the Life of British Hong Kong.* Asia 2000, 1998.

Crowfoot, Grace Mary Hood, and Louise Baldensperger. *From Cedar to Hyssop: A Study in the Folklore of Plants in Palestine.* Sheldon Press, 1932.

Cuevas, Bryan J. *Travels in the Netherworld: Buddhist Popular Narratives of Death and the Afterlife in Tibet.* Oxford University Press, 2008.

Cunningham, Graham. *Deliver Me from Evil: Mesopotamian Incantations, 2500–1500 BC.* Biblical Institute, 1997.

Curran, Bob. *Dark Fairies.* Open Road Media, 2012.

Curran, Bob. *Explore Vampires.* Heart of Albion, 2007.

Curran, Bob. *Man-Made Monsters: A Field Guide to Golems, Patchwork Soldiers, Homunculi, and Other Created Creatures.* New Page Books, 2011.

Curran, Bob. *Werewolves: A Field Guide to Shapeshifters, Lycanthropes, and Man-Beasts.* Career Press, 2009.

Curran, Bob, and Ian Daniels. *Vampires: A Field Guide to the Creatures That Stalk the Night.* New Page, 2005.

Curtin, Jeremiah. *Hero-Tales of Ireland.* Macmillan, 1894.

Czaplicka, Marie Antoinette. *Shamanism in Siberia: Aboriginal Siberia, a Study in Social Anthropology.* Forgotten Books, 2007.

Daly, Kathleen N. *Norse Mythology A to Z.* Facts on File, 2009.

Daly, Kathleen N., and Marian Rengel. *Greek and Roman Mythology, A to Z.* Infobase Publishing, 2009.

Danelek, J. Allan. *The Case for Ghosts.* Llewellyn Worldwide, 2010.

Danielou, Alain. *The Myths and Gods of India: The Classic Work on Hindu Polytheism from the Princeton Bollingen Series.* Inner Traditions/Bear and Company, 1991.

Darwin, Charles. *A Naturalist's Voyage Round the World.* John Murray, 1913.

Davenport, Richard Alfred. *Sketches of Imposture, Deception, and Credulity.* T. Tegg and Son, 1837.

David-Neel, Alexandra. *With Mystics and Magicians in Tibet.* Penguin, 1936.

Davis, Frederick Hadland, and Evelyn Paul. *Myths and Legends of Japan.* Farrar and Rinehart, 1932.

Davis, Wade. *Passage of Darkness: The Ethnobiology of the Haitian Zombie.* University of North Carolina Press, 1988.

Davison, Carol Margaret, and Paul Simpson-Housley. *Bram Stoker's Dracula: Sucking Through the Century, 1897–1997.* Dundurn Press, 1997.

Day, Peter. *Vampires: Myths and Metaphors of Enduring Evil.* Rodopi, 2006.

Daya, Dalpatram. *Essay on Demonology of Guzerat.* Bombay, India: 1849.

de Magalhaes, Basilio. *Folk-Lore in Brazil.* Imprensa Nacional, 1945.

Demetrio, Francisco R. *Encyclopedia of Philippine Folk Beliefs and Customs.* Xavier University, 1991.

Dennis, Geoffrey W. *The Encyclopedia of Jewish Myth, Magic and Mysticism.* Llewellyn Worldwide, 2007.

DePierre, David. *A Brief History of Oral Sex.* McFarland, 2017.

D'Epiro, Peter. *The Book of Firsts: 150 World-Changing People and Events from Caesar Augustus to the Internet.* Knopf Doubleday Publishing Group, 2010.

de Plancy, Jacques-Albin-Simon Collin. *Dictionary of Demonology.* Philosophical Library, 1965.

de Quincey, Thomas. *Confessions of an English Opium-Eater: And, Suspiria de Profundis.* Ticknor and Fields, 1864.

de Vere, Nicholas Tracy Twyman. *The Dragon Legacy: The Secret History of an Ancient Bloodline.* Book Tree, 2004.

de Visser, Marinus Willem. *The Dog and the Cat in Japanese Superstition.* Asiatic Society of Japan, 1909.

Dey, Lal Behari. *Govinda Sámanta, or the History of a Bengal Ráiyat,* Volume 1. Macmillan, 1874.

Dillon, Arthur Edmund Denis Lee-Dillon. *Winter in Iceland and Lapland: By the Hon. Arthur Dillon.* 2 Volumes. Henry Colburn, 1840.

Dixon-Kennedy, Mike. *Encyclopedia of Greco-Roman Mythology.* ABC-CLIO, 1998.

Do, Thein. *Vietnamese Supernaturalism: Views from the Southern Region.* Routledge, 2003.

Doniger, Wendy. *Merriam-Webster's Encyclopedia of World Religions.* Merriam-Webster, 1999.

Dorsey, F. Owen. "Tenton Folk-Lore Notes." In *Journal of American Folklore,* Volume 7 of *Bibliographical and Special Series of the American Folklore Society.* American Folk-lore Society, 1888.

Dorson, Richard Mercer. *Folk Legends of Japan.* Tuttle Publishing, 1962.

Dowson, John. *Classical Dictionary of Hindu Mythology and Religion, Geography, History, and Literature.* Trubner and Company, 1870.

Draaisma, D. *Metaphors of Memory: A History of Ideas About the Mind.* Cambridge University Press, 2000.

Drazen, Patrick. *A Gathering of Spirits: Japan's Ghost Story Tradition from Folklore and Kabuki to Anime and Manga.* iUniverse, 2011.

Drizari, Nelo. *Albanian-English Dictionary.* Frederick Ungar Publishing, 1957.

Drury, Nevill. *The Dictionary of the Esoteric: 3000 Entries on the Mystical and Occult Traditions.* Motilal Banarsidass, 2004.

Du Chaillu, Paul Belloni, and Victor Semon Perard. *King Mombo.* C. Scribner's Sons, 1902.

Dundes, Alan. *Vampire Casebook.* University of Wisconsin Press, 1998.

Dupler, Michael. *Death Explained: A Ghost Hunter's Guide to the Afterlife.* Shot in the Dark Media, 2013.

DuPrae, Levant. *The Vampires: Sodom.* Infinity Publishing, 2010.

Durham, Mary Edith. *Some Tribal Origins, Laws and Customs of the Balkans.* George Allen and Unwin, 1928.

Durrell, Lawrence. *The Greek Islands.* Viking Press, 1978.

Eason, Cassandra. *A Complete Guide to Faeries and Magical Beings: Explore the Mystical Realm of the Little People.* Weiser Books, 2002.

Eberhard, Wolfram. *Dictionary of Chinese*

Symbols: Hidden Symbols in Chinese Life and Thought. Routledge, 2006.

Echiasuksa, Chulalongkonmahawitthayalai Sathaban. *Asian Review*, Volume 2. Institute of Asian Studies, Chulalongkorn University, 2003.

Eliade, Mircea, and Charles J. Adams. *The Encyclopedia of Religion*. Macmillan, 1987.

Ellis, Peter Berresford. *A Dictionary of Irish Mythology*. ABC-CLIO, 1987.

Ellis, Stewart M. *Mainly Victorian*. Thompson Press, 2007.

Ellwood, Robert S., and Gregory D. Alles, eds. *The Encyclopedia of World Religions*. Infobase Publishing, 2009.

Elsie, Robert. *A Dictionary of Albanian Religion, Mythology, and Folk Culture*. New York University Press, 2001.

Elton, Oliver. *The First Nine Books of the Danish History*. Kessinger Publishing, 1905.

Emerton, John Adney. *Congress Volume: Jerusalem, 1986*. Brill, 1988.

Encyclopedia Americana: A Library of Universal Knowledge, Volume 3. Encyclopedia Americana, 1918.

Encyclopedia Americana or "Conversations Lexicon," being a general dictionary of Arts, Sciences, Literature, Biography, History, Ethics, and Political Economy, Volume 6. Blackie and Son, 1832.

Enright, Laura. *Vampires' Most Wanted: The Top 10 Book of Bloodthirsty Biters, Stake-wielding Slayers, and Other Undead Oddities*. Potomac Books, Incorporated, 2011.

An Ethnologic Dictionary of the Navaho Language. The Franciscan Fathers, 1910.

Falola, Toyin. *A Mouth Sweeter than Salt: An African Memoir*. University of Michigan Press 2005.

Farson, Daniel. *The Man Who Wrote Dracula: A Biography of Bram Stoker*. St. Martin's Press, 1975.

Fee, Christopher R., and Jeffrey B. Webb, eds. *American Myths, Legends, and Tall Tales: An Encyclopedia of American Folklore: An Encyclopedia of American Folklore*. ABC-CLIO, 2016.

Fierobe, Claude, ed. *Dracula: Mythe et Meta-morphoses*. Presses Univ. Septentrion, 2005.

Filipovic, Milenko S. *Among the People, Native Yugoslav Ethnography: Selected Writing of Milenko S. Filipovic*. Michigan Slavic Publications, Department of Slavic Languages and Literatures, 1982.

Fjelstad, Karen, and Thi Hien Nguyen. *Possessed by the Spirits: Mediumship in Contemporary Vietnamese Communities*. Southeast Asia Program Publications, 2006.

Flint, Valerie Irene Jane, Bengt Ankarloo, and Stuart Clark. *Witchcraft and Magic in Europe: Ancient Greece and Rome*. Continuum International, 1999.

Florescu, Radu. *In Search of Frankenstein: With Contributions by Alan Barbour and Matie Cazacu*. New York Graphic Society, 1975.

Flowers, Stephen E. *Runes and Magic: Magical Formulaic Elements in the Older Runic Tradition*. Peter Lang, 1986.

Fogelson, Raymond D., and Richard Newbold Adams. *The Anthropology of Power: Ethnographic Studies from Asia, Oceania, and the New World*. Academic Press, 1977.

Folklore Society of Great Britain. *The Folk-Lore Record*, Volume 4. Folk-lore Society, 1893.

Folklore Society of Great Britain. *The Folk-Lore Record*, Volume 6. Folk-lore Society, 1895.

Folklore Society of Great Britain. *The Folk-lore Record*, Volumes 87–88. Folk-lore Society, 1927.

Fontenrose, Joseph Eddy. *Python*. Biblo and Tannen, 1974.

Ford, Michael. *Book of the Witch Moon, Choronzon Edition*. Lulu.com, 2006.

Ford, Michael. *Maskim Hul: Babylonian Magick*. Lulu.com, 2011.

Forlong, James George Roche. *Faiths of Man: Encyclopedia of Religions*, Volume 3. University Books, 1964.

Forte, Charles. *Lo!* Claude Kendall, 1931.

Foster, Michael Dylan. *Pandemonium and Parade: Japanese Monsters and the Culture of Yokai*. University of California Press, 2008.

Frater, Jamie. *Listverse.Com's Ultimate Book of Bizarre Lists: Fascinating Facts and Shocking Trivia on Movies, Music, Crime, Celebrities, History, and More*. Ulysses Press, 2010.

Frazer, James George. *The Belief in Immortality and the Worship of the Dead: The Belief Among the Aborigines of Australia, the Torres Straits Islands, New Guinea and Melanesia*. Dawsons, 1968.

Frazer, James George. *The Golden Bough: A Study in Comparative Religion*, Volumes 2 and 11. Macmillan and Company, 1890, 1913.

Frazer, James George, and Lilly Grove Frazer. *Leaves from the Golden Bough*. Macmillan, 1924.

Frédéric, Louis. *Japan Encyclopedia*. Harvard University Press, 2002.

Froud, Brian, and Alan Lee. *Faeries*. Harry N. Abrams, 1978.

Galian, Laurence. *The Sun at Midnight: The Revealed Mysteries of the Ahlul Bayt Sufis*. Quiddity, 2003.

Gamkrelidze, Thomas V., Vjaceslav V. Ivanov, and Nichols Johanna. *Indo-European and the Indo-Europeans: A Reconstruction and Historical Analysis of a Proto-Language and Proto-Culture. Part I: The Text. Part II: Bibliography, Indexes*. Walter de Gruyter, 1995.

Garland, Robert. *The Greek Way of Death*. Cornell University Press, 2001.

Garnett, Lucy Mary Jane, and John S. Stuart-Glennie. *The Women of Turkey and Their Folk-lore*. D. Nutt, 1890.

Garry, Jane, and Hasan El-Shamy. *Archetypes and Motifs in Folklore and Literature*. M.E. Sharpe, 2005.

Gaster, Theodore Herzl. *Myth, Legend and Custom in the Old Testament: A Comparative Study from Sir James G. Frazer's Folklore in the Old Testament*, Volume 1. HarperCollins, 1970.

Gaster, Theodore Herzl. *Thespis: Ritual, Myth, and Drama in the Ancient Near East.* Doubleday, 1961.

Gaynor, Frank. *Dictionary of Mysticism.* Philosophical Library/Open Road, 2018.

Gazetteer of Bombay State, Volume 20. Government Central Press, 1954.

Geertz, Clifford. *The Religion of Java.* University of Chicago Press, 1976.

The Gentleman's Magazine and Historical Review xvi (January–June). Grant and Company, 1876.

Georgieva, Ivanichka. *Bulgarian Mythology.* Syvat Publishers, 1985.

Gerhard, Ken. *Encounters with Flying Humanoids: Mothman, Manbirds, Gargoyles & Other Winged Beasts.* Llewellyn Worldwide, 2013.

Ghosts of Glamis. Glamis Castle Publications, 2020.

Gimbutas, Marija Alseikaite, and Joan Marler. *From the Realm of the Ancestors: An Anthology in Honor of Marija Gimbutas.* Knowledge, Ideas and Trends, 1997.

Ginzburg, Carlo, and Raymond Rosenthal. *Ecstasies: Deciphering the Witches' Sabbath.* University of Chicago Press, 2004.

Glut, Donald F. *The Dracula Book.* Scarecrow Press, 1975.

Godfrey, Linda S. *Mythical Creatures.* Chelsea House Publishers, 2009.

Goss, Linda, and Marian E. Barnes, ed. *Talk That Talk: An Anthology of African-American Storytelling.* Simon & Schuster, 1989.

Goss, Michael. *Lost at Sea: Ghost Ships and Other Mysteries.* Prometheus Books, 1984.

Graham, Walter Armstrong. *Siam: A Handbook of Practical, Commercial, and Political Information.* F.G. Browne, 1913.

Grammaticus, Saxo. *The Danish History.* David Nutt, 1894.

Grauer, Armgard, and John G. Kennedy. "The Dogri: Evil Beings of the Nile." In *Nubian Ceremonial Life*, edited by John G. Kennedy. University of California Press, 1978, pp. 114–124.

Gray, Louis Herbert, George Foot Moore, and John Arnott MacCulloch, eds. *The Mythology of All Races*, Volumes 3, 10, and 12. Marshall Jones Company, 1916–32.

Grimm, Jacob, and James Steven Stallybrass. *Teutonic Mythology.* G. Bell and Sons, 1883.

Groot, Jan Jakob Maria. *The Religion of the Chinese.* Macmillan, 1912.

Guiley, Rosemary. *The Encyclopedia of Ghosts and Spirits.* 3rd ed. Checkmark Books, 1992.

Guiley, Rosemary. *The Encyclopedia of Vampires, Werewolves, and Other Monsters.* Infobase Publishing, 2004.

Guiley, Rosemary, and J.B. Macabre. *The Complete Vampire Companion.* Macmillan, 1994.

Haase, Donald. *The Greenwood Encyclopedia of Folktales and Fairy Tales.* Greenwood, 2008.

Haining, Peter. *A Dictionary of Vampires.* Robert Hale, 2001.

Hallam, Jack. *Ghosts of the North.* David and Charles, 1976.

Hamilton, John. *The World of Horror: Vampires.* ABDO Publishing, 2007.

Hammond-Tooke, W.D. *Bhaca Society: A People of the Transkeian Uplands, South Africa.* Oxford University Press, 1962.

Hard, Robin. *The Routledge Handbook of Greek Mythology: Based on H.J. Rose's "Handbook of Greek Mythology."* Psychology Press, 2004.

Harris, Jason Marc. *Folklore and the Fantastic in Nineteenth-Century British Fiction.* Ashgate, 2008.

Hartshorne, Charles Henry. *A Guide to Alnwick Castle.* Longmans, Green, Reader, and Dyer, 1865.

Hastings, James. *Encyclopædia of Religion and Ethics*, Part 5. Kessinger Publishing, 2003.

Hastings, James. *Encyclopædia of Religion and Ethics*, Part 8. Kessinger Publishing, 2003.

Hastings, James. *Encyclopædia of Religion and Ethics*, Part 24. Kessinger Publishing, 2003.

Hastings, James, and John Alexander Selbie. *Encyclopædia of Religion and Ethics*, Part 2. Kessinger Publishing, 2003.

Hastings, James, John Alexander Selbie, and Louis Herbert Gray, eds. *Encyclopædia of Religion and Ethics*, Volumes 3–4, 6, 9, and 11–12. Scribner's, 1908–26.

Hastings, James, Louis Herbert Gray, and John Alexander Selbie. *Encyclopædia of Religion and Ethics*, Volume. 13. T. and T. Clark, 1922.

Hauck, Dennis William. *The International Directory of Haunted Places: Ghostly Abodes, Sacred Sites, and Other Supernatural Locations.* Penguin, 2000.

Hayes, Bill. *Five Quarts: A Personal and Natural History of Blood.* Random House, 2005.

Hayward, Richard, and Humbert Craig. *In Praise of Ulster.* W. Mullan, 1946.

Healey, Christopher J. *Maring Hunters and Traders: Production and Exchange in the Papua New Guinea Highlands.* University of California Press, 1990.

Hearn, Lafcadio, and Keichu Takenouche. *Kwaidan: Stories and Studies of Strange Things.* Houghton Mifflin, 1904.

Heath, Pamela Rae, and Jon Klimo. *Suicide: What Really Happens in the Afterlife?: Channeled Conversations with the Dead.* North Atlantic Books, 2006.

Heinze, Ruth-Inge. *Proceedings of the Fifth International Conference on the Study of Shamanism and Alternate Modes of Healing: Held at the St. Sabina Center, San Rafael, California, September 3 to September 5, 1988.* Independent Scholars of Asia, 1989.

Heinze, Ruth-Inge. *Tham Khwan: How to Contain the Essence of Life: A Socio-psychological Comparison of a Thai Custom.* Singapore University Press, 1982.

Heldreth, Leonard G., and Mary Pharr. *The Blood Is the Life: Vampires in Literature.* Popular Press, 1999.

Henderson, George. *The Norse Influence on Celtic Scotland.* J. MacLehose, 1910.

Hertz, Wilhelm. *Der Werwolf.* A. Kroner, 1862.

Hickman, Tom. *Death: A User's Guide.* Random House Publishing Group, 2003.

Hiltebeitel, Alf, and Barbara D. Miller, eds. *Hair: Its Power and Meaning in Asian Cultures.* State University of New York, 1998.

Hock, Stefan. *Die Vampyrsagen und ihre Verwertung in der deutschen Litteratur.* A. Duncker, 1900.

Hodous, Lewis. *Folkways in China.* Arthur Probsthain, 1929.

Hoiberg, Dale, and Indu Ramchandani. *Students' Britannica India.* Popular Prakashan, 2000.

Holland, Richard. *Haunted Wales: A Survey of Welsh Ghostlore.* Landmark, 2005.

Hoops, Johannes. *Kommentar zum Beowulf.* Carl Winter, 1932.

Hopkins, Edward Washburn. *Epic Mythology with Additions and Corrections.* Biblo and Tannen Publishers, 1968.

Hori, Ichiro. *Folk Religion in Japan: Continuity and Change.* University of Chicago Press, 1974.

Houran, James. *From Shaman to Scientist: Essays on Humanity's Search for Spirits.* Scarecrow Press, 2004.

Howell, Signe. *Society and Cosmos: Chewong of Peninsular Malaysia.* Oxford University Press, 1984.

Howitt, Alfred William. *The Native Tribes of South-East Australia.* Macmillan and Company, Limited, 1904.

Hubbs, Joanna. *Mother Russia: The Feminine Myth in Russian Culture.* Indiana University Press, 1993.

Hufford, David J. *The Terror That Comes in the Night: An Experience-Centered Study of Supernatural Assault Traditions.* University of Pennsylvania Press, 1989.

Hulme, Frederick Edward. *Myth-land.* S. Low, Marston, Searle and Rivington, 1886.

Humphrey, John H. *Roman Circuses: Arenas for Chariot Racing.* University of California Press, 1986.

Hurwitz, Siegmund. *Lilith, the First Eve: Historical and Psychological Aspects of the Dark Feminine.* Daimon, 1992.

Icon Group International, Inc. *Hanging: Webster's Quotations, Facts and Phrases.* ICON Group International, Inc., 2008.

Ingpen, Robert R., and Molly Perham. *Ghouls and Monsters.* Chelsea House Publishers, 1996.

Instytut Historii Kultury Materialnej. *Ethnologia Polona,* Volumes 10–11. Zaklad Narodowy im. Ossolinskich, 1986.

Ivanits, Linda J. *Russian Folk Belief.* M.E. Sharpe, 1992.

Jackson, Nigel Aldcroft. *The Compleat Vampyre: The Vampire Shaman, Werewolves, Witchery and the Dark Mythology of the Undead.* Capall Bann, 1995.

Jackson-Laufer, Guida Myrl. *Encyclopedia of Traditional Epics.* ABC-CLIO, 1994.

Jacobs, Joseph, William Crooke, Alfred Trubner Nutt, and Arthur Robinson Wright. *Folklore,* Volume 11. Folklore Society (Great Britain), 1900.

Jakobson, Roman. *Selected Writings: On Verse, Its Masters and Explorers.* Walter de Gruyter, 1962.

Jakobson, Roman. "Slavic Gods and Demons." In *Selected Writings: Contributions to Comparative Mythology: Studies in Linguistics and Philosophy, 1972–1982,* edited by Stephen Rudy. Mouton Publishers, 1985.

Jastrow, Morris. *The Religion of Babylonia and Assyria.* Ginn and Company, 1898.

Jobes, Gertrude. *Dictionary of Mythology, Folklore and Symbols.* Scarecrow Press, 1961.

Jocano, F. Landa. *Folk Medicine: In a Philippine Municipality.* National Museum Publication, 1973.

Johnston, Corker. *Acheri Demon Haunting: The True Story of Paranormal Case 263.* CreateSpace Publishing, 2013.

Johnston, Sarah Iles. *Restless Dead: Encounters Between the Living and the Dead in Ancient Greece.* University of California Press, 1999.

Joly, Dom. *Scary Monsters and Super Creeps: In Search of the World's Most Hideous Beasts.* Simon & Schuster, 2012.

Jones, David E. *Evil in Our Midst: A Chilling Glimpse of Our Most Feared and Frightening Demons.* Square One Publishers, 2001.

Jones, Ernest. *On the Nightmare.* Hogarth Press, 1949.

Jones, Griffith Hartwell. *The Dawn of European Civilization.* Kegan Paul, Trench, Trubner, 1903.

Jordan, Michael. *Dictionary of Gods and Goddesses.* Infobase Publishing, 2009.

Journal of the Gypsy Lore Society. The Gypsy Lore Society, 1939.

Journal of Slavic Linguistics, Volume 14. Indiana University Linguistics Club, 2007.

Joya, Moku. *Mock Joya's Things Japanese.* Japan Times, 1985.

Kalland, Arne. *Facing the Spirits: Illness and Healing in a Japanese Community.* NIAS Press, 1991.

Kallen, Stuart A. *Vampire History and Lore.* Capstone, 2011.

Kanellos, Nicolás, and Claudio Esteva-Fabregat. *Handbook of Hispanic Cultures in the United States: Literature and Art.* Arte Publico Press, 1993.

Keel, John A. *The Complete Guide to Mysterious Beings.* Macmillan, 2002.

Kelly, Sean, and Rosemary Rogers. *Who in Hell: A Guide to the Whole Damned Bunch.* Villard, 1996.

Kendall, Laurel. *Vietnam: Journeys of Body, Mind, and Spirit.* University of California Press, 2003.

Kenyon, Theda. *Witches Still Live.* Kessinger, 2003.

Kessler, Joan C. *Demons of the Night: Tales of the Fantastic, Madness, and the Supernatural from Nineteenth-Century France.* University of Chicago Press, 1995.

Keyworth, David. *Troublesome Corpses: Vampires & Revenants, from Antiquity to the Present.* Desert Island Books, 2007.

Khairunnisa, Aulia, and Mira Wardhaningsih. *A Book of Indonesian Ghosts*. StoryTale Studios, 2020.

Khanam, R. *Demonology: Socio-Religious Belief of Witchcraft*. Global Vision Publishing House, 2003.

Khanna, Rakesh, and J. Furcifer Bhairav. *Ghosts, Monsters, and Demons of India*. Watkins Media Limited, 2023.

Kiberd, Declan. *Irish Classics*. Harvard University Press, 2001.

Kiev, Ari. *Magic, Faith, and Healing: Studies in Primitive Psychiatry Today*. Free Press of Glencoe, 1964.

Knapp, Bettina Liebowitz. *Women, Myth, and the Feminine Principle*. SUNY Press, 1997.

Knappert, Jan. *Bantu Myths and Other Tales*. Brill Archive, 1977.

Koentjaraningrat and Southeast Asian Studies Program. *Javanese Culture*. Oxford University Press, 1985.

Konstantinos. *Vampires: The Occult Truth*. Llewellyn Worldwide, 1996.

Kosambi, D.D. *An Introduction to the Study of Indian History*. Popular Prakashan, 1996.

Kroeber, Alfred Louis. *Peoples of the Philippines*. American Museum Press, 1919.

Kroonen, Guus. *Etymological Dictionary of Proto-Germanic*. Brill, 2013.

Kropej, Monika. *Supernatural Beings from Slovenian Myth and Folktales*. Zalozba ZRC, 2012.

Kuhn, Philip A. *Soulstealers: The Chinese Sorcery Scare of 1768*. Harvard University Press, 1990.

Kvaerne, Per. *Tibet Bon Religion: A Death Ritual of the Tibetan Bonpos*. Brill, 1985.

Laderman, Carol. *Wives and Midwives: Childbirth and Nutrition in Rural Malaysia*. University of California Press, 1987.

Laderman, Gary. *Rest in Peace: A Cultural History of Death and the Funeral Home in Twentieth-Century America*. Oxford University Press, 2005.

Lane, Edward William, and Stanley Lane-Poole. *Selections from the Kur-an*. 1863.

Latham, Robert Gordon. *Descriptive Ethnology: Europe, Africa, India*, Volume 2. J. van Voorst, 1859.

Latourette, Kenneth Scott. *The Chinese*. Macmillan, 1934.

Lawson, John Cuthbert. *Modern Greek Folklore and Ancient Greek Folklore*. Cambridge University Press, 1910.

Leach, Maria, and Jerome Fried. *Funk and Wagnalls Standard Dictionary of Folklore, Mythology, and Legend*. Funk and Wagnalls, 1949.

Leake, William Martin. *Travels in Northern Greece*. J. Rodwell, 1835.

Leatherdale, Clive. *Dracula: The Novel and the Legend: A Study of Bram Stoker's Gothic Masterpiece*. Desert Island Books, 1993.

Le Braz, Anatole, and Derek Bryce. *Celtic Legends of the Beyond: A Celtic Book of the Dead*. Red Wheel/Weiser, 1999.

Lecouteux, Claude. *The History of the Vampire*. Editions Imago, 1999.

Lecouteux, Claude. *The Return of the Dead: Ghosts, Ancestors, and Transparent Veil of the Pagan Mind*. Inner Traditions, 1996.

Lecouteux, Claude. *The Tradition of Household Spirits: Ancestral Lore and Practices*. Translated by Jon E. Graham. Inner Traditions, 2013.

Leddon, Alan. *A Child's Eye View of Fair Folk*. Spero Publishing, 2011.

Lee, Jonathan H.X., and Kathleen Nadeau. *Encyclopedia of Asian American Folklore and Folklife*. 3 Volumes. Bloomsbury Publishing USA, 2010.

Le Roy, Alexander. *The Religion of the Primitives*. Macmillan, 1922.

Lewis, Paul White, and Elaine Lewis. *Peoples of the Golden Triangle: Six Tribes in Thailand*. River Books, 1998.

Lindahl, Carl, John Lindow, and John McNamara. *Medieval Folklore: An Encyclopedia of Myths, Legends, Tales, Beliefs, and Customs*. ABC-CLIO, 2000.

Lindsay, Alexander William Crawford. *Lives of the Lindsays; or, A Memoir of the Houses of Crawford and Balcarres*. John Murray, 1849.

Lopez, Mellie Leandicho. *A Handbook of Philippine Folklore*. University of the Philippines, 2006.

Lorentz, Friedrich, Adam Fischer, and Tadeusz Lehr-Spławiński. *The Cassubian Civilization*. Faber & Faber, Limited, 1935.

Louis, Andre J. *Voodoo in Haiti: Catholicism, Protestantism and a Model of Effective Ministry in the Context of Voodoo in Haiti*. Tate Publishing, 2007.

Lung, Haha. *Lost Fighting Arts of Vietnam*. Citadel Press, 2006.

Lurker, Manfred. *Dictionary of Gods and Goddesses, Devils and Demons*. Routledge Kegan and Paul, 1987.

Lyovin, Anatole. *An Introduction to the Languages of the World*. Oxford University Press, 1997.

Maberry, Jonathan. *Vampire Universe: The Dark World of Supernatural Beings That Haunt Us, Hunt Us, and Hunger for Us*. Citadel Press, 1996.

Maberry, Jonathan, and David F. Kramer. *The Cryptopedia: A Dictionary of the Weird, Strange, and Downright Bizarre*. Citadel Press, 2007.

Maberry, Jonathan, and David F. Kramer. *They Bite! Endless Cravings of Supernatural Predators*. Kensington Publishing Company, 2009.

Maberry, Jonathan, and Janice Gable Bashman. *Wanted Undead or Alive: Vampire Hunters and Other Kick-Ass Enemies of Evil*. Kensington Publishing Corporation, 2010.

MacCulloch, John Arnott, Louis Herbert Gray, and František Krupička. *Celtic Mythology*. Marshall Jones Company, 1918.

MacDermott, Mercia. *Bulgarian Folk Customs*. Jessica Kingsley Publishers, 1998.

MacDougall, Shane. *The Vampire Slayers' Field Guide to the Undead*. Strider Nolan Publishing, 2003.

Mack, Carol K., and Dinah Mack. *A Field Guide to Demons, Fairies, Fallen Angels and Other Subversive Spirits*. Arcade, 1998.

Mackay, Charles. *The Gaelic Etymology of the Languages of Western Europe: And More Especially of the English and Lowland Scotch, and Their Slang, Cant, and Colloquial Dialects*. Trubner and Company, 1877.

Mackenzie, Andrew. *Dracula Country: Travels and Folk Beliefs in Romania*. Barker, 1977.

MacKillop, James. *Dictionary of Celtic Mythology*. Oxford University Press, 1998.

Making of America Project. *The Atlantic Monthly*, Volume 49. Atlantic Monthly Company, 1882.

Malbrough, Ray T. *Hoodoo Mysteries: Folk Magic, Mysticism and Rituals*. Llewellyn Worldwide, 2003.

Man, Volumes 23–25. Royal Anthropological Institute of Great Britain and Ireland, 1888.

Markowitz, Judith A. *Robots That Kill: Deadly Machines and Their Precursors in Myth, Folklore, Literature, Popular Culture and Reality*. McFarland, 2019.

Marra, Michael F. *Japanese Hermeneutics: Current Debates on Aesthetics and Interpretation*. University of Hawaii Press, 2002.

Marwick, Ernest Walker. *The Folklore of Orkney and Shetland*. Rowman and Littlefield, 1975.

Marwick, Ernest Walker, and J.D.M. Robertson. *An Orkney Anthology: The Selected Works of Ernest Walker Marwick*. Scottish Academic Press, 1991.

Mass, Jeffrey P. *The Origins of Japan's Medieval World: Courtiers, Clerics, Warriors, and Peasants in the Fourteenth Century*. Stanford University Press, 1997.

Massola, Aldo. *Bunjil's Cave: Myths, Legends and Superstitions of the Aborigines of South-East Australia*. Lansdowne Press, 1968.

Masters, Anthony. *The Natural History of the Vampire*. Hart-Davis, 1972.

Masters, R.E.L. *Eros and Evil: The Sexual Psychopathology of Witchcraft, Contains the Complete Text of Sinistrari's Demoniality*. Viking Press, 1974.

McClelland, Bruce. *Slayers and Their Vampires: A Cultural History of Killing the Dead*. University of Michigan Press, 2006.

McClure, Laura K. *A Companion to Euripides*. John Wiley and Sons, 2017.

McCormack, Anthony M. *The Earldom of Desmond 1463–1583: The Decline and Crisis of a Feudal Lordship*. Four Courts Press, 2005.

McCoy, Edain. *A Witch's Guide to Faery Folk: Reclaiming Our Working Relationship with Invisible Helpers*. Llewellyn Publications, 1995.

McDonald, Beth E. *The Vampire as Numinous Experience: Spiritual Journeys with the Undead in British and American Literature*. McFarland, 2004.

McGowen, Tom. *Encyclopedia of Legendary Creatures*. Rand McNally, 1981.

McHugh, James Noel. *Hantu Hantu: An Account of Ghost Belief in Modern Malaya*. Donald Moore for Eastern Universities Press, 1959.

McKinnell, John. *Meeting the Other in Old Norse Myth and Legend*. D.S. Brewer, 2005.

McKinnell, John, and Rudolf Simek, with Klaus Duwel. *Runes, Magic and Religion: A Sourcebook*. Fassbaender, 2004.

McNally, Raymond T. *A Clutch of Vampires: These Being Among the Best from History and Literature*. New York Graphic Society, 1974.

McNally, Raymond T., and Radu Florescu. *In Search of Dracula, the History of Dracula and Vampires*. Mariner Books, 1994.

Mead, Margaret, and Nicolas Calas. *Primitive Heritage: An Anthropological Anthology*. Random House, 1953.

Melland, Frank Hulme. *In Witch-Bound Africa: An Account of the Primitive Kaonde Tribe and Their Beliefs*. Seeley, Service and Company, Limited, 1923.

Melton, J. Gordon. *The Vampire Book: The Encyclopedia of the Undead*. Visible Ink Press, 1999.

Mercatante, Anthony S. *Good and Evil: Mythology and Folklore*. Harper and Row, 1978.

Merkur, Daniel. *Becoming Half Hidden: Shamanism and Initiation Among the Inuit*. Garland Publishing, 1992.

Mew, James. *Traditional Aspects of Hell: Ancient and Modern*. S. Sonnenschein, 1903.

Meyer, Elard Hugo. *Mythologie der Germanen*. Karl J. Trubner, 1903.

Mizuki, Shigeru. *Kitaro's Yokai Battles*. Drawn and Quarterly, 2021.

Moldvay, Tom, ed. *TSR Dungeons and Dragons Fantasy Adventure Game Base Rulebook*. TSR, 1981.

Monaghan, Patricia. *The Encyclopedia of Celtic Mythology and Folklore*. Infobase Publishing, 2014.

Monaghan, Patricia. *New Book of Goddesses and Heroines*. Llewellyn Publications, 1997.

Mordell, Phineas. *The Origin of Letters and Numerals*. P. Mordell, 1914.

Morris, Katherine. *Sorceress or Witch? The Image of Gender in Medieval Iceland and Northern Europe*. University Press of America, 1991.

Mowat, Farley. *People of the Deer*. Carroll and Graf, 2004.

Muhaimin, Abdul Ghoffir. *The Islamic Traditions of Cirebon: Ibadat and Adat Among Javanese Muslims*. Australian National University Press, 2006.

Muir, Henry Dupee. *Songs and Other Fancies*. Henry Dupee Muir, 1901.

Murakami, Kenji. *Strange Japanese Yokai: A Guide to Weird and Wonderful Monsters, Demons and Spirits*. Tuttle, 2023.

Murakami, Kenji. *Yoki Jiten*. Mainichi Shimbun, 2000.

Murguia, Salvador Jimenez. *The Encyclopedia of Japanese Horror Films*. Rowman and Littlefield, 2016.

Murphy, Jan. *Mysteries and Legends of Colorado:*

True Stories of the Unsolved and Unexplained. Globe Pequot, 2007.

Murray, Gilbert. *Greek Poetry and Life: Essays Presented to Gilbert Murray on His Seventieth Birthday, January 2, 1936.* Books for Libraries Press, 1967.

Muss-Arnolt, William. *A Concise Dictionary of the Assyrian Language.* Reuther and Reichard, 1905.

Nansen, Fridtjof. *Eskimo Life.* Longmans, Green, and Company, 1894.

Nardo, Don. *Understanding Frankenstein.* Lucent Books, 2003.

Nash, Maya. *Once Upon a Fairies Wing.* Author-House, 2013.

Neale, John Mason. *A History of the Holy Eastern Church*, Volume 2. J. Masters, 1850.

Nesbitt, Mark. *Civil War Ghost Trails: Stories from America's Most Haunted Battlefields.* Stackpole Books, 2012.

New York Folklore Society. *New York Folklore Quarterly*, Volumes 29–30. Cornell University Press, 1973.

Newton, Michael. *Encyclopedia of Cryptozoology: A Global Guide to Hidden Animals and Their Pursuers.* McFarland, 2016.

The Norroena Society. *The Asatru Edda: Sacred Lore of the North.* iUniverse, 2009.

Nozedar, Adele. *The Secret Language of Birds: A Treasury of Myths, Folklore & Inspirational True Stories.* HarperElement, 2006.

Nuttall, Mark, ed. *Encyclopedia of the Arctic.* Routledge, 2005.

Nuzum, Eric. *The Dead Travel Fast: Stalking Vampires from Nosferatu to Count Chocula.* Macmillan, 2007.

O'Brien, Christopher. *Secrets of the Mysterious Valley.* Adventures Unlimited Press, 2007.

O'Donnell, Elliott. *Confessions of a Ghost Hunter.* Kessinger, 2003.

O'Donnell, Elliott. *Scottish Ghost Stories.* T. Werner Laurie, 1911.

Oehlenschläger, Adam Gottlob. *Gods of the North.* William Pickering, 1845.

Ogden, Daniel, ed. *Companion to Greek Religion.* Blackwell Publishing, Limited, 2010.

Ogden, Tom. *The Complete Idiot's Guide to Ghosts and Hauntings.* Penguin, 1999.

Oinas, Felix J. *Essays on Russian Folklore and Mythology.* Slavica Publishers, 1985.

Oldenberg, Hermann. *The Religion of the Veda.* Motilal Banarsidass Publisher, 1988.

Olsen, Karin E., Antonina Harbus, and Tette Hofstra, eds. *Germanic Texts and Latin Models: Medieval Reconstructions.* Peters Publishing: 2009.

Olsen, Karin E., and L.A.J.R. Houwen. *Monsters and the Monstrous in Medieval Northwest Europe.* Peeters, 2001.

Oman, John Campbell. *Cults, Customs and Superstitions of India.* T. Fisher Unwin, 1908.

Orel, Vladimir. *A Handbook of Germanic Etymology.* Brill, 2003.

Ostling, Michael. *Between the Devil and the Host:* *Imagining Witchcraft in Early Modern Poland.* Oxford University Press, 2011.

Ouellette, Jennifer. *The Physics of the Buffyverse.* Penguin, 2006.

Owusu, Heike. *Voodoo Rituals: A User's Guide.* Sterling, 2002.

Pacheco, Allan. *Ghosts-Murder-Mayhem, a Chronicle of Santa Fe: Lies, Legends, Facts, Tall Tales, and Useless Information.* Sunstone Press, 2004.

Pacific Discovery. California Academy of Sciences, 1961.

Paglia, C. *Sexual Personae: Art and Decadence from Nefertiti to Emily Dickinson.* Penguin, 1992.

Palgrave, Francis, Geoffrey Palgrave Barker, and Robert Harry Inglis Palgrave. *The Collected Historical Works of Sir Francis Palgrave, in 10 Volumes*, Volume 7. Cambridge University Press, 1921.

Pandolfo, Stefania. *Impasse of the Angels: Scenes from a Moroccan Space of Memory.* University of Chicago Press, 1997.

Parmeshwaranand, Swami. *Encyclopaedic Dictionary of Puranas*, Volume 1. Sarup and Sons, 2001.

Parsons, Elsie Worthington Clews. *Folk-Lore of the Antilles, French and English.* The American Folk-lore Society, 1943.

Pashley, Robert. *Travels in Crete.* John Murray, 1837.

Paulist Fathers. *The Catholic World, a Monthly Magazine of Literature and Science* 21 (April–September 1875). The Catholic Publication Society, 1875.

Peck, H.T., Selim H. Peabody, and Charles F. Richardson, eds. *The International Cyclopedia.* Dodd, Mead & Company, 1899.

Peek, Philip M., and Kwesi Yankah. *African Folklore: An Encyclopedia.* Taylor and Francis, 2004.

Pennsylvania Folklore Society. *Keystone Folklore Quarterly* 1–17. Point Park College, 1956.

Perkowski, Jan Louis. *The Darkling: A Treatise on Slavic Vampirism.* Slavica Publishers, 1989.

Perkowski, Jan Louis. *Vampires of the Slavs.* Slavica Publishers, 1976.

Perrot, Georges, Walter Armstrong, and Charles Chipiez. *A History of Art in Chaldaea and Assyria.* Chapman and Hall, 1884.

Petrovitch, Woislav M. *Hero Tales and Legends of the Serbians.* Cosimo, 2007.

Petzoldt, Ruth, and Paul Neubauer. *Demons: Mediators Between This World and the Other—Essays on Demonic Beings from the Middle Ages to the Present.* Peter Lang, 1998.

Philp, Howard Littleton, and Carl Gustav Jung. *Jung and the Problem of Evil.* Rockliff, 1958.

Phongphit, Seri, and Kevin Hewison. *Thai Village Life: Culture and Transition in the Northeast.* Mūnnithī Mūbān, 1990.

Pivarcsi, Istvan. *Just a Bite: A Transylvania Vampire Expert's Short History of the Undead.* New Europe Books, 2012.

Plutarch, and John Langhorne, trans. *Lives, Translated from the Original Greek: With Notes,*

Critical and Historical; and a Life of Plutarch. Harper and Brothers, 1860.

Plutschow, Herbert E. *A Reader in Edo Period Travel.* Global Oriental, 2006.

Polidori, John William. *The Vampyre: A Tale.* Sherwood, Neely, and Jones, 1819.

Pollack, David. *Reading Against Culture: Ideology and Narrative in the Japanese Novel.* Cornell University Press, 1992.

Porter, Enid. *The Folklore of East Anglia.* Rowman and Littlefield, 1974.

Potts, Annie. *Chicken.* Reaktion Books, 2012.

Prahlad, Anand. *The Greenwood Encyclopedia of African American Folklore: A-F.* Greenwood Press, 2006.

Prince, Albertine. *The Remains of Folklore in Shropshire.* University of Wisconsin, 1915.

Principe, Lawrence. *The Secrets of Alchemy.* University of Chicago Press, 2013.

Pringle, Heather Anne. *The Mummy Congress: Science, Obsession, and the Everlasting Dead.* Barnes and Noble Books, 2005.

Proceedings—Pacific Northwest Conference on Foreign Languages, Volume 15. Pacific Northwest Conference on Foreign Languages, 1964.

Promey, Sally M., ed. *Sensational Religion: Sensory Cultures in Material Practice.* Yale University Press, 2014.

Pulliam, June Michele, and Anthony J. Fonseca, eds. *Encyclopedia of the Zombie: The Walking Dead in Popular Culture and Myth.* Bloomsbury Publishing, 2014.

Pye, Michael, and Kirsten Dalley. *Exposed, Uncovered and Declassified: Ghosts, Spirits, & Hauntings: Am I Being Haunted?* Red Wheel/Weiser, 2011.

Radcliffe-Brown, A.R. *The Andaman Islanders.* Cambridge University Press, 2013.

Radford, Edwin. *Encyclopedia of Superstitions 1949.* Kessinger Publishing, 2004.

Rae, Simon. *Breath Becomes the Wind: Old and New in Karo Religion.* University of Otago Press, 1994.

Ralston, W.R.S. *Russian Folk-Tales.* R. Worthington, 1880.

Ralston, W.R.S. *The Songs of the Russian People: As Illustrative of Slavonic Mythology and Russian Social Life.* Ellis and Green, 1872.

Ramos, Maximo D. *The Aswang Syncrasy in Philippine Folklore.* Philippine Folklore Society, 1971.

Ramos, Maximo D. *The Creatures of Midnight: Faded Deities of Luzon, the Visayas and Mindanao.* Island Publishers, 1967.

Randles, Jenny, Peter A. Hough, and Jason Hurst. *World's Best "True" UFO Stories.* Sterling Pub. Company, 1995.

Raudvere, Catharina, and Jens Peter Schjødt. *More than Mythology: Narratives, Ritual Practices and Regional Distribution in Pre-Christian Scandinavian Religions.* Nordic Academic Press, 2012.

Ray, Brian. "Tim Burton and the Idea of Fairy Tales." In *Fairy Tale Films: Visions of Ambiguity,* edited by Pauline Greenhill and Sidney Eve Matrix. Utah State University Press, 2010, pp. 198–218.

Reader's Digest, eds. *Strange Stories, Amazing Facts: Stories That Are Bizarre, Unusual, Odd, Astonishing, and Often Incredible.* Reader's Digest Association, Inc., 1976.

Reddall, Henry Frederic. *Fact, Fancy, and Fable: A New Handbook for Ready Reference on Subjects Commonly Omitted from Cyclopaedias; Comprising Personal Sobriquets, Familiar Phrases, Popular Appellations, Geographical Nicknames, Literary Pseudonyms, Mythological Characters, Red-Letter Days, Political Slang, Contractions.* A.C. McClurg, 1892.

Redfern, Nick, and Brad Steiger. *The Zombie Book: Encyclopedia of the Living Dead.* Visible Ink Press, 2015.

Reynolds, Barrie. *Magic, Divination, and Witchcraft Among the Barotse of Northern Rhodesia.* University of California Press, 1963.

Riccardo, Martin V. *Liquid Dreams of Vampires.* Llewellyn Publications, 1996.

Riccardo, Martin V. *Vampires Unearthed: The Complete Multi-media Vampire and Dracula Bibliography.* Garland, 1983.

Ridpath, John Clark, ed. *The Standard American Encyclopedia of Arts, Sciences, History, Biography, Geography, Statistics, and General Knowledge,* Volume 7. The Encyclopedia Publishing Company, 1899.

Rink, Henry. *Tales and Traditions of the Eskimo: with a sketch of their habits, religion, language and other peculiarities.* William Blackwood and Sons, 1875.

Rivière, Jean M., and H.E. Kennedy. *Tantrik Yoga: Hindu and Tibetan.* S. Weiser, 1970.

Robbins, Richard Howard. *Global Problems and the Culture of Capitalism.* Allyn and Bacon, 1998.

Roberts, Jeremy. *Japanese Mythology A to Z.* Infobase Publishing, 2009.

Robinson, Fred C. *The Tomb of Beowulf and Other Essays on Old English.* Blackwell, 1993.

Rodd, Rennell, James Rennell, and Tristan James Ellis. *The Customs and Lore of Modern Greece.* D. Stott, 1892.

Rogers, Robert William. *The Religion of Babylonia and Assyria: Especially in Its Relations to Israel.* Jennings & Graham, 1908.

Rolfes, Steven J. *Supernatural Lore of Ohio.* History Press, 2020.

Ronay, Gabriel. *The Truth About Dracula.* Stein and Day, 1972.

Roscher, Wilhelm Heinrich, and James Hillman. *Pan and the nightmare, being the only translation (from the German by A. V. O'Brien) of Ephialtes: a pathological-mythological treatise on the nightmare in classical antiquity, together with an essay on Pan, serving as a psychological introduction to Roscher's Ephialtes by James Hillman.* Spring Publications, 1972.

Rose, Carol. *Giants, Monsters, and Dragons: An Encyclopedia of Folklore, Legend, and Myth.* W.W. Norton, 2001.

Rose, Carol. *Spirits, Fairies, Gnomes, and Goblins:*

An Encyclopedia of the Little People. ABC-CLIO, 1996.

Rose, Carol. *Spirits, Fairies, Leprechauns, and Goblins: An Encyclopedia*. W. W. Norton & Company, 1998.

Rose, Herbert Jennings. *A Handbook of Greek Mythology*. E.P. Dutton, 1959.

Rosen, Brenda. *The Mythical Creatures Bible: The Definitive Guide to Legendary Beings*. Sterling Publishing Company, Incorporated, 2009.

Roth, Henry Ling, Andrew Lang, and Hugh Brooke Low. *The Natives of Sarawak and British North Borneo: Based Chiefly on the Mss. of the Late H. B. Low, Sarawak Government Service*. Truslove and Hanson, 1896.

Roux, Jean-Paul. *Le Sang: Mythes, symboles et realites*. n.p., 1956.

Ruiz, Vicki, and Virginia Sanchez Korrol. *Latinas in the United States: A Historical Encyclopedia*, Volume 1. Indiana University Press, 2006.

Rulandus, Martinus. *Lexicon of Alchemy*. Kessinger, 1992.

Russo, Arlene. *Vampire Nation*. Llewellyn Worldwide, 2008.

Ryan, William Francis. *Russian Magic at the British Library: Books, Manuscripts, Scholars, Travelers*. British Library, 2006.

Rydberg, Viktor, Rasmus Björn Anderson, and James William Buel. *Teutonic Mythology: Gods and Goddesses of the Northland*, Volume 3. Norroena Society, 1905.

Salas, Elizabeth. *Soldaderas in the Mexican Military: Myth and History*. University of Texas Press, 1990.

Saletore, Rajaram Narayan. *Indian Witchcraft*. Abhinav Publications, 1981.

Sanday, Peggy Reeves. *Women at the Center: Life in a Modern Matriarchy*. Cornell University Press, 2003.

Saunders, G.E. *Borneo Folktales and Legends*. Borneo Literature Bureau, 1976.

Sayce, Archibald Henry. *The Religions of Ancient Egypt and Babylonia: The Gifford Lectures on the Ancient Egyptian and Babylonian Conception of the Divine Delivered in Aberdeen*. T. and T. Clark, 1903.

Scarborough, Dorothy. *The Supernatural in Modern English Fiction*. G.P. Putnam's Sons, 1917.

Schwarcz, Vera. *Place and Memory in the Singing Crane Garden*. University of Pennsylvania Press, 2008.

Schwartz, Howard. *Tree of Souls: The Mythology of Judaism: The Mythology of Judaism*. Oxford University Press, 2004.

Scott, James George, and John Percy Hardiman. *Gazetteer of Upper Burma and the Shan States*. AMS Press, 1900.

Sekien, Toriyama. *Japandemonium Illustrated: The Yokai Encyclopedias of Toriyama Sekien*. Courier Dover Publications, 2017.

Senf, Carol A. *The Vampire in Nineteenth-Century English Literature*. Bowling Green State University Popular Press, 1988.

Senn, Harry A. *Were-wolf and Vampire in Romania*. East European Monographs, 1982.

Shashi, Shyam Singh. *Roma, the Gypsy World*. Sundeep Prakashan, 1990.

Shepard, Leslie, Nandor Fodor, and Lewis Spence. *Encyclopedia of Occultism and Parapsychology*. Gale Research Company, 1985.

Sherman, Aubrey. *Vampires: The Myths, Legends, and Lore*. Adams Media, 2014.

Shipley, Joseph Twadell. *Dictionary of Early English*. Philosophical Library, 1955.

Shirane, Haruo, and Sonja Arntzen. *Traditional Japanese Literature: An Anthology, Beginnings to 1600*. Columbia University Press, 2007.

Sidky, H. *Haunted by the Archaic Shaman: Himalayan Jhakris and the Discourse on Shamanism*. Lexington Books, 2008.

Silver, Alain, and James Ursini. *The Vampire Film: From Nosferatu to Interview with the Vampire*. Limelight Editions, 1997.

Singh, Madanjeet. *The Sun: Symbol of Power and Life*. H.N. Abrams, 1993.

Skeat, Walter William, and Charles Otto Blagden. *Malay Magic: Being an Introduction to the Folklore and Popular Religion of the Malay Peninsula*. Macmillan and Company, Limited, 1900.

Smith, Jeffrey Alyn. *Moonlighter's Paradise: From the Land of Iron and Steel to the Land of Irony and Stealing*. University of California Press, 2010.

Smith, Robert John. *Ancestor Worship in Contemporary Japan*. Stanford University Press, 1974.

Son, Chang-Hee. *Haan of Minjung Theology and Han of Han Philosophy: In the Paradigm of Process Philosophy and Metaphysics of Relatedness*. University Press of America, 2000.

Sotesiri, Roj. *The Study of Puan Community, Pho Si Village, Tambon Bang Pla Ma, Suphan Buri*. Bangkok, Thailand: Office of the National Culture Commission, Ministry of Education, 1982.

Spence, Lewis. *An Enclopoedia of Occultism: A Compendium of Information on the Occult Sciences, Occult Personalities, Psychic Science, Magic, Demonology, Spiritism and Mysticism*. Dodd, Mead, 1920.

Spence, Lewis. *The Minor Traditions of British Mythology*. Rider and Company, 1948.

Spinner, Alice. "Concerning Duppies." In *The Living Age*, Volume 206, edited by Eliakim Littell and Robert S. Littell. Living Age Company Incorporated, 1895, pp. 161–169.

Stafford, Charles. *The Roads of Chinese Childhood: Learning and Identification in Angang*. Cambridge University Press, 2006.

Stefoff, Rebecca. *Vampires, Zombies, and Shape-Shifters*. Benchmark Books, 2007.

Steiger, Brad. *Real Zombies, the Living Dead, and Creatures of the Apocalypse*. Visible Ink Press, 2010.

Stein, Rolf Alfred, and Phyllis Brooks. *The World in Miniature: Container Gardens and Dwellings in Far Eastern Religious Thought*. Stanford University Press, 1990.

Stepanich, Kisma K. *Faery Wicca, Book One.* Llewellyn Worldwide, 1997.

Steuding, Hermann, Karl Pomeroy Harrington, and Herbert Cushing Tolman. *Greek and Roman Mythology.* Leach, Shewell, and Sanborn, 1897.

Stewart, Hugh Fraser, and Arthur Augustus Tilley. *The Romantic Movement in French Literature Traced by a Series of Texts.* Oxford University Press, 1921.

Stone, Jacqueline Ilyse, and Mariko Namba Walter. *Death and the Afterlife in Japanese Buddhism.* University of Hawaii Press, 2008.

Stratilesco, Tereza. *From Carpathian to Pindus: Pictures of Roumanian Country Life.* John W. Luce, 1907.

Strickmann, Michel, and Bernard Faure. *Chinese Magical Medicine.* Stanford University Press, 2002.

Stuart, Roxana. *Stage Blood: Vampires of the 19th Century Stage.* Popular Press, 1994.

Suckling, Nigel. *Vampires.* Facts, Figures & Fun, 2006.

Summers, Montague. *Geography of Witchcraft.* Kessinger, 2003.

Summers, Montague. *Vampire: His Kith and Kin.* Kessinger, 2003.

Summers, Montague. *The Vampire in Europe.* Kessinger, 2003.

Summers, Montague. *The Vampire in Lore and Legend.* Dover, 2001.

Summers, Montague. *Werewolf in Lore and Legend.* K. Paul, Trench, Trubner, 1933.

"Superstition and Knowledge." *The Quarterly Review* 29 (1823): 440–75. John Murray.

Szigethy, Anna. *Vampires: From Vlad Drakul to the Vampire Lestat.* Key Porter Books, 2004.

Taberner, Stuart, and Paul Cooke. *German Culture, Politics, and Literature into the Twenty-First Century: Beyond Normalization.* Boydell and Brewer, 2006.

Tanaka, Stefan. *New Times in Modern Japan.* Princeton University Press, 2004.

Tang, Ta Thuc, ed. "Death and Remembrance." In *Vietnam Fights and Builds, Issues 1–12.* Republic of Vietnam, 1964.

Taylor, Edward B. *Primitive Culture: Researches into the Development of Mythology, Philosophy, Religion, Language, Art and Custom.* Kessinger, 2007.

Taylor, Richard P. *Death and the Afterlife: A Cultural Encyclopedia.* ABC-CLIO, 2000.

Taylor, Timothy. *The Buried Soul: How Humans Invented Death.* Beacon Press, 2004.

Teiser, Stephen F. *The Ghost Festival in Medieval China.* Princeton University Press, 1988.

Thigpen, Kenneth A. *Folklore and the Ethnicity Factor in the Lives of Romanian-Americans.* Indiana University Press, 1973.

Thompson, Laurence G. *Studies of Chinese Religion: A Comprehensive and Classified Bibliography of Publications in English, French, and German through 1970.* Dickenson, 1976.

Thompson, Reginald Campbell. *The Devils and Evil Spirits of Babylonia, Being Babylonian and Assyrian Incantations Against the Demons, Ghouls, Vampires, Hobgoblins, Ghosts, and Kindred Evil Spirits, Which Attack Mankind.* Luzac, 1903–4.

Thompson, Reginald Campbell. *Semitic Magic, Its Origins and Development.* Luzac and Company, 1908.

Thorndike, Lynn. *History of Magic and Experimental Science.* Columbia University Press, 1941.

Thorpe, Benjamin. *Northern Mythology: Scandinavian Popular Traditions and Superstitions.* E. Lumley, 1851.

Thurston, Edgar. *Omens and Superstitions of Southern India.* McBride, Nast and Company, 1912.

Tierney, Patrick. *Highest Altar: Unveiling the Mystery of Human Sacrifice.* Penguin, 1990.

Toki, Zemmaro. *Japanese No Plays.* Japan Travel Bureau, 1954.

Tolkien, John Ronald Reuel. *Beowulf: The Monster and the Critics.* HarperCollins, 1997.

Tongue, Ruth L. *Forgotten Folk Tales of the English Counties.* Routledge and K. Paul, 1970.

Torchia, Christopher. *Indonesian Idioms and Expressions: Colloquial Indonesian at Work.* Tuttle Publishing, 2007.

Transactions of the Asiatic Society of Japan, Volumes 1–50. The Asiatic Society of Japan, 1940.

Transactions of the Gaelic Society of Inverness, Volume 14. Gaelic Society of Inverness, 1889.

Triefeldt, Laurie. *People and Places: A Special Collection.* Quill Driver Books, 2007.

Turner, Patricia, and Charles Russell Coulter. *Dictionary of Ancient Deities.* Oxford University Press, 2001.

Twitchell, James B. *The Living Dead: A Study of the Vampire in Romantic Literature.* Duke University Press, 1987.

Varner, Gary R. *Creatures in the Mist: Little People, Wild Men and Spirit Beings Around the World: A Study in Comparative Mythology.* Algora, 2007.

Verma, Dinesh Chandra. *Social, Economic, and Cultural History of Bijapur.* Idarah-i Adabiyat-i Delli, 1990.

Vicary, John Fulford. *An American in Norway.* W.H. Allen, 1885.

Vigfússon, Guðbrandur, and Frederick York Powell. *Eddic Poetry.* Clarendon Press, 1883.

Vigil, Angel. *The Eagle on the Cactus: Traditional Stories from Mexico.* Libraries Unlimited, 2000.

Vijayalakshmy, R., and Ca Ve Cuppiramaniyan, eds. *Philosophical Heritage of the Tamils.* International Institute of Tamil Studies, 1983.

Villeneuve, Roland, and Jean-Louis Degaudenzi. *Le Musée des Vampires.* Henri Veyrier, 1976.

Virtanen, Leea, and Thomas DuBois. *Finnish Folklore.* Finnish Literature Society, 2000.

Voigt, Vilmos. *Folk Narrative and Cultural Identity: 9th Congress of the International Society for Folk-Narrative Research*, Volume 1. Eötvös Loránd University, Department of Folklore, 1995.

Volta, Ornella. *The Vampire.* Tandem Books, 1963.

Voltaire. *A Philosophical Dictionary: From the French.* W. Dugdale, 1843.

Wasyliw, Patricia Healy. *Martyrdom, Murder, and Magic: Child Saints and Their Cults in Medieval Europe.* Peter Lang, 2008.

Webley, Stephen J., and Peter Zackariasson, eds. *The Playful Undead and Video Games: Critical Analyses of Zombies and Gameplay.* Routledge, 2019.

Werne, Edward Theodore Chalmers. *China of the Chinese.* Sir Isaac Pitman and Sons, 1920.

Whaley, Ben. *Toward a Gameic World: New Rules of Engagement from Japanese Video Games.* University of Michigan Press, 2023.

Wharton, Edith, Edward Everett, Henry Cabot Lodge, James Russell Lowell, and Jared Sparks. *The North American Review.* O. Everett, 1836.

White, George, ed. *Ghost Stories from the North of England.* CreateSpace Independent Publishing Platform, 2013.

White, Luise. *Speaking with Vampires: Rumor and History in Colonial Africa.* University of California Press, 2000.

White, William. *Notes and Queries, Volume 41.* Oxford University Press, 1870.

Whitelaw, Alexander, ed. *The Popular Encyclopedia: Or, "Conversations Lexicon."* Blackie and Son, 1846.

Wiggermann, F.A.M. *Mesopotamian Protective Spirits: The Ritual Texts.* Brill, 1992.

Wikipedia. "Ayakashi (yōkai)." https://en.wikipedia.org/wiki/Ayakashi_(y%C5%8Dkai).

Wikipedia. "Gjenganger." https://en.wikipedia.org/wiki/Gjenganger.

Wikipedia. "Lietuvēns." https://en.wikipedia.org/wiki/Lietuv%C4%93ns.

Williamson, Jenny, and Genn McMenemy. *Women of Myth: From Deer Woman and Mami Wata to Amaterasu and Athena, Your Guide to the Amazing and Diverse Women from World Mythology.* Simon & Schuster, 2023.

Williamson, Robert W. *Religion and Social Organization in Central Polynesia.* Cambridge University Press, 2013.

Willis, Roy G. *World Mythology.* Macmillan, 1993.

Winn, Chris. *I Never Knew That About Ireland.* Macmillan, 2007.

Wolf, Anita, ed. "dance of death." In *Britannica Concise Encyclopedia.* Encyclopaedia Britannica, Inc., 2008.

Wolf, Leonard. *Dracula: The Connoisseur's Guide.* Broadway Books, 1997.

Wood, John George. *The Natural History of Man: Being an Account of the Manners and Customs of the Uncivilized Races of Men*, Volume 1. G. Routledge, 1874.

Wood, John George. *The Uncivilized Races of Men in All Countries of the World.* J.A. Brainerd, 1882.

Woog, Adam. *Zombies.* Reference Point Press, 2011.

Wright, Dudley. *The Book of Vampires.* Omnigraphics, 1989.

Wright, Dudley. *Vampires and Vampirism.* W. Rider and Son, Limited, 1914.

Wright, Joseph. *The English Dialect Dictionary, Being the Complete Vocabulary of All Dialect Words Still in Use, or Known to Have Been in Use During the Last Two Hundred Years.* Henry Frowde, 1900.

Yashinsky, Dan. *Tales for an Unknown City.* McGill-Queen's Press, 1992.

Yassif, Eli. *The Hebrew Folktale: History, Genre, Meaning.* Indiana University Press, 2009.

Yeats, W.B. *Fairy and Folk Tales of the Irish Peasantry.* Walter Scott Ltd., 1888.

Yoda, Hiroko, and Matt Alt. *Yokai Attack! The Japanese Monster Survival Guide.* Tuttle Publishing, 2012.

Young, Kenneth. *The Greek Passion: A Study in People and Politics.* Dent, 1969.

Zak, Zuza. *Slavic Kitchen Alchemy: Nourishing Herbal Remedies, Magical Recipes & Folk Wisdom.* Watkins Media Limited, 2023.

Zell-Ravenheart, Oberon. *A Wizard's Bestiary.* Career Press, 2007.

Zelliot, Eleanor, and Maxine Berntsen, eds. *The Experience of Hinduism: Essays on Religion in Maharashtra.* State University New York Press, 1988.

Index

Main entries are shown in **bold**

www.ingramcontent.com/pod-product-compliance
Lightning Source LLC
Chambersburg PA
CBHW050240290326
41929CB00049B/3293